D0041104

WHY THEY
DO IT

WHY THEY DO IT

Inside the Mind of the
White-Collar Criminal

EUGENE SOLTES

PUBLICAFFAIRS

New York

PublicAffairs books are available at special discounts for bulk purchases in the U.S. by corporations, institutions, and other organizations. For more information, please contact the Special Markets Department at the Perseus Books Group, 2300 Chestnut Street, Suite 200, Philadelphia, PA 19103, call (800) 810-4145, ext. 5000, or e-mail special.markets@ perseusbooks.com.

Library of Congress Cataloging-in-Publication Data

Names: Soltes, Eugene, author.
Title: Why they do it : inside the mind of the white-collar criminal / Eugene
   Soltes.
Description: New York : PublicAffairs, 2016. | Includes bibliographical
   references and index.
Identifiers: LCCN 2016018444 (print) | LCCN 2016026144 (ebook) | ISBN
   9781610395366 (hardback) | ISBN 9781610395373 (ebook)
Subjects: LCSH: White collar crimes. | Commercial crimes. | Commercial
   criminals—Psychology. | BISAC: BUSINESS & ECONOMICS / Business Ethics. |
   BUSINESS & ECONOMICS / Workplace Culture.
Classification: LCC HV6768 .S65 2016 (print) | LCC HV6768 (ebook) | DDC
   364.16/8—dc23
LC record available at https://lccn.loc.gov/2016018444

First Edition

10 9 8 7 6 5 4 3 2 1

To my two darling girls,
Jennifer and AB

CONTENTS

PART III

THE BUSINESS OF MALFEASANCE

Managing in the Gray

It is hard to understand why someone who has reached the
pinnacle of success would risk all that for more.
—US DISTRICT JUDGE RICHARD SULLIVAN

You never really understand a person until you consider things
from his point of view—until you climb into his skin and walk
around in it.
—ATTICUS FINCH, *TO KILL A MOCKINGBIRD*

I N 1999, TWO of the world's leading executive headhunters teamed
up to write *Lessons from the Top: The Search for America's Best
Business Leaders*. Their book profiled fifty executives who exempli-
fied, in the authors' view, the defining characteristics of great leaders.
They encouraged readers "to learn from and pattern themselves" after
those they profiled in order to improve their own management acumen.
"We are confident in saying," they wrote, "that these 50 individuals are
collectively among the very best—and most successful—business leaders
in America."

With decades of combined experience, the headhunters had filled hundreds of chief executive positions for the largest and most prestigious
multinational corporations. Making their list was a significant achievement. Yet, within just a few years, three of those selected—Kenneth Lay
(the chairman of Enron), Dennis Kozlowski (the CEO of Tyco), and Bernie Ebbers (the CEO of WorldCom)—were convicted of white-collar
crimes and headed to prison. Three more were charged with overseeing

fraudulent practices and collectively fined over $20 million. And Rajat Gupta, the former managing director of McKinsey and Company, who provided a glowing testimonial describing the book as "truly ground-breaking," was himself convicted of insider trading.

The dramatic fall of leaders once held in such high esteem is startling. These were the same people who spoke at university commencements, graced the covers of *Fortune,* and donated generously to charities. They had prided themselves as being role models for employees and aspiring business school students alike. Their failure surprised even those who knew these executives and had watched their careers blossom. My colleague Clayton Christensen remarked of Jeffrey Skilling, his business school classmate and the former CEO of Enron, that "the Jeffrey Skilling I knew of from our years at HBS [Harvard Business School] was a good man. He was smart, he worked hard, he loved his family. . . . When his entire career unraveled with his conviction on multiple federal felony charges relating to Enron's financial collapse, it not only shocked me that he had gone wrong, but how spectacularly he had done so." Each time another celebrated executive unexpectedly descends into the netherworld of criminal activity, we are perplexed and stuck asking "why." Why do they do it?

WHILE FLIPPING THROUGH the television channels late one evening almost a decade ago, I stumbled across *Lockup* on MSNBC. Somewhere between a documentary and a reality television show, *Lockup* featured interviews with felons at prisons around the country. The inmates described their lives before prison and the circumstances that led them to commit brutal and often violent crimes such as assault, murder, and rape. Not surprisingly, financial troubles, drug addiction, and gang affiliations provoked many of their offenses.

While watching the show, I began to think about a different group of offenders whose motivations were far more puzzling. The names of once-respected corporate titans from Enron, Tyco, and Computer Associates regularly led the business news. Then, as now, it was a rare week when the *Wall Street Journal* didn't feature a story about some miscreant executive. Yet, none of these white-collar offenders lived the harsh lives of those discussed on *Lockup.* In fact, before their crimes, many lived extraordinarily comfortable lives, both personally and professionally. Despite all their privileges, these executives engaged in criminal activities that had deleterious consequences not only for themselves and their families but also for their employees, investors, and companies.

Driven by curiosity, I decided to write to several former executives who were now in prison. I typed a brief letter with the first dozen questions that came to mind. What were the most significant pressures they faced? How did the way they were compensated influence their decision making? What were their intentions once they were released? I found their addresses online using the surprisingly convenient Federal Bureau of Prisons inmate locator website and dropped the letters into the mail the following day. I went back to my other research and soon forgot about my letters.

A month later, I unexpectedly started to receive responses. One executive offered to speak with me if I visited him in prison, another volunteered to discuss over the phone, and several others wrote to say that they would consider carrying on a correspondence by mail.

One particularly poignant response came from Stephen Richards, a former senior executive at Computer Associates. Richards sent me a somber letter written in elegant cursive describing the challenges he had faced in the software industry. As global head of sales, Richards helped backdate contracts that were signed by clients after the quarter officially ended. His actions inflated quarterly earnings and temporarily propped up the firm's

Introduction to the letter from Stephen Richards.

stock price. When the deception was ultimately revealed, eight executives from Computer Associates, including Richards, were convicted. "Unfortunately the world is not black and white," Richards concluded at the end of his letter. "Senior managers spend most of their life in the gray regardless of their responsibility and that can be a dangerous and hard place to be."

I wrote a case study based on Richards' letter that became part of the MBA and executive education curriculum at Harvard Business School. The intimacy of Richards' comments sparked lively debates. Some students harshly criticized Richards for the ease in which he had succumbed to institutional and market pressures. Others appreciated that what he did was wrong, but also imagined themselves facing similar challenges in their own careers. It was easy to rationalize why Richards deserved to be punished for breaking an accounting rule, but whether a sales contract was dated Friday or Monday didn't create a strong feeling of anger or indignation among many students. There was an uncomfortable disconnect between what we all intuitively felt and what we intellectually believed was right and wrong.

Struggling to resolve these questions myself, I started searching for explanations. I soon found a bewildering number of theories about why white-collar criminals "did it." Some people argued that criminality stemmed from psychological aberration. Others said it might be due to overconfidence or stress. Still others argued that it was simply a result of excessive greed or ambition. Many different reasons were suggested by prosecutors, scholars, and the media, but often with little concrete evidence or support. Much had been written about the decisions that led to these executives' success, but surprisingly little was understood about the choices that led to their downfall.

In the years that followed, I began to correspond with and visit more than four dozen of the most senior executives who oversaw some of the most significant corporate failures in history. Some, like Bernie Madoff, had gained celebrity status and were effectively serving life sentences in prison. Others, like Sam Waksal, the founder of ImClone who was convicted of insider trading, had managed to rehabilitate themselves and reignite their careers. Many I would get to know only from the confines of their cell, but others I spent time with before and after their incarceration, at home and with their families.

Investigating how these former executives made decisions required getting to know them as people—their personalities, desires, and temperaments. I shied away from formal interviews in favor of interactions that were more conversational and casual. We often discussed recent financial news and politics, topics I was teaching in my classes, and books we both read. I sought to place myself in their positions and to understand the world as they saw it. It sometimes took months, even years in several instances, before we developed a relationship that gave them the comfort to discuss their views more frankly. But over time, many removed the superficial veils that they had become accustomed to wearing. These former executives opened up about the frustrations and personal challenges they faced during their professional careers and current predicaments. I was given an opportunity to intimately see how they viewed themselves and the world around them.

Incarcerated and coping with the stigma associated with their criminal conduct, many of these executives were not the confident men they had once been. Life in prison was humbling. "I receive only nine cents per hour as a tutor for inmates studying to take the GED exam," sighed Russell Wasendorf, a CEO who previously ran one of the most successful futures brokerage houses in the United States. "I have to work about six hours to earn enough money for a postage stamp." A few former executives were reluctant to speak about their experience—in some cases, because they, too, were struggling to understand their own behavior.

Several provided commentary that differed from, even conflicted with, their court testimony. In many instances, executives who testified against others in return for leniency were more concerned with appeasing prosecutors than with accurately describing the complexities of working in a highly charged corporate environment in an unbiased way. In court, they often reduced the complexity of the real world to make matters appear black and white. During one discussion, a CEO casually described to me the hours he had spent with his attorney rehearsing how to express contrition in preparation for his parole hearing. While he felt little reason to repent, his attorney advised him that he needed to effectively convey penance to improve his chances of parole. After much practice, the former CEO was soon able to present a convincing, albeit false, display of remorse.

The deliberate distortion of narratives by cooperating witnesses to win over prosecutors not only undermines the judicial process but also contorts our understanding of what the executives thought and felt while their crimes unfolded. During our discussions, however—now that these events were behind them and there was no longer a need to maintain a particular narrative—many described far rawer motivations, emotions, and expectations to me. In these unencumbered discussions, a different and more nuanced picture of why executives engage in malfeasance emerged.

MANY PEOPLE, federal prosecutors, scholars, and media commentators claim that executives make decisions, including criminal ones, through explicit cost-benefit calculation. Although such deliberate reasoning is consistent with the way many business decisions are made, this explanation seems at odds with how these former leaders made choices that eventually led them to prison. Many were not mindfully weighing the expected benefits against the expected costs. If they had been, even the remote chance of being caught and sent to prison, upending their otherwise comfortable lives, would have weighed heavily on their conscience. But I didn't see this. Instead, I found that they expended surprisingly little effort deliberating the consequences of their actions. They seem to have reached their decisions to commit crimes with little thought or reflection. In many cases, it was difficult to say that they had ever really "decided" to commit a crime at all.

I struggled to understand why they didn't anticipate the adverse and often extraordinary consequences of their decisions. Their failure to see the personal and professional consequences of their choices seemed deeply myopic and inconsistent with the very traits that made their prior success possible. Even if they had total disregard for the well-being of others, it seemed inexplicable that they would want to potentially risk their personal wealth, reputation, and family to acquire more. It was not that they simply believed they wouldn't be caught and they could engage in corporate crimes with impunity, either. It was a broader lack of recognition of the consequences of their actions.

Over time, I began to understand the reason for this shortsightedness. They put little effort into these decisions because they never deeply felt that the decisions were actually harmful to themselves or others. Because they didn't perceive this harm, they had little reason to pause and reconsider their course of action. It wasn't that these executives recognized that other people were going to be harmed and simply didn't care. Rather, they never even stopped to consider that their actions would harm, even devastate, real people.

It may seem hard to believe that an intelligent executive could fail to see the harm created by fraud, embezzlement, or price-fixing. To victims, the negative ramifications of such crimes are readily apparent. However, while manipulative corporate conduct has the same financial effect as stealing money from an investor's wallet, there is a crucial difference between these types of crime from the perspective of the perpetrator. Stealing money from another's pocket involves a high degree of intimacy. The perpetrator sees the victim, physically touches his property, and witnesses his immediate reaction after being robbed. But manipulative corporate conduct lacks all these sensations associated with theft. Executives never need to get close—physically or psychologically—to their victims. Instead, the victims of financial crimes often remain distant and amorphous.

The distance between individuals in modern business dealings creates a problem for managers and executives. The human ability to sense the potential for harm is significantly affected by physical and psychological proximity. Just consider your own reaction to harm or suffering. Your instinctive response to seeing those you are closest to suffer produces a much stronger emotional reaction than similar harm caused to strangers. Similarly, if you witness suffering firsthand, you have a much stronger desire to relieve it than if you simply hear or read about suffering in some far off part of the world, even if this suffering afflicts many more people. Proximity deeply affects our instinctive ability to sense and react to harm. As distance grows, our ability to empathize with others shrinks. In business, where many transactions occur at "arm's length" among unrelated parties, there is often no natural tendency to empathize with individuals on the other side of a transaction, let alone those derivatively affected second- or thirdhand. The nature of modern commerce has made it perilously easy to wander into the penumbra—that "gray zone" between right and wrong.

Ultimately, these are not simply tales of hubris, greed, or ambition. While those who falter often display such characteristics, so too do many successful executives whose lives are not described in these pages. This

also isn't a story about executives just suffering from psychological aberrations or deploying careful calculated reasoning to motivate breaking the
law. Instead, I'll describe people just following their intuitions and primitive gut feelings—poor guides to the straight and narrow in the modern
business world.

IF THIS BOOK had been written a hundred years earlier, much of the business misconduct described here would not have been illegal. To the extent
that the law prohibited this conduct, violations produced little public condemnation and few prosecutions. Remarkably, just a half-century ago, the
public often stood behind executives who were prosecuted for white-collar
offenses. Throughout the twentieth century, however, public sentiment
grew increasingly unsympathetic toward deceptive business practices and
regulators increasingly designed and enforced laws to restrict this behavior. Part I of this book tells the story of how white-collar crime came to be
criminalized.

After describing these changes, I begin exploring the "why." For centuries, people sought to explain criminal conduct by appealing to physical
aberrations and psychological abnormalities. After researchers realized
that individuals were not necessarily bound by their biology, crime became viewed as a choice. Among federal prosecutors, economists, criminologists, and many in the media, cost-benefit analysis became the favored
rationale for understanding corporate malfeasance. In Part II, I explore
these explanations and how the cost-benefit explanation of executive deviance fails to fit the evidence.

Drawing from research in psychology, neuroscience, legal theory, and
philosophy, I then investigate how poor managerial intuitions, rather
than failed reasoning, can motivate fraudulent behavior. Explaining misconduct in this way allows us to understand how intelligent, even brilliant, executives can commit fraud—often without perceiving the harm
they cause.

The chapters in the final section of the book focus on my conversations
with former executives and how they reflect on their actions. Readers especially keen on hearing from these executives can begin with Part III.
While the historical circumstances underlying white-collar criminality
and the theories explaining this misconduct provide the context for these
narratives, the later chapters can be enjoyed without this background.

Some of the conduct described in this book can stir strong emotions. Hearing these individuals describe their actions dispassionately will inevitably inflame these emotions for some of my readers. Although the book is an attempt to better explain why these executives perpetrated these acts, it is emphatically neither a defense of their actions nor an attempt to reduce their culpability. Ultimately, this book represents an attempt to study and hopefully learn from the mistakes they made.

THIS PROJECT HAS a distinctly personal aspect for me as a business school professor. With few exceptions, no one leaves a leading business school or embarks on a new career with the aspiration of doing harm. And after becoming wealthy, most successful executives don't set out to engage in fraud during the final years of their careers. Yet we sometimes see people of extraordinary talent and promise doing just that. Among the several dozen Harvard Business School graduates who ended up in prison, something must have happened along the way.

In a sense, then, this book is not just about "them" but also about "us." Part of what I hope to illustrate is that the errors made by these executives are ones that we are all susceptible to. Obviously, this is not to say that we'd all necessarily behave similarly if placed in their situation. Rather, my point is that, in our own small ways, we are all susceptible to making the same mistakes as these former executives. Fortunately for us, the consequences are considerably less significant in most instances for ourselves and others. At the same time, by illustrating how we all share certain limitations, I hope the following pages instill some degree of humility.

We devote plenty of time and thought to the factors that contribute to making our careers and personal lives a success but much less time pondering what might undermine these accomplishments. By better understanding how and why these executives failed, I hope that we can begin a more thoughtful dialogue about how we too might err.

PART I

THE STRUGGLE TO CRIMINALIZE

1

Not . . . bucket-shop operators, dead-beats, and fly-by-night swindlers

Pillars of the Community

B Y 2013, SCOTT London had much to be proud of. Nearly two decades earlier, at the age of thirty-two, he had made partner at KPMG, one of the largest and most prestigious accounting firms in the world. Out of the nearly one hundred others who started at KPMG at the same time, he was the only one to reach the partnership rank.

London now led KPMG's practice for the entire southwestern United States, with prestigious clients like the footwear company Deckers, maker of UGG boots. More than fifty partners and nearly five hundred professional auditors worked under his leadership. His position paid generously, too—he expected to take home at least $900,000 annually. London was a leader in the accounting world.

In his personal life, London felt equally lucky. He had been married for over twenty-five years. A recruiting visit to his alma mater as a junior accountant for KPMG led him to a fortuitous encounter. "I ended up recruiting a wife instead of a new candidate for the firm," London fondly remembered. He and his wife had a son and a daughter, both in college. His daughter enthusiastically looked forward to following her father into the accounting profession. "Although our lives were all busy, we were a very close family," London recalled. "I had an incredible family and felt very lucky both personally and professionally."

The morning of Thursday, March 7, 2013, began like many others for London. He planned to spend the day in KPMG's satellite office, some twenty-five miles outside Los Angeles. With the office close to home, London looked forward to avoiding LA's notorious traffic and headed to the gym before arriving at the office around 9 a.m. After a few hours of routine administrative work, he met a few partners at a local food court before taking a short drive to meet an old friend, Bryan Shaw. "It was an unremarkable day," said London. "I never knew it would change my life forever."

London and Shaw had originally met more than a decade earlier playing golf at a local country club. Over time they connected over common interests, and soon the two started going out socially to dinner with their spouses. They attended concerts—Bruce Springsteen was a favorite—and traveled with friends to Las Vegas. Both London and Shaw enjoyed debating issues in the news and other topics that most of London's other friends and colleagues avoided. "We were good friends," London felt. "I could say anything and he did the same. I believed I could act without holding back. He provided an outlet that I did not have elsewhere."

Following the 2009 recession, Shaw's family-run jewelry business encountered difficulties. Around this time, he also started asking about London's work. It began as gentle inquiries over dinner and on the golf course into how things were going at the office. Over time, Shaw asked more pointed questions about specific clients and how they were performing. "It slowly developed and evolved into something," London remembered. A few months after these discussions started, London offered more detailed information about a particular client. Shaw traded on it, said he made $20,000, and gave London a couple thousand in return. "Once it happened and it worked, then it became easier for both of us," London explained. In the coming months, London provided Shaw additional pieces of actionable intelligence that Shaw traded on. "Once I saw that nothing was happening, my standards became lower," London admitted.

On that fateful spring afternoon in 2013, London met Shaw in a Starbucks parking lot. After a cursory greeting, Shaw handed London a small black bag containing a manila envelope. "I think we made a little bit more on Deckers than we anticipated," Shaw explained. The company had announced record fourth-quarter earnings the prior week and the stock had jumped 15 percent in response—much as Shaw expected, since he relied on information provided by London. As a KPMG client, Deckers' earnings were available for London to view ahead of their public release to the market.

Inside the manila envelope was $5,000 in cash. Shaw apologized that he had *only* $5,000 with him. London told him to keep the money and they'd "figure it out later," but Shaw persisted and London took the envelope. Shaw asked London what he thought he should do with the remaining options he still had on Deckers. "Sell it and take the profits?" Shaw asked. London paused briefly, then responded: "Yeah, sell it and take the profit. . . . trust me, we're gonna have . . . more . . . opportunities, so why risk losing anything of the profit that you got."

Had London and Shaw been alone in the parking lot that afternoon, this brief interaction would have been quickly forgotten. But they weren't alone. Not far away was a van with FBI agents armed with a camera and telephoto lens. They snapped a photograph of London, on the left, accepting the envelope and conspiring to provide inside information to Shaw. Shaw, someone whom London considered a close friend, wore a wire during their entire conversation.

Figure 1.1: Scott London, on left, accepting a payment from Bryan Shaw.

A week and a half later, London answered a knock at his door at 8:15 in the morning. Two men wearing suits presented their identification as FBI agents. At London's kitchen table, the agents told him that they were aware of his discussions with Shaw and the profits Shaw had made by trading on this information. To the agents' surprise, London quickly admitted his guilt. "I knew straight away that my KPMG career was over. Regardless of whether I fought it and sought advice from an attorney first, the likely outcome was set." After twenty minutes, the agents left and London steeled himself for a difficult discussion with his wife and children. London would soon begin to prepare for the next, more difficult chapter in his life.

To most outside observers, London's offense is obvious. In providing information to Shaw, London violated the confidentiality he owed his clients. Confidentiality was a sacred pillar at KPMG, as it was among all auditors. "In an elevator, in a restaurant—in any public place—you don't talk about anything sensitive that's client related. Those rules were firmly ingrained," explained London. "I knew those rules and I was expected to set an example for everyone that worked for me." Yet London supplied a friend with advance notice of upcoming news about several clients. Why would London violate the confidentiality rules that he himself had long preached to others and engage in insider trading? He had a prosperous career with an annual income nearing the seven-figure mark and an enviable family life. In return for the information he provided Shaw, he received some concert tickets, a Rolex watch, and a few envelopes containing cash—together valued at less than $70,000. London's thirty-year career as a successful auditor ended on April 5, 2013, the day he was arrested and terminated by KPMG.

Today, we would take KPMG's decision to fire London for granted—a professional does not violate the confidence of clients, and those who do deserve to be punished. However, this turns out to be a startlingly modern view. In the early 1960s, when Robert Morgenthau was the US Attorney for the Southern District of New York, one of the most prestigious and powerful prosecutorial positions in the United States, arresting an accountant was tantamount to turning on one's own. "The general policy was not to indict and try lawyers and accountants on the ground they are professional people and that this would be too harsh a step," Morgenthau recalled.

Actions that today earn long jail sentences, from insider trading to the manipulation of financial statements, were not widely seen as criminal until the middle of the twentieth century, when an academic from a midwestern university began proclaiming that everybody had it all wrong.

Illuminating Executive Misconduct

On the evening of December 27, 1939, Edwin Sutherland took to the podium to deliver his presidential address at the fifty-second annual meeting of the American Sociological Society. Soft-spoken and admired for his scholarly objectivity, Sutherland had distinguished himself as a conservative yet influential sociologist. Many in the audience knew him from his popular university textbook *Principles of Criminology*. Based on his past work, few of the distinguished sociologists and economists in attendance were prepared for Sutherland's provocative remarks that evening.

Sutherland began his speech by arguing that much of what his colleagues understood about crime was "misleading and incorrect." By relying on public criminal records, Sutherland chided his fellow criminologists for mistakenly concluding that crime was restricted to the streets and largely committed by individuals in the lower social classes. In Sutherland's view, much of the most serious crime was being committed not by the poor or the "delinquent" but, instead, by society's most well-known and respected business leaders. Deviance committed by "respected business and professional men" was simply overlooked because people of high socioeconomic standing were not usually convicted in criminal courts. During his talk, Sutherland even coined a new term for this class of deviance: "white-collar crime."

In what was a rare privilege for an otherwise obscure academic presentation, several leading newspapers covered Sutherland's speech the following day. The *Philadelphia Inquirer* noted that his speech "heaved scores of sociological textbooks into a waste basket" and that sociologists in attendance were "astonished" by his remarks. The *New York Times* credited Sutherland for giving an address "which discarded accepted conceptions and explanations of crime." The article, echoing Sutherland's speech, noted that "the financial cost of white-collar crime is probably several times as great as the financial cost of the crimes which are customarily regarded as the crime problem." As evidence, the *Times* article gave one of Sutherland's examples about a grocery store executive who embezzled $600,000 (the 2016 equivalent of more than $10 million) in just one year. This was six times the entire amount from five hundred robberies that occurred at the same chain of stores during the year.

This professional malfeasance, in Sutherland's mind, was hardly an isolated phenomenon. Although he lacked broad statistical evidence at the time, Sutherland offered detailed examples of manipulative practices across every major industry—banking, utilities, insurance, oil, real estate—that he believed were just as disruptive and harmful as most street offenses against people and property. He insisted that this white-collar criminality was not restricted to "ambulance chasers, bucket-shop operators, dead-beats, and fly-by-night swindlers" but, rather, was present within many of the leading corporations in America. To his surprised audience, Sutherland went so far as to compare some of these corporate practices to the "legitimate rackets" operated by Al Capone, the notorious Chicago mobster. "White-collar crime is real crime," he contended. "It is not ordinarily called crime, and calling it by this name does not make it worse, just as refraining from calling it crime does not make it better than it otherwise would be."

The concerns Sutherland expressed about pervasive malfeasance perpetrated by the leaders of corporate America stood in stark contrast to the widespread veneration of businessmen only a few years earlier. In 1928, a well-known advertising executive named Earnest Calkins wrote in his book that "the most admirable and efficient piece of work being done today is the work business is doing. No king or general or priest is accomplishing so much, even in terms of his own *métier,* as the captains of industry. . . . Business is doing its job, and as much cannot be said of the traditional and historic leaders of mankind." The executive was credited in popular media as being the "most influential man in our time," and entering the field of business could hardly sound more attractive and glamorous when described as "something of the glory that in the past was given to the crusader, the soldier, the courtier, the explorer, and sometimes to the martyr." Much of this ebullience toward business could be attributed to the rising stock market, which nearly doubled in value between 1926 and early 1929. The wealth created by the market ushered in an era of prosperity, carrying with it executives who enjoyed the public's admiration and respect.

There was a dramatic shift in this perception when the stock market crashed in October 1929. Between August 1929 and June 1932, the S&P Composite Index lost 86 percent of its value. More than simply dampening the public's enthusiasm toward business, the once infallible executives who gained almost heroic status in the 1920s now found themselves the targets of blame for the nation's economic woes. The chairman of the country's largest bank, Charles Mitchell, was lauded by one New York paper as the "ideal modern bank executive" in May 1929. Six months later, he found himself chastised as one of the individuals most "responsible for this stock crash" and the subsequent economic turmoil.

During the backlash against the business elite in the early 1930s, Sutherland developed his scholarly interest in corporate malfeasance. This attention arose from his personal misgivings about the behavior of executives and the outcome of one trial in particular. In the fall of 1932, a well-known Chicago utility executive, Samuel Insull, was charged with twenty-five counts of mail fraud and embezzlement. As the trial unfolded Insull insisted that he'd acted as any businessman would have and, therefore, that there was nothing wrong with his actions. During his cross-examination, when asked about one of the allegations, Insull exclaimed: "I would do it again—I would do it today!" Following the two-month trial, Insull won a complete dismissal of all charges. According to Marshall Clinard, a student in Sutherland's graduate seminar and later a respected criminologist himself, Sutherland was outraged. Sutherland was baffled that someone in Insull's position could be acquitted since, in his view, Insull's behavior was so obviously criminal.

Soon thereafter, Sutherland began taking a scholarly interest in professional deviance. Inspired by his reading of E. A. Ross' book, *Sin and Society,* Sutherland came across the concept of the "criminaloid," people who commit acts that are not necessarily illicit but nevertheless undermine societal well-being. In Ross' depiction, the criminaloid prospers "by flagitious practices which have not yet come under the effective ban of public opinion." "But," as Ross wrote, "since they are not culpable in the eyes of the public and in their own eyes, their spiritual attitude is not that of the criminal." According to Ross, a criminaloid is a man who "murders with an adulterant instead of a bludgeon, burglarizes with a 'rake-off' instead of a jimmy, cheats with a company prospectus instead of a deck of cards, or scuttles his town instead of his ship, [and] does not feel on his brow the brand of a malefactor." Picking up on Ross' description of the criminaloid soon after the Insull trial, Sutherland wrote in the 1934 edition of his text-book that "these white-collar criminaloids . . . are by far the most danger-ous to society of any type of criminals from the point of view of effects on private property and social institutions." Sutherland further alluded to criminaloids in several additional articles before finally giving his own detailed interpretation of malfeasance by professionals and others of high social standing in his 1939 presidential address.

Corporate deviance had been historically overlooked by criminologists because it was not actually considered criminal in most instances. This circumstance arose, in part, from the lack of regulation prohibiting injuri-ous behavior in the conduct of business. Except for some laws regulating competition and the sale of adulterated products, the federal government largely left individual states free to enact their own regulation to protect consumers and investors. These state laws were commonly referred to as "blue-sky" laws, after the belief that without them "financial pirates would sell citizens everything in [the] state but the blue sky." Despite their intent to protect investors, blue-sky laws were often ineffective. The laws them-selves were weak, and enforcement was even weaker—deliberately so in some cases, because state legislators did not want to lose licensing fees to other states with more lenient regulation.

Despite the ill effects created by deviant executive behavior, there was little effort to rein in corporate conduct and limit destructive behavior at the federal level in the 1920s. Although support for additional regulation grew in the immediate aftermath of economic downturns, subsequent im-provements in conditions muted support for the passage of additional legislation. Ten weeks after the stock market crash of October 1929, six members of Congress introduced legislation to regulate corporate finan-cial reporting and securities trading. However, this legislation was passed over during a modest, but short-lived, recovery in early 1930. When the stock market began another deep slide in the summer of that year, Presi-dent Hoover anxiously chided the private governing bodies of the securi-ties markets to enact their own changes, but he resisted efforts to take federal action as part of his desire to champion a laissez-faire, pro-business philosophy.

Seizing on Hoover's inaction, Franklin D. Roosevelt promised swift adoption of federal securities legislation during his 1932 presidential

campaign. Capitalizing on the public's anger, President Roosevelt highlighted the dangers posed by irresponsible business practices and proposed regulation to control executives, or "privileged princes" as he once
called them. Not surprisingly, many executives were opposed to the proposed regulation. During the congressional inquiry into the causes of the
1929 stock market crash, *Time* magazine revealed that "bankers high &
low throughout the land, while not condoning the acts of 1929, loudly
proclaimed that last week the greater villains were U.S. Senators who
would risk the credit of the U.S. by putting scandal into the headlines
when Confidence had already received body-blows."

Despite strong resistance by corporate leaders, legislators eventually
recognized a need to address weak state blue-sky laws, which led to the
creation of the first major pieces of federal securities regulation—the Securities Act of 1933 and the Securities Exchange Act of 1934. The 1933 Act
mandated the disclosure of accurate financial information to investors
prior to selling securities. The 1934 Act created sweeping legislation governing the financial markets and controlled how securities could trade in
the United States. To help restore investor confidence, the 1934 Act also
created a new agency, the Securities and Exchange Commission (SEC), to
regulate securities offerings and corporate reporting.

Despite these advances in regulating business conduct, Sutherland was
deeply unsatisfied. He lamented the fact that executives who perpetrated
injurious conduct and violated criminal law usually avoided criminal
prosecution. By doing so, they fortuitously avoided the stigma of being
labeled as a "criminal." Sutherland believed that this favored administration of justice insulated corporate offenders from more serious criminal
prosecution. He argued that "the crimes of the lower class are handled by
policemen, prosecutors, and judges, with penal sanctions in the form of
fines, imprisonment, and death." But "the crimes of the upper class either
result in no official action at all, or result in suits for damages in civil
courts, or are handled by inspectors, and by administrative boards or
commissions, with penal sanctions in the form of warnings, orders to
cease and desist, occasionally the loss of a license, and only in extreme
cases by fines or prison sentences."

Sutherland attributed the development of this alternative punitive system to the fact that respected individuals used their power and influence
to determine not only what laws were passed but also "how the criminal

law as it affects themselves is implemented and administered." Even the newly minted SEC, which was created in 1934 to explicitly police fraudulent investment practices, had only the power to sanction executives, file civil suits, and levy fines. It could not bring criminal charges against firms or individuals itself. Rather, if officials at the SEC believed a case warranted criminal indictment, they were required to refer it to prosecutors at the Department of Justice, who in turn chose whether to pursue it or not. As a result, Sutherland found that "white-collar criminals are segregated administratively from other criminals, and largely as a consequence of this are not regarded as real criminals by themselves, the general public, or the criminologists."

With limited regulation of professional behavior and even less effort to prosecute this behavior criminally in his opinion, Sutherland compared executives to the clergy in medieval society who could act with relative impunity. According to the official statistics, criminal activity seemed to be largely restricted to street crimes such as murder, assault, and burglary. This led to one unequivocal, but misleading, conclusion—that criminal activity had a very high incidence among individuals in the lower social classes and a low incidence among people of high socioeconomic standing. By Sutherland's estimate, over 98 percent of documented crime occurred among people of the lower classes.

Relying on these statistics on the incidence of crime, Sutherland rejected the widespread notion among criminologists of the 1930s that "since crime is concentrated in the lower class, it is caused by poverty or by personal and social characteristics believed to be associated statistically with poverty, including feeblemindedness, psychopathic deviations, slum neighborhoods, and 'deteriorated' families." He fervently sought to overturn this belief by arguing that "businessmen are generally not poor, are not feebleminded, do not lack organized recreational facilities, and do not suffer from the other social and personal pathologies." The theory that poverty caused crime simply captured the fact that regulation usually excluded deviant activities undertaken by people of the upper or professional classes. Sutherland later likened this approach by criminologists to collecting data only on criminals with red hair and then erroneously finding that red hair caused criminal behavior.

Despite Sutherland's deliberate attempt to appear objective in his address, he could not remain detached. Underneath the veil of his academic style, he deeply believed that it was insufficient to simply classify executives who perpetrated socially injurious acts as criminal in a scholarly sense. He believed that deviant executives ought to be condemned and prosecuted as criminals without any special regard for their prior accomplishments or esteemed social status.

A Futile Effort

In the ten years following his speech in Philadelphia, Sutherland labored to create his magnum opus on white-collar crime. For $60 a month, he hired graduate students to laboriously hand-collect every violation and legal decision against seventy large firms. Using court records, reports from federal agencies, and articles from the *New York Times,* Sutherland's students recorded every action, both civil and criminal, against each firm. Incredibly, Sutherland found that every single firm in his sample had at least one decision against it. Furthermore, 60 percent of the firms were convicted in criminal court, each with four convictions on average. Sutherland's analysis provided sobering evidence, as he later noted, that "the ideal businessman and the large corporation are very much like the professional thief."

All of Sutherland's findings were published in his book, *White Collar Crime,* in 1949. Sutherland's disheartening assessment of business and the gall it took to identify certain business activities as criminal, which were not prosecuted as such at the time, were provocative. As one reviewer of the book from Yale University put it, Sutherland was "daring to call criminal a phenomenon which neither the Chicago Police Department nor the Federal Bureau of Investigation or the Attorney General's Department list under that heading. This is as daring as a medieval philosopher discarding Aristotle and the Church Fathers." Sutherland believed that "an unlawful act is not defined as criminal by the fact that it is punished, but by the fact that it is punishable."

Sutherland's contentious conclusions were not well received in all quarters. When Sutherland approached his publisher with the draft of his book, the publisher demanded that he remove the names of firms from the text, worrying that it would face libel suits. Administrators at Sutherland's school, Indiana University, further appealed to him to remove the names of firms out of fear that it could offend wealthy donors to the

school. Eventually, Sutherland acquiesced to these demands and he removed the names of firms from his book.

Despite the absence of firms' names in the published book, academic
reviewers were nearly unanimous in recognizing that Sutherland's contribution was significant. Now that the pervasiveness of deviant corporate behavior had been explicitly quantified, few could dispute
Sutherland's basic argument that there were undesirable activities occurring at the highest echelons of society.

There was an immediate flurry of academic scholarship in the wake of
the book's publication, but its influence on policy and the public perceptions of corporate behavior was considerably less significant. *Harper's
Magazine*, the only major mainstream periodical to review Sutherland's
book, found his analysis less compelling. In particular, the reviewer noted
that "institutional crimes can never have the emotional impact of personal crimes, though the former may be just as—or more—reprehensible
and injurious to society." The objectionable corporate practices that
Sutherland saw as deplorable were decidedly less apparent to others.

Unlike Sutherland, it seemed as though the public had largely forgotten, or at least overcome, the anger toward business leaders that emerged
during the depression of the 1930s. The economy was improving rapidly
following the end of World War II, and there was little fervor to mark im-
pudent executives as criminals. When misconduct occurred, it did not
necessarily represent a serious affront to social norms. "Most of the studies
of white-collar crime in the 1950s," noted two prominent criminologists,
"portrayed an economy where criminal activity was tolerated and desired
by corporations." One survey conducted every decade from the late 1920s
to the late 1950s found corporate misconduct *increasingly* tolerated by the
public over time. In 1958, more respondents condemned a firm for not
paying a respectable wage than for committing outright financial fraud.

To the satisfaction of at least some executives who believed that it was
best not to draw attention to infractions, lest it create a bad reputation for
business, the media continued to largely overlook corporate wrongdoing.
The amorphous harms that Sutherland bemoaned years earlier in his
speech tended to make business misconduct an unattractive topic. Without the urgency that characterized most street crime, white-collar offenses
usually lacked the sensational appeal that made front-page news. The lack
of media interest was further compounded by the fact that most journalists

lacked the technical knowledge needed to write about the intricacies that arose in complex white-collar litigation.

Business proceeded as it desired. Business*men,* as they predominately were at the time, had the opportunity to sidestep any inconvenient broader responsibilities associated with their actions. Ted Levitt, a marketing consultant and, later, a Harvard Business School professor, expressed this sentiment well in a 1958 *Advertising Age* article. "The cultural, spiritual, social, moral, etc., consequences of his actions," Levitt wrote, "are none of his occupational concern. . . . If what is offered can be sold at a profit (not even necessarily a long-term profit), then it is legitimate."

Sending Gentlemen to Prison

Two decades after Sutherland's speech, there were few indications of any significant shift in attitudes about executive misconduct. Fines might be levied on a company, but individual accountability—let alone criminal prosecution—was still exceedingly rare. Something extraordinary needed to occur to rouse a change in sentiment.

In 1961, The Great Electrical Conspiracy seemed to be exactly what was needed to catalyze public perception. As Anthony Lewis of the *New York Times* wrote at the time, "Here were the classic elements of the great criminal case: charges of the most serious skullduggery, involving vast sums of money; powerful, highly respectable defendants; disclosures raising moral questions not just for the defendants but for society at large."

The events began rather innocuously in mid-1959, when federal regulators received complaints from the Tennessee Valley Authority that manufacturers had submitted identical bids for electrical power equipment. This struck officials as unusual since the bids were submitted via sealed envelope to ensure secrecy. Even more curiously, in several instances the biggest manufacturers of electrical equipment, General Electric and Westinghouse, turned in identical offers even though the distance between the manufacturing facilities and the Tennessee Valley Authority operations differed by hundreds and even thousands of miles. The delivery cost alone should have created significant variation in the bids. The likelihood that manufacturers coincidentally submitted the same "secret" bids to competitive contract auctions seemed increasingly improbable as more evidence was collected.

Under the Sherman Antitrust Act, firms were expressly forbidden from colluding on prices. The federal government investigated the allegations of price collusion and soon uncovered a sophisticated price-fixing arrangement that engulfed the entire electrical equipment industry. In an effort to stabilize prices and preserve their profit margins, managers from each of the electrical firms clandestinely met and decided on a price for their products. One firm would be selected to "win" the contract, and managers at other firms would tacitly agree to place less competitive bids. To decide which firm would win each contract, managers utilized a variety of schemes that differed among product lines. In one case, the market was divided up and each firm received a predetermined amount of market share: General Electric received 42 percent, Westinghouse 38 percent, and lesser shares went to the smaller niche firms. In another division, each firm won all contracts from a particular geographic area. To maintain the discreetness of these operations, details of the meetings were coded. Attendance records were referred to as the "Christmas card list," and the rotating strategy to determine which firm would win each contract was labeled colorfully as the "phases of the moon."

When the defendants were finally brought in front of the presiding justice over the case, Judge J. Cullen Ganey, he summarized the findings as a "shocking indictment of a vast section of our economy." A list of twenty charges alleged that twenty-nine firms, including industry leaders General Electric and Westinghouse, conspired to fix prices on everything from "tiny $2 insulators to multimillion-dollar turbine generators." Forty-five individual executives were listed as conspirators in the price-fixing scandal.

The onslaught of media attention, directed not just at the firms but also at the individual executives involved, was unrivaled in the history of journalism. Robert Kennedy, the attorney general of the United States who led the prosecution, explained his desire to seek criminal sanctions against the executives in this case:

In the past 30 years the government has won a number of antitrust suits. But in these earlier cases the punishment was usually in the form of fines, and after it was over, business went on as usual. The businessman who participated was not treated as though he had done anything really wrong. He was just following the accepted practices of big business in the 20th Century U.S.A. He was accepted as usual at the country club, he was appointed as usual to be the chairman of the community charity-drive.

Kennedy sought criminal prosecutions of these executives because, in his view, he saw this case as one "where the small businessman is exploited, where the consumer is disregarded, [and] where the government is defrauded."

This innovative and ultimately more severe prosecution of executives did not sit well with those involved. One defense attorney questioned the government's desire to punish executives for practices that were so pervasive that they were essentially norms of practice in the industry. Another attorney called the prosecutor's demand to send his client, a General Electric executive, to prison "cold-blooded." Further pleading with the judge, the attorneys for the defense questioned the need to incarcerate a "fine man" with other "common criminals," which included "crooks, gangsters, pimps, and prostitutes."

Despite these protests, seven executives were sentenced to prison and another twenty-four received suspended jail sentences. George Burens, a forty-year veteran of General Electric, spoke to journalists as he waited to call his wife after being sentenced to thirty days in prison. "There goes my whole life," exclaimed Burens. "Who's going to want to hire a jailbird? What am I going to tell my children?" The nationally renowned periodical *Life* printed a photograph of one of the executives confined behind bars. The image of the respected, distinguished executive who was infallible was permanently shattered.

The investigation and ensuing sentencing captured not only the attention of the public but also that of President John F. Kennedy. At a news conference held two days after the sentences were handed down, Kennedy suggested that it would be worthwhile if the business community could develop standards to restrain managers from undesirable corporate conduct. Luther Hodges, Kennedy's secretary of commerce, took the lead on the president's idea and formed an advisory council with representatives from the business and educational communities as well as the clergy. They decided to develop a system of guidelines to help managers grapple with some of the ethical challenges facing business leaders. Six months later, in

Figure 1.2: Edwin Jung,
former Vice President of
Clark Controller, looking
out from confinement.

January 1962, Hodges' group produced *A Statement on Business Ethics and a Call to Action,* which raised a variety of issues around managerial conduct.

After meeting with Hodges and reading over the *Call to Action,* President Kennedy optimistically believed that the business community would respond favorably to the council's findings. Hodges started the campaign with roundtable discussions with leading business figures. Almost immediately, he encountered a starkly unfavorable response from the prominent businessmen in attendance. "Two or three people spoke out against making public the work of the Ethics Council," Hodges recalled. "One industrialist argued very forcefully that it was bad to issue a statement like the *Call to Action* because, he contended, it makes the public feel that all business is unethical." In the end, "not a solitary soul stood up to support the proposed program or to endorse our view that the business community should get actively interested in this problem."

Although Attorney General Kennedy thought that the electrical equipment case was "not something we can forget after sending some of these men to jail," it ultimately did not instigate a widespread and lasting moral condemnation of corporate deviance. In fact, several prominent individuals even came to the defense of the electrical equipment executives.

Arnold Bernhard, founder of the popular *Value Line Survey,* expressed the dilemma that executives faced with antitrust laws:

> If he fixes prices or stabilizes them, he may be guilty of conspiracy to violate the antitrust laws. On the other hand, if he observes this section of the law and is governed only by the law of supply and demand, he soon destroys all his competition and emerges as the monopoly power in his field and a violator of Section II of the same law.

Bernhard's argument expressed the contradictory nature of economic regulation designed to promote competition rather than protect physical welfare or public safety. Economic regulation did not always prohibit widely agreed-upon harms. In fact, there was often considerable debate among regulators, courts, and even the authors of the legislation about what specific behavior ought to be prohibited by such regulation.

Sutherland, like Robert Kennedy, believed that punishing executives criminally would lead to public censure. What they failed to understand was that criminal prosecution was itself insufficient to lead to this condemnation. Society also had to view their offenses as morally reprehensible. Yet, many regulatory offenses lacked this stigma. "Without moral wrongfulness," the legal scholar Stuart Green wrote, "one might conclude that defendants who violate such laws do not 'deserve' to be punished."

In a later interview with *Fortune* magazine, one of the General Electric managers involved in the price-fixing incident conveyed this distinction as he understood it. "Sure, collusion was illegal," he explained, "but it wasn't unethical. It wasn't any more unethical than if the companies had a summit conference the way Russia and the West meet. Those competitor meetings were just attended by a group of distressed individuals who wanted to know where they were going."

Despite the intense scrutiny of Westinghouse's practices by the press and politicians, the company's reaction to the convictions provided a revealing depiction of the perceived gravity of these crimes from the perspective of the business community. In an announcement, Westinghouse's president and CEO, Mark Cresap, stated that he did not plan to take punitive action against any of the managers criminally convicted in the price-fixing scandal. Each manager would remain in his current position. Cresap declared that "these men did not act for personal gain, but in the belief . . . that they were furthering the company's interest." He went on to say that "each of these individuals is in every sense a reputable citizen, a respected and valuable member of the community and of high moral character."

Unlike Westinghouse, General Electric dismissed its indicted executives. Yet, there is little evidence that those dismissals significantly stymied those executives or their careers since they soon found managerial-level positions at other firms. William Ginn, one of General Electric's youngest vice-presidents and the highest paid individual indicted, joined Baldwin-Lima-Hamilton in Philadelphia and soon became its president. Another executive, Lewis Burger, became president of LeTourneau-Westinghouse. The decision to dismiss them wasn't even widely accepted. When a panel of young businessmen assembled at the University of Pennsylvania's Wharton School of Business in June 1961, they were asked whether they would have dismissed the managers involved if they were an executive at General Electric. Nearly two-thirds of those in attendance said no.

The overarching public ambivalence toward the Great Electrical Price Conspiracy didn't mean that crime as a whole was ignored during the 1960s. On the contrary, crime was a rising domestic policy concern. President Johnson established a commission to study crime in America, and in 1967 the group released its report titled *The Challenge of Crime in a Free Society*. The report speculated that the cost imposed on the public by the price fixing of the twenty-nine electrical companies exceeded the aggregate cost of all reported burglaries reported during the year. Yet, despite these costs, the report devoted only 6 of its 814 pages to discussing white-collar criminality. "The public tends to be indifferent to business crime or even sympathize with the offenders when they have been caught," the authors of the report concluded.

Attorney General Kennedy's assessment that the perception of white-collar crime would change significantly if some prominent executives were sent to prison was mistaken. While this publicity may have exposed managerial misconduct more broadly than in the past, white-collar criminality itself lacked the fear factor associated with street crime. As a result, such offenses were seen as neither especially harmful nor deeply offensive to the public's moral sensibility in many instances. "It is essential that the public becomes aware of the seriousness of business crime," argued the authors of the commission's report. "Without such awareness and the resulting demands for action, legislatures, courts, and administrative agencies will continue, as is now usually the case, to treat business offenses as relatively minor mistakes."

BY THE CLOSE of the 1960s, the idea of branding senior executives as criminals and sending them to prison was still a foreign and uncomfortable idea. "Forces in the criminal justice system today have combined to minimize the prospect that the white-collar offender will receive any significant jail sentence or fine," lamented the federal prosecutor Robert Ogren. It was possible, as with the case with executives from Westinghouse, to break laws, be convicted, and still be rehired after completing a stint in prison. "Few would choose to live in a society in which there were no criminal laws prohibiting fraud and corruption," reflected one prosecutor at the time. "The nagging question is whether, as a practical matter, we are not today perilously close to functioning as though there were no such laws."

It would take more time—but not all that much—before white-collar crime would be widely perceived as serious misconduct in both the United States and elsewhere.

2

Guys . . . don't drop out of windows for no reason

Creating the White-Collar Criminal

I N 1972, THE fallout from the burglary of the Democratic National Committee offices riveted Americans. Prosecutors traced money carried by the burglars to a fund created to reelect President Nixon. When it was discovered that many major corporations, including American Airlines and Goodyear Tire, had made illegal campaign contributions to this reelection fund, the Watergate scandal soon began to ensnare American business.

Like many Americans, Stanley Sporkin, deputy director of the SEC's division of enforcement, watched the hearings on television. "What bothered me . . . was that I didn't understand how these companies were making these payments," Sporkin recalled. "How did a publicly traded corporation record such an illegal transaction?" Sporkin put an investigator informally on the task and soon "discovered that the use of company funds was not confined to illegal political contributions. . . . Secret funds were used to make many other forms of illicit payments, including payment of bribes to high officials of foreign governments." A hunch soon turned into a full-fledged investigation.

These discoveries were fresh in Sporkin's mind on the morning of February 3, 1975, when Eli Black jumped from the 44th floor of the Pan Am building in New York City. Black was chairman of United Brands, a multibillion-dollar conglomerate best known for its Chiquita banana brand. Sporkin called several of his attorneys, including Ralph Ferrara, into his office after hearing about Black's untimely death. "Ralph," Sporkin told him, "Guys don't die like this, don't drop out of windows for no reason. I want you to call up and find out what's going on."

After considerable prodding by Sporkin's lawyers, attorneys for United Brands finally revealed that in 1974 Black paid $1.25 million to the president of Honduras, General Oswaldo López, for a reduction in Honduras' banana export tax. Black committed suicide soon after depositing the funds into a Swiss bank account. Within two weeks of this bribery becoming public, the Honduran military ousted President López in a coup.

The disclosures did not end with United Brands. With relatively limited resources available through the SEC, Sporkin knew that his staff could not undertake its own investigations to unearth these hidden political payments. Creatively, Sporkin offered executives a choice: they could undertake their own internal investigation and disclose these payments, or the SEC would sue them for violation of federal securities law and force their firm to undergo a costly court-ordered audit. Hundreds of firms complied with Sporkin's offer to "voluntarily" disclose their payments.

To the irritation and embarrassment of many executives, Sporkin's ingenuity yielded considerable evidence that investigators began to comb through for potential cases of corporate mischief. Many of the largest companies found themselves revealing substantial sums they had paid to conduct business around the world. When Lockheed Martin disclosed tens of millions of dollars paid to heads of state, it became front-page news. The company used a variety of arrangements to hide its transgressions, including issuing a payment of "one hundred peanuts" to the office of the prime minister of Japan. Lockheed executives made other payments to Indonesian military officials in a disguised account called "The Widows and Orphans Fund."

The *New York Times* decried the practice of spending "hundreds of millions of dollars each year for agents' fees, commissions and outright payoffs to foreign officials." Hypocritical behavior on the part of executives only served to further raise corporate cynicism. Robert Moore, the CEO of Castle & Cooke, one of United Brands' largest competitors, told the *Wall Street Journal* that Black's bribery payment at United Brands was "a deplorable development" that he was at a "loss to understand." Remarkably, Castle & Cooke would later reveal that it had made its own illicit payments to Latin American officials. Despite the fact that this bribery was widely perceived by the public as unacceptable corporate behavior, it wasn't actually illegal. There was simply no explicit law prohibiting inducements and kickbacks in the conduct of business.

Foreign bribery was hardly the only type of corporate mischief that came to the fore in the 1970s. All of a sudden white-collar crime filled the news, and it seemed as though "lawless behavior—including price-fixing, illegal political contributions to domestic and foreign governments, environmental damage, and health and safety violations—was the norm rather than the exception." Led by consumer advocates like Ralph Nader, executive conduct came under increasing public scrutiny and once well-regarded business leaders transformed into villains. From a car manufacturer's explicit decision to leave a faulty fuel tank in place, to a chemical company knowingly discharging pesticides into waterways, corporate America became increasingly defined by its dubious ethical standards.

The damage created by this managerial malfeasance caught the attention of the media like never before. The distinguished legal scholar John Coffee noted in 1977 that "the business pages of American newspapers have carried a continuing story of corporate misconduct with the same daily regularity as the sports pages have reprinted the baseball box scores." What had changed was not just the frequency with which articles about managerial deviance appeared but also the fact that the tenor of press coverage was anything but sympathetic, in stark contrast to the coverage of the price-fixing scandal a decade earlier. *Fortune* magazine wrote that "crime in the executive suite has come to command media attention of a sort formally reserved for ax murders." By the late 1970s, managerial deviance had acquired such interest that it even briefly became the subject of its own comic-book series, *Corporate Crime Comics*.

With all this media coverage focused on business misconduct, the reputation of business leaders—once revered by the public—began to plummet. When Gallup asked 1,500 adults to rate the honesty and ethical standards of various professions, doctors and engineers ranked at the top with 55 percent and 48 percent approval ratings, respectively. But only 19 percent of survey respondents felt similarly optimistic about the ethical standards of business executives.

Figure 2.1: The cover of the second issue of *Corporate Crime Comics*.

Unlike earlier decades, the desire to prosecute white-collar criminality was no longer a sentiment held by a lone professor or isolated prosecutor. The rising public backlash against business misconduct made it a political issue on the agenda of federal investigators and prosecutors. In 1974, the FBI's annual report listed white-collar crime as its own separate subheading for the first time. Even so, two years later, one prominent US attorney ridiculed the FBI publicly for being "out of step," charging that the Bureau was unwilling to investigate economic crime because of its interest in "quantity—not quality" of prosecutions. But by 1980, the FBI had tripled the resources it devoted to investigating white-collar crimes to nearly a quarter of its overall budget. More agents were assigned to white-collar cases than to any other unit in its entire force outside national security.

The growth of white-collar prosecutions by the end of the 1970s also manifested itself in other unexpected ways. The head of the American Bar Association's Section on Litigation remarked that white-collar criminal defense was the fastest-growing legal specialty by the late 1970s. "Attorneys employed by such defendants are not constrained by resources," wrote legal scholar William Genego. "They are able to present comprehensive and vigorous defenses. . . . These attorneys devote large amounts of time to defense preparation; they hire private investigators, defense experts, and consultants both before and during trial." Despite the formidable legal defense that white-collar defendants could muster, the Department of Justice officially made white-collar crime a top priority in 1978, as more federal prosecutors grew willing to take on these challenging cases.

Emboldened by the growing mistrust of business practices, legislators passed new regulations significantly restricting corporate behavior that the public felt was not just unethical but criminal. Most prominently, Congress passed the Foreign Corrupt Practices Act (FCPA) in 1977, making bribery of foreign officials a criminal offense for the first time. Corporate executives who violated the FCPA could spend up to five years in jail, while their companies could incur fines up to $1 million. Prior to the FCPA's passage, foreign bribery not only was not explicitly illegal but was actually tax deductible so long as the foreign government in question "acquiesced" to the payments.

The Supreme Court also issued a landmark ruling in 1975 that made executives responsible for conduct that fell outside of their direct supervision.

The laws themselves as well as the vigor of enforcement pivoted dramatically by the end of the 1970s. Punishments for violating the Sherman Act were ratcheted up, with individuals now facing up to three years in prison. When *Business Week* described the growing legal accountability that executives now faced, one executive sarcastically remarked that many firms "are thinking about hiring a vice-president in charge of going to jail."

Pushing the Envelope

Opening their *Wall Street Journal* on Friday, February 13, 1987, readers were thrust into an unusually dramatic scene:

> At 10:30 a.m. yesterday, federal vans pulled up to the downtown Manhattan skyscraper headquarters of Goldman, Sachs, and Co. and Kidder, Peabody and Co. . . . A brigade of federal marshals and postal inspectors descended on the office of Richard Wigton, the head of arbitrage and over-the-counter trading. In full view of the firm's stunned traders, he was placed against the wall, frisked and handcuffed, and led away in tears.

This sort of story typified Rudolph Giuliani's style of conducting a white-collar arrest. And few district attorneys were more aggressive in supporting the new paradigm against white-collar criminality in the 1980s than Giuliani, the United States Attorney for the Southern District of New York and later mayor of New York City. Giuliani quickly gained notoriety for being tough on crime by going after not only the major New York Mafia bosses but also prominent securities traders. In his first four years in office Giuliani charged more than fifty individuals for securities violations, and he gained a particularly infamous reputation for pioneering the "perp walk" to humiliate those he indicted.

Giuliani's strategy for pursuing white-collar criminals was simple. Anyone charged with committing a corporate offense would be not only coaxed into confessing his wrongdoing but also compelled into providing evidence against his colleagues and business associates in return for leniency in sentencing. Giuliani cast a wide net, intimidating potential white-collar offenders who faced the criminal justice system for the first time in their lives. While usually effective, Giuliani occasionally met resistance, prompting even greater creativity in his pursuit. In one case, Giuliani sought the executives at the Princeton/Newport investment management company on charges of "stock parking"—a form of deception that entails holding the stock in another person's name for tax benefits. Despite the fact that lower-level staff members were presented with substantial evidence against them, they were unwilling to confess the wrongdoings of higher-level executives at the company.

Giuliani realized that it would take an innovative strategy to go after the leaders of Princeton/Newport. He introduced what would be his greatest—and most controversial—contribution to pursuing white-collar criminals by employing the Racketeer Influenced and Corrupt Organizations statute (RICO) to yield prosecutions. RICO was originally devised to prosecute members of organized crime rings like the Mafia, in which middlemen in seemingly legitimate operations made it difficult to pursue those in leadership positions. RICO allowed prosecutors to indict all individuals involved in a criminal organization as part of a racketeering enterprise and gave regulators authority to seize assets of offenders even prior to trial. If convicted, even assets gained through noncriminal means could be seized by the government.

RICO's application to a financial entity was so potent that Princeton/Newport shut down prior to a trial as clients such as Harvard University's endowment and McKinsey & Co. worried that their assets could be frozen, or perhaps even seized, in the ensuing prosecution. Applying RICO's potency to corporate criminality enabled Giuliani, according to one legal scholar, "to drop the equivalent of a nuclear bomb on any target, at any time, no matter how trivial or harmless the underlying conduct." The Justice Department, however, concluded that applying RICO in the Princeton/Newport case was so extreme a step that it blocked the use of RICO in future cases involving relatively mundane tax disputes.

In his effort to pursue corporate offenders, Giuliani contorted preexisting laws to pursue people he believed were committing crimes even when the crime was vaguely defined and difficult to prove. He generated significant coverage for successfully pursuing charges against Ivan Boesky, one of Wall Street's wealthiest and most successful stock arbitrageurs. While nearly thirty years earlier, the judge in the electrical equipment conspiracy had noted that for most white-collar defendants, "long probationary periods where a watchful eye can be kept on their activities and fines will suffice for their first offense," the judge sentencing Boesky deemed that "the time has come when it is totally unacceptable for courts to act as if prison is unthinkable for white-collar defendants, but a matter of routine in other cases. Breaking the law is breaking the law."

By the end of the 1980s, other prosecutors had begun to follow Giuliani's lead, marking an overall shift in sentiment toward white-collar crime in the United States. This aggressiveness was evident from creative new strategies for uncovering and pursuing white-collar criminals. In operations colorfully named "Hedgeclipper" and "Sourmash," the FBI placed undercover agents on the floor of the Chicago Board of Trade and Mercantile Exchange. These agents made recordings of traders cheating their customers, ultimately leading to convictions of nearly fifty people. Criminal sanctions coupled with prison had now become an accepted norm for executives perpetrating misconduct. Even in cases where experts believed that prosecutors, such as Giuliani, were overly aggressive in applying statutes to bring those accused of corporate misconduct to justice, prosecutors continued to gain public support. In response to criticism that he was being too tough on nonviolent offenders, Giuliani stood firm. "The rules apply to mob big shots like Fat Tony Salerno, and they apply to big shots at Goldman Sachs, too."

A Worldwide Response

In 1944, Edwin Sutherland laid out three impediments that he believed were holding back a more aggressive stance toward white-collar misconduct. He was hopeful that regulators, the public, and the business community eventually would come to surmount these obstacles. More than seven decades later, what can be said about our vigilance against corporate malfeasance?

The social status of businessmen that seemed to protect them from recrimination was Sutherland's first concern. Historically, prosecutors did not want to antagonize business leaders, because of their prominence and respectability in society. Regulators feared the accused. But these sentiments shifted dramatically, as more regulators and politicians sought to define themselves as taking a tougher stance against conduct condemned by their electorates.

In just five years, beginning in 2002, federal prosecutors in the United States secured convictions against more than 200 CEOs, 50 CFOs, and 120 vice presidents. Across the world, status and wealth, while once providing a source of protection, often now prove to be a vulnerability. Nations that historically had a reputation for not prosecuting business leaders, or suspending their sentences if convicted, have changed their sentiments. In Spain, for instance, a wealthy developer charged with evading nearly 1 million euros in taxes went to his sentencing hearing in 2012 with the expectation that he would pay a fine and return to his daily routine. Instead, he was sentenced to three and a half years in prison. "He had the money in the bank to pay," noted his surprised defense attorney, "but the judge didn't want it."

In South Korea, a country notoriously lenient toward its business leaders, the chairman of Hyundai Motors was arrested for embezzlement and bribery. As many predicted, his appeals judge ordered him released "in consideration of the huge economic impact that could result from imprisonment." It seemed to one British-based Korea expert that the heads of the country's conglomerates "are so important they can do what they damn well please." But even these sentiments have begun to change. In 2013, Chey Tae-won, one of Korea's wealthiest executives, was sentenced to four years in prison for embezzlement. Even within emerging and industrializing economies, the tendency to prosecute powerful executives is shifting. In Oman, the CEO of the national oil company was sentenced to twenty-three years in prison for bribery in 2014. In Brazil, Eike Batista, once worth $30 billion and estimated to be the seventh-richest person in the world, was charged with financial manipulation in 2014.

Sutherland was equally concerned that white-collar offenders, even if convicted, would not be effectively punished. He believed that sanctions against white-collar offenders were designed much like those against juvenile delinquents. Laws and procedures avoided labeling young offenders as criminals to prevent placing a negative stigma over their lives. Sutherland believed that legislators had similarly designed laws to avoid "unfairly" stigmatizing executives. Here, too, the modern trend has tilted the other way. One study found that the average CEO charged with financial misrepresentation in the United States was sentenced to nearly six years in prison. "The number of individual prosecutions has risen—and that's not an accident," noted Mark Mendelsohn, the Justice Department's former chief prosecutor of foreign bribery. "That is quite intentional on the part of the Department. . . . People have to go to jail."

Once unthinkable, prison is no longer an uncommon place for wayward executives. Consider the article titled "Going to Jail" published in the *Financial Times* quarterly *Wealth* magazine in 2014 that described "how to soften the blow if your financial dealings land you in jail." While *Wealth* normally offers a planning section with advice on estate succession, butlers, and living at luxury hotels, this piece offered readers ten tips to help prepare for life inside a British prison. There is even a burgeoning industry of white-collar prison consulting firms that offer courses and consultation to help the newly convicted adapt to prison conditions. The founders of these firms have usually spent time in prison themselves and offer modularized training programs to prepare former executives for the challenges they will face during incarceration, including learning prison slang and how to navigate the prison black market.

Some commentators have even begun to ask whether sanctions are now too harsh. Kate Stith, a scholar at Yale Law School, offers an example of how drastically sanctions for white-collar criminality have risen in the United States. A defendant who pled guilty to inflating earnings and causing a $12.5 million loss to shareholders would have had a recommended prison sentence of 30–37 months in 1987. But by 2003, a defendant committing the same crime would have faced a recommended sentence of 151–188 months—a quintupling of penalties equating to nearly an additional decade in prison. It's for this reason that the *Wall Street Journal* remarked that "there may never have been a worse time to be a corporate criminal."

The final hindrance, in Sutherland's eyes, to more vigorous white-collar prosecution was the general indifference of the public toward white-collar offenders. Efforts by prosecutors and regulators to crack down on bribery, corruption, and fraud have led to significant changes in the public perception of white-collar crime. Movements like Occupy Wall Street, in which thousands of people took over Zuccotti Park in New York City's Financial District, provide visceral evidence of the changes in attitude. Holding signs with slogans that read "Go Directly to Jail!" and

"Hungry? Eat a Banker," they demanded greater punishment for Wall Street executives engaged in alleged misconduct. The Supreme Court, writing in 2010, noted that "economic crimes are certainly capable of rousing public passions, particularly when thousands of unsuspecting people are robbed of their livelihood and retirement savings."

Of course, there remains a well-founded concern that not all executives deserving of criminal sanctions are prosecuted. The German public was up in arms when the billionaire Formula One chief executive Bernie Ecclestone settled criminal charges of bribery, which could have led to as many as ten years of jail time, by paying a German court $100 million. The business-section headline of the *Frankfurter Allgemeine Zeitung,* one of Germany's most popular newspapers, cried "Obscene Deal." Criticism rained from above as well, with Germany's former justice minister exclaiming that "this is something we would massively criticize in other countries."

The widespread outrage at the lack of high-level individual prosecutions in the aftermath of the 2008–2009 financial crisis in the United States is further testimony to just how much opinion has changed. "The failure of the government," noted prominent federal judge Jed Rakoff, "to bring to justice those responsible for such a massive fraud bespeaks weaknesses in our prosecutorial system that need to be addressed." President Obama himself was put on the defensive to explain the lack of prosecutions, awkwardly arguing "a lot of that stuff wasn't necessarily illegal, it was just immoral or inappropriate or reckless."

Despite occasional waxing and waning in resources to prosecute business leaders, executives can hardly feel immune to punishment as they once did. The transnational reach of regulators means that laws—and the ensuing sanctions—in one country can often be applied to those in others. While this practice is controversial, one nation's borders no longer insulate individuals from the consequences of perceived misconduct in another. Today, norms and rules in one jurisdiction are routinely applied to conduct elsewhere.

The public, the judiciary, prosecutors, and elected officials all take white-collar crime seriously in a way that would have been unthinkable eighty years ago. Much has changed even if punishment is not always doled out as effectively, or as often, as desired by the public.

THE SIGNIFICANT CHANGES in the response to corporate misconduct prompt an obvious question. If white-collar crime is punishable by prison, and those convicted are branded as social pariahs, why would people in a position of wealth and privilege risk everything to commit such a crime? Why do they do it?

PART II

NATURE OR NURTURE? REASONING OR INTUITION?

3

Inherently inferior organisms

Bad People Making Bad Decisions

O N A GREY November morning in 1870, Cesare Lombroso approached the body of a deceased felon named Giuseppe Vilella. Lombroso had just carefully begun his post-mortem examination, as he had done hundreds of times before, when he was struck by an insight. "At the sight of the skull," Lombroso recalled, "I seemed to see all of a sudden, lighted up as a vast plain of a flaming sky, the problem of the nature of the criminal—an atavistic being who reproduces in his person the ferocious instincts of primitive humanity and the inferior animals."

Lombroso's revelation wasn't an indiscriminate hunch but, rather, one built on the enduring idea that a person's disposition could be assessed by examining his physical appearance. In ancient Greece, the esteemed mathematician Pythagoras chose his friends and students on the basis of their appearance, believing it depicted their true character. Aristotle wrote extensively on how disposition could be deduced from physical character, declaring that "there was never an animal with the form of one kind and the mental character of another." A well-regarded text of the Italian Renaissance furthered this idea by comparing men to the animals they most closely resembled. Mapping specific physical characteristics to particular dispositions was a topic of serious inquiry and lively debate.

By the late eighteenth century, the practice of assessing an individual's character based on his physical likeness had become a full-blown "science"

47

Figure 3.1: An illustration from Giovanni Battista della Porta's
sixteenth-century work comparing men to animals.

known as physiognomy. After the Swiss pastor Johann Lavater published
his book on physiognomy in 1775, it became a worldwide sensation with
over one hundred and fifty editions in half a dozen languages. A broad,
square forehead, Lavater said, provided a clear indication of a good memory. Or, if a person's eyebrows were situated unusually high on the forehead, the person would be incapable of reflection. The idea gained such
mainstream acceptance that in the mid-nineteenth century one magazine
even claimed that it would be ill-advised to hire an employee until that person's features had been compared with one of the well-known physiog-
nomic manuals available at the time.

   Amidst this intellectual backdrop, Lombroso began his systematic investigation of identifying the physical characteristics of criminals. He
conducted detailed physical examinations using an array of newly invented tools to measure every aspect of felons from the angle of their ears
to their sensitivity to pain. Lombroso compiled details of thousands of
criminals and published his findings in his magnum opus *L'Uomo Delin-
quente,* or *The Criminal Man.*

   Lombroso argued that criminals exhibited numerous physical anomalies of a primitive origin. Preserved in modern "savages," according to

Lombroso, were elongated arms reminiscent of those used by apes for walking and climbing, hooked noses that resembled the beaks possessed by birds of prey, and supernumerary teeth like those of snakes. "All these characteristics pointed to one conclusion," said Lombroso's daughter: "atavistic origin of the criminal, who reproduces physical, psychic, and functional qualities of remote ancestors." Such men were prehistoric evolutionary throwbacks who were inherently unable to abide by modern societal laws. They were simply born criminal.

While most of Lombroso's analysis would be dismissed as pseudoscience today, his basic premise that some people are deeply and fundamentally flawed—that they are "born criminal"—continues to resonate. Pressed to explain the deviant executive behavior following the collapse of Enron, President George W. Bush responded that "there are some bad apples." The Chamber of Commerce handbook on white-collar crime describes how some individuals who commit fraud are "simply 'rotten apples' . . . who have an inborn predisposition to defraud." Bernard Madoff's attorneys said they "represent a deeply flawed individual" at his sentencing hearing. And graduates of University of Pennsylvania's Wharton School of Business contended that a spate of their alumni convicted of insider trading were simply "bad eggs" who fundamentally differed from other graduates. Ultimately, "because the public is constantly exposed to financial debacles and evidence of corporate excess and CEO greed," argued the criminologist Sally Simpson, "a bad apple image of offenders has been cemented in the public consciousness."

These explanations point to the idea that corporate criminality arises not from an act of mistaken judgment or some situational influence but, rather, from a deviant nature that is innate and simply waiting to exploit an appropriate opportunity. In being themselves, these individuals are the cause of the crime. While the expression "bad apple" may, at times, be applied casually with little consideration of its implications, this chapter explores whether corporate misconduct might be the inevitable result of inborn processes. Can the onslaught of executive malfeasance be understood by seeing these former leaders as unscrupulous to their very core?

It's worthwhile to step back and appreciate the serious implications if there is something innate that deterministically leads people to criminality later in life. Criminal prosecution relies on establishing *mens rea*— that the accused intended to commit a wrongful act freely and willfully.

We generally believe that prosecution and punishment are reserved for those who have not only an "evil-doing hand" but also an "evil-meaning mind." Someone "born criminal," however, lacks this volition. Their crimes would not be committed voluntarily but, rather, would be caused by biological factors that lay beyond their control. The choice to commit the criminal activity was already, in a biological sense, made for them.

Punishing people for behavior that they are unable to control has long been viewed as unjust. At the same time, there is a desire to prevent supposedly "bad apples" from inflicting even greater social harm. To many, rehabilitation instead of retribution is usually viewed as the more appropriate and humane response. But it was precisely under the guise of rehabilitation and, later, prevention that many of the twentieth century's most oppressive social policies were created. For instance, preventing people deemed socially unfit from having children fueled the eugenics movement in America. The Supreme Court Justice Oliver Wendell Holmes Jr. wrote in 1927 that "it is better for all the world if, instead of waiting to execute degenerate offspring for crime . . . society can prevent those who are manifestly unfit from continuing their kind." By 1937, thirty-two states had passed laws sterilizing prisoners and others deemed unfit to procreate. "Criminals are organically inferior . . . ," wrote one prominent scholar during this rise of eugenic based regulation. "It follows that the elimination of crime can be effected only by the extirpation of the physically, mentally, and morally unfit, or by their complete segregation in a socially aseptic environment." While such radical ideas are out of sync with social policy today, the ramifications of viewing some individuals as "bad apples" are potentially significant.

A Focus on the Body

Lombroso's ambitious and detailed work made him a late-nineteenth-century celebrity. Rather than appealing to a hodgepodge set of maladies ranging from social ills to evil spirits in order to explain criminal conduct, Lombroso provided a systematic set of causes to identify criminals. For this contribution he is often cited as the "father of modern criminology."

In spite of all this favorable attention to Lombroso's work, a group of English scientists led by Charles Goring emerged as ardent critics. After conducting his own set of physical examinations on English convicts, he defiantly concluded that "this anthropological monster has no existence in fact. . . . There is no such thing as an anthropological criminal type." Comparing Lombroso's scientific methods to medieval alchemy, Goring attacked the assertion that there was a distinct criminal subspecies separate from "normal man." He found that if he did a more careful comparison between criminals and noncriminals that took age and stature into account, all of a sudden the criminals didn't look so different from their noncriminal brethren. Goring saw criminals not as freakish evolutionary throwbacks but as regular people who simply had subtle differences in their disposition toward committing crime.

It appeared that Goring's "devastating critique," in the words of one reviewer, might close the door on the idea of the biologically driven criminal type. Curiously though, Goring still interpreted the physical differences between criminals and noncriminals as a sign of the former's inferiority. For all Goring's talk about scientific objectivity, his peculiar interpretation was deeply colored by the eugenics movement, which was well in vogue at the time. Goring simply replaced Lombroso's atavistic "savage" with a different individual who was born with inferior weight, stature, and mental ability.

Across the Atlantic in his office at Harvard University, Earnest Hooton was "disgust[ed] with the sanctimonious statistical deviousness of Goring." Hooton was not a criminologist but, rather, a celebrated anthropologist who specialized in the physiological variation between ancient and modern people. He began his own foray into the world of criminality when he started teaching a course at Harvard in 1916 titled "Criminal Anthropology and Race Mixture." After reviewing the criminological literature himself, Hooton believed that Goring was deeply prejudiced against Lombroso and that Goring had purposely obfuscated an important relationship between physical characteristics and criminality.

Supported by a large and well-funded research lab, Hooton decided to undertake a major study to tease out possible physical differences between criminals and noncriminals. Graduate students scoured prisons around the country, compiling nearly two dozen measurements on more than ten thousand convicts—more than 10 percent of the entire male prison population at the time. The copious amounts of data recorded about each subject led Hooton's study to become one of the largest and most ambitious investigations of criminals ever undertaken.

More than a decade after beginning the project, Hooton triumphantly concluded not only that there were differences between criminals and noncriminals but also that he could identify physical differences between criminals convicted of different offenses. The differences, Hooton argued, "almost justify the generalization that short, fat men rape; short, thin men steal; tall, thin men kill and rob; tall, heavy men murder and forge." The white-collar offenders in his sample, forgers and fraudsters, were shown as having thin hair, a medium-sized nasal bridge, thicker lips, and lack of teeth wear. He largely dismissed environmental factors as an explanation used by those who "appraise human conduct sympathetically rather than intellectually," and he largely reverted to Lombroso's view of the born criminal. "You may say that this is tantamount to a declaration that the primary cause of crime is biological inferiority," Hooton wrote, "and that is exactly what I mean."

Despite the abundance of data Hooton offered in support of his arguments, there were doubts that specific bodily measurements—sloping foreheads, snubbed noses, and long necks—represented some sort of physical inferiority and could be connected to criminal behavior in some meaningful and predicable way. Hooton's discussions around the

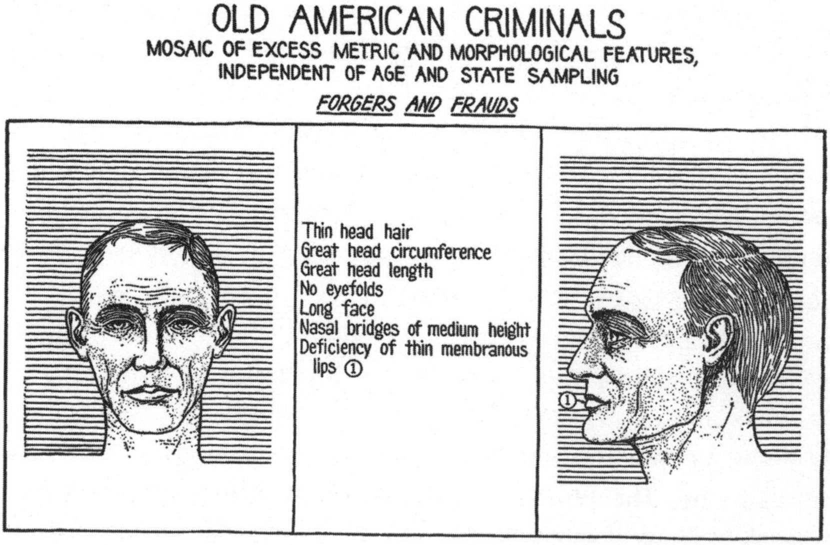

OLD AMERICAN CRIMINALS
MOSAIC OF EXCESS METRIC AND MORPHOLOGICAL FEATURES,
INDEPENDENT OF AGE AND STATE SAMPLING
FORGERS AND FRAUDS

Thin head hair
Great head circumference
Great head length
No eyefolds
Long face
Nasal bridges of medium height
Deficiency of thin membranous
lips ①

Figure 3.2: Earnest Hooton's depiction of a white-collar criminal.

"inherently inferior organisms" and the "ruthless elimination of inferior types" were viewed not as those of a distinguished professor relying on his data but, rather, as those of a man bent on preaching eugenic principles. Even if criminals were constitutionally distinct, there was no evidence in support of the argument that these differences were inferior or necessarily the cause for their criminality. Reflecting the deep skepticism that gripped Hooton's line of reasoning, one prominent reviewer called his book "the funniest academic performance that has appeared since the invention of moveable type."

By the 1950s, interest in relying on purely physical differences to differentiate individuals had declined and scientists who continued to believe in its promise became increasingly isolated. One prominent sociologist aptly summed up the prevailing sentiment by saying that "except for Professor Hooton and a few of his followers, no one today takes seriously the proposition that there are demonstrable physical differences between those who commit crime and those who do not."

The wide skepticism that criminals were visually differentiable from noncriminals did not eliminate the enthusiasm for finding some biologically rooted factor that could explain criminal conduct. Researchers still had the hunch that criminals were somehow fundamentally different from noncriminals. With newer and more sophisticated tools available, the search simply moved from the external body to the internal mind.

A Lack of Control

At the French bank Société Générale, Jérôme Kerviel was assigned to trade fairly low-risk securities. As he gained more experience, Kerviel began to dabble in riskier transactions. One of his first higher risk trades was in 2005, when he took a multimillion-euro position on a global insurance company. Coincidentally, he placed the trade prior to the terrorist attack on London's subway system, and it soon generated significant profits. Fueled by this early win and encouragement from others at the bank, Kerviel went on a spree, taking increasingly large and more speculative financial positions. The positions were worth hundreds of millions and eventually billions of euros. By 2008, Kerviel held positions worth approximately €50 billion, more than the market capitalization of the entire bank.

When internal systems finally detected this extraordinary exposure, Société Générale tried to quickly unwind the trades. In the process, the bank
incurred nearly €5 billion in losses.

Questions circulated about what drove a trader at a prestigious bank to
take such radical and reckless positions. His trades nearly destroyed one
of France's largest and most respected banks. When Kerviel later went to
trial, the judge pointed to results from a psychological assessment as explanation for his wild trading: Kerviel had low self-control.

In line with the judge, numerous prominent criminologists have also
argued that crime—including the white-collar variety that Kerviel engaged in—can be explained in terms of deficiencies in self-control. Their
basic premise is that people with lower self-control have greater difficulty
resisting temptation and restraining reckless behavior, and eventually
some of this rash and opportunistic behavior is likely to end up as criminal conduct.

Over the last thirty years, the question of why some people have less
control than others has been a subject of considerable debate. Some researchers initially believed that low self-control was caused by poor parenting, while others argued that it was largely due to heredity. But whether
self-control is driven by nature, nurture, or a combination of both, once
set, self-control remains largely stable for the remainder of a person's life.
In a well-known set of experiments from the early 1970s children were
given the choice of receiving one marshmallow immediately or two if they
waited until the researcher returned to the room. When experimenters
reexamined children who had participated in the original experiments
decades later, they found significant differences between those who immediately ate the marshmallow and those who had the willpower to wait.
As adults, those who delayed gratification in childhood exhibited higher
educational achievement, had better relationships, and were less likely to
be overweight. Such research helped solidify the idea that those with little
self-control during their youth similarly begin their professional careers
with impaired self-control.

While different from external, physically discernible aberrations like
those proposed by the likes of Lombroso and Hooton, the idea that crime
is caused by insufficient self-control similarly regards managerial misconduct as arising from personal deficiency. In some of the most highly cited
research by criminologists, Michael Gottfredson and Travis Hirschi

argued that people with low self-control are more likely to engage in deviant behavior throughout their entire life. According to this argument, executives with impaired self-control shouldn't just engage in corporate misconduct but their low inhibitions should tempt them to engage in all sorts of reckless behavior. This includes ordinary street offenses like drug-usage and assault, but also noncriminal behaviors like excessive gambling and promiscuity. Anything that can provide temporary pleasure, relief, or excitement is potentially attractive.

It's easy to find anecdotal examples of corporate leaders lacking self-control outside their work. Jonathan Burrows, a managing director making an estimated £1 million a year at investment management behemoth Blackrock, was caught skimping on his train fare—by nearly £15 a day—for more than five years. Once he was caught, regulators in London took the unprecedented step of permanently barring Burrows from the financial industry for life because of his lack of "honesty and integrity."

More compelling evidence that executives who engage in fraudulent behavior engage in other sorts of deviant conduct comes from a comprehensive analysis of the criminal backgrounds of CEOs named in accounting frauds by Robert Davidson, Aiyesha Dey, and Abbie Smith. Their investigation found that of the CEOs facing sanctions by the Securities and Exchange Commission, 11 percent had serious prior criminal charges. The offenses included felony drug possession, domestic violence, and reckless endangerment.

While it may be surprising that so many executives gained leadership positions after engaging in criminal conduct, if all CEOs convicted of malfeasance had lifelong impairments to their self-control, we'd expect that number to be even higher. But some of these former executives do not comport with the archetype of a reckless individual. In fact, their ability to achieve considerable professional success often relied on their restraint and self-control. Echoing this observation, during the sentencing of a pharmaceutical CEO for fraud, the judge noted that "there's nothing about this particular defendant . . . that would suggest that he has made this trip before and come close but not stepped over the line before, or that's he's been stepping over the line regularly or anything like that. . . . The facts seem to suggest to the contrary." The judge struggled to sentence the executive precisely because the charges seemed to be at odds with the conservative character of, and otherwise disciplined choices made by, that executive throughout his life.

Rather than seeing self-control as a permanent impairment, some argue that malfeasance might be better explained as caused by temporary lapses in control. Supporting this, more recent research suggests that self-control, while broadly stable throughout life, might actually function like a muscle that becomes depleted when it's continually exerted. Experiments posed in a variety of settings show how stress, noise, and overtiredness can rapidly deplete self-control and inhibit restraint. These lapses make individuals temporarily more prone to lie and cheat.

However, if managerial misconduct is caused by fleeting lapses in self-control, it would be incorrect to categorize deviant managers as "bad apples." Put another way, deviance could arise among executives endowed with normal or even above-average levels of self-control, and situational forces could dominate any innate factor in influencing their criminal behavior. Thus, criminality would not be inevitable as suggested by the "born criminal" idea, since it would be caused by transitory lapses and changes rather than by a permanent deficiency.

Whatever the true nature of self-control, there are aspects of the theory that are compelling. But to understand the origins of executives' malfeasance, we still need to dig deeper, since self-control is more of a label than an explanation. It is easy to assert after a white-collar crime is committed that if the executive had high self-control, he would not have engaged in the misconduct. It inevitably follows, then, that crimes are caused by low self-control. In the words of the prominent criminologist Gilbert Geis, the "absence of self-control causes all crimes except those that it does not cause." Given its tautological nature, this theory does not lead to clear predictions of which executives will engage in malfeasance. If researchers had hopes of finding a biological basis for white-collar crime, they needed to probe even further inside the human mind to understand what drives psychological differences between executives who engage in misconduct and those who do not.

Inside Our Body

Many biologically rooted explanations suffer from the same problem. Whether referring to a violent street offense or to a carefully planned white-collar transgression, they generalize that all crime is caused by the same set of physical or psychological aberrations. But there is no obvious reason to suppose that white-collar and street offenses ought to be explained similarly. White-collar offenses often require considerable planning, are not especially thrilling, and have the potential for considerable financial benefit—critical differences from many street crimes. Executive-level offenders also tend to be driven individuals who care deeply about their success. Exploring, rather than minimizing, these differences seems essential to any theory seeking to explain white-collar criminality.

Detecting subtle differences that might distinguish white-collar offenders from other criminals meant putting away the blunt instruments used by early investigators like Lombroso. These early tools were effective for recording surface pathologies and anomalies, but the structure and function of our most important inner hardware—the brain—eluded measurement. This all began to change in the 1990s as advances in brain imaging created new opportunities to resurrect the search for the biologically motivated origins of criminality. Neurocriminology, as it would become known, utilizes the methods of neuroscience to investigate the criminological origins of antisocial behavior. At the forefront of this new science is Adrian Raine, a criminologist at the University of Pennsylvania. "I do believe," says Raine, "that Lombroso . . . was on the path toward a sublime truth."

Raine's research focuses on how neurobiological abnormalities, ways the brain may be compromised in some way during its development, can correlate with criminality. In one study, for instance, Raine saw that murderers exhibited considerably lower activation of the prefrontal cortex, the part of the brain used to regulate emotion and personality expression. Additional research showed that men convicted of spousal abuse were less able to suppress negative emotions due to an inhibited connection between the frontal and limbic regions in the brain. In study after study of violent behavior, Raine found differences in the brain structure and activity of criminals, leading him to conclude that they were "constitutionally different than other men."

With the help of William Laufer, a colleague specializing in business ethics, Raine turned his attention to examining people who engaged in white-collar crimes. From the start, Raine and his co-authors argued that white-collar offenders were likely to be less impulsive and more calculating than other criminals. They also believed these differences might be detectable within an offender's brain. "Rather than conceiving these characteristics as deficits," the researchers wrote, "they more likely aid them in accommodating the structure, function, and culture of an organization, allowing white-collar offenders to engage in elaborate calculations." They saw these neurological differences as possible advantages, rather than as impairments, in the business context.

When the researchers examined brain scans of individuals, some of whom engaged in white-collar crimes and others who did not, they began to see several differences in the white-collar offenders. One brain region suggested that the white-collar offenders had greater cognitive control, useful for creating and acting on goals. Another area that differed between the groups suggested that the white-collar offenders would be driven more by abstract rewards like money. Taken together, the evidence led the researchers to the preliminary conclusion that "white-collar criminals have information-processing and brain superiorities that give them an advantage in perpetrating criminal offenses in occupation settings." Such findings suggest that the brains of white-collar offenders have several potential constitutional differences that distinguish them from others.

Brain imaging is one way of exploring our inner selves to reveal differences relating to potential criminality, but another is genetics. Although humans share 99 percent of their genes with one another, the remaining 1 percent that differs can create extraordinary variation. To put this 1-percent difference in perspective, consider that chimpanzees differ from humans by only 2 percent. Genes influence virtually every part of our psychology and contribute to whether we're ambitious, shy, impatient, and caring, among other personality traits. Not surprisingly, antisocial tendencies that facilitate criminality are also affected by genetic makeup.

Using a variety of clever strategies, it is possible to identify the contribution of genes toward creating antisocial tendencies. One persuasive way of investigating this question is to examine identical twins who were separated at birth and reared in different environments. Since identical twins have 100 percent of their genes in common, differences in antisocial behavior and criminality can be attributed to differences in environment and upbringing. Not surprisingly, this type of research is difficult to undertake, given the rarity of the desired research subjects. But when one set of researchers managed to gather enough participants for such a study, they found that 29 percent of the separately reared twins engaged in anti-social behaviors—evidence of a significant genetic influence. Other investigations using fraternal twins and adoptions further supported the significance of genetic influences, with estimates ascribing 40–60 percent of antisocial behavior to genetics. Although the specific contribution differs by individual, this research suggests that genes have the opportunity to play a significant role in forming major determinants of personality, some of which contribute to criminality.

One way this genetic variation sways behavior is through its influence on bodily hormones and regulatory biochemicals. Greater levels of testosterone, for example, have long been hypothesized to lead to more aggressive and egocentric behavior. Following research that linked high testosterone levels to increased cheating, several business school researchers decided to investigate whether high testosterone levels could help explain the tendency for some executives to more aggressively push the boundaries of acceptable conduct. Could high testosterone levels also be responsible for some executives' decision to engage in financial fraud?

This was a provocative hypothesis, but the challenge is that most executives would not be willing to subject themselves to a physical examination to test such a proposition. Luckily, testosterone not only influences human behavior but also manifests itself in the development of facial structure. Utilizing a method that harkens back to the physical measurements done by Lombroso and Hooton, the researchers relied on facial measurements taken from photographs of male executives—in place of direct measurement.

As they hypothesized, the researchers found that executives with the most masculine facial features, indicative of higher testosterone levels, were nearly twice as likely to manipulate their firm's financial statements. The researchers also found evidence indicating that more masculine executives were more likely to engage in other risky activities including opportunistic trading and options backdating. While these findings are still preliminary, they suggest one pathway that variation at the genetic level could manifest itself in deviant managerial behavior.

DOES SOME OF the more recent brain-imaging and genetic evidence prove that there is an underlying biological cause for white-collar criminality and, therefore, truth to the "bad apple" theory? The answer comes down to separating correlation from causation. The observed differences between white-collar offenders and others suggest that there are some potential biological correlates with white-collar crime. However, correlation does not necessarily imply causation. The fact that people tend to carry umbrellas when it rains creates a high correlation between umbrella carrying and rain showers. However, it is obvious that choosing to carry an umbrella does not cause rainfall. Asserting that something is a cause of a phenomenon requires demonstrating how observing "A" leads to "B." The brain-imaging and testosterone studies provide some intriguing correlations but no definitive evidence for a biological cause for corporate misconduct.

In addition, there are cases in which the "bad apple" label just doesn't seem to aptly describe the lifelong conduct of those convicted of managerial misconduct. Rajat Gupta, the former managing director of McKinsey and Company, was convicted in 2012 for securities fraud. During his sentencing, former friends and associates wrote on his behalf, describing his personal contributions throughout his career. Kofi Annan, the former secretary-general of the United Nations, wrote that Gupta "is a person who has conducted his life with an admirable sense of purpose and desire to improve the lives of people in trouble around the world." Bill Gates wrote that "many millions of people are leading better lives—or are alive at all—thanks to the efforts [Gupta] so ably supported." Prior to imposing a two-year prison sentence on Gupta, even the federal judge assigned to his case noted that he "never encountered a defendant whose prior history suggests such a devotion, not only to humanity writ large, but also to individual human beings in their time of need." It would be cavalier and unreflective to apply the "bad apple" label to Gupta as a means of explaining his offense.

WE'RE NOT BORN with a "blank slate," nor do inherited or genetic dispositions entirely determine our behavior. Biology manifests itself in behavior by predisposing individuals, some more than others, toward certain tendencies. But it's how these biological influences interact with the environment and surrounding culture that determines how such tendencies manifest themselves. Under the right circumstances, these dispositions can be accentuated or nullified.

Consider the role that empathy—the ability to identify and appropriately respond to the feelings experienced by others—may play in an executive's capacity to engage in—or avoid—misconduct. In times of need or crisis, some people display an extraordinary capacity to identify with the strife of those in trouble, while others struggle to relate compassionately. A number of still poorly understood biological factors contribute to variations in the level of empathy displayed by different individuals. Women, for instance, tend to innately exhibit higher displays of empathic understanding and behavior than men.

Executives who are less empathic lack the ability to appreciate the emotional impact of their actions on others. As a result, they are less likely to feel the same natural tendencies of guilt or remorse that ought to accompany wrongdoing. At its most extreme, this lack of empathy manifests itself in a clinical condition known as psychopathy.

The psychologist Robert Hare and his colleagues assessed a group of business executives and managers on the prevalence of psychopathic traits. They found that a greater number of executives display psychopathic characteristics than the population at large. Specifically, 3.5 percent of the executives they examined fit the profile of a psychopath compared to only 1 percent in the general population. Perhaps most intriguing was the fact that those displaying greater psychopathic characteristics were rated as having more effective communication skills, being more creative, and displaying greater strategic thinking—characteristics usually associated with more effective management.

To the extent that corporate misconduct harms both investors and employees, it would not be entirely surprising to find a correlation between having a lower level of empathy and an individual's propensity to engage in corporate misconduct. Yet, a lack of empathy does not inevitably give rise to criminality. As with other personality characteristics like ambition, pride, risk-aversion, and narcissism, these individual characteristics will be moderated or accentuated by circumstances and environment. Constitutional factors contribute to understanding an executive's behavior, but they cannot be interpreted in isolation.

The trick is to separate out the influence of these innate personality characteristics from the broader background context—a difficult task. The challenge is further accentuated when examining managerial deviance, since the crime is committed within an environment that potentially influences the propensity of a person to engage in criminal activities. One important study managed to separate these comingling factors, albeit by focusing on petty criminality. The researchers assessed subjects' genetic predisposition by looking at whether their parents had committed crimes, and measured the effect of environmental factors by the affluence of the home in which they were raised. Using these data, the researchers examined the likelihood that men who were adopted at a young age would later commit offenses.

The researchers found that among men without a genetic or environmental disposition, fewer than 3 percent engaged in criminal behavior. However, when they examined men with both genetic and environmental dispositions, this incidence jumped fourteen-fold to 40 percent. Genetic and environmental factors each independently contributed to increasing the propensity to commit crime. But the multiplicative effect occurred only when individuals with a biological predisposition were placed in an environment that further cultivated this tendency. Innate biological characteristics were important, yet it was the surrounding cultural environment that served as the essential fuel for the fire.

Summing It Up

Humans are complex creatures. If we want to understand why executives who otherwise seem so successful commit deviant acts, we can't rely on simplistic labels. Lombroso may have been right to advance his idea that biological characteristics matter for describing an individual's propensity to engage in crime, but he was wrong to broadly categorize all felons as "born criminals" who were destined to offend. Appealing to the "bad apple" label obscures the significant role played by context and the surrounding culture.

One thing that makes the managerial misconduct by prominent executives like Rajat Gupta so difficult to comprehend is that these individuals not only resembled but actually seemed to be individuals who merited the admiration they received. "This is a deepening mystery in my work," declared Judge Alvin Hellerstein at the sentencing hearing of a banking executive. "Why do so many good people do bad things?"

If Judge Hellerstein is correct in suggesting that many of those sentenced for white-collar crimes are actually good people, we need to take a step back from focusing on the characteristics of the individuals involved and focus on the decisions being made by managers instead. Perhaps their failures arise not from "bad character" but, instead, from poor decisions made by otherwise typical individuals.

To explore this idea, let's see how one prominent executive found himself becoming a white-collar criminal.

4

I thought it was all going to pass

A Press Release with Consequences

O N A FRIDAY afternoon in the summer of 2002, Scott Harkonen, CEO of InterMune, eagerly awaited the clinical trial results that could determine the future of his company. Over the previous two years, the California-based biotechnology firm had been engaged in a major trial of Actimmune, InterMune's treatment for a rapidly debilitating and fatal lung condition known as idiopathic pulmonary fibrosis (IPF). The disease is "like a slow-burning grassfire in your lungs that within a few years suffocates you to death," explained Harkonen. "It's a horrible, horrible disease with no known treatment."

The genesis for the clinical trial had begun almost three years earlier, in the fall of 1999. Returning home from a trip, Harkonen glanced at the cover of the *New England Journal of Medicine*. A research team at an Austrian medical school had just completed a study employing gamma interferon, the same naturally occurring molecule that InterMune marketed as Actimmune. Incredibly, patients taking gamma interferon showed substantial improvement in lung function with relatively few side effects. "I didn't even have my overcoat off yet," Harkonen recalled, " . . . and I was like holy smokes."

InterMune had the exclusive rights to distribute Actimmune in the United States and Canada. The Food and Drug Administration (FDA) had already approved Actimmune to treat chronic granulomatous disease, an

illness that makes individuals prone to severe infection, and malignant os-
teoporosis, a bone disorder. Yet, with only eight hundred people in the
United States suffering from these two diseases, the market for this use of
Actimmune was tiny. In comparison, more than fifty thousand people suffered from IPF in the United States.

Demonstrating the efficacy of Actimmune with IPF patients could have
a major impact on Harkonen's fledgling company. The treatment cost
$50,000 a year per patient, a price in line with many other genetically engi-
neered drugs. "We were building the company brick by brick with 4 million here and 5 million there and all of a sudden we had a $250 million
market," Harkonen recalled. "And then we said, wait, check the zeros. It's a
freakin' $2.5 billion market." If Actimmune's application to IPF worked, it
had the potential to entirely transform InterMune.

Gaining approval to market Actimmune for the treatment of a new disease was costly and time consuming. Instead of undertaking a clinical trial
for Actimmune to treat IPF patients, some of InterMune's advisors suggested pursuing a different strategy. Since Actimmune was already approved
by the FDA to treat several other diseases, it could be prescribed to patients
to treat other diseases unofficially—"off-label" as it was called by doctors.
Pharmaceutical companies commonly employ this strategy with 20 percent
of all medications prescribed off-label. In fact, some drugs gain almost all
their sales from non-FDA-approved off-label treatments. Thalomid, a drug
approved to treat leprosy for instance, received more than 90 percent of its
$200 million plus in annual sales through off-label cancer treatment.

The problem with relying on off-label sales was that InterMune could
not advertise Actimmune as an effective treatment for IPF. "The feeling
was that if you could get it on-label and promote it, the difference in the
market opportunity might be five- or ten-fold," Harkonen explained. "InterMune had $7 million in revenue at the time; if the off-label usage
brought this up to $100 million, by anyone's script that would be a huge
success for a start-up. . . . But I didn't want to run a company that was de-
pendent on off-label sales."

Even if the drug was sold off-label, InterMune could still support the
drug by funding studies that would make physicians aware of its potential
benefits to patients. Yet, Harkonen believed this wasn't the right strategy
for the company or for patients suffering from IPF. After two months of

discussion and after finding an investor willing to sponsor a costly clinical trial, Harkonen and his team reached a decision: they would go ahead with tests to gain full FDA approval.

THE CLINICAL TRIAL lasted nearly two years, cost over $25 million, and involved more than three hundred patients afflicted with IPF. As the study neared its conclusion in August 2002, the anticipated results seemed to be all anyone wanted to discuss. When the results of another InterMune trial focusing on tuberculosis became the topic of conversation at a board meeting, one of InterMune's major institutional investors was up in arms. "They couldn't understand why we were talking about anything except IPF," Harkonen recalled. "At the meeting, they said it was just a waste of time."

During its initial public offering in 2000, InterMune raised $125 million. Flush with this infusion of cash, Harkonen actively invested these proceeds to expand research and development at InterMune. "I was leveraging the value of Actimmune and IPF to parlay that into other products. But at the time of the clinical trial, I would go to Wall Street and they would say 'Don't talk to us about anything except IPF,'" Harkonen recalled. "But hell, by 2002, we had a Phase III antibiotic for staph infections, another drug using interferon for hepatitis. . . . We had five products."

Harkonen understood the consequences if the drug failed. Similar failures at other biotechs sent their shares plummeting and sometimes threatened the firms' very existence. Shares in one biotech firm named Connetics plummeted by 79 percent in a single day after the company's new drug failed its Phase III trial. Nevertheless, Harkonen was optimistic about the future prospects of InterMune regardless of the trial's outcome. "I'd be standing on stage at a podium and imagining the curtain coming down if there was an IPF failure," Harkonen explained, "but behind that we'd have a lot of other products. I could say that InterMune has a tomorrow and a next year. There's a lot else here. It's not just Actimmune."

In preparation for the IPF trial results, the public relations team at InterMune readied for three possible outcomes—"positive," "equivocal," and "negative." The team presented their different strategic responses to the board of directors at their June 2002 meeting.

Strong, positive results supporting the beneficial effects of Actimmune would make life easy. Actimmune could be positioned as the "gold standard" for safely and effectively treating IPF. "In my mind, I already did the walk on the beach with the big company CEOs about acquisition if the trial turned out to be a huge success," Harkonen described wistfully. "A billion-dollar product takes all your troubles away in biotech and no one is counting paper clips anymore."

Managing negative results would also be straightforward. "As CEO I led the company thinking or assuming that the IPF trial would be a failure. . . . Most trials fail. . . . That's why I wanted a pipeline of drugs behind IPF." Doctors would still be able to utilize the drug off-label if desired by patients, but InterMune would expect sales to decline. "If it would have been an abject failure, it would have been hard to take, but you're done and move on."

"Mixed or equivocal results . . . that just made me grimace," noted Harkonen. "There was already pressure from investors about spending money on other products. But now that we're going to have to grind through another Phase III trial of Actimmune, spending money on any other product was going to be hard."

HARKONEN'S INTEREST IN medicine was sparked at a young age when he was diagnosed with a rare metabolic disease affecting his kidneys. Worried that they would fail, Harkonen enrolled in medical school at the University of Minnesota, where he began conducting research on kidney aliments. He quickly demonstrated his acumen as a researcher by publishing a piece in the *American Journal of Medicine* as the lead author.

After finishing medical school, Harkonen worked as a practicing physician for two years. He decided to return to laboratory work when he was offered a prestigious research fellowship focusing on experimental therapeutics. In the mid-1980s, researchers had begun to see the potential for genetically engineered drugs and Harkonen had the opportunity to be at the forefront of this research.

After completing his fellowship, Harkonen was quickly hired by a biotech firm that funded one of his studies. In his first major success, Harkonen discovered that WinRho, a drug originally designed to treat a rare ailment in which the mother and baby have different blood types, could

actually treat another rare disease called immune thrombocytopenic purpura (ITP). Children with ITP were known to suffer from bruising, nose-
bleeds, and, in some cases, life-threatening cranial bleeding. In 1995,
WinRho became the only biologic approved by the FDA to treat ITP.

Later, Harkonen helped find a treatment for osteopetrosis, a genetic
disorder causing bone enlargement that eventually leads to deafness and
blindness in children. Osteopetrosis is especially rare, with only one to
two dozen children born with the disease in the United States each year.
Since the market is so small, pharmaceutical companies tended to be less
inclined to create treatments for these so-called orphan diseases. "There
was no financial gain" in developing and testing a treatment, noted Harkonen. "At best, it would be a wash." But the treatment Harkonen helped
develop prolonged the time before a patient started deteriorating by three-
fold. The National Organization for Rare Diseases presented Harkonen
and his team an award for developing a drug aimed at an especially small
population that "otherwise had no hope."

Harkonen spent his career moving from biotech firm to biotech firm
helping to design new and innovative treatments. In the years that followed, Harkonen's efforts would lead to FDA approval for three more
biologics—all for orphan diseases.

During his career, Harkonen also experienced some significant and
costly setbacks. Years before beginning at InterMune, which bought the
rights to Actimmune, Harkonen was especially excited about the drug's
prospects for treating another disease, severe eczema. "There was a study
out of Harvard that was published in the *New England Journal of Medicine* showing a clinical benefit. . . . We did a big Phase III trial, which was
really expensive. We had to set up standardized cameras and lighting at
each clinical site to monitor redness, since this was a skin disease." But
then the results starting coming back: "It was a complete failure. . . . We
saw no signal in any of the endpoints. There was no change in redness—
none. It just didn't work."

After overseeing more than a hundred clinical trials in his career,
many of which failed, Harkonen was accustomed to tests not succeeding.
It was the nature of scientific research. But it was this challenge that motivated Harkonen. "I was always the R&D guy," Harkonen said. "That's
what I loved."

It was Michael Crager, InterMune's senior biostatistician, who brought Harkonen the trial results that Friday afternoon in 2002. Together, they began reviewing the data.

Prior to starting the trial, progression-free survival had been selected as the objective to assess Actimmune's efficacy, known in scientific circles as the primary endpoint. Progression-free survival measured the drug's effectiveness in attenuating the worsening of lung function and prolonging life. Crager's notes showed that there was an 11 percent improvement in the rate of progression-free survival for those receiving Actimmune. While the results went in the desired direction of showing a positive effect, they were not statistically significant.

As Harkonen and his team dug deeper into the data, they found another promising trend: 16 of the 162 patients treated with Actimmune died as compared with 28 out of the 168 in the placebo group. It was a 40 percent reduction in mortality. "Cancer trials often target a 20 percent reduction in mortality. When we got a 40 percent reduction in mortality, it was totally unexpected," Harkonen recalled. "Our chief medical officer called these initial results an off-the-fence triple." This finding was closer to being statistically significant, but it still did not achieve the level typically demanded for broad approval by regulators.

Over the following days, Harkonen and his team continued to scrutinize the data. They analyzed the prognosis of individuals in the mild to moderate stages of IPF. After excluding patients whose condition was already severe, they found a stunning 70 percent reduction in mortality. Notably, these results were statistically significant.

There were several trends favoring patients taking Actimmune, but failing to achieve the primary endpoint at the level of statistical significance demanded by the FDA led Harkonen and his team to deem the study as equivocal. "When I got the mixed results I knew that it wasn't going to be easy. On one hand, we had the sales, but on the other hand they are off-label and we can't promote it," noted Harkonen. "You're stuck in the middle." Harkonen and his team prepared a press release describing the results of the trial and their additional analyses. On August 28, InterMune issued the release that Harkonen and others on his team prepared:

INTERMUNE ANNOUNCES PHASE III DATA
DEMONSTRATING SURVIVAL BENEFIT
OF ACTIMMUNE IN IPF

—Reduces Mortality by 70% in Patients with Mild to Moderate Disease—

BRISBANE, Calif., August 28, 2002—InterMune, Inc. (Nasdaq: ITMN) announced today that preliminary data from its Phase III clinical trial of Actimmune* (Interferon gamma-1b) injection for the treatment of idiopathic pulmonary fibrosis (IPF), a debilitating and usually fatal disease for which there are no effective treatment options, demonstrate a significant survival benefit in patients with mild to moderate disease randomly assigned to Actimmune versus control treatment (p = 0.004).

Immediately after the release, Harkonen hosted a conference call with analysts and investors. Their reaction was much as Harkonen had anticipated. One biotech analyst wrote that the "preliminary results from a Phase III study of Actimmune were mixed—as we expected. Data missed the primary endpoint of progression-free survival, but demonstrated a considerable survival benefit in mild-moderate IPF patients." Analysts from Morgan Stanley were somewhat more optimistic. They titled their report "InterMune Hits a Double" because the study showed a positive trend in mortality for one important subgroup, but it fell short of showing a statistically significant progression-free survival effect for all study participants.

A WEEK AFTER issuing the press release, Harkonen received a letter from Thomas Fleming, the external chairperson monitoring the Phase III trial of Actimmune. Fleming was a well-respected statistician and chair of the biostatistics department at the University of Washington. Fleming was outraged.

"I was stunned by the misrepresentation in the News Release of the results from the clinical trial," Fleming wrote. "The claims of the established survival benefit . . . are so fallacious that they would provide a humorous illustration of an absurd misrepresentation of exploratory statistical analyses if not for the serious consequences to patients, caregivers, and the investment community who might be misled in their therapeutic or financial decision-making process."

"I was shocked," Harkonen recalled in reaction to Fleming's complaints. "He was really mad and I didn't understand why."

Fleming's anger centered on the all-important "p-value" describing the statistical significance of the trial results. In the Actimmune trial, researchers sought to determine whether patients taking Actimmune fared better than those who took a placebo. The p-value described the probability that health improvements of patients taking Actimmune and those on the placebo were simply by happenstance. The lower the p-value, the less likely that this difference occurred by chance.

In clinical trials, the p-value takes on crucial importance since it indicates whether a trial can be described as "statistically significant" to regulators at the FDA. For medical trials, a standard, but somewhat arbitrary, guideline suggested that the p-value needed to be .05 or smaller to be deemed statistically significant. Although the study showed a 40 percent reduction in mortality of IPF patients, the p-value was 0.084 (meaning there was an 8.4 percent chance that the reduction in morality was by happenstance)—too high for Actimmune to be described as having a statistically significant effect, according to this guideline.

In the reanalysis of the data for patients with mild to moderate IPF in whom researchers observed a 70 percent decline in mortality, the p-value was statistically significant at 0.004: there was only a .4 percent chance that the reduction in mortality was by happenstance. However, this analysis was not specified prior to undertaking the study. Fleming argued that because the InterMune team was testing a new hypothesis after they had already conducted their clinical trial, specifically whether Actimmune would be effective on patients with mild to moderate IPF, the finding could not be considered statistically valid. Although both results were described in the press release, Fleming objected that the second and more significant finding was highlighted in the opening sentence without any indication of when the hypothesis had been specified.

After Harkonen read the distraught letter from Fleming, he flew out to meet him in person to address his concerns. Fleming was known as being an outspoken researcher and someone not afraid to voice a critical opinion. In an FDA advisory meeting for another drug in 2003, he was outvoted 14 to 1 when he wanted to reject the treatment because its statistical results were mixed. To help address Fleming's concerns, Harkonen agreed to let Fleming review and comment on slides for a major upcoming presentation at the European Respiratory Society, when the more complete results of the study would be unveiled.

The presentation of the trial's results in Stockholm three weeks after the initial press release was well received. "I got a bear hug from one of the steering committee members. . . . It was the first time people had seen promising results around fatality for IPF, so people were saying congratulations," Harkonen remembered fondly. InterMune issued another press release after the meeting in Stockholm describing the results of the study in greater detail. "After the second press release, I thought Fleming was placated," Harkonen recalled.

In the months that followed, another study from a team in Greece provided additional results suggesting that Actimmune could improve the survival of IPF patients. Some investors and InterMune board members thought that Harkonen should seek approval from the FDA based on the three studies to date that showed a positive trend for IPF patients taking Actimmune. Although the studies did not provide the conventional level of statistical significance for approval, the FDA often approved promising drugs that did not meet the usual cutoffs for diseases with small patient populations.

Harkonen nonetheless felt Actimmune needed an additional Phase III trial that would clearly demonstrate its efficacy. It was the only way Harkonen saw Actimmune gaining widespread use for patients suffering from IPF. In the months that followed, he began preparing for the new trial. However, after lowering Intermune's 2003 sales forecasts and watching the stock steeply decline due to lower-than-expected sales of Actimmune, Harkonen agreed to step down as CEO. He would move to another biotech firm before a new Actimmune trial got under way.

It was spring of 2007—almost four years after Harkonen had left Inter-Mune. "I was at another biotech company when I heard that the second IPF trial came out negative. I remember thinking in the back of my mind—'uh-oh.'"

Following the negative trial results, governmental prosecutors began an investigation into InterMune's public statements related to Actimmune's efficacy. "I thought it was all going to pass," Harkonen recalled. "Whatever they wanted to look at, I thought it was all going to pass because we got the mixed results."

It didn't pass. "Lawyers at the Department of Justice and FDA saw the second trial, and to them that was proof that the drug didn't work," Harkonen explained in frustration. On March 18, 2008, Harkonen received a formal indictment. Prosecutors charged him with creating and disseminating false information about the efficacy of Actimmune. At the forefront of these charges was the 2002 press release stating that the original Phase III trial "demonstrated" benefits for IPF patients. For this offense, the government would eventually seek a ten-year prison sentence for Harkonen.

There was never any doubt about the facts within the press release. Even the prosecutors acknowledged that the data presented in the release were correct. It was a matter of how the contents of the release could be interpreted by patients, investors, and doctors. In his defense, Harkonen's lawyers and fellow doctors argued that there existed legitimate disagreements among scientists about how to interpret the initial findings. "I believe that I bent over backwards to make sure the results of the trial were thoroughly reviewed inside and outside the company by experts," lamented Harkonen. The Justice Department, however, argued that although Harkonen had not falsified any data, he had intentionally falsified the study's interpretation—all as part of a plan to encourage more off-label prescriptions of Actimmune.

After a seven-week trial, the jury found Harkonen guilty of wire fraud, but acquitted him of misbranding. The Department of Justice issued a press release lauding his successful prosecution. The FBI Special Agent in Charge announced that "Mr. Harkonen lied to the public about the results of a clinical trial and offered false hope to people stricken with a deadly disease. Manipulating scientific research and falsifying test results . . . undermines public trust in our system for drug approval."

Harkonen was astonished by the verdict. "I never in a thousand years thought it would end up like this."

"It would be easier to live with if I was distracted and ran a red light causing some injury and got sued for that," Harkonen reflected. "A camera would show that I ran a red light and I'd say I made a mistake. . . . But in this, I don't think I made a mistake."

"ALL LIES ARE false statements, but not all false statements are lies," argued the philosopher Thomas Carson. Executives, for instance, are regularly observed making exaggerated statements that are not considered lies. For years, Esso, the oil company, famously advertised its petrol with the slogan "put a tiger in your tank." No driver expected an actual tiger to be placed in their gas tank; rather, drivers interpreted the expression to mean that Esso's gasoline would boost their car's performance. In another case, Bayer, the pharmaceutical company, advertised its pain reliever as the "world's best aspirin" that "works wonders." Again, while Bayer's aspirin would cure an unpleasant headache, most consumers would not consider this so wondrous.

Such statements are generally regarded as puffery—vague statements of corporate optimism that are simply promotional. They are viewed as acceptable because consumers interpret the statements figuratively rather than literally.

Yet, it's easy to imagine how touting can go from the merely promotional to the deceitful. Courts often assess this distinction on the basis of whether a statement is viewed as material or not. Materiality is assessed on the basis of whether a reasonable consumer or investor would be motivated to change his or her behavior—which product to buy or which stock to invest in—on the basis of the statement. The challenge is that generalizing the mentality of a "reasonable" consumer is itself fraught with difficulty since there are considerable differences in how people interpret information.

To better understand how individuals view statements made by executives, the legal scholar Stefan Padfield took announcements made by CEOs in several security class action cases and asked business and law students to evaluate whether they felt the information was material. In one scenario, Padfield presented statements from the CEO of Tellabs, a fiber-optic cable equipment manufacturer, announcing a $100 million contract for its TITAN networking system. Not long thereafter, Tellabs' CEO boasted to investors that customer demand for the TITAN system "is exceeding our expectations." The CEO went on to say that "we feel very, very good about the robust growth we're experiencing."

In the coming months, the company announced slowing sales and struggled to meet its growth expectations. Management cut its earnings projections and announced that it was shuttering a project and embarking on cost-cutting measures. In response to this series of discouraging announcements, Tellabs' stock price fell from \$67 to less than \$16 a share. Plaintiffs alleged that the CEO's earlier optimism was unwarranted amidst the negative information that they alleged management knew, but only later revealed publicly.

However, the judge in the case stated that CEO's statements were "essentially . . . meaningless," and concluded that "this is precisely the type of statement that the marketplace views as pure hype and accordingly discounts entirely." Nevertheless, 62 percent of the participants in Padfield's research found the CEO's first statement about the TITAN system exceeding expectations material. Thirty-three percent of participants found the second statement about the firm's robust growth material. Together this provided clear evidence that not all "reasonable" people would dismiss the statements by the CEO as trivial or meaningless.

Padfield presented other examples of statements made by executives that were deemed immaterial in court, but in each case a significant percentage of participants disagreed, finding them material for their own

Figure 4.1: Rice Krispies box promoting the cereal's immunity boosting benefits.

decision making. Where some people saw a simple piece of promotional sales talk, others saw a piece of actionable data that influenced and potentially distorted their decisions. Such subtle or, sometimes, not-so-subtle puffery can influence opinions.

The ability of exaggerated claims to materially influence perceptions is why regulators seek to sanction those who disseminate false or misleading promotions paraded as fact. In one of the more egregious cases, when a swine flu epidemic hit the United States in 2009, Kellogg advertised its popular Rice Krispies cereal by saying that it "now helps support your child's immunity." Soon thereafter, the Federal Trade Commission took action against the firm for making claims of health benefits without any scientific basis.

As the philosopher Francis Bacon put it four centuries ago, "It is not the lie that passeth through the mind, but the lie that sinketh in and settleth in it, that doth hurt." Bacon identified the key concern regarding deceptive speech and promotions: it's not the literal message but the impact that message has on decision making that's the issue. "Put a tiger in your tank" creates little harm because it does little to distort consumers' behavior by making them ill-informed. Harm arises when individuals purchase products that they would otherwise not buy if they were more accurately informed about the quality of the products.

In Harkonen's case, prosecutors described several specific groups they believed were misled and harmed by inclusion of the word "demonstrate" in the press release. Among these, they claimed, were veterans who had been harmed because the costly and ineffective treatment diverted resources away from the effective care that veterans would otherwise have received. Additional critically ill patients were allegedly harmed when Harkonen offered them "false hope" with an ineffective treatment. It was not only that Harkonen damaged patients financially, according to prosecutors, but even more fundamentally, he undermined their psychological well-being.

As Harkonen created the release, "the initial thought was how would investors interpret this. If they see a headline that says 'Actimmune Trial Fails,' they are going to sell. In biotech, a lot of companies only have one product and whether it succeeds or fails, it is a binary event. A lot of trials fail and then you see their stock crash and they lose 80 percent of their value in 24 hours. . . . We felt pretty strongly that this is not truth. There is a positive signal here." At the same time, press releases are read by investors, doctors, and patients, each with their own interests and differing abilities to interpret nuanced evidence from a scientific study.

The clinical trial was not an abject failure. Supporting this conclusion, Donald Rubin, the chair of Harvard University's statistics department, argued that "a study with estimates that include a 40% reduction in mortality—particularly for a rapidly progressing, inevitably fatal disease for which there is no effective treatment—is not a 'failure.'" At the same time, the fact that the trial was *not* a failure also did not affirm it as a success.

IPF was a fatal disease with no known treatments. Doctors, even many of those scrutinizing the data most critically, believed that there were some potentially promising trends observed in the first clinical trial.

"The dilemma is how could it have been said differently?" asked Harkonen. It often seemed as though Harkonen's conviction stood on the use of one particular word in the release. "People talk about using the word 'suggest' instead of 'demonstrate,'" Harkonen reflected, "but I don't think that would have occurred to us then."

Consumers couldn't act on the release alone, and doctors prescribing the medication were primarily academic clinicians who understood how to interpret scientific findings. The FDA noted that its panel would never rely solely on a press release to make a decision on whether or not to prescribe a particular medication to patients. "At worst," Harkonen conceded, "maybe it was puffery." However, Harkonen never saw how the release could harm patients.

The government sought a ten-year prison sentence for Harkonen on the basis of being able to provide specific victims. It was, however, a futile search. "We can't even figure out who a victim is in this case, and whether the victims were benefited in some way," noted Judge Marilyn Patel.

Under these circumstances, it was difficult for the judge to render what felt like an appropriate sentence. "There aren't that many offenses that you could compare it to. . . . There's no real way of determining if there is restitution and to whom it would be paid or how it would be determined." The judge finally came to a conclusion. Against the prosecutors' wishes, there would be no prison time for Harkonen. Instead, he'd face three years' probation in closing a contentious case.

WAS HARKONEN'S DECISION to issue the disputed press release the result of being influenced by the way other executives touted their products? Did he see how others might interpret the press release as dishonest? Was the final release a result of Harkonen weighing the costs against the benefits and being concerned about Wall Street's reaction if the release appeared more negative?

These are the issues taken up in the next chapter as we explore how reasoning might contribute to executives engaging in malfeasance.

5

If you don't take it then you will regret it forever

The Triumph of Reason

IN MARCH 2014, over two dozen salesmen appeared outside the Shanghai offices of the pharmaceutical manufacturer GlaxoSmith-Kline (GSK). The employees were angry that GSK was not reimbursing them for bribes they paid to doctors and hospitals, as they customarily had been. At the protest, the salesmen unrolled a banner that read "Return my hard-earned money." As instructed, they had routinely provided fake receipts as documentation of the cash payments they made. "All the expenses were approved by the company," noted a letter by the group. "The expenses were paid with our own money," noted another upset GSK salesman, "and although the receipts were not compliant, it was our managers who told us to buy the fake receipts." From their superiors at GSK, the salesmen had learned not only the illegal practice of paying bribes to boost drug sales but also how to get reimbursed using fake receipts.

Today, it seems quite sensible to view people who commit crimes as having learned to do so from others. However, this was not always a widely held belief. As discussed in a previous chapter, biological anomalies were often relied on to explain criminal conduct. Even more than a century ago this troubled one man named Gabriel Tarde. A budding French sociologist and provincial judge in the nineteenth century, Tarde had a voracious intellectual appetite and read widely in the fields of psychology, criminology, biology, and law. Influenced by his extensive reading and experience on the judicial bench, Tarde criticized the explanation that some people were "born criminal." Instead, he argued that criminal behavior was learned by observing others, just as people emulate the style of how others dress. The more frequent and intense the contact with those engaged in criminal conduct, Tarde believed, the greater the likelihood for imitating that behavior oneself.

Scholars eventually picked up on Tarde's work and this theory came to be called "differential association," because it suggested that a person's propensity to become a criminal depended on how much one associated with other criminals. Differential association seemed well suited to explain corporate malfeasance because many, if not most, white-collar offenders grew up in stable neighborhoods, supported by good parents, and attended prestigious schools. It was only later, after exposure to crooked

Figure 5.1: From *The Atlantic* by Sage Stossel.

business practices in the course of their profession, that these same people found themselves committing criminal offenses and encouraging subordinates to do the same.

The trouble with this idea is that if criminality spreads from exposure like a virus, it's not clear why some people heavily exposed to illicit practices behave otherwise. Why doesn't everyone associating with white-collar offenders adopt similar criminal tendencies? Something—or someone—must be halting certain people from becoming criminals and not others.

Decades after Tarde, Donald Cressey picked up on this question. Cressey, a graduate student of Edwin Sutherland—the sociologist who coined the term "white-collar crime"—focused his attention on one group of white-collar offenders, embezzlers, who were unlikely to suffer from having grown up in "broken homes" or "bad neighborhoods." Cressey wanted to dispense outright with explanations based on the circumstances of a criminal's upbringing. He decided to head to penitentiaries to investigate why people embezzle from their firms.

Drawing on his extensive conversations with more than a hundred inmates convicted of embezzlement, Cressey hypothesized that there were three conditions needed to motivate someone to embezzle. First, the person needed a financial problem that could not be shared with others. One businessman, for example, described feeling that he could not tell his colleagues about their firm's disappointing performance. "There are very few people who are able to walk away from a failing business. . . . Most of us don't know when to quit. . . . Whether you call this bull-doggedness or hard-headedness or whatever it is, it exists. And we consider it a good characteristic in most cases." For these managers, pride often stood in the way of resolving their difficulties legally.

The second condition for Cressey was the person's realization that his nonshareable problem could be solved secretly. In many cases, Cressey observed embezzlers employing the same knowledge to embezzle funds that they once used productively for the firm's benefit. "I learned all of it in school," recalled one embezzler. "In school they teach you in your advanced years how to detect embezzlements, and you sort of absorb it. . . . I did not use any techniques which any ordinary accountant in my position could not have used; they are known by all accountants."

The final condition, rationalization, was the crucial step that Cressey said either led the individual into trouble or kept him out of it. Cressey's subjects wanted to maintain their self-image as respected members of their firm and society. When Cressey's embezzlers encountered a non-shareable financial problem that they could solve secretly, they were not motivated to go ahead until they figured out how to view their actions as essentially noncriminal. As one real estate salesman recalled, "In the real estate business you have to paint a pretty picture in order to sell the property. We did a little juggling and moving around, but everyone in the real estate business has to do that." The rationalizations the embezzlers described were not explanations produced after the offense took place. Rather, Cressey believed that individuals devised rationalizations prior to perpetrating their illicit acts. These explanations helped to artificially maintain the embezzler's self-image as a trusted and respected individual while committing the offense. "If he cannot do this," Cressey wrote, "he does not become an embezzler."

Cressey published his findings in his 1953 book, *Other People's Money.* Reviewers unanimously appreciated the detail of his study and expected it to spur additional research, especially since it showed that "much can be learned about the processes of criminal behavior from the study of prisoners." Yet, despite high praise from scholars when it was released, the book failed to stimulate sustained interest and soon went out of print. It was among the few significant intellectual disappointments in Cressey's otherwise illustrious career.

Decades later, however, Cressey's thesis experienced an unexpected revival. In the late 1970s, an accounting firm gave several researchers a grant to study ways to improve fraud detection. After examining a group of convicted fraudsters, they soon concluded, much as Cressey had, that there were three major forces underlying the decision to commit fraud. Building on Cressey's work, they called these three factors pressure, opportunity, and rationalization. These three forces—together called the "fraud triangle" by the authors—could explain not just embezzlement but deceptive business conduct more broadly.

Easy to understand and neatly framed, the "fraud triangle" received much attention. The Association of Certified Fraud Examiners added the model to its training curriculum for examiners. Securities regulators included it into accounting standards to describe when fraudulent behavior was likely to arise. Textbooks adopted the "fraud triangle," and it became a theory commonly discussed in business school classrooms. While

Cressey may have been disappointed that his research initially received little attention, it laid the foundation for what would ultimately become one of the most widely cited theories to explain managerial deviance in the twenty-first century.

Making Unethical Decisions

Tarde, Sutherland, and Cressey described circumstances that led professionals to engage in crime, but their theories failed to explain the decision-making process that led people down this path. According to the theory of differential association, individuals discovered their deviant values through associating with other criminals. And the "fraud triangle" offered a description of the conditions—motivation, opportunity, and rationalization—ripe for criminal behavior to arise. Yet, why a person would choose to resolve a problem criminally when legal options were potentially available was still unclear. Given the potential consequences, how does someone reason his way toward believing that the illegal choice is the most appropriate course of action?

Suppose a sales manager loses an important contract after negotiations break down on the final day of the quarter. His colleagues counted on him to get the deal signed by quarter-end. In the best-case scenario, reporting this failure would simply be a setback to possible promotion and prompt a loss of his bonus. However, the manager worries that the more likely outcome of reporting the botched negotiation is that he will be fired and not have a chance to try again the next quarter.

To a righteous outside observer, there is not much of a decision to make here. Reporting the failed negotiation seems so obvious that the issue is how to report the failure, not whether to report it. But suppose the vice-president is sure that the client is just playing hardball because it is near quarter-end. He is confident that the client will sign the contract the following week when it becomes clear that there is no more room for negotiation. If he can just temporarily create the illusion of a successful negotiation, he figures he can overcome this uncomfortable situation and avoid the negative ramifications created by anxious investors. With his job and financial well-being on the line, falsifying a few documents begins to look surprisingly attractive. But he also realizes that he would be engaging in exactly the kind of behavior he has spent his career condemning. How does he finally make the decision to forge a document or not?

To psychologists, there is something special about the decision to commit a criminal offense like the one described in this dilemma. White-collar crimes such as embezzlement, financial fraud, and bribery violate well-established social norms. Embezzlement is a professionalized form of stealing. Wire fraud uses lying to deprive other people of their property. And bribery relies on both cheating and disloyalty. Even the Federal Bureau of Investigation, the primary agency tasked with investigating federal crimes in the United States, defines white-collar crime as "illegal acts which are characterized by deceit, concealment, or violation of trust."

All of these violations—lying, cheating, and stealing—are offenses universally perceived as morally wrong because they affront our basic notions of fairness and honesty. The decision to commit a white-collar crime is not just a choice between committing an illicit act or not. Rather, it is also a decision about whether to violate a deeply held notion of morally acceptable behavior.

How we develop our moral sense of telling right from wrong has long fascinated psychologists. Lawrence Kohlberg, one of the most prominent in the field, developed his own interest in understanding how human morality arises while serving in the American Merchant Marine during World War II. After witnessing the atrocities committed by the Nazis, Kohlberg was determined to help those who had survived the Holocaust. He volunteered to smuggle Jewish refugees to freedom in Palestine as an unpaid engineer on a freighter, but his ship, with two thousand refugees on board, was seized by the British Navy for violating a blockade. Kohlberg was taken into custody, but he escaped and made his way to Palestine before finding his way back to Europe. The experience left Kohlberg shaken and raised difficult questions for him about potential disparities between morality and legality. When could it be appropriate to ignore laws? When was it permissible to use violence to achieve supposedly just ends? With this experience and these questions fresh in his mind, Kohlberg returned to the United States to study philosophy and moral psychology at the University of Chicago.

Kohlberg explored how people reach moral judgments by presenting vignettes of moral dilemmas to research participants. In one example,

Kohlberg described a woman who was dying from a rare disease. A nearby pharmacist had found a cure, but its price was prohibitively expensive. The women's husband, Heinz, tried everything possible to borrow the money he needed to pay for the treatment but managed to collect only half the medication's cost. Heinz explained to the pharmacist that his wife was dying and requested a discount or an opportunity to pay later, but the pharmacist declined. In desperation, Heinz broke into the pharmacist's store at night and stole the remedy to save his wife.

After presenting the dilemma to participants, Kohlberg asked a series of probing questions. Should the sick woman's husband have stolen the drug? Which was worse—stealing or letting someone die? Can something be wrong which everyone would do? Kohlberg elicited responses and then scored participants on the depth of their thinking. Through an analysis of their responses, Kohlberg hypothesized that individuals advance through six stages of moral development. They begin by evaluating actions on the basis of avoiding punishment and satisfying their own needs. Later, individuals make judgments based on societal expectations. By the sixth and highest stage of moral development, individuals would respect the rights of others by appealing to abstract principles of universal justice.

Kohlberg argued that each successive stage of moral development is superior to the stage before it. For instance, if asked why cheating on a test is wrong, one person might say that it's because the perpetrator might be punished. Someone else might respond that cheating is wrong because it creates mistrust that can undermine societal well-being. The latter explanation exhibits greater moral maturity, in Kohlberg's analysis, since it captures broader societal concerns and not the individualist ideal of avoiding punishment. Each successive stage of moral development is better than the last because it implies more sophisticated distinctions about respecting individual rights.

By placing the individual's capacity to reason at the center of moral decision making, Kohlberg's thesis ignited a revolution: morality could effectively be taught. Kohlberg was so confident in his ideas that he even helped create schools to foster his vision of moral development. Business leaders were also attracted to his research. Some believed that corporate misconduct, viewed as a series of ethical dilemmas, could be reduced through cultivating better moral reasoning in managers.

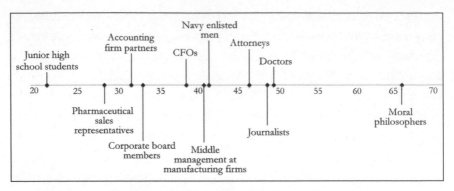

Figure 5.2: Moral development by profession.

However, the all-important question was whether more sophisticated moral reasoning actually led to more ethical behavior. Executives might be able to describe a sophisticated and carefully reasoned argument against engaging in fraud, but would those who could more capably do this actually be less inclined to engage in fraud in practice? In hundreds of studies following Kohlberg's work, researchers tried to understand the moral development of groups from college students to military personnel. As expected, there was considerable variation in these groups. Adolescents and prison inmates ranked near the bottom. Business professionals ranged across the scale depending on their area of expertise, with more seniority often being inversely related to their moral aptitude. But it was moral philosophers, ethicists by profession, who showed the highest level of moral development. If "superior" moral reasoning leads to better moral behavior, then professional ethicists, the highest-ranking cohort, ought to be more virtuous in their behavior when compared to others.

In a clever series of studies, the experimental philosophers Eric Schwitzgebel and Joshua Rust decided to test the actual behavior of moral philosophers in a variety of ethical contexts. Their conclusion: Professional ethicists behave no better than other similarly educated professionals. In fact, in some cases, their behavior was noticeably worse. In one study, the researchers found that ethics books, those likely to be exclusively read by faculty and advanced doctorate students in moral philosophy, were missing from the library more often than other philosophical texts, and the most advanced books on ethics were 50–150 percent more likely to be missing than comparable texts. Whether the books were missing due to outright theft or just negligent treatment, moral philosophers appeared considerably less righteous in practice than was suggested by their moral development scores.

These studies, along with additional empirical evidence, questioned the association of more sophisticated moral judgment with behaving more ethically. There seemed to be a discrepancy between people's supposed moral development and their actual behavior in ethically charged situations. At least in some circumstances, people could be quite comfortable pontificating about principles, but then they would act less virtuously when confronted with an actual decision to make.

The inconsistency between moral judgment and behavior suggested that the specifics of the situation play a far more significant role in determining behavior. The ability to behave morally isn't necessarily as ingrained in a person's character as researchers once thought.

As further support, researchers asked students at the Princeton Theological Seminary to give a short talk on the biblical parable of the Good Samaritan. The parable describes several individuals hurrying past an injured person, before one Samaritan finally stops to take care of the despondent man—an act that Jesus commends. Seminarians were asked to deliver a talk on the parable in an adjacent building, on whose path the researchers had positioned a groaning "victim" slumped over in the doorway. The seminarians were precisely the kind of individuals who espoused that they would stop to help.

Under time pressure, however, many of the seminarians ignored the victim or were not inclined to offer aid. In several instances, they even literally stepped over the victim as they rushed to give their talk on the parable of the Good Samaritan. Seminarians were so engaged with delivering their speech that they failed to even recognize the moral dilemma directly in front of them. Helping the victim required not only believing that it is one's abstract duty to help but also recognizing the problem in the first place.

This experiment, along with others like it, helped psychologists see that moral decision making is actually far more complicated than they initially envisioned. People have to successfully complete a whole series of steps—becoming aware of a problem, forming a judgment, establishing intent, and engaging in moral behavior—to behave ethically. Those prone to succeed at one step might find themselves overlooking at others, and failing at any one step leads to failure at the end.

Consider identifying which step Gregg Ritchie, one of KPMG's senior tax partners, failed when he advised his firm not to register a tax shelter with the IRS as required by law. In a memo to colleagues, Ritchie explained his thinking: "First, the financial exposure to the Firm is minimal. Based upon our analysis of the applicable penalty sections, we conclude that the penalties would be no greater than $14,000 per $100,000 in KPMG fees." After pointing out the financial benefits of not registering, he went on to reassure his colleagues that they were simply following the norm in the industry. "There are no tax products marketed to individuals by our competitors which are registered," Ritchie wrote. He concluded:

> Any financial exposure that may be applicable can easily be dealt with by setting up a reserve against fees collected. Given the relatively nominal amount of such potential penalties, the Firm's financial results should not be affected by this decision. . . . The rewards of successful marketing of [the tax structure] product (and the competitive disadvantages which may result from registration) far exceed the financial exposure to penalties that may arise.

Nowhere did he evaluate the ethical ramifications of advocating an illicit act. By overlooking the ethical question, Ritchie, much like the students who stepped over the groaning victim at the seminary, failed to recognize that he faced a moral decision in the first place. Without seeing any moral component to the decision, he never arrived at the stage of balancing moral considerations against other objectives when forming his opinion.

The idea that successful moral decision making employs an elaborate series of steps raises the broader question of what really makes something a moral decision at all. If moral issues are present whenever there is the potential to help or harm another person—as there often is in a managerial context—almost every decision can be construed as a morally relevant one. What executive-level decision doesn't impact other people? Raising prices on products can benefit employees and shareholders at the expense of customers. Laying off staff can benefit employees staying on at the expense of those being let go. Short-term cutbacks can benefit current shareholders at the expense of long-term shareholders.

All choices inevitably involve trade-offs between competing interests and priorities that are not just moral but also economic, legal, environmental, and personal. Accordingly, perhaps we need to question whether there's anything really distinctive about "moral" decisions as compared to many others that are made every day in business. Perhaps we should consider the possibility that illegal business decisions—moral decisions in their own right—are actually made much like any other kind of decision.

Analyzing the World Through Cost-Benefit

Struggling to make a decision, David Messer, a twenty-nine-year-old bank manager in Tampa, Florida, sat down to make a list. Down the left side of his yellow legal pad, he wrote the cons of stealing from his bank: "Fugitive on the run. . . . Money won't last forever. . . . If caught, will go to jail." On the right, he wrote the pros: "Travel anywhere. . . . Live on islands. . . . Meet many women. . . . Party and prevent heart attack." At the bottom of the list Messer gave himself a final charge: "Dave, let's face the hard facts that you are a loser. . . . If you don't take it then you will regret it forever and you won't get another chance again I promise."

With that, Messer made his decision. He packed up his brown Oldsmobile with money orders, traveler's checks, and more than $150,000 in stolen cash. He skipped town, ready to enjoy the life he envisioned on the right side of his list.

Messer is different from most white-collar offenders. Most do not actually write down a list of the potential merits and drawbacks before perpetrating a crime (or if they do, they certainly don't leave it behind for investigators to find!). Yet, the basic idea that executives decide to commit crimes by weighing the potential benefits against the expected consequences is regularly cited in the pages of *The Economist* and by pundits on CNBC. One editorial in the *Wall Street Journal* noted, for instance, that "unlike the tempestuous and murderous spouse or the impoverished and desperate mugger, suite criminals are sophisticated and deliberative businessmen who engage in crime only after carefully calculating the benefits and costs."

Making trade-offs through cost-benefit analysis has long been regarded as a basic core competency in business. Benjamin Franklin wrote to a friend in 1772 that he employed the method to resolve problems. "My way is to divide half a sheet of paper by a line into two columns; writing over the one Pro and the other Con." Franklin suggested that his friend do the same. As a way to determine whether a venture is profitable, managers regularly employ cost-benefit analysis to select which projects to undertake. Its application to making business decisions is clear, but how did cost-benefit analysis also become commonly applied to explain the decision to commit white-collar crime?

As a young economics professor at Columbia University in the early 1960s, Gary Becker normally put his car in the parking lot. One day while running late to administer an oral examination to graduate students, he asked himself whether he should just park illegally on the street closer to campus. Becker recalled doing a quick calculation of the likelihood of getting a ticket, its cost, and the time he could save. After balancing these trade-offs, he came to the conclusion that it made more sense to park illicitly on the street. Becker quickly nabbed a space and made it to the exam room, where the first question he posed to the nervous graduate students was how they would explain the decision to commit such an offense.

Luckily for Becker, he didn't get a parking ticket. More significantly, the event also spurred him to start thinking more carefully about crime. Much of the dialogue around explaining criminal behavior at the time of his fateful parking choice emphasized anomalous psychological deficits and oppressive social forces. Becker was perturbed by the idea that criminals were "helpless victims." In his view, offenders got themselves into trouble through their own doing. He didn't see the basic motivation of criminals as necessarily all that different from those of anyone else. Perhaps people who committed criminal offenses simply weighed the benefits and costs and decided that it was worth the risk.

As Becker continued to study the problem, he took inspiration from a much earlier social philosopher. Working in the late eighteenth century, Jeremy Bentham was a brilliant and eccentric scholar troubled by Europe's harsh penal systems. In England there were more than two hundred listed capital offenses, for crimes as diverse as forgery and stealing cattle. Executions in the 1780s were overwhelmingly carried out against those who committed property crimes and other economic offenses. Bentham argued that punishment needn't be so excessive and if the specter of hanging an effigy of a man was enough to deter future crime, then actually hanging a man was unnecessary. He believed that if punishments could merely be set slightly greater than the perceived benefit of committing a particular crime, it would serve to deter the offense.

A central axiom of Bentham's theory of punishment was that individuals were constantly maximizing their well-being through rational calculation. Bentham argued that we are all constantly weighing pleasure against pain—a process he called "felicific calculus." He even described fifteen factors contributing to pleasure—riches, friendship, reputation, power, and hope, among others—and wrote a similar list of factors contributing to pain. These forces drive our behavior in the most general sense and "govern us in all we do, in all we say, in all we think." By understanding how individuals weigh pleasure against pain, Bentham believed he could carefully design policies to nudge people toward better conduct. By studying moral decisions with the same precision used to study the natural sciences, he aspired to become the "Newton of the Moral World."

A century and a half later Becker, too, sought a more scientific understanding of human behavior. He dispensed with Bentham's more arcane views about the specific pleasures and pains that individuals experience and instead focused on the basic assumption that individuals tend to maximize their own general well-being—what economists call "utility." Individuals pursue activities that are utility increasing and avoid those that are utility decreasing. Becker didn't specify or assume anything about the particular behaviors that would be utility increasing or decreasing. These were ultimately a function of the individual, his motivation, and the set of circumstances he faced. Choosing to get married, have children, smoke, and skip school could all be rationally explained by appealing to the basic notion that individuals would pursue activities that were welfare enhancing as they subjectively perceived it.

Under this theory, crime could also be viewed as arising from the same rational calculus. From the perspective of a potential perpetrator, the way to make the decision would be to compare the utility of committing an illicit act against the utility gained by committing the same amount of time and resources to other legitimate activities. Viewed in this way, a criminal is not criminal by nature but, rather, someone who simply perceives the costs and benefits of illegal decisions differently from another person.

In the decades that followed, Becker's seminal work—"Crime and Punishment: An Economic Approach"—became one of the most highly cited papers in economics. When he was awarded the Nobel Prize in 1992, the committee specifically noted Becker's contributions to understanding crime. Interest in employing a rational choice approach also crept outside economics into other disciplines including sociology, criminology, political science, and legal theory. Its surge in popularity was principally due to the fact, as one legal scholar noted, that the theory was perceived as "the most complete and coherent account of human decision making in the social sciences." Not surprisingly, criminologists saw the relevance of Becker's theory to white-collar crime. If the theory was applicable to street offenders, it seemed even more applicable to executives who worked in environments that promoted the use of cost-benefit analysis.

Though lauded in many circles, Becker's theory attracted criticism in others. Detractors claimed that by placing criminal acts on the same ground as other decisions, it appeared to remove any moral content from the choice to commit a criminal offense. Such a sentiment was expressed, for instance, by Richard Horton, editor-in-chief of *The Lancet,* one of the oldest and most prestigious medical journals in the world. "Economists have stripped morality from economics. . . . The assumption is that human beings make cost-benefit decisions based only on self-interest." From this perspective, the welfare of others, the fundamental basis of morality, was essentially excised from consideration by economists.

But individuals have a rich set of motivations, and it's clear that not all decisions are solely driven by narrow monetary or egocentric considerations. As Becker argued, the rational choice model merely says that "individuals maximize welfare as they conceive it." Altruism, loyalty, vengefulness, and fairness are all motivations that can play a role in an individual's decisions under different circumstances.

Morality, rather than being stripped away in rational choice, is incorporated as just another motivation in a cost-benefit decision. Committing a moral violation comes into the equation as an additional cost alongside the pecuniary and other personal costs that accompany a decision. For example, recall the dilemma that Kohlberg described to his research subjects. Explaining that a husband decides to steal an antidote to save his dying wife through rational choice does not diminish the moral content of the decision. Before deciding to break into the shop, the husband, Heinz, knew that there was some chance he'd be caught and spend a few very uncomfortable years in prison. But this wasn't the only cost or drawback that Heinz thought about before breaking into the shop. Heinz prided himself as being an upstanding citizen who obeyed laws, and stealing the medicine from the pharmacist violated his ethical principles and undermined the example he wanted to set for his children. Yet, Heinz concluded that the utility of seeing his wife rejuvenated, his family intact, exceeded the disutility associated with potentially being caught and the personal disrepute of violating the pharmacist's rights. Another person might have similarly valued his family and the potential disutility from being caught, but placed a higher cost on violating the pharmacist's rights. This person would not have broken into the shop, since the higher moral cost of doing so would have exceeded the benefit. The moral content of a decision is ultimately taken into account, but without appealing to any special moral decision-making process.

People often struggle to view moral decisions under the rational choice framework because they view morality as sacrosanct. The prospect of viewing the moral content of a potentially unethical decision as just some additional cost in the decision-making process somehow cheapens morality itself. Yet, in practice, few moral tenets are actually inviolable. Consider the killing of another human being—one of the most significant moral transgressions which virtually all people resolve never to do. But place a parent in the position where he would need to kill an intruder to protect his child, and few parents would see the ethical and psychic costs of killing another human being outweigh the benefits of saving their child. Rational choice recognizes that even deeply rooted moral beliefs can be violated in circumstances where the expected benefits outweigh the expected costs.

In short, rational choice models cannot be dismissed for being "amoral," as they have been by some critics. But this still leaves the question of how well it captures how individuals behave. As often interpreted, rational choice seems to say something about the actual mental process people use to make choices. But do people always, or even usually, consciously calculate when making decisions?

Perhaps surprisingly, early economists who studied and promoted the idea of utility maximization didn't actually care whether it really captured how people thought. The model was designed to predict aggregate behavior by groups of people. Whether or not the model accurately captured the psychological process of specific individuals was irrelevant.

To make their point, Milton Friedman, a Nobel Prize–winning economist and Gary Becker's colleague, offered the example of trying to predict shots made by an expert billiards player. A scientist could write out a set of equations describing the precise speed and direction needed to hit each ball. These equations would be incredibly complex in calculating how the movement of one ball would impact all the others. Correctly written, they would accurately describe each shot made by the professional billiard player. Yet, it's obvious that billiard players do not employ such complex mathematical formulas to determine the angle, speed, and direction for their next shot. However, for the purposes of predicting where each ball would go when hit by a professional, it would be reasonable to assume *as if* the billiard player was using these formulas when deciding how to take the next shot.

The rational choice model was developed and tested as a prediction model, not as a model of human cognition. It only mattered that people behaved "as if" they calculated the costs and benefits when making decisions. This subtle but important "as if" distinction was lost in later discussions. The model evolved into one that not only predicted behavior but also described the psychological decision-making process.

This transformation occurred as people interpreted the model to be one about reasoning, echoing Bentham's early writing that "all men calculate." For instance, the entry on white-collar crime in the *Encyclopedia of Criminological Theory* states that rational choice describes how "individuals consciously and deliberately choose criminal behavior." But the popularization of this impression was not limited to those who misunderstood the theory. Even those most knowledgeable about its assumptions perpetuated this impression, perhaps unintentionally. Gary Becker, in a *Business Week* editorial, wrote that "executives contemplating whether to commit a crime take into consideration not only the punishment they face if caught, but also their chance of being apprehended." By asserting that executives contemplate criminal actions before undertaking them, the rational choice theory as popularized in the preceding examples presupposes a particular psychological state.

The description of the rational and reasoning executive offender also entered the legal domain. One of the most influential people tasked with prosecuting white-collar crime is the United States Attorney for the Southern District of New York. The position's purview over Wall Street gives this US Attorney particular prominence in the fight against white-collar crime. Preet Bharara, the attorney who assumed the position beginning in 2009, has prosecuted well in excess of one hundred executives during his first six years in office. In public speeches, Bharara often describes executives as cost-benefit calculators. Those he prosecutes, Bharara explains, "are highly skilled at cost-benefit analysis" and they "weigh the risk of getting caught against the potential reward, and they decide it's worth the risk." Bharara holds press conferences to help raise awareness of the costs of engaging in corporate malfeasance and, more specifically, to "convince rational business people that the risk is not worth it."

The impression that executives explicitly weigh costs and benefits when considering an illicit act is not limited to abstract scholarly discourse. In fact, this notion motivates much of the discussion around how to deter deviant managerial behavior. As pointed out during a Senate Judiciary Committee hearing, lengthening prison sentences is often seen as the most fitting solution because executives rely on "cold and careful calculation" when considering whether or not to commit an illicit act. Not surprisingly, increasing the severity of punishment is viewed as a particularly effective form of deterrence since, according to the *Harvard Law Review*, executives "know the available punishments and recent comparable sentences for their contemplated crimes, and they incorporate those potential downsides into their decision-making process." Likewise, a former Department of Justice's fraud section chief argued that "one of the principal assumptions about the white-collar criminal is that he is calculating and therefore highly deterrable." The prevailing ideas around reducing white-collar criminality rely on the assessment that executives are reasoning and calculative when they decide to commit an illegal act.

The emphasis on viewing cost-benefit analysis as a psychological model of choice rather than as simply a description of behavior has led to a particular notion of why once successful and intelligent executives commit white-collar crime—namely, that these executives make thoughtful and deliberative calculations to break the law when doing so serves their needs and desires. They are not making hasty decisions with clouded judgment. Their personal failure lies in reasoning that the illicit choice is the "appropriate" one.

As we'll see in the next several chapters, the trouble with this theory is that it doesn't seem to match especially well with how executives who engage in white-collar crime actually think.

6

I never once thought of the costs versus rewards

Intuitive Decisions

A CCORDING TO POPULAR belief, executives commit crimes through cool, calculated reasoning. But consider how Scott London, the senior partner at KPMG who provided trading information about his clients to a friend, described what he thought about while engaging in securities fraud. "At the time this was going on, I just never really thought about the consequences," London explained. "The money was nominal, really nominal. . . . I was on three charitable boards and I had to step off of all of them. I will probably lose my CPA license and I can't practice in front of the SEC. None of these things were going through my mind. . . . I never once thought about the costs versus rewards."

Where was the careful contemplation? Why was there no apparent deliberation of the risky consequences? Even if the risk of being caught was improbably small, the possible magnitude of those consequences ought to have spurred some thought. In fact, London believes it is very unlikely that he would have shared confidential information if he had ever taken the time to stand back and think about the ramifications on his family, professional life, and friends.

This apparent lack of contemplation wasn't unique to London, either. Similar accounts emerged again and again during my conversations. "You just don't think like that when you're making this kind of decision," another executive convicted of insider trading confided to me. Most of the former executives I spoke with were not denying that they had engaged in illicit conduct. Rather, they were stumped trying to understand their decisions through formal logic.

The more time I spent exploring the decision-making processes of prominent leaders and executives who engaged in misconduct, the less it looked like these decisions were made with deep, thoughtful deliberation of the consequences. And I wasn't the only one who observed this: at the trial of a Canadian minister accused of forging a document to receive an illicit reimbursement, a judge stated that "while I am perplexed as to why a man of such accomplishments might choose to take these actions . . . I have long ago abandoned the notion that motive results from a logical cost-benefit analysis."

This chapter explores how we often rely on intuition, not deliberative reasoned calculation, to make decisions. It turns out that even when we think we're employing effortful analytical reasoning to reach a judgment, we are actually just searching for additional evidence in support of an earlier intuitive judgment. The research I'll describe in this chapter sets the stage for understanding how our minds are not always well adapted to the challenges, pressures, and opportunities that people face in the modern business world.

Decision Making Behind the Scenes

Think about your typical morning. After the alarm clock goes off, you can choose to hit the snooze button or not. Then there's how hot to set the shower, what to wear, whether to eat breakfast at home or to take it on the road. By the time you've reached work, how many decisions have you made? Dozens? Hundreds? If you tried disassembling each action into its component choices, the number would be overwhelming.

Choices like these don't require much effort or reflection. For instance, choosing when and how big a sip of coffee to take while reading the newspaper doesn't actually seem like a decision. As you approach a red light or as a car suddenly comes to a halt in front of you, pressing the brake pedal is more of an instinctive response than a careful choice. While these actions don't require much in the way of active deliberation, they are still decisions since you could have acted differently.

With so many choices available, we inevitably make many more decisions than we're aware of. Between the five basic senses, estimates suggest we take in more than 11 million bits of information a second. Yet, we consciously process only around 16 bits a second, the tiniest sliver of all this material. Much of the information we process and many of our choices are made with little effort, almost as though they are being made automatically.

With so many decisions to make and so much information to process, the question is whether a deliberative model of balancing costs and benefits appropriately represents how decisions are made. Remember that according to the popular interpretation of the rational choice model, it wasn't just illicit choices that are made via cost-benefit analysis but all decisions in life. "The economic approach does not draw conceptual distinctions," noted Gary Becker, "between major and minor decisions, such as those involving life and death in contrast to the choice of a brand of coffee."

Yet, even just a brief inspection of our daily life shows that we make many decisions without any formal calculation or reflection. We can, of course, also recall decisions that seemed effortful and required deliberation. However, even in those instances, can we really be sure we understand the process used to reach our final judgment?

Nearly a century ago, a psychologist at the University of Chicago named Norman Maier demonstrated how people can mistakenly believe a judgment arises from a conscious reasoned analysis—like cost-benefit—when it actually comes about from a less mindful process. In a clever experiment, Maier hung two ropes from the ceiling of a large room and challenged participants to tie the ends together. The ropes were hung sufficiently far apart so that a person holding the end of one rope could not reach the other. Maier placed a variety of objects including poles, clamps, pliers, and extension cords around the room for participants to use. While three of the solutions were easy for participants to figure out, one was far more difficult and eluded most people. After watching them try for ten minutes, Maier would casually walk up to one of the ropes and gently put it in motion without saying a word. Quickly, many participants found the more difficult solution, which involved tying a weight to one rope so that it could be swung closer to the other.

After completing the experiment, Maier asked participants how they came up with the idea of using one of the ropes as a pendulum. They offered a variety of explanations: "It just dawned on me," "it was the only thing left," and "perhaps a course in physics suggested it to me." A professor of psychology offered an especially colorful account of his reasoning process: "Having exhausted everything else the next thing was to swing it. I thought of the situation of swinging across a river. I had imagery of monkeys swinging from trees. This imagery appeared simultaneously with the solution. The idea appeared complete." The people involved in Maier's experiment were oblivious to the fact that Maier had helped them by putting the rope in motion.

Maier's participants attributed their actions to their own cleverness and reasoning, while overlooking the actual impetus that prompted them to figure out the solution. The real reason they figured out how to tie the ropes together, the gentle swing started by Maier, remained inaccessible and unidentifiable.

Since we are not entirely conscious information processors, we're often tempted to behave like Maier's participants and falsely describe more than we know. The motivations for our actions often appear clear, even obvious, even when that is not the case. Yet, accepting the idea that unconscious processes might play a more significant role in our behavior is both uncomfortable and perplexing. Even as we utilize information that lies outside our awareness to inform our opinions and judgments, we believe that conscious processes lead to our decisions. We like to feel as though it is our conscious self that compels our actions and judgments even when this is not the case.

An especially powerful demonstration of the degree to which we are unaware of how nonconscious processes influence our actions was observed by exploring the simplest body movement: the flicking of a finger. The physiologist Benjamin Libet asked participants to occasionally move a finger and to take note, on a nearby clock, of the exact moment that they consciously intended to move it. By observing measurements of their brain activity, Libet found that the participants' brains were already preparing to act 300–500 milliseconds before they reported the decision to act.

If our actions originate in consciousness, the decision to move our finger ought to occur simultaneously with our conscious decision to move it. Put another way, brain activity for a particular action should begin at the onset of conscious volition. But Libet's findings suggest otherwise. Unconscious processes precede conscious decisions. Yet, we're oblivious to the role played by these unconscious processes because we are simply not aware of them.

It's one thing to acknowledge that lifting a finger or figuring out how to tie two ropes together is not driven by entirely conscious processes, but quite another to accept the idea that more consequential decisions in life can be influenced by those same processes. This idea is disconcerting and doesn't sit well with how we usually view our own behavior or that of others.

Moral decisions—the kind that generate judgments like "this is wrong" rather than simply "I don't like that"—are also usually presumed to be based on reflection and deliberative analysis. Decisions tinged with morality generate considerable fervor because they are not just expressions of personal tastes but evaluations about right or wrong that concern the well-being of others.

Generally, when we deem something immoral, we believe there are good reasons to support this judgment. After all, we're usually willing to condemn people, often quite harshly, for immoral conduct. But consider the following scenario posed by the social psychologist Jonathan Haidt:

> Julie and Mark are brother and sister. They are traveling together in France on summer vacation from college. One night they are staying alone in a cabin near the beach. They decide that it would be interesting and fun if they tried making love. At the very least, it would be a new experience for each of them. Julie was already taking birth control pills, but Mark uses a condom too, just to be safe. They both enjoy making love, but they decide never to do it again. They keep that night as a special secret, which makes them feel even closer to each other. What do you think about that? Was it ok for them to make love?

Almost everybody immediately responds that Julie and Mark's actions were wrong. When asked why, most say that incest could lead to birth defects. But once people are reminded that Julie and Mark used multiple forms of birth control, there's usually an awkward pause, followed by the proposal of another explanation—maybe their relationship will be damaged. Yet, as noted in the hypothetical story, Julie and Mark actually believed their actions improved their relationship. Most people, after having this pointed out, relent and say something like "I don't know, I can't explain it, I just know it's wrong."

It may be difficult for people to pinpoint exactly what makes Julie and Mark's consensual behavior wrong. But most still quickly arrive at the unequivocal conclusion that there's something wrong with the choice made by these siblings. When pressed to explain their reasons and shown why each is unjustified, most people are still deeply reluctant to change their mind.

We like to believe that our assessments of right or wrong come about from careful and deliberate reasoning. But reasoning isn't always the impetus for our judgments. It's often possible to come to a judgment quickly and effortlessly without being able to accurately describe the underlying process used to make it. It's like asking someone to remind us of his or her name. While the answer will appear immediately in their consciousness, it's impossible for them to describe the actual process they used to retrieve it from memory.

As the basis for our judgments, the power of deliberative reasoning tends to be significantly overestimated. "Most of a person's everyday life is determined not by their conscious intentions and deliberate choices," write the psychologists John Bargh and Tanya Chartrand, "but by mental processes that are put into motion by features of the environment and that operate outside of conscious awareness and guidance."

This isn't to say that reasoning has no role to play in decision making. On the contrary, over the last several decades, researchers working in psychology and neuroscience have found compelling evidence of two distinct processes at work during decision making. Much of our behavior is driven by automatic and intuitive processes that are quick, fast, and effortless, but there's also a second set of processes that are controlled and effortful. These reflective processes are slow by comparison and bounded by the capacity of working memory. Such reflective processes are at work when, for example, you try to compute the expected monthly lease for a new car. It's just that we more closely identify with this slower reflective decision-making system since we are consciously aware of some of the steps in its process.

Our ability to engage in effortful, reflective decisions is limited, however, because we're unable to take on more than one reflective decision at a time. To manage all the decisions that confront us moment to moment, we inevitably rely on our intuitive system, which handles decisions in parallel. When the reflective system spots an inconsistency or an error, it can step in to help the intuitive system. But that doesn't mean the reflective system always or even usually catches errors made by the intuitive system. It's simply too costly and time consuming for the reflective system to monitor each routine decision being made. Consider, for example, this question: "A bat and ball cost $1.10. The bat costs $1.00 more than the ball. How much does the ball cost?" If you responded that the ball costs 10 cents, as more than half the students at MIT, Harvard, and Princeton did, you were incorrect. The correct answer is 5 cents, but the tendency to respond intuitively—and incorrectly—is commonplace. Although it requires only a few seconds of reflective thinking, many people say 10 cents, following their mistaken intuitions.

The popular interpretation of cost-benefit analysis sees reflective processes as the dominant means of decision making. However, research suggests that reflective thought is much less pervasive in practice. Unless there is some specific reason to slow down and employ this more controlled and effortful system, decisions arise from intuitive processes.

IF EXECUTIVES OFTEN make decisions—even criminal ones—without engaging in careful and time-consuming deliberation, it doesn't make sense to broadly characterize those involved in corporate malfeasance as "deliberative businessmen who engage in crime only after carefully calculating the benefits and costs." While their actions are no less harmful, viewing their deviance as arising from a failure in intuition, rather than a failure in reasoning, has the potential to better reflect the psychological process they employed.

But if executives engage in criminal conduct by relying on their intuitions, we need to better understand how the intuitive system operates and when it may falter. Specifically, why would intuition motivate a person to choose one action—one that is potentially harmful and criminal—over another? It's only by understanding why intuitions might sometimes fail these otherwise successful people that we can have greater faith that poorly attuned intuitions might ultimately be at fault for their white-collar crimes.

Much of our knowledge about what drives our intuitions comes from a small group of people who have had an unfortunate accident or injury causing damage to a particular and critical portion of their brain. By observing the difficulties they face in their day-to-day decision making, we can see the importance that gut feelings play in successful decision making.

Affective Inputs

On September 13, 1848, an athletic twenty-five-year-old railroad foreman named Phineas Gage was clearing away rock from a construction site in rural Vermont. Gage was known as an energetic and careful boss, well-liked by his men. After pouring gunpowder into a blasting hole, Gage accidently began patting down the powder with his iron rod before sand was placed on top to contain the explosion. Unexpectedly, the gunpowder went off.

The blast immediately turned the iron rod into a potent weapon. It shot through Gage's left cheek, entering his skull and passing through his brain, before finally exiting the top of his head. Smeared with blood, the iron rod finally came to rest more than a hundred feet away. "Horrible Accident" cried the headline in the *Boston Daily Courier.*

Gage fell to the ground but remained, against all odds, alive and coherent. Remarkably, just an hour after the incident he was telling his story to bystanders while being examined by a doctor at a local inn. Over the weeks that followed, Gage's body fought off infection after infection. Incredibly, less than two months later, the doctor pronounced Gage cured.

Despite his extraordinary physical recovery and seemingly intact mental faculties, Gage's personality had changed in an unusual way. Once regarded as one of the best and most efficient workers at the site, he now proved unable to plan for the future. He showed less concern for his fellow workers and had bouts of profanity, all uncharacteristic of Gage before the accident. He worked a series of different jobs but was fired from or quit each one. No one could understand the reason for this profound shift in his demeanor. According to friends and acquaintances, "Gage was no longer Gage."

After Gage's death, his skull was deposited in Harvard Medical School's library, where researchers some 130 years later decided to more closely examine the specific brain regions damaged in the accident. Gage's ventromedial prefrontal cortex (vmPFC), a region of the brain that sits just above the eye sockets, was particularly damaged. This was the same kind of neurological damage that Antonio Damasio, a neuroscientist at the University of Southern California, studies in modern patients, most of whom suffer vmPFC damage from brain tumors. Like Gage, Damasio's patients often exhibit the same remarkable personal transformations after their injury.

Elliot, one of Damasio's patients, had a promising job in business along with a caring, stable family before he was diagnosed with a benign brain tumor that damaged his prefrontal lobes. Soon after the tumor was removed, Elliot's life began falling apart. He lost his job, then his life savings. Elliot's wife left him and another marriage failed. Similar to Gage, Elliot's ability to successfully make and execute plans for the future were markedly impaired after his vmPFC was damaged.

When Damasio subjected Elliot to a barrage of examinations—language, memory, attention—he consistently performed like someone with a normal, even above-average, intellect. But when Elliot recounted experiences in life, even tragic ones following the removal of his tumor, he did so without the least bit of emotion. "I found myself suffering more when listening to Elliot's stories than Elliot himself seemed to be suffering," Damasio wrote. While Elliot could remember what it felt like to be sad, angry, or joyous, he was no longer capable of experiencing those emotions in new situations following his operation. "We might summarize Elliot's predicament," Damasio explained, "as to know but not to feel."

We often dismiss emotion as a hindrance to effective decision making. "Emotion clouds judgment" and "cool heads make wiser decisions" are common pieces of advice. But what Damasio saw in his patients was an inability to function in the most basic way when a part of their brain that dealt with emotional processing was impaired. Without the tug of emotion, easy decisions became surprisingly difficult to resolve. Since no outcome ever felt just right for Elliot, he jostled back and forth between options. He was unable to effectively make choices and tended to make choices poorly when he came to any decision at all.

Most of us tag everything we encounter automatically with some affective judgment. "We do not just see 'a house,'" explained Robert Zajonc, an influential psychologist who argued that affective reactions are rapid and omnipresent. "We see 'a handsome house,' 'an ugly house,' or 'a pretentious house.' . . . The same goes for a sunset, a lightening flash, a flower, a dimple, a hangnail, a cockroach, the taste of quinine, Saumur, the color of earth in Umbria, the sounds of traffic on 42nd Street." However, the particular part of the brain damaged in people like Gage and Elliot led them to suffer from an unfortunate condition that interfered with their ability to incorporate these affective signals into their decision making.

While we consciously experience emotions like anger, fear, or disgust, quick, simply affective flashes are far broader and more ubiquitous. Often our affective reactions to phenomena and the accompanying emotional states remain outside our conscious awareness.

Unconscious signals provoke important physical changes—changes in heart rate, blood flow, and hormone excretion—that profoundly influence behavior. Imagine that while out for a walk you see a thick, coiled object in your path. If you had to think carefully about whether it's foliage, rubbish, or a venomous snake, it would be too late to jump back to avoid being struck. Instead, when you see something potentially harmful that looks snake-like, you instinctively jump back even before you're consciously aware of exactly what the object is. Your heart and respiratory rates increase, adrenaline is secreted, and your mind focuses on the immediate threat. In fact, the brain is wired to deliver crude visual information directly to the amygdala, an emotional core of the brain, to immediately initiate action before additional time is taken to fully process the information in the visual cortex. The crucial time saved by a rapid affective response helps you suddenly jump back from a potentially dangerous curled object before it's too late. In the same way, you don't need to think about removing your hand when it's accidently placed on a hot stovetop. You'll remove it before you consciously realize that the stove is too hot to touch. In this way, affective evaluations serve as an early "danger detector" that innately leads us away from decisions and behaviors that are detrimental to our well-being.

But affective evaluations are not simply about avoiding stepping on snakes or touching hot stoves. Such evaluations serve a far broader role in a whole range of everyday decisions by helping us quickly eliminate undesirable or detrimental options. Damasio proposed something called the "somatic marker hypothesis" to explain how our body rapidly figures out the expected consequences of different options and helps us choose the most advantageous response. "When the bad outcome connected with a given response option comes into mind, however fleetingly," Damasio explains, "you experience an unpleasant gut feeling." These gut feelings are recalled whenever the same situation is encountered or imagined again. If the prior experience led to a safe and successful outcome, there will be a positive gut feeling associated with it. Conversely, if the prior experience led to a negative experience, it provokes an unpleasant gut feeling.

Even though we are not often consciously aware of it, our body has a remarkable ability to rapidly learn which behaviors are undesirable and should be discontinued. Researchers demonstrated this unconscious ability by devising a clever experiment using a game known as the Iowa Gambling Task. In the experiment, players were given four decks of cards and instructed to turn over the top card of any deck of their choice, one card at a time. Each time a participant turned over a card, it revealed a gain or, occasionally, a loss of money. Participants were challenged to earn as much money as possible by turning over cards from different decks.

Unbeknownst to the participants, the decks were rigged in a very particular way. Two decks offered cards with higher immediate gains than the others, but these decks also led to greater losses over time. While the participants were playing, the researchers monitored their palms for tiny beads of sweat—a good indicator of stress. After merely a dozen cards had been drawn, the researchers began observing an increase in the players' hand sweat before a subsequent draw from a money-losing deck. Participants' bodies knew to steer clear of the money-losing decks even before their conscious minds could articulate why.

The researchers then had patients with vmPFC damage—like Gage and Elliot—play the game. They did far more poorly. Lacking the usual "gut feelings," they did not experience heightened sweatiness before drawing from the negative decks. In fact, these participants continued to draw from the bad decks even after they could articulate how the decks were stacked—consistently choosing the decks that offered higher immediate rewards even though doing so led to greater losses in the end. The bodies of patients with vmPFC damage were unable to guide them in the right direction. As the authors of the study concluded, these participants "may 'say' the right thing, but they 'do' the wrong thing." Conscious awareness of the properties of the different decks was not sufficient to motivate choosing from the better ones. Rather, it took a physical gut feeling about a forthcoming bad decision to support making the better decision.

The importance of gut feelings in evaluating risks and making appropriate decisions becomes clear by observing the difficulties faced by individuals like Gage and Elliot who lack the ability to predictably make affective evaluations. Gut feelings protect us from taking unnecessary risks, facilitate social interaction and planning, and keep us out of harm's way.

Our intuitions help nudge us to act in certain advantageous ways, but one question that remains is whether these feelings serve to strictly benefit us. Put another way, if our intuitions simply help us behave in a manner that selectively benefits and protects us personally, it would be natural to find people engaging in behavior that offers attractive personal benefits but causes harm to others. Socially destructive conduct would be quite common, both in our personal lives and in the corporate world, if our affective judgments were driven by personal benefit and myopic financial rewards. Executive misconduct could be seen as a manifestation of these selfish intuitions.

But when we look at human behavior generally—and even at business conduct more specifically—it's clear that not all people are motivated to steal from and deceive one another. Something is driving our gut feelings beyond shortsighted personal gains and protection. As described in the next section, our intuitions evolved all the way down to the genetic level to simultaneously promote our own well-being and moral behavior.

Our Deepest Inclinations

Whether people are predisposed toward good or evil is among humanity's longest-running intellectual debates. Early Christian theologians argued that we are indelibly corrupted because of Adam and Eve's original sin. Later philosophers and scientists, such as Thomas Hobbes and Thomas Huxley, came to a similarly disheartening view, albeit through different logic that man was brutish and largely apathetic toward the well-being of others. The niceties of fairness and altruism, the roots of morality, were thought to be nothing more than a thin coat of veneer covering our fundamentally egotistical nature.

The idea that man has little concern beyond his immediate well-being was often bolstered by misunderstandings of Darwin's theory of natural selection, especially in its later application to genetics. So-called Social Darwinists described a brutally competitive landscape in which the strongest members of a species defeated the weakest.

Metaphorically, genes can be "selfish" in seeking their own replication and survival by promoting advantageous traits that are passed on over time. From this it might seem to follow that selfish genes lead to selfish people and that even apparently altruistic acts are self-serving. Yet, "this interpretation," as pointed out by one researcher, "amounts to the claim that Mother Teresa follows the same basic instinct as any inside trader or thief." As molecular units, genes themselves are not endowed with any intrinsic motivation or intention.

Instead, genetic forces serve to support human interaction in complex communities. As with other social species, it's not uncommon to observe humans engaging in self-sacrificial acts that seem to be in conflict with a person's own well-being. It is here that we see the roots of altruism appear. In so-called kin altruism, people engage in self-sacrificial acts toward family members since it makes little difference whether a gene is passed to the next generation by its immediate owner or by a relative. And among unrelated people, humans also engage in reciprocal altruism, the "you scratch my back and I'll scratch yours" type because doing so mutually improves the success of both parties in the long run. Thus, humans are intrinsically endowed with tendencies that promote altruistic social behavior.

Affective evaluations and gut feelings help support these altruistic tendencies. Social interaction is riddled with complexity, yet it often demands immediate decisions. Affective evaluations help us rapidly respond. When someone is in need, sympathy prompts a helping hand. When someone provides assistance, we express gratitude. People who take without reciprocating find themselves targets of anger. And a sense of guilt motivates us to rectify relationships after lapses in good behavior. All of these affective responses serve as commitment devices to promote harmonious relationships between people and restrain potentially destructive behavior. These feelings also arise automatically, whether we want them to or not. Perhaps it's not surprising then that individuals who are deprived access to such emotional signals through disease, handicap, or injury have such trouble in social contexts. Emotions are critical to our ability to thrive in those settings.

These ingrained responses also benefit others and serve as the foundation for moral behavior. Suppose someone cheats you. When I hear about it, I'll be less inclined to engage with that person in the future—not only because I'll be protecting myself, but also because I will empathize and share in your resentment. I'll be displeased to see this person violate a basic tenet of honesty that I believe ought to be widely upheld. Taking on the perspective of another person and envisioning how you would feel in his place is central to the most basic and universal moral tenet, the golden rule: "Do unto others as you would have them do unto you." We vicariously respond to the feelings of others as part of a coordinated emotional experience. Not only are you upset when you are cheated, but you feel similar indignation, albeit perhaps not as strongly, when you see someone else being cheated.

"Distress at the sight of another's pain is an impulse over which we exert little or no control," wrote the renowned primatologist Frans de Waal. "It grabs us instantaneously, like a reflex, without time to weigh the pros and cons." De Waal, who has devoted much of his career to studying and writing about the empathetic behavior of our closest ancestors, has provided compelling evidence that empathetic behavior is not something that arose uniquely in humans but is instead something rooted in our earlier ancestors, including apes and monkeys, just as Charles Darwin suggested in the mid-nineteenth century.

These inclinations against causing harm to others are especially potent in human behavior. One study measured the vital signs of people engaging in a variety of realistic but simulated acts of violence like smashing someone's hand or smacking the body of a baby against a table. Participants knew that these acts were only simulated and would not cause any harm. Nonetheless, merely pretending to engage in barbaric actions produced an adverse biological reaction: participants experienced a significant constriction of their peripheral blood vessels, a classic physical symptom of what is often called "cold feet." Our natural aversion to causing harm is so deep that just the perfunctory simulation of violent acts triggers revulsion. Humanity is perhaps better-natured than some philosophers and theologians in the past have made us out to be.

The universality of certain moral sensibilities has led numerous scholars to draw comparisons between moral development and language development. The pioneering linguist Noam Chomsky argued that we're innately endowed with a "universal grammar" that provides the capacity to speak and understand language without being consciously aware of all its underlying complexities. Drawing on this work, several scholars have proposed that we also have a "universal moral grammar" that provides the capacity to intuitively judge right and wrong. It's an intriguing proposition that implies that we're endowed with at least some rudimentary sense that tilts us to behave less adversely toward one another.

Of course, this is not to say that every person has the same moral sensibilities. While we're ingrained with a variety of tendencies that help support and maintain our ability to cooperatively support one another, there is still significant variation among individuals' capacity to empathize. Nonetheless, the collective evidence supports the idea that humans have an innate system of affective reactions and related moral emotions that promotes social behavior.

Reconciling the Good and the Bad

If we are innately inclined to be moral, then why are immoral acts—such as those committed by the former executives discussed in this book—so pervasive? For all the acts of altruism and self-sacrifice rejoiced over in newscasts and daily papers, there are also plenty of destructive feats that violate the basic precepts of avoiding actions that harm others. As the writer Michael Shermer aptly put it, "Humans evolved to be moral animals, but by no means always moral. There are times when we are amoral or even immoral." Each time an executive inflicts economic harm to others by committing fraud, engaging in embezzlement, or trading on insider information represents another instance of just such damaging conduct.

Although some of the affective, automatic reactions supporting moral behavior are innate, they are also fragile. Many of the conditions under which we developed these affective reactions differ from those that we confront today. For most of human history, we lived in close physical contact with one another in small communities. Relationships among individual members were well known, and we stuck together protecting those in our own group. It was under these conditions that we developed our affective evaluations about which things to approach, which things to avoid, and how to instinctively behave toward one another. In the limited time since then—on an evolutionary time scale—relatively little modification of the human mind has occurred. And therein lies the problem. Both the world and what's needed to interact successfully within it have changed significantly more, and in far more profound ways, than our minds have.

We still rely on automatic intuitive responses to facilitate many of our decisions, but we're now operating outside the familiar contexts in which these systems evolved to produce successful behavior. In today's globalized world we are much more likely to interact with people outside our immediate community and to do so in ways other than through face-to-face encounters. Executives convicted of insider trading, such as Scott London or McKinsey's Rajat Gupta, never met the victims of their crimes.

Our instinctive reactions may no longer produce the behavior best suited to succeed in the modern business environment. The desire to avoid failure, maintain our reputation, and trounce competitors creates circumstances that challenge our tendency to behave morally. The next chapter explores how failures of intuition create the prospect for corporate malfeasance.

7

I never felt that I was doing anything wrong

Overlooking Harm

I N MAY 2008, a horrific earthquake struck Sichuan Province in western China. Nearly 70,000 people were killed, 18,000 more were missing and presumed dead, and another 370,000 were injured. The magnitude 7.9 quake was among the worst in China's history, and papers around the world carried news of the devastation. The BBC aired footage of sobbing parents outside collapsed schools waiting for their children to be rescued from the rubble. Poorly constructed buildings crumbled during the aftershocks, leaving millions of people homeless.

Two and a half centuries earlier, Adam Smith, the celebrated Scottish Enlightenment philosopher asked his readers to imagine just such a disaster striking China in his book, *The Theory of Moral Sentiments*:

> Let us suppose that the great empire of China, with all its myriads of inhabitants, was suddenly swallowed up by an earthquake, and let us consider how a man of humanity in Europe, who had no sort of connexion with that part of the word, would be affected upon receiving intelligence of this dreadful calamity.

Individuals living far away from China, then as now, reading about such a disaster would feel sorry for the deep misfortune of those affected.

Smith conjectured about how someone hearing news of the disaster would feel.

> He would, I imagine, first of all, express very strongly his sorrow for the misfortune of that unhappy people, he would make many melancholy reflections upon the precariousness of human life, and the vanity of all the labours of man, which could thus be annihilated in a moment.

Today, if such an event struck, some people might be moved to donate money online to an aid organization. Others might go online to read about the events, see pictures, and discuss the tragedy with their friends and family. Heads of state would send their condolences, and leaders of multinational firms would offer to donate food and other goods to those affected. Yet, as Smith appreciated, these emotions and the ensuing responses would be fleeting. "And when all this fine philosophy was over, . . ." Smith wrote, "he would pursue his business or his pleasure, take his repose or his diversion, with the same ease and tranquility, as if no such accident had happened."

Such indifference to human suffering would strike some as rather crass. Surely, they would argue, people would be moved to do more if there was such terrible suffering abroad. It's an optimistic thought, but one not necessarily borne out by our behavior. To put this tragedy in perspective, Smith asked readers to imagine if some loss, like losing our little finger, was to befall us personally. This trivial "disaster," by comparison to a massive earthquake in China, would keep us up late into the night, worrying about its consequences. The earthquake that led to the deaths of thousands "seems plainly an object less interesting to him, than this paltry misfortune of his own," noted Smith. With this example, Smith identified a fundamental dimension of human nature: our ability to empathize with others is directly related to their proximity to us. The farther away the harm, the more fleeting our emotions. As the saying goes, "out of sight, out of mind."

To understand how our affective reactions to committing harm do not always function as we'd expect, consider your own reaction to a hypothetical dilemma. Suppose a trolley car is running out of control and heading toward five people making repairs to the tracks. You happen to be standing

Figure 7.1: Runaway trolley and the track-switch dilemma.

next to a rail switch. If you flip it, the trolley will be diverted to another track killing only one worker rather than five. Would you choose to flip the switch?

With little hesitation, the vast majority of people—almost 90 percent in one large survey—say "yes," they would flip the switch. To most, saving five people, at the expense of killing one, seems quite sensible.

But consider your judgment in another scenario. Suppose you're a surgeon and five patients are acutely in need of one organ each. Two patients need a lung, two need a kidney, and one requires a heart. All five will die today if they do not get these organs, but there's little chance that matching donor organs will be found in time. Coincidentally, your nurse calls to say that another patient has arrived at your clinic for his routine annual checkup. The nurse's preliminary examination shows that he's in perfect health, and even has the right blood type—he's the perfect donor. All you'd need to do is quickly sedate him, bring him to the operating table, remove his healthy organs, and distribute them to your other patients. He'd die, but you'd save five other people. Would you go ahead with the procedure?

Figure 7.2: Runaway trolley and the footbridge dilemma.

Quickly and confidently, the vast majority of people respond that they wouldn't kill the healthy individual to save five others. Thus, people are content flipping the switch to save five people at the expense of one, but uncomfortable taking the organs from one man to save five others. Why should our judgments be so apparently inconsistent?

To further highlight this distinction, consider another version of the trolley scenario. Suppose you're standing on a bridge alongside a large man. You again see a runaway trolley rushing toward the five workers on the tracks. You realize that if you push the man over the rail, he'd stop the trolley. Although he'd die, you'd save the five others. Would you push the man over the rail?

Like those choosing not to remove the organs from the healthy man, the vast majority of people say they wouldn't push the man over the rail. In fact, in the same survey where almost 90 percent said "yes" to flipping the switch (resulting in only one death), nearly 90 percent said "no" to heaving the man onto the tracks (thus resulting in five deaths). It's as though there is an internal emotional response that screams out to us saying, "No, I just cannot push an innocent man in front of an oncoming trolley!"

The potential trade-off—one life weighed against saving five others—is identical in these scenarios, but there is also a crucial difference. Taking organs or pushing a man over a rail involves an intimate act of violence. Even though the deliberate demise of one person will prevent the death of others, it still has all the sensation of deliberately killing someone, which rings an internal chord telling us not to proceed. It seems that we have a basic aversion to this kind of direct and intimate killing of another human being, even if it could save others.

Curiously, if we take away the physical contact of pushing someone and replace it with pulling a switch, we become more comfortable with following through. The death of the man in the switch dilemma is impersonal since we feel it's the switching of the tracks that's causing the one man's death—not us. The incidental and more distant harm caused by flipping the switch doesn't immediately engage our emotional senses in the same strong way as pushing someone off a bridge or removing a healthy man's organs. In fact, when people are placed in an fMRI machine and given these scenarios, this difference in emotional engagement is exactly what's observed in the brain. The prospect of pushing the man over the railing sets off significant activity in the ventromedial prefrontal cortex, the part of the brain associated with emotional engagement and compassion—the same area damaged in Phineas Gage's accident. But when individuals consider the switching case, there is comparatively little activity in this area.

Humans have always harmed one another. From slapping, pushing, and hitting to killing in combat, harming other people has been for most of humanity's existence an intimate affair. Although violence has occurred throughout human history, evidence also suggests that it is not something we're especially keen on doing. The statistics are controversial, but several military historians have offered data suggesting that soldiers in many of the major modern conflicts, from the American Civil War to World Wars I and II, were deeply averse to directly firing on enemy combatants. For instance, one estimate suggests that fewer than half—with some estimates as low as 20 percent—of riflemen discharged their weapons directly onto enemies during World War II, even when their compatriots were at risk. While alarming for a general trying to create an effective fighting force, such statistics say something important about our deep aversion to causing direct harm, just as people are averse to pushing the man over the bridge.

Until quite recently in our history, it was difficult to cause direct harm to another person unless that individual was physically close to us. Harm was not only physical but intimate. As the ability to communicate and influence others from greater distances became possible, however, new and different ways of inflicting harm emerged as well. Notably, these innovations permitted the perpetration of newfangled kinds of harm against individuals—namely, economic harms, which are less physical and more abstract. Economic harms fundamentally differ from other acts in that they do not trigger gut feelings of actually doing harm, as was the case with intimate, physical harm. Yet, they injure others—albeit economically rather than physically—all the same.

The difference between the age-old physical harms and the newer economic harms is easily observed by looking at how one commits financial fraud. In many cases, the modern financial crime simply involves changing a few numbers on a spreadsheet. In perpetrating a fraud at the publisher ProQuest, regulators alleged that Scott Hirth, its CFO, employed an especially crude computer trick. To boost earnings, Hirsh made fraudulent adjustments to the firm's financials in a white-colored font. Hirsh also entered fictitious journal entries to the spreadsheet using the "Hide" function. When viewed or printed out, these multimillion-dollar adjustments were invisible. Coupled with a few other spreadsheet adjustments, Hirsh inflated pre-tax earnings by more than 30 percent over four years.

While such conduct causes significant damage—ProQuest's shareholders lost $437 million in market value when Hirth's fraud was revealed—it does not engage the same emotional circuitry in the brain as does physical violence. Like most business misconduct, the dash of a pen or the click of a mouse creates a distant and impersonal kind of harm. Yet, the deleterious consequences can be just as devastating to those affected. One need only ask the victims of Bernard Madoff's Ponzi scheme who lost much of their life savings, or any of the thousands of employees who lost their jobs when WorldCom shuttered its operations.

It's often from the perspective of the victim that we approach the question of why an executive would commit misconduct. Why would someone so successful seek to injure another person? But the trouble with this approach is that it assumes that the executive considered the victim's suffering in the first place. Victims have compared, for instance, the actions of Jeffrey Skilling, Enron's CEO, to that of a rapist, an Al Qaeda terrorist, and even an axe murderer. "I know how awful it would be to lose the pension you depend on," said one Houston resident. "Hurting that many elderly people so severely is, I feel, the equivalent of being an axe murderer."

Such a characterization might reflect how a victim feels, but it does little to explain what the executive actually thought or felt while perpetrating the fraud. It also doesn't illuminate the actual reasons why someone as intelligent as Skilling would engage in a complex multibillion-dollar act of corporate misconduct. "The emotions of the victims are not a valid guide to those of the perpetrators," noted the social psychologist Roy Baumeister. "Indeed perpetrators may feel little or no emotions at all."

To understand managerial malfeasance, then, we need to examine the problem from the perspective of the manager. Why was he able to proceed with committing an act that was harmful not only to others but also, in the end, to himself? Why didn't he feel compelled to stop and choose an alternative path, one that wasn't illicit? To answer these questions, we need to consider how intuitions can fail to appropriately detect the harm our actions may cause.

Distancing the Executive

There was once a time when virtually all businesses were financed by a single person or small group. Investors served as operators, and the firm's owner and manager were one and the same. Managers had little incentive to misappropriate assets since that would simply mean moving money from one pocket to another. "Corporations were rare," wrote historian Glenn Porter, "and business had a very personal tone."

Over time, larger and more ambitious business ventures began to uproot this basic structure. By the sixteenth century, the expansion of global trading networks, especially in spices, minerals, and other exotic goods that could be profitably sold back home, contributed to these changes. Voyages lasted months, even years, and required significant upfront investment. With tremendous risks associated with these ventures, groups of investors would bind together to underwrite the expeditions, sharing both the potential risks and the rewards. These shareholders, who had neither the time nor the expertise to manage the firms they owned, left the specifics to managers experienced in running similar operations. Thus began the slow march toward separating the manager who controlled the day-to-day operations from the owner of the business.

Although the owners and managers evolved into separate roles, business still relied on a close-knit community. In seventeenth-century New England for instance, owners often brought in a mix of family members, in-laws, and friends to train and later manage operations. The relationship between owners and managers continued to be an intensely personal one. But increasingly over time, this relationship became less intimate as firms needed to raise even greater amounts of capital to support more complex and dispersed operations. Some firms began trading on the burgeoning securities exchanges that sprang up in cities like Amsterdam and London, permitting members of the public to buy shares and become partial firm owners. Still, the number of individuals invested in a firm continued to be fairly small. For corporations registered in New York in 1826, for instance, the number of shareholders ranged from a paltry 3 for one turnpike developer to 560 for a major bank. Many of these investors had familial ties with the firms they invested in, and 90 percent lived in New York.

But what started as a few dozen shareholders became hundreds, and eventually thousands upon thousands. By the early twentieth century, prompted by the perceived opportunities to expand one's wealth by holding securities, the number of shareholders owning stakes increased dramatically. AT&T, the iconic firm founded by Alexander Graham Bell, the inventor of the telephone, had 7,000 shareholders at the turn of the twentieth century, 140,000 by 1920, and nearly 600,000 by 1930. Almost 90 percent of shareholders held fewer than a hundred shares, with managers themselves holding larger, but similarly limited, numbers of shares.

For all the business advantages offered by the rise in dispersed ownership, this financial innovation marked the demise of the personal relationship between executives and investors. Not only did managers and investors not physically interact, but executives were often shielded from even knowing who their investors were. Executives communicated to investors through brief annual letters, and shareholders became strangers who were anonymously connected to executives only through amorphous legal contracts.

Executives whose business was once supported by communal and even familial ties now found themselves working for investors and with employees with whom they shared no relationship other than a contractual one. This diffusion in ownership and personnel also meant that actions

Office of
THE PROCTER & GAMBLE COMPANY

Cincinnati, Ohio, August 15, 1919.

To the Stockholders of The Procter & Gamble Company:

The total volume of business done by this Company and constituent Companies for the fiscal year ended June 30, 1919, amounted to $193,392,044.02.

The net earnings for the year, after all reserves and charges for depreciation, losses, taxes (inclusive of Federal and State Income and War Taxes), advertising and special introductory work had been deducted, amounted to $7,325,531.85.

We shall take pleasure in furnishing further information to any accredited stockholder who is interested and who will apply, in person, at the Company's office in Cincinnati.

Yours respectfully,

THE PROCTER & GAMBLE CO.,

Wm. Cooper Procter, President.

Figure 7.3: Procter & Gamble's annual report for 1919.
Requests for additional information need to be made in person in Cincinnati.

that once might have affected only a handful of people now had the capacity to affect thousands. Harmful conduct committed by an executive was no longer against a specific group of individuals known to the executive but, instead, against an ill-defined and little-known mass. This not only increased the magnitude of the harm that the executive had the capacity to inflict but it also fundamentally shifted the psychology of harm. By divorcing executives from contact with the individuals directly impacted by their actions, executives were shielded from experiencing the emotional feedback that arose from their decisions.

Mother Theresa once supposedly said, "If I look at the mass I will never act. If I look at the one, I will." She was moved to help the gravely ill because of the emotional impact their suffering had on her. Through an inversion of this sentiment, business malfeasance often lacks a parallel emotional punch. It doesn't motivate strong feelings because individuals—investors, employees, consumers—become obscured within an anonymous mass. With the harm neither present nor visible, the affective system does not whirl into gear to promote avoidance of harmful action. There isn't an internal signal that warns *"Stop!"* and prompts the executive to choose a different course of action.

When Carl Kotchian, president of Lockheed, admitted paying millions in bribes to foreign dignitaries during the 1970s—payments that would eventually lead to the imprisonment of Japan's prime minister—he felt little in the way of guilt. Kotchian reflected on these payments:

> Some call it gratuities. Some call them questionable payments. Some call it extortion. Some call it grease. Some call it bribery. I looked at these payments as necessary to sell a product. I never felt I was doing anything wrong.

Kotchian expressed little remorse because to him these payments were simply a cost of doing business: 2 to 5 percent of sales in East Asia and 7 to 15 percent in the Middle East. The broader negative societal ramifications that corruption had on the well-being of others from such payments never occurred to him.

The difference in reactions between specific and diffuse harms can even be observed in how police and federal agents charged with protecting the public see different offenses. If federal investigators unearthed a plot that endangered the physical or financial well-being of a specific person, agents would seek to protect the potential victim by stopping the assailant prior to the crime taking place. Yet, for diffuse white-collar crimes where the harm is spread across many anonymous victims, investigators are sometimes willing to stand aside and watch the misconduct occur in order to ensure a successful conviction.

In the summer of 2014, federal agents grew suspicious of the irregular trading activity of Michael Lucarelli, a director at an investor relations firm in New York City. As the head of market intelligence, Lucarelli was privy to firms' press releases prior to their public release. Relying on the confidential information in these news releases, Lucarelli was suspected of purchasing securities before this information was announced publicly, in violation of insider trading laws.

In July 2014, federal agents entered Lucarelli's office on a search warrant and copied files of a preliminary earnings release they found inside his locked briefcase. The agents placed the files back in exactly the same position they found them, believing that Lucarelli would utilize the information to place trades. As they suspected, Lucarelli began purchasing tens of thousands of shares from investors who unknowingly sold them to him over the coming week. Once earnings were released, Lucarelli dumped the stock to net nearly $90,000 in profits. For the governmental agents and prosecutors, the desire to improve the chances of a successful conviction outweighed the harm to a diffuse set of anonymous victims.

In contrast to assault, rape, and other violent offenses that target a specific individual as the object of the crime, the harm created by financial misconduct might be better thought of as an incidental, albeit significant, effect of the executive's actions. Harming investors or employees is not the intention behind engaging in misconduct but, rather, an inevitable corollary or externality. This distinction is important since it helps explain why, from the standpoint of the executive, misconduct doesn't necessarily lead to the sensation of taking or stealing anything from anyone.

Steven Garfinkel, the former CFO of DVI Inc., a medical equipment financing company, described his reaction to signing false collateral reports and double pledging assets, a fraud that would ultimately send him to prison for twenty-six months. "I know this is going to sound bizarre, but when I was signing the documents I didn't think of that as lying."

For Garfinkel, lying on paper was a distinctly unemotional event. At the same time, he clearly recognized that this deception felt different from directly lying in-person to another individual. Notably, it was this difference that led Garfinkel to decide to proceed no further with the fraud. During a meeting with bankers from Goldman Sachs, they asked Garfinkel if there was anything else they needed to know about DVI's financials. This question was an important turning point for Garfinkel. Either he had to lie directly to them to further cover up DVI's fraud or he'd have to reveal that some of the information the bankers were relying on was fraudulent. "At that point, I said I can't lie to the guy face-to-face. . . . I said wait a second, I went down the hall, told the CEO that I'm telling Goldman about this, and turned around and walked out."

Garfinkel had signed off on reports in the past attesting to the fraudulent collateral. Although his actions allowed lenders and investors to believe that DVI had appropriately designated more collateral than it actually had, the reports never instigated the feeling of deception and harm that lying to DVI's banker in person did. "There was a difference between filling out a form and flat out looking someone in the eye and lying to them and saying no, there is nothing else you should know about," Garfinkel explained. "I don't know why that seemed different, but it was."

It's often a convoluted path from an executive's decision to the impact on investors. Even in the most blatant misconduct, an executive's actions can seem far removed from the eventual negative repercussions on others or the erosion of trust among the public at large. There is no gut feeling associated with inflicting harm because the executives don't actually witness the harm their actions cause.

It is even possible for some fraudulent actions to cause deaths in such a diffuse manner that they are unlikely to resonate with those perpetrating the crime. In 2015, regulators revealed that Volkswagen had illicitly installed software in numerous diesel car models causing these vehicles to report artificially low emissions readings. In reality, the cars produced nitrogen oxides—dangerous emissions that have been closely linked to lung disease— at levels up to forty times above emissions standards. When researchers from MIT and Harvard teamed up to model the effect of this additional pollution on public health, they estimated that Volkswagen's extra emissions were responsible for fifty-nine early deaths. However, for those individuals who installed this deceptive software and for the executives who knew about its existence, the true effects of this malfeasance are hidden: they will never know, or even be able to identify, the fifty-nine people they killed.

A Temporal Gap

With business malfeasance, it's not just that those who are economically injured are physically and psychologically distant. Victims, too, are temporally removed from the actual acts. This occurs because of the lag between the time when the executive engages in the malfeasance and the time when the negative consequences are experienced by those affected.

A simple analogy can put this delay into perspective. If you smack someone on the shoulder, he will recoil in pain and look at you for an explanation. It'll be obvious right away that you inflicted harm. You'll quickly realize the mistake, apologize, and avoid doing it again.

Financial crime lacks this instantaneous feedback. The harmful consequences of such crime may follow months, even years, after the initial actions, so it's easier for the perpetrator to be ignorant of the harm he caused. It's as if you smacked someone but saw no reaction until you hit him twenty times. By then, you'd have already caused considerable harm and missed the window of time to halt.

In the late 1990s, WorldCom had become one of the largest telecommunications companies in the world, with annual revenues topping $30 billion. In 1996, the *Wall Street Journal* ranked the firm as having the best ten-year performance out of a thousand companies surveyed. By late 1999, however, executives faced with declining margins made several material accounting changes in an attempt to obfuscate this deterioration in performance. Billions in expenditures were incorrectly booked as assets rather than as expenses. These "adjustments" temporarily propped up WorldCom's performance but were eventually exhausted. When this deceit was finally revealed, the share price tumbled from over $90 a share in the fall of 1999 to less than $1 a share in the summer of 2002. Nearly $80 billion would need to be written off its balance sheet. In the ensuing bankruptcy, tens of thousands of employees were laid off and upward of 100,000 people are believed to have lost money in their pension plans. As significant as this fraud was, none of the devastation was viscerally anticipated by the executives making these adjustments.

David Myers, WorldCom's controller who oversaw the firm's accounting and the preparation of financial statements, recalls how the fraud began: "We closed the books and the results were nowhere near where expectations were." Some executives suspected that this might be due to an accounting error, so they agreed to make a "correcting entry" to the financial statements that quarter in anticipation of finding the mistake later. "We thought there was an error that we were going to fix," recalled Myers. "Once you fixed it you'd be understating expense in one quarter and you'd just overstate it in the next quarter and get it all back to zero. . . . No harm, no foul."

The problem was that there wasn't an accounting mistake. Soon enough the executives began entering figures, often in the hundreds of millions of dollars, to make the accounting books balance correctly. "We knew what earnings *needed* to be, we knew what revenue was, and we knew all the other expenses . . . and the amount it took to get there was the amount we capitalized." While engaging in the fraud and still seeking to run a successful firm, Myers recalled spending much of his time "thinking that you're helping people and doing the right thing" instead of thinking about the eventual consequences of his actions. "It was just shortsighted by not trying to understand what the true outcome was going to be."

Ironically, investors may unknowingly applaud these actions while simultaneously being defrauded. At the peak of Enron's financial manipulation, for instance, its chief financial officer and the architect of many of its dubious schemes, Andrew Fastow, was given the prestigious CFO of the Year award by *CFO Magazine*. Scott Sullivan, WorldCom's CFO, and Mark Swartz, Tyco's CFO, were similarly recognized with awards in the midst of their misconduct. After these numerous frauds were revealed, the magazine decided to scrap the award entirely.

Receiving these accolades while at the same time engaging in misconduct is analogous to getting positive reinforcement after striking someone. Rather than getting a negative response, you are encouraged by this feedback to do it again and again. Without experiencing any negative consequences, you're unlikely to feel that you're committing harm. In fact, with all the positive reinforcement you're getting, the offending act begins to resonate positively. It's only later, when all of a sudden the truth is revealed, that the harm becomes evident. But by then, it's too late. The harm has already been done.

Our Natural Limitations

Imagine placing yourself in the position of Andrew Fastow or David Myers. Why, you might ask, didn't they feel what I think I'd have felt that would have stopped me from committing a crime?

It's easy to imagine that we should have some strong intuition telling us *"No!"* when faced with the choice to engage in wrongdoing. Yet this impression overlooks our basic human nature, which can easily fail to recognize distant and temporally offset harms. Each kind of corporate misconduct has facets that make it resonate less intuitively. With financial reporting fraud, the effects are not felt until long into the future and the victims are often applauding the perpetrator's behavior until the deception is revealed. With insider trading, it's difficult to identify precisely which investors are harmed. And with tax evasion, the reduction to government coffers makes the harm to specific individuals so diffuse that it no longer feels salient to say it harmed any individual person. Each white-collar crime has different dimensions that make the harm more psychologically distant than even the most rudimentary physical harm.

While encountering a situation like the trolley dilemma in real life is unlikely, this scenario does illustrate something fundamental about our intuitions. "Throwing a switch that diverts a train that will hit someone bears no resemblance to anything likely to have happened in the circumstances in which we and our ancestors lived," pointed out philosopher Peter Singer. "Hence the thought of doing it does not elicit the same emotional response as pushing someone off a bridge."

New situations and new technology influence our affective evaluations in ways that are not always in our own or the public's best long-term interests. The trolley dilemma helps illustrate the problem with the psychologically distant harm that people routinely encounter in the modern business world. The fact that our intuitions are poorly attuned to the potential for harm in such settings raises the prospect of corporate malfeasance.

There are some executives with lower capacities to appreciate the harm they cause to others, like Bernard Madoff, whom we'll meet in a later chapter. These individuals may have a stronger innate proclivity to engage in malfeasance when the opportunity arises. But most people in the business community don't engage in misconduct even when a situation ripe for such behavior presents itself despite facing the limitations and weaknesses described in this chapter. To explain this, there must be other forces that mitigate misconduct when the internal affective alarm fails. The next chapter focuses on how we've come to learn and adapt to some of the challenges we face in the modern business world. Understanding what those forces are, how they function, and where they can fail helps explain why malfeasance is more pervasive in some firms and industries than in others.

8

If there was something wrong with this transaction, wouldn't people have told me?

The Difficulty of Being Good

S UPPOSE THERE IS no legal prohibition against murder. If you killed someone, no police officer would whisk you away to prison. Legally speaking, it would be "okay." Would you murder someone? Would your friends? Would your community suddenly be swept up in a surge of unrelenting violence?

Such dramatic social upheaval is unlikely. Even without legal ramifications, the overwhelming majority of people would not kill another human being. Our intuitions tell us that murder is wrong and we don't need a law to prevent us from engaging in it. We would still avoid killing even if there is little chance of being caught or punished.

In contrast, there are many illegal acts, some with potentially serious consequences and a high likelihood of being caught, that people routinely commit. Illicit substances, for instance, are consumed widely in the United States. One estimate showed that as many as 9 percent of the adult population have consumed some illicit drug or medication within the past month. Despite the war on drugs, the decision to consume or avoid these substances has little to do with the law for most people. An analysis of the choice to use or avoid drugs found that less than 5 percent of this decision can be explained by the chance that people think they will be caught and punished.

At first glance, the choice between which laws to follow and which to break is inconsistent. In some instances, people will voluntarily follow laws even when there is little prospect of being caught. In other cases, individuals will flagrantly violate laws even when doing so poses significant risks to themselves and others. The Yale Law School professor Tom Tyler has studied this discrepancy and found that the tendency to comply with a law has less to do with the potential punishment and much more to do with attitudes about the legitimacy of that law.

Tyler's research suggests that merely prohibiting something doesn't stop people from seeking to engage in that behavior. To be effective, legal prohibitions need to be consistent with individuals' moral intuitions. People naturally comply with laws when breaking them violates their internal sense of right and wrong. Tyler's analysis explains why dropping the prohibition against murder wouldn't dramatically change most communities: a law is not needed to tell most people not to go out and kill one another.

In contrast, much of the discussion around deterring corporate malfeasance focuses on the possibility of being caught and punished. Preet Bharara, the federal prosecutor for the Southern District of New York, often argues that the most effective way to deter white-collar crime is to show offenders the ramifications of misconduct. "If you show them the consequences of bad conduct and you show them that you are engaged in enforcement," Bharara told CNBC, " . . . over time rational people who have gone to business schools and understand quantitative models will come to the inevitable conclusion that I shouldn't commit that crime. . . . That's part of the message that I think we want to send to people who are thinking about committing that crime."

But even when there are no laws against manipulating financial figures or insider trading, most executives remain honest. With potentially much to gain and little to lose, these executives cannot simply be reasoning that the potential monetary or reputational costs outweigh the benefits. Instead, they must have developed some values, some moral proclivities, that encourage them to behave in a certain way even when they are unlikely to be punished.

How do these values arise? The decision to avoid illegal acts such as price-fixing or bribery is not evolutionarily hard-wired or innate. The abstract and often ambiguous nature of the harm created by such conduct—types of harm that became possible only recently—must make aversion to this conduct something new.

At least in theory, both intuition and reasoning have the potential to motivate executives toward compliance with regulation and away from malfeasance, but they also represent very different ways of reaching a decision. To understand why some executives sometimes behave destructively, we need to understand why most behave well—and obey the laws that govern corporate conduct—most of the time. Exploring these difficult issues is the task of this chapter.

Manufacturing Morals

Being a United Nations diplomat has a number of perks. Among these privileges is immunity from parking violations in New York City. Park anywhere you want in the Big Apple—in a loading zone, doubled-up in front of your favorite restaurant, in front of a fire hydrant—and an orange violation will likely appear under your front windshield wiper. But for a United Nations diplomat, the ticket could simply be ignored.

If enforcement—or lack thereof—drives behavior, diplomats from every country should be racking up similarly large numbers of violations. But when two economists looked at the number of tickets received by United Nations diplomats, they found that some had virtually none while others had many. There was also a clear pattern describing which diplomats received the most violations. Diplomats from high-corruption countries—Chad, Sudan, Pakistan, Mozambique, Bulgaria—received the most parking tickets. Diplomats from low-corruption countries like Norway and Canada received the least.

The economists explained this finding by describing how the country that each diplomat hailed from provided each with a sense of identity and culture. Some diplomats came from cultures that tacitly permitted corrupt behavior—like parking wherever they want to and not paying the fine—as acceptable for someone of their stature. Others came from countries whose culture implored them to respect local regulations even when they faced no likely sanctions for violating the rules.

Culture is a set of shared assumptions that guides members of a community toward a particular set of attitudes and beliefs. It arises within groups—some as broad as the citizens of a country, others as narrow as a handful of friends who meet weekly for a game of poker. And within every culture, there are also subcultures. In the workplace, subcultures arise among individuals who operate in the same industry, work at a particular firm, or share an office, and repeatedly confront similar dilemmas and experiences.

Culture imbues all aspects of workplace life—whether communication is confrontational or collaborative, whether emotional expression is encouraged or condemned, and whether disappointing news is perceived as a threat or as a development opportunity. Marvin Bower, the famed management consultant, once gave one of the clearest and most parsimonious descriptions of firm culture when he described it simply as "the way we do things around here." More than just affecting the atmosphere and mood, differences in firm culture can influence whether a business is able to innovate and succeed in a competitive market. Employees at one firm may address emerging challenges with a sense of urgency and vigor while those at another may sluggishly avoid external threats and pressures.

While some aspects of culture focus on internal dynamics, other dimensions transcend the firm and affect competitors, customers, investors, and the general public. By potentially improving or detracting from the well-being of others, cultural influences are often imbued with some moral element.

Consider some predicaments that commonly arise in corporate life whose responses are shaped by workplace culture. If asked for a side payment to win a lucrative contract, would an employee be willing to pay it? When quarterly sales targets are reached a few days before a quarter ends, does a manager wait to officially book new contracts until the next quarter begins? When results from a recent product test are disappointing, does an engineer describe the failure openly or seek to hide it within some fine print? Would managers seek to include a costly safety feature for a product even if consumers are unlikely to fully appreciate its inclusion?

Responses to dilemmas like these are usually consistent among people operating within a subculture. Providing a payoff to a local official might seem like an efficient and sensible solution to managers at one firm but an egregious offense to managers at another. The response that immediately strikes a manager as the "right one" is a product of the environment that the person belongs to and identifies with.

Culture thus provides a set of norms that guide groups of individuals toward particular practices and away from others. These norms consist of tacit rules that guide conduct and create cohesiveness among individuals. People appeal to these norms to figure out how to appropriately respond—by the standards of the group—when a particular dilemma or problem arises.

Even at the most senior level of an organization, there are significant differences in norms and these are shaped by the particular subcultures that executives belong to. One global survey of executives found that 10 percent of chief financial officers believed it was acceptable to illegally backdate a contract to meet a financial target. In contrast, only 3 percent of chief compliance officers felt this was tolerable. The acceptance of illicit practices also varies dramatically by geography. More than a quarter of respondents in Vietnam and Indonesia approved misstating financial performance to survive an economic downturn, while no executives in the UK or Switzerland expressed such approval. One's perception of what's appropriate or inappropriate depends heavily on what culture one identifies with.

When the norms of one subculture differ from those held by the public, conflict is likely. Financial advisors, for instance, often tout in marketing materials that they "put customers first." In practice, though, many offer clients products charging higher fees that provide them with generous commissions rather than identical products lacking these kickbacks. According to one estimate, the pervasive pushing of these higher-fee products costs investors an average of 1 percent annually on their retirement savings accounts. Not surprisingly, many outside the financial advisory industry have found these practices deceptive and irresponsible. After years of effort, new regulation forcing advisors to more genuinely place the client's interest ahead of their own was passed in 2016. Once these rules are in effect, financial advisors who do not change their norms and continue pushing products that benefit themselves at the expense of clients will run afoul of both public expectations and the law.

WHEN EXISTING NORMS conflict with laws and regulations, people can seek to inculcate new ones. Imagine a firm where some managers have gained a sense of entitlement from their position and begin expropriating the firm's assets for their own use. These could be minor, like sending the occasional piece of personal mail through the company's post, or significant, like booking a personal vacation on the company's credit card. By inappropriately diverting resources away from a firm and its shareholders, these activities constitute embezzlement, albeit at different degrees of magnitude.

To combat the growth of such expropriation, the firm's leaders might seek to build stronger norms around separating personal benefits from company assets. Managers could, for instance, be instructed to carry separate mobile phones for personal and work-related calls. By introducing such practices for even minor expenditures and reminding employees of this expectation regularly, leaders can begin to normalize the idea that any use of firm resources for personal use will not be tolerated. Activities that once inspired little thought, like using a company's phone for a personal long-distance call or booking the company livery service on a personal trip, would start to feel wrong. When this perception becomes widely shared and viewed as part of the basic routine by members of the organization, the practice becomes an organizational norm. Through persistence and reinforcement over time, some norms become especially powerful and begin operating at a visceral level. These deep-seated norms that operate automatically and affectively are intuitions.

It may seem obvious that executives ought to have intuitions that are consistent with regulation. To those outside the unique subculture of a company, it seems ludicrous to employ managers who possess intuitions that run contrary to the law. Yet it's important to recognize that many corporate norms are superficial. They are simply rules and policies that lack an affective component and are never internalized as intuitions. These artificial norms masquerade as aspirational credos that executives pay homage to during good times but quickly deviate from when pressed during more difficult periods.

A lawsuit against the investment bank Goldman Sachs illustrates the gap that can arise between touted norms and actual intuitions. Fabrice Tourre was a trader at Goldman Sachs who specialized in creating complex mortgage-backed securities—an area of finance that fell into disrepute after the collapse of the mortgage market in 2008–2009. On the afternoon of April 16, 2010, Tourre learned that he had been personally

Final Termsheet	**ABACUS 2007-AC1, Ltd.**								July 2, 2007
	(Incorporated with limited liability in the Cayman Islands)								
Goldman Sachs	**ABACUS 2007-AC1, Inc.**								
	(Co-Issuer for the Class SS, Class JSS and Class A-1 Notes)								Capital

USD 2,000,000,000 Structured Product Synthetic Resecuritization

Referenced to a Portfolio of RMBS Securities selected by ACA Management, L.L.C.

Note: The Class SS Notes, the Class JSS Notes, the Class A-1 Notes, the Class A-2 Notes (together with the Class A-1 Notes, the "Class A Notes"), the Class B Notes, the Class C Notes, the Class D Notes and the Class FL Notes (collectively, the "Notes") have not been registered under the Securities Act of 1933, as amended (the "Securities Act"), and are being sold (a) in the United States only to qualified institutional buyers ("QIBs") in reliance upon the exemption from the registration requirements of the Securities Act provided by Rule 144A and who are also qualified purchasers as defined in the Investment Company Act of 1940, and (b) outside the United States to non-U.S. persons in reliance on Regulation S.

Tranche	Expected Ratings (Moody's/S&P)	Initial Notional Amount (USD MM)[3]	Initial Issued Amount (USD MM)[5]	Initial Tranche Size[1]	Initial Tranche Subordination[1]	Interest Rate	Portfolio Selection Fee Rate	Approximate Issue Price	Expected WAL[2]
Class SS	[Aaa]/[AAA]	1,000.00	[ ]	50.00%	50.00%	USD 1m LIBOR +[ ]%	NA	[ ]	3.4
Class JSS[4]	[Aaa]/[AAA]	100.00	[ ]	5.00%	45.00%	USD 1m LIBOR +[ ]%[4]	NA	[ ]	3.9
Class A-1	Aaa/AAA	200.00	50.00	10.00%	35.00%	USD 1m LIBOR +[ ]%	0.25%	[ ]	4.0
Class A-2	Aaa/AAA	280.00	142.00	14.00%	21.00%	USD 1m LIBOR +[ ]%	0.25%	[ ]	4.2
Class B	[Aa2]/[AA]	60.00	[ ]	3.00%	18.00%	USD 1m LIBOR +[ ]%	0.50%	[ ]	4.3
Class C	[Aa3]/[AA-]	100.00	[ ]	5.00%	13.00%	USD 1m LIBOR +[ ]%	0.50%	[ ]	4.4
Class D	[A2]/[A]	60.00	[ ]	3.00%	10.00%	USD 1m LIBOR +[ ]%	1.00%	[ ]	4.6
Class FL	[NR]/[NR]	200.00	[ ]	10.00%	0.00%	USD 1m LIBOR +[ ]%	NA	[ ]	5.1

[1] As a percentage of the Initial Reference Portfolio Notional Amount
[2] Based upon the Modeling Assumptions set forth in the "Notes – Summary" section of the Offering Circular
[3] The Issuers shall be authorized to issue more than the Initial Notional Amount of each Class of Notes. The amount of Notes issued on the Closing Date may differ from the Initial Notional Amount. See "Additional Issuance" herein.
[4] The JSS tranche may be offered in unfunded credit default swap or in credit linked note format
[5] Notes issued on the Closing Date

Figure 8.1: ABACUS termsheet noting that
the securities were "selected by ACA Management."

named as a co-defendant along with his employer, Goldman Sachs, in a securities fraud suit by the Securities and Exchange Commission.

According to the complaint, Tourre misled clients who purchased a complex security, a synthetic collateralized debt obligation known as ABACUS 2007-AC1. The deal's documentation stated that a neutral party, ACA Management, had selected the underlying portfolio of securities whose movement affected the value of ABACUS. In reality, however, a well-known and successful hedge fund, Paulson and Company, which stood to profit from the decline in the value of ABACUS through its "short" position, had played a critical role in selecting the underlying portfolio. According to the suit, Tourre's deception ultimately caused investors who purchased the security to lose over $1 billion. Judge Katherine Forrest, presiding over the case, summarized the allegations as "Tourre handed Little Red Riding Hood an invitation to grandmother's house while concealing the fact that it was written by the Big Bad Wolf."

Goldman Sachs soon settled its case for $550 million, the largest fine ever paid by a Wall Street firm up to that time, and admitted that ABACUS disclosures "contained incomplete information." Tourre, however, maintained his innocence and decided to take his case to trial. Nothing struck Tourre as intuitively wrong with the transaction he helped design. He believed it complied with the law. In fact, waiting in his attorney's office for the verdict, Tourre reflected on the charges against him. "If there was something wrong with this transaction," Tourre asked, "wouldn't people have told me?"

The jury returned with a unanimous verdict: guilty. Tourre struggled to understand how his gut had misled him about the propriety of the transaction. If the ABACUS transaction was so overtly fraudulent, why didn't any of his superiors or colleagues at Goldman Sachs tell him? He was hardly the only one who helped put together and market this deal.

Another lawsuit filed while these proceedings were ongoing offers some insight. Ilene Richman, a Goldman Sachs shareholder, sued Goldman Sachs and four of its senior executives, accusing them of defrauding shareholders in conjunction with ABACUS. Richman described the frequent public statements made by Goldman's executives explaining how important integrity was to the firm. For instance, according to Goldman's statement of its own Business Principles and Standards, they said "we are dedicated to complying fully with the letter and spirit of the laws, rules, and ethical principles that govern us. Our continued success depends upon unswerving adherences to this standard." Richman argued that by misleading the ABACUS deal to its clients, Goldman had defrauded its own shareholders by not abiding by the firm's statements about its integrity and desire to follow the "letter and spirit" of the law. Put simply, by lying to its clients, Goldman also lied to its shareholders.

In response, Goldman sought to have the suit dismissed. Attorneys on behalf of the firm and its executives argued that

> the vast majority of the supposed "misstatements" alleged in the complaint—e.g., regarding the firm's "integrity" and "honesty"— are nothing more than classic "puffery" or statements of opinion.

In short, the firm's statements about its ethics are little more than gimmicky marketing. These principles do not actually set standards for those at the firm, and investors are not supposed to literally believe them. Remarkably, this admission came from Goldman Sachs itself.

ALTHOUGH EXAMPLES OF superficial norms being touted by executives are commonplace, people can develop genuine intuitions that help enable compliance with the law. The day-to-day ability of some senior leaders to comply with laws and regulations without hesitation, even when there are opportunities to behave differently, attests to this. However, sustaining these intuitions in the face of competing pressures can be difficult.

Our views of appropriate conduct are shaped by the varying subcultures that we belong to and identify with. We're influenced by our colleagues, people we meet at social gatherings, and competitors. As we interact more frequently with others who have different practices and values, we may begin adopting their norms. In some cases, these new norms can undermine the ones that served us well in sustaining law-abiding behavior in the past.

To the extent that a corporate workplace can develop its own strong and supportive culture, the global strategy consultancy McKinsey and Company serves as an exemplar. The firm celebrates its consultants' role as trusted advisors to senior executives at leading firms around the world. The modern incarnation of McKinsey is largely the creation of Marvin Bower, the firm's managing partner in the 1950s and 1960s and a figure who continues to be revered within McKinsey today. Bower transformed the identity of McKinsey consultants through the creation of a set of professional norms. These norms describe how McKinsey consultants should act, engage, and present themselves. Bower identified five criteria that embody the McKinsey consultant: placing the clients' interests above the firm's, superior competence, adherence to truthful and ethical practices at all times, the protection of client confidences, and the maintenance of professional independence. Through the rigorous adherence to this set of principles, Bower believed that McKinsey consultants would be imbued with a respected professional identity much like a doctor, lawyer, or military officer.

McKinsey's culture continues to cultishly embrace and reinforce these values. "We have an indoctrination program," Bower once proudly boasted during an introduction to new McKinsey hires. Bower helped institutionalize these norms through the meticulous selection of new employees, a rigorous "up or out" promotion process, and regular exercises in self-reflection and analysis for associates and partners. To many within McKinsey, it is the faithful adherence to these norms that have supported

McKinsey's distinctive culture and its extraordinary success as a consultancy for decades. It is also for this reason that when two of the most senior members of its organization, former managing director Rajat Gupta and senior partner Anil Kumar, were caught on wiretaps directly undermining these principles in 2009, it made front-page news. How did these two prominent leaders seemingly dismiss the values that they practiced, cherished, and even taught to others for decades? Anil Kumar's evolving interactions with one outspoken hedge fund manager provide clues.

Kumar's career at McKinsey began in the spring of 1986. A decade later, he became a senior partner, a highly sought after and prestigious position garnered by only one out of every hundred analysts who join the firm. He opened the firm's New Delhi office and founded McKinsey's lucrative e-commerce and off-shoring practices. The work was grueling—it was not unusual for Kumar to fly 30,000 miles in a single month to meetings around the globe. Despite these demands Kumar found the work incredibly satisfying, both personally and professionally. Among the reasons he felt privileged to be part of McKinsey was that even with the workload expected of him, there were still opportunities for Kumar to pursue other projects he personally cared about. "I don't think that there are too many institutions in the world where I could actually work, but spend 10–20 percent of my time doing things that were my passions." It was during this pursuit that Kumar formed a relationship with Raj Rajaratnam, the head of the Galleon Group hedge fund, that ultimately unraveled his career.

Whereas Kumar was reserved and had an almost scholarly demeanor, Rajaratnam was brash and enjoyed displaying his bravado. Rajaratnam often played the role of the stereotypical trader by making crude jokes laced with sexual innuendo and handing out cash to employees who consumed the most shots at a bar. Kumar had originally met Rajaratnam in the early 1980s, when both were new immigrants attending the University of Pennsylvania's Wharton School of Business. While never exactly friends, they remained in contact over the years through their mutual interest in the burgeoning technology industry emerging on the West Coast. The two lost touch when Kumar moved to New Delhi for McKinsey, but Kumar rekindled the relationship in 2000 when he sought backers to fund a new business school in India that he was helping to build. Unexpectedly, Rajaratnam volunteered to anonymously contribute a million dollars to the school. Kumar was impressed by his largesse.

A year after donating to the Indian School of Business, Rajaratnam inquired about enlisting McKinsey's help with a project for his hedge fund. "He was being generous," Kumar recalled, "but I was already onto much bigger clients—SAP, Vodafone, really substantial companies." For McKinsey's partners, the prominence and prestige of their clients was everything. "You can get twenty million dollars a year in billings from some podunk company that no one's ever heard of and you will get zero credit," Kumar explained. "And you can get one million from Google and you'll get enormous credit." Not only was Rajaratnam's hedge fund unlikely to generate significant fees, but it also lacked the cachet of a firm like Google. However, needing to respond to Rajaratnam's inquiry, Kumar assigned a lower-level engagement manager to make the pitch. There was little response after the proposal was sent—it fell on deaf ears.

Several months later, Kumar and Rajaratnam ran into each other at a charity event and Kumar inquired about the McKinsey proposal. Rajaratnam expressed disappointment at the pitch. "He said it wasn't what he wanted . . . those guys aren't that smart. They wrote a proposal which wasn't all that meaningful." McKinsey's proposal vaguely described its ability to provide industry trends and background, but Rajaratnam was looking for something different.

In their conversations about the tech industry over the years, Rajaratnam had always been very complimentary, even deferential, toward Kumar's intellect. "He would tell me how he valued my insights. . . . He'd just say 'you really have a good grasp on the whole industry' or 'it's amazing how you see things that other people don't.'" As a result, it was not altogether surprising when Rajaratnam proposed a different arrangement to Kumar. "You're the smart fellow. I'd like to retain you."

Kumar was initially reluctant. Kumar had always focused on serving clients through McKinsey, and this arrangement struck him as unconventional. "You work very, very hard, you travel a lot, you are underpaid," Rajaratnam persisted. "People have made fortunes while you were away in India and you deserve more." Rajaratnam proposed that Kumar simply speak to him every four to six weeks to share his insights on the tech industry. "Just keep track of your knowledge in the industry and share it with me."

Rajaratnam was insistent that Kumar be paid. "If I didn't get money," Kumar recalled Rajaratnam telling him, "I would not remember to call him up and give him ideas." As long as this side project wouldn't detract from his work at McKinsey or be viewed as competing with McKinsey, Kumar knew it wasn't forbidden by his contract. Kumar was aware of other McKinsey partners who worked on projects outside their official capacities. Rajaratnam also proposed providing payments through an account held by Kumar's housekeeper to further alleviate Kumar's concerns about directly receiving payments for non-McKinsey work.

Rajaratnam offered to pay Kumar a half-million dollars a year for his advice. The amount was generous, but it wasn't the money that attracted Kumar. Despite a multimillion-dollar salary from McKinsey, Kumar lived quite frugally. "I viewed this as a guy who was trying to tap into my mind, brains, and happened to want to appreciate it more monetarily than others," Kumar noted. "I didn't ask for a half-million. He could have said a hundred thousand or he could have said two million. It was just formal validation. . . . The benefit was not the monetary value; it was the psychic value that someone valued my advice."

Kumar agreed. With the arrangement consummated, he began to periodically call Rajaratnam. "I read different sources and I have insights about certain things," explained Kumar. "I can see patterns."

By describing the trends he saw to Rajaratnam, Kumar believed he was validating the worth of his strategic intellect. "I took pride in what I told him. I told him Amazon is going to do really well in online retailing because I had done digital and e-commerce. I told him about Huawei because I saw all these telecom operators building 3G and 4G networks buying their equipment. . . . I gave him five or six long-term companies, every one of which did spectacularly well." During these dialogues, they got to know one another better, too. "Raj had become a friend of mine. Our conversations became more personal in nature—he would talk about his frustrations, his joys, his family."

"I was giving him general advice, but he would always ask, 'So what about AMD?,'" Kumar recalled. AMD, a large publicly traded semiconductor company, was pitted against Intel to dominate the computer processor market. Rajaratnam had long followed the firm, first as an analyst and now as a trader. Kumar also knew the company well: as Kumar's client for McKinsey, AMD was in the midst of a significant transformation. Kumar sat in on many of AMD's senior executive meetings and was privy to significant amounts of confidential information. "You are being very vague about what your client is doing and you're architecting the transformation?" Kumar recalled Rajaratnam exclaiming. Kumar responded again quite vaguely about AMD by saying that "the glass is half-full," to which Rajaratnam retorted, "What are you talking about? I know much more about exactly what's going on over there."

Despite Kumar's prior success in pleasing McKinsey clients, he was faltering in his ability to deliver to Rajaratnam. "Raj says, 'Look, I feel like Muhammad Ali. I am in the ring and I am getting beat up here.'" Kumar took a lot of pride in satisfying the demands of clients. Failing to meet their needs was not something he was accustomed to. Kumar was more used to being praised for going beyond their expectations. "I would kill for my client from the standpoint of really going the extra mile. I helped clients with children's admissions to school, . . . recommendations, . . . personal counseling on their life, on their wife—you know, on everything. I was this one-bucket-everything guy. . . . I think I was overzealous at times. I mean, metaphorically, I would kill for my clients."

To Rajaratnam, trading was not about understanding a long-term industry trend or an emerging line of products. Instead, it was about having an edge. He particularly sought information that allowed him to correctly take a contrarian view against the market. For Rajaratnam, the best source of this information was company insiders who had access to proprietary information and data. These contacts provided him with specific intelligence—earnings would be higher than expected this quarter or the firm is preparing for an acquisition—that he could use to make a quick trade. Over the years, Rajaratnam had carefully cultivated a network of insiders who provided this type of high-value information. Whether simply oblivious or naïve, Kumar thought that Rajaratnam would be satisfied with his strategic analyses and the advice he provided. "I thought that most of my inputs are these brilliant insights, but he kept asking for more and more specific information," Kumar said. Patterns and emerging trends weren't what Rajaratnam really wanted.

Rajaratnam already knew a lot more about AMD than other outsiders—he had cultivated another contact who was in an intimate relationship with the CEO. Rajaratnam loved impressing Kumar with just how much he knew about AMD. "He didn't ask me questions," Kumar said. "He told me answers. He started by telling me about AMD. . . . Frankly, for my clients, for most of McKinsey, I actually thought this was pretty neat. This guy is actually telling me all their plans."

Kumar's relationship with the senior management at AMD was a source of great personal satisfaction. "I was a confidant and an advisor to the CEO. I took some pride in feeling like I was architecting the transformation of AMD. The head of corporate strategy commissioned McKinsey work—CEOs rarely do that."

Kumar felt personally obligated to validate his prowess to Rajaratnam. In response to Rajaratnam's increasingly specific questions, over time Kumar started divulging information that more closely appealed to Rajaratnam's interests. In 2005, for example, AMD began considering an acquisition of a major graphics chip maker, either Nvidia or ATI Technologies. As befit Kumar's position as a confidant to AMD's senior management, he joined the highly confidential strategy meetings to discuss the potential acquisition code-named "Project Super Nova." Kumar learned that ATI would be the target.

"It is astonishing that AMD would do something like this," Rajaratnam replied when Kumar told him the news. "Are you absolutely sure it is ATI?" This kind of tradable intelligence was exactly the kind Rajaratnam lusted for. "I told him this was red hot and that it just should not be discussed." Kumar was genuinely excited about AMD's bold and potentially transformational move that he was helping to bring to fruition.

During Kumar and Rajaratnam's later phone conversations, Rajaratnam obsessed over the progress of the deal. "I would let him know the rough parameters of the timing." Kumar said. "I would just say it is progressing. . . . Sometimes I would say there is a delay, but not to worry, it is going ahead." Later, as the acquisition came closer to completion, the conversations began to focus on the price that AMD would pay for ATI's shares. The share price was critically important to Rajaratnam since it allowed him to figure out how many shares he could profitably purchase. When Kumar initially told Rajaratnam the price that AMD was prepared to pay, Rajaratnam was stunned. "I can't believe that AMD is going to do it. Are you absolutely sure?" After confirming, Kumar heard the kind of satisfaction that he had long sought from those he helped: "Wow, this is very useful."

On July 24, 2006, the deal was announced and ATI's stock price jumped. Rajaratnam called Kumar at home. "I just wanted to thank you. That was fantastic. We are all cheering you right now." Raj made nearly $23 million from the rise of ATI's stock based on the confidential information that Kumar shared with him—information that Kumar acquired by virtue of being a McKinsey partner with access to ATI's senior management.

Kumar's case illustrates how even well-developed intuitions can be influenced, and ultimately overridden, by interactions with individuals who hold different norms. Examining Rajaratnam's interactions with Kumar shows how intuitions can evolve. If Rajaratnam had simply asked Kumar to give him proprietary information about his client during their initial conversation, Kumar would almost certainly have been taken aback and declined.

Intuitions, especially those that describe behavior as morally right or wrong, are emotionally charged. Appealing to direct or overt persuasion, even if rationally compelling, will usually fail to inspire a change in intuition because it does not trigger a change in affective sentiments. Rajaratnam's appeal that Kumar "deserved more" would hardly have been sufficient for Kumar to dispense with the principles around client confidentiality that he'd honed for more than two decades with McKinsey. Instead, Rajaratnam more effectively appealed to Kumar's sense of worth. By conveying all that he already knew, Rajaratnam transformed himself into what appeared to be an insider at the firm, putting Kumar at ease. He cleverly challenged Kumar to provide something of value to him, something that Kumar had historically never had trouble doing. Failing to deliver for a client didn't feel right to Kumar.

The most important transition arose when Rajaratnam transformed information that needed to be protected into information that needed to be conveyed. Confidentiality became an opportunity to identify which information was valuable. Ironically, the more confidential the information, the more that delivering these insights felt like the best way to appeal to Rajaratnam.

By effectively changing Kumar's intuition, Rajaratnam nudged Kumar to adopt his norms. Unfortunately for Kumar, adopting Rajaratnam's intuitions around the appropriate use of information led not only to his dismissal from McKinsey but also to his later conviction for securities fraud.

DIRECT PERSUASION IS not the only way to influence our intuitions. The judgments of friends, colleagues, and those we seek to emulate often influence our behavior even without overt attempts to change our minds. By simply identifying with their behavior, we can begin imitating different norms. This process can shape intuitions about what constitutes appropriate, or inappropriate, conduct.

Executives often seek to emulate the behavior of other prominent business leaders whom they perceive to be successful. Depending on the target of their admiration and how they see them achieving their goals, executives may develop intuitions that lead to compliance with the law or incline them toward illicit conduct.

In the 1990s, few executives were more venerated than Jack Welch, the chairman and CEO of General Electric (GE). Over the course of his tenure as CEO, GE's market capitalization grew from $14 billion, in 1980, to over $400 billion in 2001. And despite the fact that GE operated numerous cyclical businesses and its revenues topped 1 percent of US GDP, Welch managed to deliver stable earnings growth year after year. In fact, by the late 1990s, GE's growth became so consistent that the firm met or beat earnings estimates twenty-nine consecutive quarters in a row. Despite its size, GE defied naysayers with its reliable and predictable earnings—and investors celebrated Welch for it.

Executives such as Dennis Kozlowski, the CEO of Tyco, revered Welch as well. Kozlowski would later be convicted of embezzlement, but while sitting in prison, he described how he sought to emulate GE's management of earnings—a practice that the SEC would later deem illegal—that was so celebrated under Welch's tenure.

WHEN KOZLOWSKI TOOK over Tyco in 1992, it was a modest industrial conglomerate that made products like fire-sprinklers and medical equipment. In the years that followed, Kozlowski rapidly expanded Tyco by prolifically acquiring companies—sometimes making multiple acquisitions in a single week. Earnings rose by nearly 50 percent a year from 1997 to 2001, and Tyco soon boasted a market capitalization greater than that of Boeing, 3M, or Pepsi.

Despite Tyco's growth, Kozlowski lacked the rock-star status enjoyed by Welch and other celebrated business leaders. In 1999, the same year that the title of "manager of the century" was bestowed on Welch by *Fortune* magazine, *Barron's* described Kozlowski as toiling in "relative obscurity." That would soon change, however. Kozlowski had turned to emulating

Welch's efforts at GE to increase Tyco's earnings and boost his own recognition in the process. "We studied their financials. We studied their proxies. We modeled GE," Kozlowski recalled. "I thought Jack Welch had a good thing going at GE. . . . I mean, we said if it's good enough for Jack, then it's good enough for me."

Although GE, like Tyco, owned many cyclical businesses, GE managed to defy the natural volatility associated with operating in those industries. GE's reported earnings grew smoothly and predictably quarter over quarter, pleasing both analysts and investors. Kozlowski, on the other hand, saw Tyco's quarterly performance intertwined with, even determined by, the prevailing economic conditions. Forecasting Tyco's future earnings was difficult because of the bumpy and unpredictable nature of its businesses.

"I envied GE because everything went into this big black box," Kozlowski recalled. "There was very little disclosure, but you knew that when GE was having a difficult quarter . . . you knew that GE Capital probably re-capitalized or went mark-to-market on one of their financial products and, voilà, out came a big fat profit."

Kozlowski's assessment of GE was only partly an exaggeration. The difference in earnings predictability could easily be observed just by comparing the stability of earnings growth during the Welch years with those of his predecessor. "When a new CEO took over at GE and they could no longer mark-to-market . . . all of a sudden GE lost their way," Kozlowski noted.

Welch prided himself on being able to hit the targets expected by analysts. When GE discovered that a trader in its Kidder Peabody subsidiary had falsely booked over $300 million in profits, Welch explained how he was "damn mad" that this scheme would "break our more-than-decade-long string of no surprises." Welch's inability to plug the resulting earnings gap in the final days before earnings were released was not due to a lack of effort, either. One solution proposed by his managers to address this shortfall was to "find" additional income in one of its operating units. "Even though the books had closed on the quarter," Welch wrote, "many [business unit heads] immediately offered to pitch in to cover the Kidder gap. Some said they could find an extra $10 million, $20 million, and even $30 million to offset the surprise." And as much as Welch abhorred unexpected losses, he also sought to avoid unexpected gains. In 1993, GE booked a $1.43 billion profit by selling its aerospace business. At the exact same time, GE took a $1.01 billion charge to close "certain production, service, and administrative facilities world-wide." Once taxes were taken in account, the gain and loss "coincidentally" matched the exact same amount—$678 million.

"It was all GE Capital," Kozlowski asserted. GE Capital was a financial services subsidiary that offered financial and leasing services.

The financial freedom and flexibility seemingly offered by GE Capital gave Kozlowski an idea. "We said if GE can have a capital company, then we should have a capital company." In 2001, Kozlowski and his team began scouting financing and leasing companies for a potential acquisition. Through one of Tyco's directors, Kozlowski was introduced to CIT Group, which Tyco soon bought for over $9 billion. "We changed the name to Tyco Capital," Kozlowski added. "We thought we were really doing well, like GE. . . . I couldn't wait till our first bad quarter so we could mark-to-market some of those assets and make our year."

Such management of quarterly reported earnings, explained Kozlowski, is "totally within the purview of accounting rules and everything else." However, these were the same techniques that Arthur Levitt, the chairman of the SEC at the time, lambasted as manipulation. "In the zeal to satisfy consensus earnings estimates and project a smooth earnings path," Levitt noted in one speech, "wishful thinking may be winning the day over faithful representation." Levitt argued that such practices were harming financial markets and investors. "Managing may be giving way to manipulation," he warned. "Integrity may be losing out to illusion."

Some of the earnings management practices that leaders at both Tyco and GE trumpeted as being acceptable also turned out to be fraudulent. Tyco was charged with employing improper accounting practices to inflate results by over a billion dollars. At nearly the same time, GE was also charged with misleading investors by employing a variety of noncompliant accounting practices that allowed it to avoid missing analysts' forecasts. Robert Khuzami, then the SEC's director of enforcement, described GE's financial manipulation by saying that it "bent the accounting rules beyond the breaking point."

It turned out that Kozlowski had little time to enjoy the acquisition of CIT as well. "It blew up," Kozlowski lamented, "and that was the beginning of the end." Prosecutors charged and later convicted Kozlowski for misusing funds from Tyco to support his lavish lifestyle. As with the emulation of Welch's earnings management, Kozlowski defended his use of company funds on the basis of the behavior of others he admired: "Every CEO before me had short-term purchases that they were doing." Kozlowski was fired from Tyco and spent more than eight years in a New York state penitentiary.

Reason—Explorer or Defender?

The extraordinary power accorded to reasoning is based on the assumption that the reasoning process is designed to provide different—and better—judgments than intuition. The reasoning process, however, is not always in the business of exploring alternative perspectives and reassessing intuitive judgments. Instead of reasoning our way to new judgments, we more often come up with rationalizations for judgments we have already made.

In the 1970s, researchers gave people with strong views about whether the death penalty deterred violent crime two articles to read. One article provided evidence that the death penalty effectively deterred crime, while the other provided evidence to the contrary. The researchers wanted to see if those taking part in the study would come away with the impression that the evidence was, at the very least, more muddled or nuanced than they had originally thought.

The reaction was almost exactly the opposite. Participants applauded the scholarship of the article that was consistent with their views and assailed the one that ran counter to them. Minor methodological errors were derided as critical flaws and held up as reasons to reject the opposing argument outright. Subjects held their original point of view even more strongly after reading the article that provided conflicting evidence. Instead of making people more open to alternative views, the reasoning process simply found explanations for them to support and justify their earlier beliefs.

It's uncomfortable to encounter dissonant information about ourselves or our views. Rather than struggle to objectively resolve the tension, it's often far easier to muster evidence to support a preexisting narrative that we're already comfortable with. This can even be witnessed in the portions of the brain active during "reasoning" exercises. In one experiment, when people were placed in an MRI machine and given credible threatening information that undermined the political candidates they supported, researchers found a surprising lack of activity in the parts of their brain associated with objective reasoning. Instead, they observed lively activity in the emotional part of the brain. The people comfortably maintained support for their candidate in light of explicit, conflicting evidence by appealing to emotional, rather than evidentiary, support of their candidate.

We often imagine business leaders acting like philosophers who employ reasoning to ponder decisions thoughtfully and objectively in search of the most appropriate actions. However, like most people, their reasoning is often used not to search for the truth but, instead, to support preexisting intuitive views. Take Fabrice Tourre, the Goldman Sachs trader who read an article in the *Financial Times* in January 2007 describing the significant and growing risks in the credit markets. The markets were beginning to roil and Tourre reflected on his position. As he e-mailed the article to a friend, Tourre explained:

> You should take a look at this article . . . Very insightful . . . More and more leverage in the system, the entire system is about to crumble at any moment . . . the only potential survivor, the fabulous Fab . . . standing in the middle of all these complex, highly leveraged, exotic trades he created without necessarily understanding all the implications of those monstrosities!!! Anyways, not feeling too guilty about this, the real purpose of my job is to make capital markets more efficient and ultimately provide the US consumer with more efficient ways to leverage and finance himself, so there is my humble, noble and ethical reason for my job ;) amazing how good I am in convincing myself!!!

By recounting how he spent his long days in the office, Torre engaged in reasoning, albeit not of a form that sought to deeply envision the potential consequences of his behavior. He didn't make a significant effort to explore the potential dissonance between his increasingly precarious position structuring mortgaged-backed securities and the mounting credit crisis rooted in those very same securities. Instead, his reasoning was closer to self-justification: Tourre comfortably explained his behavior by sarcastically citing the capital efficiency supposedly created by his endeavors.

This isn't to deny the human capacity to employ reasoning to change or override initial judgments and impressions. It's just that the process we call "reasoning" plays more than one role. The first of these is akin to a lawyer's defense strategy. It strategically operates in a way similar to that expressed, only partly in jest, by the British politician Lord Molson: "I will look at any additional evidence to confirm the opinion to which I have already come." This form of reasoning is neither exploratory nor capable of leading to new and superior judgments. Instead, it simply offers support for prior judgments, thereby supporting our self-image and maintaining our psychological well-being.

Reflective reasoning, however, also has the capacity to play a second role as an explorer. It's this more reflective and thoughtful role played by reasoning that gets most of the attention and credit. Through the consideration of different alternatives, reasoning can produce judgments that can conflict and even overturn judgments reached intuitively. Yet, since there's more than one role being played by our reasoning system, it would be incorrect to presume that the decision-making process will necessarily engage this more enlightened version. In fact, there's little reason to expect that reflective reasoning is more likely to come into play. Engaging in such reflective thinking takes time and effort. When an easier solution is available, the lazier "justifier" kind of reasoning is more apt to prevail.

Under what circumstances is the second, "smarter" variety of reasoning likely to arise and triumph? Psychologists from Stanford and Harvard decided to more deeply investigate by reexamining the story about Julie and Mark, the hypothetical brother and sister with the incestuous relationship discussed in Chapter 6. Before being asked about the morality of the siblings' actions, half of the participants in the study were given a weak argument to support the morality of their actions and the other half were given a much stronger argument based on sophisticated evolutionary evidence about disgust and morality. One might expect that the strength of the argument would influence participants' views about the morality of Julie and Mark's behavior. Yet, when pressed to provide a response after immediately reading the story and either of the two arguments, the sub-jects condemned their behavior just as strongly. To the extent that the subjects engaged in "reasoning" after reading these arguments, it served only to echo their original intuitive judgments about the immorality of Julie and Mark's behavior.

Then the psychologists added a twist. They asked some participants to wait two minutes before responding, requesting that they think more carefully about the arguments during this time. When queried again about their views, those given the weak argument were just as likely to continue to judge Julie and Mark's actions as immoral. But when the researchers queried participants who were given the stronger argu-ment, they witnessed changes in judgment: these participants were much less likely to see Julie and Mark's behavior as immoral. These participants overrode their initial intuitive judgment condemning Julie and Mark and reasoned their way toward a different judgment. Time—to think, reflect, and reconsider their initial intuitive response—was the critical ingredient in facilitating this more enlightened, objective reasoning.

It takes neither a psychologist nor a philosopher to appreciate when the conditions are right for more reflective reasoning. "Given time and conscious appraisal," wrote Alan Greenspan, the former chairman of the Federal Reserve, "we often revise our less thoughtful initial reactions and sometimes completely reject them." The problem is that many executives are constantly engaged in a whirlwind of meetings, travel, and e-mails. With incessant demands on their time, they take few opportunities to slow down, ruminate on their judgments, and engage in this more reflec-tive thinking.

In the 1970s, the famed management scholar Henry Mintzberg studied how managers utilize their time and make decisions. After extensively studying the day-to-day activities of managers over the course of several weeks, Mintzberg concluded that managerial "activities are characterized by brevity, variety, and discontinuity, and that [managers] are strongly oriented to action and dislike reflective activities." The majority of mana-gerial decisions, even those that were organized, occurred rapidly and concluded within minutes. In the decades since Mintzberg's original study, managerial life has become, if anything, even busier and more hectic. In describing the changes in managerial activities since Mintz-berg's study, the psychologist Dolly Chugh pointed out that managerial work "has gotten more, not less, messy." In short, none of the demands on managerial time promote the kind of thoughtful, objective reasoning that is likely to overturn instinctive intuitive judgments about the appropriate course of action.

The inattentive engagement of behavior that often characterizes mana-gerial life has been described by the social psychologist Ellen Langer as a state of "mindlessness"—actions and behavior without thoughtful aware-ness of one's behavior or its consequences. Mindlessness arises when peo-ple fail to actively engage and critically evaluate their actions. In one early experiment in the late 1970s, Langer and her colleagues sent a comically nonsensical memo: the only content on the paper was the request to re-turn it ("This memo is to be returned to Room 247.") A mindful reader might have questioned why anyone would have sent around such a ridic-ulous document and tossed it into the trash. But most employees were so used to mindlessly obeying memos that they seemed not to consider the illogical nature of the request. Lulled into their usual routine, 90 percent sent the memo back.

People have a tendency to simply follow their prior habits automati-cally, with little consideration about whether their behavior is appropri-ate. This, too, promotes mindless automaticity. Gertrude Stein, the celebrated novelist, actually became aware of this phenomenon over one hundred years ago as a psychology student at Radcliffe. Stein and her co-author, Leon Solomons, tested their ability to undertake multiple com-plex tasks simultaneously to show that one of those tasks could be done without explicit attention. They studied activities like reading a book while another book was read aloud to them. Although their methods would not be seen as scientific by today's standards, Solomons and Stein's conclusions, which were published in the prestigious *Psychological Review* in 1896, still resonate today: "We may sum up the experiments by saying that a large number of acts ordinarily called intelligent, such as reading, writing, etc., can go on quite automatically in ordinary people. We have shown a general tendency on the part of normal people, to act, without any express desire or conscious volition, in a manner in general accord with the previous habits of the person."

The challenge is that much managerial activity consists of sets of routinized activities—such as the creation of the so-called "TPS reports" in the popular comedy *Office Space*—that promote mindlessness. Managers rely on past experiences to ascertain the level of effort needed to respond effortlessly in the present. As long as everything is congruent with those past experiences, information is processed uncritically. While the mindless following of routines when returning a pointless memo is of little consequence, mindless behavior in a corporate setting can be very significant. Consider Dennis Kozlowski's description of his routine of signing documents—the same ones that prosecutors argued he authorized to forgive himself over $100 million in company loans. "Twice a month I had folders with yellow stickies that were this big," Kozlowski recalled as he spread his arms wide to indicate the immense stack awaiting his signature. "I signed everything, but it was the same thing that I had been doing since 1976. . . . I had the company tell me what it was and I signed it. So how's that criminal?"

Kozlowski signed papers without carefully considering how others, including some members of his own board, would perceive the forgiveness of millions of dollars in loans. With decades of mindless signatures behind him, Kozlowski never thought to stop and carefully consider whether, even if he could sign a document, doing so was appropriate use of his authority.

Breaking the cycle of mindlessness requires some novelty that forces an individual to step back to reconsider his or her actions. Recall the experiment that Langer performed with the nonsensical office memo. When the memo was formatted in the same way as those that were usually sent around, 90 percent of the employees sent them back. However, when Langer and her colleagues made a minor formatting adjustment so that the memo appeared visually different, only 60 percent returned it. A small format change, an ostensibly trivial adjustment, was enough to force people to become more aware, or mindful, of what was in front of them and the ludicrous nature of the request. By actively confronting the memo's absurdity, many more chose to appropriately discard it.

When routines that drive mindless behavior are interrupted, people are forced to confront the novelty of the situation and reengage their critical faculties. Discrepancies between intended actions and personal beliefs create a form of uncomfortable tension. This "cognitive dissonance," as pointed out by Leon Festinger, the psychologist who coined the term, is analogous to hunger. When we feel hungry, we engage in a specific behavior—namely, eating—to resolve that hunger. Similarly, when we sense an inconsistency between our beliefs and actions, we seek to eliminate that unpleasant inconsistency. In the context of corporate misconduct, this can lead to the rationalizing and contorting of an illicit action to make it seem more appropriate and attractive, thereby reducing dissonance.

During a routine audit in 1993, regulators from the Commodity Futures Trading Commission office found a possible violation in the way that customer funds were invested at the Peregrine Financial Group, a futures brokerage founded by Russell Wasendorf. Peregrine made the appropriate adjustment, but regulators performed six additional audits in the coming months and found another violation—one indicating that Peregrine had occasionally fallen below its required capital reserve. Although the regulators didn't file a formal complaint, they made it clear that they would more carefully scrutinize Peregrine's capital reserves in the future.

Wasendorf interpreted the audits not as evidence of regulatory due diligence but, rather, "as punishment and . . . retaliation." In the note written before his unsuccessful suicide attempt, Wasendorf rationalized his later decision to commit fraud. "The forgeries started after I was in a battle with the Kansas City Commodity Futures Trading Commission's Office," he explained. "The cost of an Attorney and the requirement to maintain a greater capitalization pushed us into a financial crisis, I had no access to additional capital and I was forced into a difficult decision: Should I go out of business or cheat?" Over the next two decades, Wasendorf would go on to fabricate bank statements for Peregrine. When the fraud was exposed, investigators would reveal that Peregrine's statements were overstated by over $200 million.

Dissonance can cause individuals to identify contradictions between their beliefs and judgments, compelling them to slow down, take time, and reduce this threat. Yet for Wasendorf, there was no sustained uncomfortable dissonance that forced a reckoning. Instead, regulatory scrutiny intended to improve controls actually fueled Wasendorf's fraudulent behavior by providing a convenient rationalization that it was the regulators who caused the problem, not him. "I have to say I don't feel bad having deceived the Regulators. . . . During the last 30 years that I have been exposed to them they have become more and more mean spirited. *They* made the decision to be my enemy," Wasendorf wrote. "They have successfully put another Firm out of business."

Realizing Too Late

Responding to an exploding number of financial scandals, Congress passed the Sarbanes-Oxley Act in 2002. As part of the new law, regulators sought to make executives think more carefully about the reliability and accuracy of their firms' financial statements. The regulators believed that if senior executives were forced to personally attest to the accuracy of their firms' statements by signing the financial report, executives might second-guess their decision to file a fraudulent report. Their signature was a final opportunity to reflect—and reconsider—the consequences of filing a fraudulent financial statement.

But for Steven Garfinkel, the CFO of DVI convicted of financial fraud, the signing of this paper did little to change his judgment. "I just sat there and stared at the damn thing. I stared and stared and stared. I didn't know what to do . . . so I just said sign it and move on with life." For Garfinkel, "signing a piece of paper to me was so different than lying to someone's face." Garfinkel felt the need for a reckoning only when he was confronted with lying to another individual in person, but this was too late. He was one of the first executives convicted for signing off on fraudulent financial disclosures under the Sarbanes-Oxley Act.

Surrounded by conflicting incentives, managerial efforts to sustain better intuitions can easily be undermined. By the time a manager appreciates that he should have made a decision differently, it's often too late.

"I never thought about the consequences honestly because I didn't think I was doing anything blatantly wrong," reflected Michael Lucarelli, an executive at an investor relations agency. But in the early morning of August 2014, agents arrived at his home to arrest him. The evidence against Lucarelli would later make it clear that he had engaged in illicit insider trading. Agents brought Lucarelli to the courthouse, where he posted a half-million-dollar bail.

It was only when Lucarelli prepared to exit the courthouse that the full scope and consequentiality of his actions finally sank in. "I was left all alone with only one exit and not briefed by anyone of what waited for me outside." A group of reporters emerged to question and admonish him. Lucarelli was overwhelmed. He took off running, losing his sandals in the process, to escape a mistake that now was so obvious to him.

Figure 8.2: Michael Lucarelli dashing away from
the courthouse in New York City.

PART III

THE BUSINESS OF MALFEASANCE

Unlike burglary or assault, white-collar crimes usually lack videotape or wiretap evidence depicting the crime as it occurred. Viewed in isolation, any individual piece of evidence can often be dismissed as circumstantial or explained away as misinterpretation. White-collar criminal cases generally need to be built by the tedious and laborious accumulation of documentation and the triangulation of facts. But every once in a while, a recording clearly captures malfeasance as it unfolds.

The London Interbank Offered Rate, or LIBOR for short, is among the most important financial numbers in the world. Over $300 trillion in contracts, equivalent to $45,000 for every human being on the planet, is pegged to LIBOR. Home mortgages, student loans, and interest rate swaps are all based on LIBOR. The ubiquity of LIBOR makes the process by which it is set crucial to the efficient functioning of the modern financial system.

LIBOR's calculation has always been surprisingly simple. Each weekday at 11 a.m., traders from leading banks send their estimates of the costs to borrow different currencies for varying amounts of time. A computer program discards the top and bottom 25 percent of submissions, and the average of the remaining estimates determines LIBOR. Underscoring how even small movements in LIBOR can create significant financial shifts, if LIBOR rates were lowered by a mere 1/10th of 1 percent on average for a year, total interest payments would fall in excess of $300 billion.

The magnitude of LIBOR's importance to the maintenance and integrity of the entire financial system is what made the revelation of a small cabal of traders rigging the calculation so extraordinary. Traders from UBS, Deutsche Bank, Rabobank, Barclays, and other top investment banks sought to collaboratively move LIBOR higher or lower depending on what best suited their trading positions. Most surprisingly, the actual rigging was caught in explicit detail over instant message communications. For instance, one of the conversations between traders at the Royal Bank of Scotland went like this:

> Yen Trader 3: where's young [Yen Trader 1] thinking of setting it?
> Yen Trader 1: where would you like it [,] libor that is [,] same as yesterday is call
> Yen Trader 3: haha, glad you clarified! mixed feelings but mostly I'd like it all lower so the world starts to make a little more sense.
> Senior Yen Trader: the whole HF [hedge fund] world will be kissing you instead of calling me if libor move lower
> Yen Trader 1: ok, i will move the curve down 1bp maybe more if I can
> Senior Yen Trader: maybe after tomorrow fixing hehehe
> Yen Trader 1: fine will go with same as yesterday then
> Senior Yen Trader: Cool

By 2016 global banks paid over $9 billion in fines for this collusion, and dozens of traders became enmeshed in civil and criminal charges on both sides of the Atlantic. One estimate suggests that total fines and payments for damages could top $35 billion. But what made the LIBOR rigging so unusual is that it occurred so overtly and was plainly visible once investigators looked at the traders' messages.

For most white-collar crimes, physical evidence is far more convoluted. Much of the background behind corporate misconduct—conversations, personal interactions, and institutional dynamics—can't be readily observed through examinations of physical evidence. Without this additional context, it is difficult to even begin to understand what the executives involved were thinking. Eventually the "why" becomes obscured and speculation abounds.

To overcome these limitations and better understand why a successful executive might seek to engage in misconduct, it is necessary to reconstruct events in much the same way as investigators do after a transportation disaster. After a plane crashes or a train derails, transportation officials attempt to piece together exactly what happened by incorporating data from different sources, taking into account all the systems that may have failed, leading to an accident. Central to any transportation investigation is careful review of the "black box" recordings of the dialogue of the pilots at the time of the mishap and, if possible, interviews with the pilots. In piecing together the evidence, investigators try to understand, for example, why it made sense to a pilot to pull up on the control stick when he or she should have pushed down.

As the financial economist Andrew Lo has observed, no similar investigation occurs after corporate disasters. Prosecutorial cases and bankruptcy proceedings—the proceedings in which we try to understand corporate crime—are very different sorts of investigations. Instead of seeking to gain a holistic understanding of the causes in hopes of preventing similar failures in the future, the adversarial procedures in a courtroom are designed to assign blame and apportion responsibility.

Faulty equipment or adverse environmental conditions are often to blame in plane or train disasters, and investigators can conclude that there wasn't any pilot error. However, with corporate malfeasance there's always "pilot error." External circumstances can contribute to executives' illicit judgments, but ultimately the blame is theirs. In the following chapters, I attempt to provide an understanding of malfeasance from the perspective of the executives by describing their sentiments and objectives as they were making decisions.

NEARLY ALL THE former executives described in this book have been convicted of criminal offenses. In several instances, however, I spoke with executives who were sued for civil violations or acquitted at trial. I include these discussions of noncriminal offenses to the extent that their cases help elicit a greater understanding of managerial conduct than I believe is possible simply by focusing on cases where an executive was criminally convicted. I also use the actual names of executives throughout the book, with two exceptions. The personal reflections of these two former executives could compromise their defense in pending legal matters, hence I preserved their anonymity. Nonetheless, as with the other executives interviewed, their quotations are preserved in entirety and the details of their professional lives are neither disguised nor altered.

Women are conspicuously absent from the ranks of prominent white-collar criminals. Of the few female managers convicted of white-collar crimes, one study showed that they tended to hold lower-level managerial or clerical positions and the magnitude of the harm they caused was considerably less than that associated with the average male offender. Women were also found to be less likely to be proactive in developing schemes and tended to be accomplices to duplicitous acts led by men. The lack of high-profile female offenders can no longer be attributed to the scarcity of women holding leadership positions either. These findings raise some important questions to consider about the proclivity of malfeasance by gender. The narratives in the following pages are thus almost invariably those of men. Throughout the book, I've deliberately used the pronouns "he" and "him" for this particular reason.

EACH CHAPTER INCLUDES extensive dialogue from my conversations with the executives involved. Hearing these individuals describe events from their perspective means that we do not have to speculate about how their actions looked to them. At the same time, there are limitations to relying on individuals' stated reports and memories. Aside from possible biases, even with the best attempts to describe events openly and honestly, human memory is both partial and fallible. Wherever possible, I sought out additional evidence to corroborate accounts of particular events.

Despite the inevitable limitations of oral history, what emerges is a far rawer picture of corporate malfeasance. In viewing their own actions, the executives exhibit a consistency across their accounts that begins to reveal what underlies their conduct. In many of these cases, there isn't any elaborately sinister plot. Instead, the crime might more aptly be described as a mundane sequence of "everyday" decisions. In fact, rather than feeling concern about the destructive consequences of their actions, these executives often convey a sense of pride that their actions were sustaining their firms during difficult or challenging circumstances.

In a sense, it's the routine unremarkableness of their actions, even to themselves, that makes this malfeasance all the more important to understand. Luigi Zingales, the former president of the American Finance Association and a professor of finance at the University of Chicago, aptly described this misconduct more broadly while reflecting on the LIBOR fixing. "There is no attempt to hide what they are doing, no sense of guilt," Zingales wrote. "It is ordinary business."

9

You can't make the argument that the public was harmed by anything I did

Misleading Disclosure

ANYONE BUYING A car knows haggling will be involved. The dealer will say that he can't go any lower than one price and you'll respond that you can't afford to pay a dime more than a substantially smaller amount. You and the dealer recognize that these are negotiation tactics, not objective facts. At some point, however, the dealer will insist that it's the lowest price he can give, or you'll explain why you've hit your maximum, and the negotiation comes to a close. It is the signal that someone needs to accept the other's price, or shake hands and part ways.

When the dealer says "I'm giving you the best price I can," however, we don't normally think that it's literally the lowest price he could possibly offer. Few would think the seller acted wrongly if he had the authority to lower the price even further—we'd just say that the buyer should've negotiated more aggressively. Few would accuse the dealer of outright fraud since what he said is understood as simply part of the negotiation process.

These kinds of literal misstatements are routine in many everyday transactions, but in some markets these statements can court controversy and lead to serious consequences. From 2008 to the end of 2011, Jesse Litvak worked at the investment bank Jefferies & Company trading residential mortgage-backed securities (MBS) with investors at other banks and investment funds. Unlike equity markets, where it's easy to look up prices online, information about MBS prices is not readily accessible. Litvak's customers had to rely on their valuation models to determine whether to buy or sell at the prices he quoted. As with buying a new car, there was some haggling over the price, too.

To improve his negotiating position, Litvak sometimes told clients that sellers were demanding higher prices than they actually were. For example, in June 2011, Litvak told an investor at AllianceBernstein that he had bought a particular MBS they were interested in for $67.66. "If you guys want em you can have em. . . . if not . . . that's ok too . . . ," Litvak messaged the investor. AllianceBernstein offered $67.78, paying the usual markup. Unbeknownst to AllianceBernstein, Litvak had actually purchased the bonds for $67.47, making a .46 percent profit rather than .18 percent. By misrepresenting his acquisition price for the security, Litvak made an additional $10,000 on the trade.

At other times, he created the illusion of furious negotiations to help bolster his margins. In November 2010, Litvak told an investor at Magnetar Capital that he found an investor willing to sell him a particular MBS for $55. The investor at Magnetar told Litvak that he was willing to pay $50.50, and inquired about the seller. A money manager, Litvak responded, suggesting that the investor might have more room for price negotiation. Litvak said he'd message Magnetar back after getting in touch with the seller. "He came off 1 pt to 54," Litvak messaged. "i am getting the sense that he really doesnt want to sell bonds that much lower than that . . . based on my last conversation." The Magnetar investor asked, "you tell me—isn't it a low 50's bond?"

After some further exchanges, Litvak's Magnetar contact raised the price he was willing to pay to $52.50, adding, "definitely do not want to pay more than what I have to. . . . " Thirty minutes later, Litvak wrote back that the investor was at $53.50. "i beat him up pretty good to get that . . . and think we are getting to the end of the rope with him. . . . " Magnetar raised its offer again to $53 and Litvak confirmed that he got the investor to agree to the price. Boasting how hard he had to work for the deal, Litvak messaged:

alright dude . . . he sold me bonds at 53 . . . but it was painful getting him to do it! he literally was talking about bwic'ing them . . . and I was like dude . . . u cant . . . so whatever the case . . . i bot bonds at 53 . . .

Believing that Litvak acquired the bonds at $53, the investor agreed to purchase them at $53.25, providing Litvak a modest markup for his diligent work. But Litvak's supposed negotiations were entirely fictitious: Jefferies had bought the securities four days earlier for $51.25 a piece. By pretending to negotiate with a "money manager" and raising the price on Magnetar, Litvak made an additional $90,000 on the trade.

A year later, in November 2011, one of Litvak's colleagues inadvertently e-mailed a spreadsheet detailing the prices Litvak actually paid to one of the traders at AllianceBernstein. After seeing the discrepancy between what Litvak paid and what he'd told AllianceBernstein, the trader reported Litvak to regulators. On the morning of January 28, 2013, Litvak was arrested for defrauding his clients. He would eventually be sentenced to two years in prison for securities fraud.

PEOPLE MISSTATE, MISREPRESENT, and exaggerate all the time in business. Sometimes these practices are tolerated as acceptable—as in negotiations for a new car—and sometimes they're fraudulent and possibly constitute crimes—as in the bond market. The legal ramifications are radically different, but the distinction between these different kinds of deception isn't always so clear.

How do executives view such misstatements? Do they see them as simply part of how business is done, much like a car dealer does? Do they regard them as actually misleading? Do they see such statements as causing harm?

In Chapter 4, we began to address these questions by exploring the case of Scott Harkonen, the CEO of the biotechnology company Inter-Mune. In this chapter, we'll investigate these questions further by looking at Paul Bilzerian, a former "corporate raider." Both Harkonen and Bilzerian faced criminal sanctions for issuing misleading disclosures: Harkonen for a press release and Bilzerian for a regulatory filing. While these men operated in two completely different industries, they both viewed their actions dramatically different than others did.

For a Greater Cause?

Throughout 2009, President Obama traveled the country building support for an unprecedented overhaul of the United States health care system. The proposed legislation offered affordable health care insurance to millions of Americans for the very first time, but many who already had insurance were concerned that the proposed modifications could lead to the cancellation of plans they were already happy with.

President Obama and congressional leaders sought to assuage these concerns. "No matter what you've heard," President Obama noted during an address in August 2009, "if you like your doctor or health care plan, you can keep it." Individuals who already had insurance wouldn't need to change plans or be adversely impacted by the new law—or at least that was how the new regulation was touted.

When the new health care legislation went into effect in late 2013, millions of Americans began receiving cancellation notices. Immediately, criticism mounted that consumers had been duped and that those with preexisting coverage would be unexpectedly harmed by the law. "The whole episode is a window into a fundamentally dishonest presidency," cried one op-ed in the *Washington Post*.

It surprised neither the president nor Congress that some insurance plans were cancelled once the new regulation went into effect. Some White House aides tried to modify the pitch, but they were overruled on the basis that it could clutter the message. To gain support for a piece of legislation that the president's team felt was in the best interests of the country, they considered it acceptable to deviate from the literal truth.

The ancient Greek philosopher Plato called these kinds of misstatements "noble lies." Leaders, Plato argued, "will have to use frequent doses of lies and deception for the benefit of their subjects." Such misstatements are made under the pretense of altruistic intentions often in the name of saving lives and protecting nations.

In 1940, President Franklin Delano Roosevelt reassured nervous citizens about the prospect of the United States entering the growing conflict in Europe by asserting that "your president says this country is not going to war." Secretly, however, Roosevelt had ordered American destroyers to aid in the effort to track and destroy German U-boat submarines. Soon, an American ship was fired upon during one of these missions. "I tell you the blunt fact," Roosevelt stated during one public address, "that this German submarine fired first . . . without warning and with deliberate design to sink her." Sidestepping the deliberate efforts to provoke the U-boat, Roosevelt relied on the incident to step up engagement in the conflict and support America going to war.

As historians later observed, had Roosevelt told the American public that the U-boat actually fired in self-defense and that Germany was not immediately intent on attacking the United States, Roosevelt would not have gained the support he needed to move America toward war. Potentially only once Britain, or later Russia, came closer to defeat would Roosevelt have gotten the additional support he desired. However, this delay could have proven catastrophic—Germany might already have largely won the war. Roosevelt believed he understood the risks facing the United States better than Americans themselves. Accordingly, he felt that this deception was justifiable for the good of the American people.

While "noble lies" may confer some immediate or near-term benefits, there are often negative long-term ramifications. Later presidents would rely on the precedent created by Roosevelt to justify lying in other, less righteous circumstances. Speaking in 1971 about President Lyndon Johnson's (LBJ) use of deception to justify increasing America's engagement in Vietnam, Senator William Fulbright argued that "FDR's deviousness in a good cause, made it much easier for LBJ to practice the same kind of deviousness in a bad cause."

Lying is easier when it is viewed as having some prosocial motivation, something we are all familiar with in our personal lives. When receiving a gift we do not want or like, we feign happiness. Or when friends ask whether they look good in a new outfit, we might offer a compliment even when it's not exactly to our taste. We believe these kinds of fibs are appropriate since they make people we care about feel more appreciated or happier.

The broader ramifications of little white lies are obviously insignificant in comparison to similar actions in matters of state, but lying to a relative about a present and lying to constituents in hopes of passing new legislation appeal to the same underlying rationalization—that deception can be appropriate when it serves some greater cause. Dishonesty can feel acceptable, even honorable, because those affected appear to be beneficiaries, not victims. Such lies can be rationalized by the perceived, albeit sometimes artificial, benefit that they confer to others.

There are also personal benefits to deception. A politician who mis-
states details to facilitate passage of legislation will gain greater political
legitimacy from its enactment. Similarly, when we compliment a friend in
a manner that is not forthright, it can help us maintain a positive self-
image as a kind, appreciative, and thoughtful person. The feeling of righteousness associated with telling these kinds of lies relies on thinking
about the perceived social benefits while ignoring the self-serving motives
that may actually instigate the dishonesty.

The presence of perceived beneficiaries and the absence of victims often mitigate the sensation of wrongdoing in the telling of noble lies. Yet,
the supposed benefits might simply be an illusion. Our views of what
makes other people feel better may differ from what actually does. We are
presumptuous to believe that we know what's in the best interests of those
we're deceiving. And even when people do benefit from deception in its
immediate aftermath, victims can arise later when other acts of deception
go awry. Successful deception helps rationalize further dishonesty, but the
mere fact that it worked in one instance does not mean it will again.

As we have seen, deception is commonly justified by ulterior social
motives in government, politics, and even our own social lives. But business leaders, too, can rationalize the acceptability of deception based on
the greater cause they believe it serves.

IN THE EARLY 1980s, the American economy was in the depths of a recession. The securities market was in the doldrums and some stocks in the
oil industry were selling for half their appraised values. Inefficiency
abounded, and astounding wealth awaited investors who figured how to
close this gap.

Paul Bilzerian, a veteran of the Vietnam war who later attended Stanford and Harvard, was one of these investors who sought to benefit from
these emerging opportunities. By his early thirties, Bilzerian had already
proven his acumen by making a fortune in the Florida real estate market.
In 1983, he turned his attention to publicly traded companies, where he
saw even larger opportunities abound.

"The US was the laughing stock in the world," Bilzerian recalled.
"Executives running our companies were a joke. They ran them as their
own little piggy banks and didn't give a rat's ass about the shareholders."
Even with this mediocre performance, most executives had historically

little to fear from outside investors. "The shareholders were diffuse and mostly institutional so no one was going to challenge management. You had a recipe for incredible mediocrity."

The appearance of "junk bonds" as well as other innovative forms of financing in the early 1980s enabled individual investors like Bilzerian to mount ambitious takeover bids. If management failed to utilize their firms' assets effectively, an investor could swoop in to purchase a firm's assets cheaply and redeploy them in a more profitable manner.

In May 1984, Bilzerian spotted his first major takeover opportunity—a California-based pharmaceutical company called Syntex Corporation. "I concluded that this company had to sell five of its six divisions, pull out cash, and invest it in the profitable pharmaceutical division. If you did that, you'd have a company earning $250 million a year with $600 million in cash." Bilzerian flew out to meet with Syntex's management, but he was quickly dismissed. "I walked out of there thinking they could care less about the shareholders—maybe I should just try to buy the whole company, run it properly, and make 2 billion dollars."

Bilzerian flew around the country pitching his takeover idea to potential investors and a number of prominent bankers offered to back him. However, a problem quickly emerged. As Bilzerian talked up his ideas for Syntex to secure financing, investors began buying the stock themselves. As they bought, the stock price rose so much that it made Bilzerian's takeover impractical. This leakage of his tactical intentions was a problem that Bilzerian would seek to never repeat again.

During the early 1980s, investors who sought to take over mismanaged firms regularly roused suspicion and public condemnation. To repay the massive borrowings that fueled takeover attempts, successful acquirers often liquidated firms they acquired by closing down divisions and selling off others to the highest bidder. Some of the most prominent investors, such as Carl Icahn and T. Boone Pickens, acquired the notorious title of "corporate raider" as they acquired and then dismantled firms. Bilzerian, a relative newcomer on the scene, had little public reputation until his next attempt.

In the fall of 1985, Bilzerian targeted Cluett, Peabody, & Company, a well-known apparel company and maker of the popular Gold Toe socks and Arrow shirts. Bilzerian quietly amassed shares over several weeks before publicly announcing his bid of $40 a share. The management at

Cluett resisted, and Bilzerian's efforts soon became lead news in the *Wall Street Journal* and the *New York Times*. After several months of deliberation, another textile manufacturer—West Point-Pepperell—unexpectedly bid $41 a share, besting Bilzerian's offer. Despite losing the takeover, Bilzerian's ownership stake still led to an $8 million profit in the share price run-up.

After seeing Bilzerian doggedly pursue Cluett, when Bilzerian approached Hammermill the following year, the company's management and other investors immediately took note. After purchasing more than 3 million shares at an average price of $47, Bilzerian offered $52 a share for the rest of the paper conglomerate. Hammermill's management soon rejected the offer, but Bilzerian offered to raise his offer to $57 if some additional conditions were met. Nevertheless, the management of Hammermill was reluctant to take Bilzerian's offer and sought other suitors. Soon International Paper emerged as a competing bidder and offered $64.50 a share. To avoid being bought by Bilzerian, Hammermill accepted International Paper's offer. The aggressiveness with which Bilzerian went after firms led *Forbes* magazine to call him "one of the more voracious creatures stalking corporate prey these days." And despite again losing out to another bidder, Bilzerian and his fellow investors still made nearly $60 million through the appreciation of their Hammermill shares.

"All of a sudden managers started saying geez if we don't get our stock price up, if we don't start making money, if we don't start utilizing these assets, if we don't start shedding assets that are no longer useful, this guy is going to come after me and throw me out," Bilzerian boasted. "We changed the game."

Launching a takeover required maneuvering at breakneck speed. "God, I worked hard . . . I was just a crazy man," recalled Bilzerian. After selecting a target, Bilzerian began quietly buying stock. Bilzerian would enlist brokers to purchase blocks of stock on his behalf to avoid alerting others in the market. Once Bilzerian surpassed a five percent ownership stake, he was required to notify the Securities and Exchange Commission within 10 days. This notification, known as a 13(d) filing, immediately alerted other investors to Bilzerian's intentions.

Bilzerian's tactics were simultaneously admired and decried. Like other corporate raiders who sought undervalued and poorly managed firms, Bilzerian terrified managers as he often seemed to arrive at their doorstep by stealth. How Bilzerian managed to successfully conceal his interest in firms and quietly buy shares until he was ready was cause for great speculation. In an interview with *Forbes* at the time, Bilzerian boasted, "We use every trick. . . . We use whatever creative ways we have. No single person knows what I'm doing. Not even my wife has a clue." Bilzerian knew that secrecy and stealth were essential for a successful takeover.

For Bilzerian, his efforts were far more than just about making money for himself and shareholders—he saw them as bettering corporate America. "We let incompetent, selfish, self-centered people who employ thousands and thousands of people rip off shareholders because they can. We let them take jobs for twenty years and then take a $35 million dollar parachute going out the door at retirement. That's where corporate America was when we stepped in, but we brought a different mindset to the business community."

In 1988, Bilzerian succeeded in acquiring the defense conglomerate Singer. As he strategized how to profitably sell off its divisions, Bilzerian was hit with a federal criminal indictment. Prosecutors charged him with concealing his true level of ownership as he amassed shares in the firms he targeted for takeover. It was considered a landmark case since no one had been criminally charged by prosecutors for misstating ownership on a 13(d) filing before. In the Cluett and Hammermill transactions, prosecutors alleged that Bilzerian had enlisted the help of brokers at Jefferies & Company to accumulate stock for Bilzerian under its name. By placing Jefferies as the record holder rather than himself, Bilzerian delayed the filing of the 13(d) by five days in the Cluett deal and by more than two weeks in the Hammermill takeover attempt.

"The question would be—even if that were true—so what?" argued Bilzerian. "You can't make the argument that the public was harmed by anything I did. Give me a theoretical victim . . . there were no victims." Many investors consistently profited from his transactions—even those the government alleged were defrauded. "All the shareholders, they love you. They didn't spend a dime, they didn't do any analysis, they didn't do anything. . . . They just made money."

Bilzerian would eventually be convicted on nine counts of conspiracy, securities fraud, and making false statements, and be sentenced to four years in prison and over $30 million in disgorgement in both civil and criminal penalties. Although he vigorously denies the charges against him, he does concede the possibility that some technical errors were made during these blazingly fast and complex transactions. "I pushed everything to the limit. . . . Are you going to make some mistakes? Just think of all the moving parts to do these transactions."

Deception can feel harmless when it appears necessary and no one is immediately made worse off. When viewed as fostering some greater beneficial purpose, it can even feel righteous. To Bilzerian, he was pursuing a great goal—one that enriched both himself and the shareholders of the firms he invested in. "If you're managing a baseball team and there's someone better to play second base, they will replace him in a heartbeat. Why should it be any different for companies that are so much more important than sports teams?"

Prosecutors perceived Bilzerian's secrecy in accumulating shares as securities fraud. But rather than seeing himself as someone who deceived thousands of shareholders and undermined investor confidence in the securities markets, as prosecutors charged, he believes he both enriched shareholders and improved the functioning of corporate America.

"In my heart of hearts, those of us that were out there doing this changed the entire way corporate America functioned. We made management responsible to shareholders. We helped to create values. We got rid of the incompetence. We brought a different mindset to the business community," Bilzerian argued. "But I'm the criminal? The truth is, the government has it upside down."

10

Unfortunately, the world is not black and white

Financial Reporting Fraud

THE PROSECUTING DISTRICT attorney Kurt Meyers began by comparing financial statements to a scoreboard at a sports game in the fraud trial of Michael Rand, former chief accounting officer of Beazer Homes. "You show how much money you're making on the scoreboard. What your expenses are, what your revenue is," Meyers stated. "The defendant was supposed to act like an umpire. You got to call balls and strikes . . . you're not supposed to look at the scoreboard as an accountant before you decide how much to book. You're supposed to report the numbers as the numbers."

Financial reports are created to provide accurate information to investors about a firm's financial position and performance. As Meyers sought to point out to the jury, nudging results toward a desired target undermines the financial reporting process by biasing those results.

In practice, an impartial accounting estimate can be difficult to provide when a transaction requires judgment. For example, any manager selling a product inevitably knows that some customers will not pay for some of the goods as invoiced. Whether it is because customers are unwilling to pay or are simply unable to, these accounts will need to be written off. Managers are expected to make an appropriate estimate of the amount they expect will not be collected to help investors get a better sense of the actual amount of revenue the firm will ultimately make. Determining this estimate can present a challenge.

Managers could simply assume that the amount will reflect a level proportional to prior years. But this approach is unlikely to produce the best estimate since there are other factors that lead to different levels of receivables that should be written off from year to year. "Some of the other things that need to be taken into account include the context of the general economy—stable, upturn, or downturn—and what is happening in the particular industries of the company's customer/buyers," noted William Parfet, the CEO of MPI Research. "Are the customers' markets healthy and growing, or shrinking, with thinning profit margins? Is the climate one of stable established companies, proliferating new startups, or industry consolidation?" All of these factors contribute to figuring out the appropriate allowance, but all entail significant managerial judgment as well.

Accounting rules often offer some guidance, but the subjective nature of estimates ultimately leaves considerable room for individual discretion. Even experienced professionals might come to significantly different conclusions. Consider this scenario:

> Your company is a defendant in a large new civil suit. You approach 3 different attorneys to provide estimates of the potential costs of settling the litigation. Each believes he is providing an appropriate estimate, but they range from a low of $300,000 to a high of $2 million. All the attorneys have an equally good track record of estimating the company's exposure in the past. What is the appropriate projection of losses from litigation to record in the financial statements?

If the first attorney you approach produces what seems to you to be an unreasonably high estimate and you find a second attorney who produces a much lower estimate, is there any obligation to acknowledge the estimate from the first attorney? Does it matter that exerting more effort to find estimates from additional attorneys influences what amount you disclose to investors in the end? Scenarios like this are common and create opportunities for managers to have discretion in what they report to shareholders.

Unless managers plan to resolve such decisions with the flip of a coin, providing a neutral estimate entirely free of managerial judgment is impossible. Inevitably, estimates will reflect some upward or downward bias. The question, then, is how these judgments tend to get resolved.

Executives make accounting choices surrounded by the relentless expectations created by Wall Street analysts, media, and institutional investors. They are pressured and incentivized to meet targets, or "the numbers." Increasing the stock price, building credibility with the market, reaching bonus benchmarks, maintaining credit ratings, and reducing stock price volatility are all rewards for hitting financial goals.

To the extent that managers have discretion in their financial reporting choices, it's not surprising that many use their discretion to nudge estimates toward meeting their desired benchmarks. Business scholars John Graham, Campbell Harvey, and Shiva Rajgopal surveyed more than four hundred financial executives to better understand the significance of hitting earnings targets. In one question, they asked executives: "Near the end of the quarter, it looks like your company might come in below the desired earnings target. Within what is permitted by Generally Accepted Accounting Principles (GAAP), which of the following choices might your company make?" Executives were asked whether they agreed with a variety of choices including drawing down reserves, booking revenue now rather than later, or providing an incentive for customers to buy more product this quarter.

More than a quarter of the executives surveyed said they would use their professional discretion to make accounting adjustments to hit their desired earnings target. These actions included drawing down on reserves previously set aside (28 percent of respondents), postponing taking an accounting charge (21 percent), and altering an accounting assumption on an allowance or pension rate (8 percent). Notably, all these actions are precisely the same as the ones that Meyers sought to describe to Rand's jury as impermissible and wrongheaded—"you are not supposed to make that judgment by looking first at what your earnings are going to be and then make the decision later."

However, this survey suggests that many executives are willing to look at their firm's earnings and, if they are short of the desired target, to reexamine their accounting choices to find some additional revenue to record or an expense to postpone. These actions are normally permitted so long as the adjustments can be rationalized as staying within the accounting rules. At the same time, deliberately dressing up a firm to satisfy market expectations strikes many investors—and, certainly, regulators—as deceptive. Making a firm appear better off than it actually is fits the commonsense notion of fraud. No one wants to buy a new Ferrari, only to pop the hood and see a used Yugo engine.

In his opening arguments, Meyers accused Rand of engaging in deception by falsely depicting the performance of Rand's firm, Beazer Homes. There was a twist to Rand's case, though. Unlike most cases of financial fraud in which individuals are accused of exaggerating earnings, Rand was accused of manipulating earnings downward to make Beazer's performance look worse on paper than it actually was.

THANKS TO THE rapidly growing housing market in the United States in the late 1990s, the performance of Beazer Homes was stellar. Through its operations spanning the country, Beazer purchased empty land to develop into picturesque residential communities. While the firm initially struggled to find its footing after going public, by the time Rand was promoted to corporate controller in 1998, Beazer was breezing through its earnings estimates quarter after quarter. By the third quarter of 1999, Beazer announced earnings of $1.15 per share as compared with analysts' expectations of only $0.97.

Following this success, executives at Beazer set an aggressive five-year target to double earnings per share by 2005. Already by January 2002, however, Ian McCarthy, Beazer's CEO, was boasting that "we set an ambitious five-year target to double our EPS to $9.00 per share by 2005. We have now exceeded this target three years early."

Although reaching this goal was unquestionably positive news, in the week prior to the release, e-mails between David Weiss, Beazer's CFO, and Rand described their apprehensiveness about reaching the target so soon. After Rand sent Weiss an e-mail indicating that earnings for the final quarter of 2001 were anticipated to be between $2.46 and $2.47 a share, Weiss responded:

From: David Weiss
To: Mike Rand
Sent: Thursday, January 17, 2002 9:39 AM

Spoke to Ian. We are happy with $2.46. That gives us $9.03 for calendar 2001 ($9.11 before extraordinary item). We made our $9.00!!!!!

From: Mike Rand
To: David Weiss
Sent: Thursday, January 17, 2002 10:51 AM

i may be able to nudge south of that . . . we'll talk at end of day . . .

From: David Weiss
To: Mike Rand
Sent: Thursday, January 17, 2002 11:36 AM

I have now convinced him that the $9.00 story for calendar 2001 works well for us. So don't nudge too hard

The record earnings announcement came on top of the concerns of some executives that Beazer was exceeding its forecasts too significantly in prior quarters. Beating expectations by such margins could bolster expectations to unrealistic levels that management would have trouble meeting in the future. At the very least, exceeding targets—even because business was doing so well—could suggest that senior management didn't have a good grip on the economics of its business or the industry. With a muted market reaction to better-than-expected earnings over the last several quarters, Beazer's executives broke their $9-a-share goal by being anything but aggressive in their accounting.

The consolidation of the financial reports across Beazer's many divisions fell to Rand as its corporate controller and, later, its chief accounting officer. Among Rand's many duties was to determine the appropriate amounts to place into two important reserve accounts—called "land allocation" and "house cost-to-complete." Beazer bought land and developed it into housing subdivisions, complete with streets and sewer systems. These costs were divided up and placed into land allocation accounts. Each house also accumulated a variety of unexpected expenditures for additional cosmetic improvements and property fixes. To account for these charges, some of which resulted simply from cost overruns, Beazer placed an estimate into a house cost-to-complete reserve. Although

Beazer had over thirty operating subdivisions, each with its own reserve estimates, Rand had the ultimate responsibility for determining whether the reserves appropriately reflected the economics of the business.

As Beazer went through its especially strong period of growth and record-breaking earnings, Rand sent numerous e-mails to divisional heads urging them to nudge their earnings downward and bolster their reserves.

From: Mike Rand
To: Brendan O'Neill
Sent: Friday, June 30, 2000

i'm relying on each division to hit their revised forecast. It's dangerous to many involved—namely you and me if we strive towards something else. If you have more than 100k extra, hide it.

From: Mike Rand
To: Jovan Tseng
Sent: Wednesday, August 16, 2000

To achieve the 'goal' $ for this year, let's squirrel $ away in places which will turn around in the next year, not be so 'open', and also which will not result in timing differences for tax purposes

From: Mike Rand
To: Todd Mitchell
Sent: Thursday, September 21, 2000

We may have $5 million to squirrel away, so if you have any ideas, let me know. Joavan's cookie jar has no more room.

From: Mike Rand
To: Tara Shipley
Sent: Tuesday, January 08, 2002

Ian gave me a target for the quarter which is considerably less than what I think our Divisions will initially report . . . in the aggregate. . . .
Accordingly, I have reviewed closing, overheads, etc . . . and am giving you the following quarterly EBIT target and not to exceed target for the quarter. . . . Please review your land allocations, house contingencies, etc. accordingly. . . .

EBIT Target. . . . . 1.45 million
not to exceed 1.55 million

From: Mike Rand
To: Tara Shipley, Jovan Tseng, Brendan O'Neill
Sent: Thursday, January 10, 2002
Subject: Set aside all the reserve you reasonably can. The quarter is too high.

PROSECUTORS ARGUED THAT Rand deliberately sought to overstate reserves during Beazer's booming growth phase. As a result, Beazer's earnings were understated. When Beazer later encountered more challenging economic times, these accumulated reserves were then drawn down to help prop up earnings. Prosecutors argued that this conduct manipulated Beazer's financial reports and deceived investors. Ultimately, a jury would find Rand guilty of these charges and he'd be sentenced to a decade in prison for this and related obstruction-of-justice charges.

Rand deeply disagreed with the verdict and sought to appeal the sentence. He appreciated that he made directional adjustments but notes that he did so only after assessing whether the adjustments were within the range of reasonable estimates. To see his perspective, Rand offered an example:

Over the last year, cost overruns averaged $1,500 per house. Due to increased efficiencies and a better prediction model, overruns were reduced to $800 per month over the last six months and only $300 in the prior month. But frantic building during the final month of the fiscal year has always tended to lead to higher costs. Historically, these overruns have cost upwards of $2,000 per house.

At year end, divisions have set aside $1,000 on average in contingency funds for potential overruns. However, some divisional heads set aside as little as $0, while others set aside as much as $3,000. The pre-contingency profit is only $5,000 per house so increasing/decreasing the adjustment will have a material effect on end-of-the-year earnings.

With this background, Rand asks: Suppose you ask the divisions to set aside $2,000 on average at the end of the year—is that appropriate or fraudulent? What about if you ask the divisions to set aside $300 on average—is that appropriate or fraudulent? Both of these estimates fall within the historical range. Do you have the discretion to select a contingency reserve anywhere in the range of $300 to $2,000?

In theory, the answer is yes. All these estimates would be justifiable and in accordance with accounting rules based on the historical data. But what if a colleague—say, the CEO or CFO—comes to you and asks if you could increase the reserve to help the company come closer to quarterly targets? Before this conversation, you were ready to settle on keeping the reserve at $1,000 a house on average. Surely, if you took another look through the reserve estimates you'd find some division for which you could justify increasing the reserve. Does the fact that your colleague spoke to you affect whether you have discretion to change the reserve?

"If the reason you can't make a discretionary change is because the CEO asked you to, that doesn't make sense," Rand pointed out. "You get different accounting results based on the existence or nonexistence of communication."

You may object because the reserve is being changed to more closely match a target, as Meyers argued at the beginning of his trial. Suppose, then, that your colleague only asked you to stay late and double-check each division's reserves, knowing that inevitably someone had overlooked some risk factor when setting aside the reserve. If you just spent enough time looking, you'd find a reason to justify increasing reserves, although the only reason you'd be doing this additional checking is to help hit a target. Following this line of reasoning, Rand argues, it's acceptable to make adjustments to help hit a target so long as the estimates stay within the justifiable range at the end of the day.

Therein lies the challenge. How can a manager be accurately showing the economics of the business while also trying to nudge results toward some target? These objectives conflict with one another. A manager cannot achieve one without some sacrifice to the other.

Rand argues that the estimates he produced were reasonable. "Reasonable" suggests that an estimate can be rationalized by data. "Reasonable," however, is not necessarily a "best approximation"—a term suggesting that the estimate reflects the best efforts and knowledge of the individual preparing the figure. As argued by Rand's prosecutor, financial reporting strives toward the production of estimates that are not simply reasonable but represent the best approximation of the preparer.

For managers, this distinction can easily be lost. An executive like Rand can act in literal accordance with the accounting rules by producing a reasonable estimate while at the same time undermining the spirit of those very same rules by seeking to nudge estimates upward or downward. Estimates must be produced with reasonable judgment, but "reasonable" is not the only criterion to evaluate whether it is appropriate. This apparent contradiction is the one that eventually played out in court for Rand, and it is the one he ultimately lost. It turns out that an estimate can be both reasonable and fraudulent.

Transforming Legitimate Practices into Illegitimate Practices

At the checkout lane of any supermarket, department store, or discount retailer, there is a bar-code scanner. Chances are that the red laser running over the bar code that produces the familiar beep was produced by Symbol Technologies.

Symbol was a tech company long before technology became associated with online or dot.com. Its engineers created the first bar-code scanner in 1980, and the company grew to become the dominant laser bar-code scanning firm, with many of the largest retailers including Walmart, Target, and Home Depot as customers. As early as 1995, analysts estimated that Symbol controlled nearly 75 percent of the worldwide bar-code scanner industry. In 2000, Symbol Technologies was awarded the National Medal of Technology, the highest honor bestowed for technological innovation, for "creating the global market for laser bar code scanning." By producing a technology that transformed the retail industry, Symbol Technologies was able to grow more than ten-fold during the 1990s.

Unlike the executives at many other tech firms that saw their future economic prospects disappear as soon as the technology bubble collapsed in 2001, those at Symbol remained deeply optimistic—they argued that Symbol was not like other technology firms. During the announcement of its first-quarter results in 2001, Tomo Razmilovic, Symbol's president and CEO, said that "unlike many technology companies that are reporting dramatic revenue fall-offs, we expect to produce robust year-over-year revenue and EPS growth for 2001 and beyond." The senior leadership prided themselves on having met or beat analyst expectations for thirty-one quarters in a row, and they planned on continuing that streak.

Symbol had long used its dominant market position to help it meet market expectations. "We had a significant market share, so we could put pressure on people even when they didn't want to take equipment," remarked Symbol executive Bob Jones. "If they wanted to be in good standing with us—they'd take the equipment." When Jones felt a customer was reluctant to accept a large equipment order or sought to reduce an order, he'd tell them: "If you don't pay us, we're going to stop shipping to you." Jones reminded resellers that Symbol wouldn't deliver critical parts or models when needed if they didn't capitulate. "I would have shut them off," Jones asserted. Symbol placed the burden of figuring out how to sell more equipment to its resellers. It was an aggressive sales practice, but one that historically allowed Symbol to smoothly maintain its revenue growth.

As markets began to slow during the 2001 recession, pushing resellers to sell more of Symbol's equipment was no longer a viable strategy. "We were shoving inventory down their throats," Jones explained. "The problem is we got to the point where we rammed them so hard that they said I can't take anymore, I really don't want it." Symbol executives nonetheless wanted to continue meeting analysts' expectations—"the number"—as they always had in the past. Symbol had recently won its largest contract to date by outfitting 300,000 US postal workers with scanning devices for priority mail, so expectations for Symbol's future growth were higher than ever. Yet, its ability to acquire new business and sell more scanning equipment became increasingly strained as economic conditions cooled. "I'm a solutions-oriented person," Jones said. "So ultimately what happened is that I came up with different ideas about how we might get to the number."

Jones appreciated that they needed to incentivize resellers to take more of their products. Resellers also needed to feel comfortable about not being stuck with large volumes of inventory they could not sell. "We knew that they weren't going to be able to sell all that inventory and we had to give them the right to return," Jones said, "or they would say at some point 'we're not going to take it' no matter how much pressure we put on them." The solution seemed simple enough. Symbol could continue to give resellers extra equipment to sell, and to the extent that they were unsuccessful in finding a customer for it in the end, they could return it.

However, Jones knew that these return privileges would dampen reported sales. Symbol could only recognize revenue only once equipment was shipped and payment was reasonably assured. If Symbol offered resellers the right to return inventory, Symbol would be able to recognize only a portion of what it actually shipped to resellers during the quarter on its income statement. If a reseller sold additional inventory in later quarters, Symbol would be able to recognize additional revenue when it was paid, but Jones was looking for a way to meet this quarter's expectations.

"We'd get to the end of the quarter and we knew we really needed some more revenue. We'd try to encourage customers to take an order without having any return rights, and we'd give the reseller a discount—a point or two—to get them to take an order," Jones explained. "It's like running a sale at the end of the quarter. They were often more than happy to do it because they knew they could sell it down the line with a greater margin on it." But Jones and the other Symbol executives realized that they couldn't meet ambitious revenue expectations by relying on discounts alone. To help Symbol reach its quarterly revenue targets, Jones created a practice that executives would refer internally to as "stock rotation rights."

The idea of "stock rotation rights" started with a legitimate premise. "If you were a reseller, you sometimes took product you didn't have a hard order for but you wanted to have available if an order came in," explained Jones. Symbol had always allowed resellers to exchange a portion of its stock with other items in Symbol's warehouses to help refresh their inventory. This practice helped resellers better match their current stock with the demands of their customers. "There was a fee, but it was a valid business practice to give resellers some flexibility."

But as pressure built to hit higher revenue targets, Jones and other executives at Symbol decided to offer far more attractive "stock rotation rights" to resellers. Not only would resellers have the right to return any unsold product without fees, but—critically—the reseller didn't have to pay Symbol until the equipment was sold. The policy was a very liberal return policy couched as "stock rotation rights." These special terms were offered orally to customers and were not written on any contracts or invoices. Not surprisingly, some resellers wanted written confirmation of this valuable arrangement. For example, one reseller e-mailed Robert Asti, vice-president of sales, to confirm that "as we discussed, 'stock rotation' as used in your e-mail of the terms means complete stock return privilege."

By expanding the return privileges that Symbol offered to resellers, but continuing to recognize revenues as soon as equipment left its warehouses, Symbol's sales grew immediately. But neglecting returns made the practice fraudulent by distorting the level of equipment genuinely being sold each quarter. "It expanded on a practice of running some sales at the end of the quarter in order to push revenue for real sales without any return rights. . . . We just kinda morphed it," explained Jones. "We were just trying to disguise it to some degree without saying outright that it was a return right. So we tried to mask it with the term 'stock rotation rights.'"

EXPANDING STOCK ROTATION helped Symbol bring in additional revenue. "It was all about having an environment where we kept hitting the numbers," noted Jones. But keeping up with analysts' expectations led Jones and other executives to devise additional revenue-boosting practices. "We'd go to the reseller and say there's an end customer, but they can't take it right now," explained Jones. But Jones would tell the resellers that if they purchased the equipment now, Symbol would entice them by offering them a very attractive price on the equipment or provide other financial inducements, internally known as "sugar." There was one more catch, though.

"Underneath that, we'd say to them, we're not shipping directly to you. You have to buy it from a distributor," Jones said. Telling a reseller to buy equipment from a distributor, rather than directly from Symbol, was obviously a circuitous process, but one with a deliberate goal in mind. "We'd go over to the distributor and say, look we're turning a reseller over to you and you're going to get, say, $2 million in business that you wouldn't have had before. But for us to turn that reseller over, you need to buy $4 million worth of stuff from us—2 million for them and 2 million from us."

Jones knew that this complicated arrangement, which Symbol executives internally referred to as "candy deals," created significant purchases of equipment and appeared good on paper, but he also knew that it had one critical hitch. "We did all this stuff—we made a reseller order from a distributor, a distributor order from us—but where it fell apart was the reseller never had anywhere to go with the stuff to start with," Jones pointed out. "The stuff they were ordering wasn't the stuff they needed for the end customer. The end customer might have wanted the newer model and we didn't have it, so we were trying to force movement of stale inventory." Shipping stale, old, or unneeded inventory to resellers and distributors had an inevitable consequence: "It would just end up coming back directly to us," said Jones. Symbol simply shifted the timing of earnings by inflating earnings in one quarter when all the equipment was shipped out and then depressing earnings the next quarter when it would all come back.

"We morphed a whole bunch of different practices that were valid at one point into something we wanted them to be," observed Jones. "It started out relatively small but when we didn't let our foot off the pedal, the only way we could make it was to fabricate it and every quarter you did it, you have to fabricate even more. You had to make up what you did in the prior quarter because product was going to come back and you had to hit a higher number." Between the "stock rotation rights" and the "candy deals," executives at Symbol were already engaging in several illicit revenue recognition policies. Unless they wanted to concede failure, they couldn't stop there. "It was a snowball that kept coming down the hill," sighed Jones.

The increasing challenge to hit analysts' expectations led to the most audacious revenue recognition policy of all—what executives referred to as "ship-in-place" deals. "Ship-in-place initially started when we were actually trying to help our customers," Jones explained. "Customers were saying that we want you to reserve this stuff because we think we'll have a need for it in the future." In these deals, customers would pay for the equipment and legally own it. Symbol would warehouse the equipment for the customer, and the customer would pay additional storage charges until it was shipped out. "So we created an inventory location within our facility for inventory that was owned by some of our customers," Jones explained.

"But then ship-in-place got convenient for us to expand because if we just got the customer to sign a letter that said he was willing to take it, we recorded revenue," Jones explained. "Especially as you got down to the last two to three hours at the end of the quarter, what we wanted to do is say if you'll sign a ship-in-place letter for us, we'll be able to record revenue." If anything happened to the equipment, Symbol would bear the loss since ownership didn't transfer until it was actually received by the customer.

The customer could also "return" the equipment before it was even shipped, meaning that the transaction never generated any actual sales.

Like most of Symbol's fraudulent reporting practices, ship-in-place expanded significantly beyond anything Jones had anticipated. "It started out as something where we were trying to help the customer and we kind of blew it up."

"I WASN'T THINKING about the investors," Jones lamented. "I never meant to hurt anybody. My motivation was for the company to do well." But when this deception was eventually revealed, Symbol's stock fell by 18 percent and thirteen of its executives were indicted. The company's CEO fled to Sweden, where he had citizenship. Wanted posters advertising a $100,000 reward for information leading to his apprehension were posted, but Sweden does not extradite individuals for white-collar offenses outside the European Union, and he remains a fugitive to this day.

WANTED
U.S. POSTAL INSPECTION SERVICE

$100,000 reward for information leading to the arrest and conviction of Tomo Razmilovic

Violations:	Conspiracy to commit securities fraud, 18 USC 371. Thirteen counts of securities fraud, 15 USC 78j(b), 78m(a) and 78ff.
Case No.:	1144-1366960-FC(1)
NCIC No.:	W306000777
FBI No.:	none
Warrant No.:	Issued on May 28, 2004, by U.S. District, Eastern District of New York, Brooklyn, NY
Aliases:	none
DOB:	May 31, 1942, Split, Croatia
Description:	5' 11", 205 lbs., gray hair, blue eyes
Occupation:	Corporate executive
Misc. Info.:	Photograph taken September 1994

Tomo Razmilovic is the former CEO of Symbol Technologies, Inc., a public company. He is accused, with others, of carrying out a securities-related accounting fraud scheme wherein the investing public lost more than $200 million. He is now believed to be in Sweden.

TAKE NO ACTION TO APPREHEND THIS PERSON YOURSELF

Figure 10.1: Wanted poster for Tomo Razmilovic, CEO of Symbol Technologies.

As with most financial frauds, the time between the fraudulent activity and the time of its impact are offset. "There were a crapload of people—and I'm not talking about inside Symbol—that made a crapload of money while all this was going on. There were people once it came to light that got hurt, but there were also a lot of people that made a lot of money," Jones argued. "The stock went up and was maintained. It should have gone down way before that because we couldn't hit the numbers. But someone was benefiting from us continuing to hit the numbers, and it wasn't just insiders."

For Jones, explaining what happened at Symbol comes down to how he thought about his position. "You have a career of being able to find solutions, being successful, and doing it the right way. Before I had this job, I worked in the industry for twenty years, and we always figured stuff out. We always did well . . . you can't switch gears about trying to find a solution. It's just a question of the ethical side," Jones said. "But you have to understand, it comes from a career of trying to find solutions to things. We never grew up with someone saying you can't do it and therefore you're not going to hit a number. We always tried to come up with a solution whether it was for hitting a number or whether it was a solution for making computers work right. We always came up with solutions. . . . Whatever it took, you did it and you got success from it."

Is It a Matter of Intent?

Name _____

Date _____

Most of the time, there's little thought given to the date line on a contract. Next to or below the signature space, the date merely denotes when a signature was placed on the page. The ubiquity of this detail belies its potential consequences. For Stephen Richards, Global Head of Sales at Computer Associates, and six of his senior colleagues, it would be the date line that would significantly upend each of their lives.

Throughout the 1990s, Computer Associates, known as CA for short, prospered as a global software firm that provided database, financial management, and other enterprise software. Within its industry it trailed only Microsoft and Oracle in size, and 95 percent of Fortune 500 companies relied on its products. CA was also heralded as one of America's "most admired" companies by *Fortune* magazine, which ranked it at the top of its social-responsibility category.

In a little more than a decade with the firm, Richards quickly rose through the ranks. When he became the global head of sales, he led more than seven thousand employees in negotiating contracts and managing customer relationships. Richards loved his job, but he always knew that the last few days of each quarter would be hectic and stressful. Looking to negotiate the most favorable terms with CA, clients often waited until CA's sales team was down to the last few days of the quarter. Customers knew that salespeople were expected to meet quarterly sales targets, and they'd often try to take advantage of this during negotiations. "This approach has resulted in significant problems for both software companies and investors," explained Deutsche Bank analyst Alex Brown in one of his notes to investors. "Customers learned, or were advised by consultants, that the later into a quarter they waited to sign a contract, the more likely they were to get a better deal (bigger discounts, extended payment terms, free services, etc.). . . . The bigger the deal, the more likely that the prospect would use such delaying tactics." Inevitably, Richards said, "customers would transact towards the end of the quarter," and sometimes 80–90 percent of an entire quarter's sales would be logged in during the final ten days of the quarter.

"You think there are ninety days in a quarter," explained Richards, "so there's ninety days to do those transactions. But realistically, the majority of transactions are done within the last seven to ten days. We'd do roughly $2 billion a quarter. If you say you're doing 80–90 percent of that in the last seven days, that's a hell of a lot of money to be chasing."

Not surprisingly, Richards expected his sales team to go to significant lengths to get contracts completed. "Sales guys would sit in their cars outside the front of the client's house waiting for them to sign a contract," Richards recalled. "Clients would go away on holiday and we'd fly the sales guy to where the client was with the contract to drive up to the resort to get the contract executed. I once did a forty-eight-hour negotiation with a financial institution—with only toilet and meal breaks—to get a deal done. The pressure in these environments is absolutely incredible."

This perverse end-of-quarter rush to finalize deals arose from the collision between accounting rules and market expectations. According to

Generally Accepted Accounting Principles (GAAP), software firms recognized licensing fees once a contract was signed, software was delivered, and payment was reasonably assured. Once these conditions were met, software firms could recognize the entire value of the licensing fees as revenue on their financial statements. The ability to immediately recognize in one quarter all licensing proceeds from a multiyear software contract created a make-or-break situation for CA's sales team that became known as the "hockey stick effect." Revenue would be flat throughout the quarter and then rise dramatically at the very end as huge deals were signed.

While signing a contract created a revenue windfall for CA, narrowly missing a contract at the end of the quarter could create a gaping hole in its finances. For multimillion-dollar contracts, failing to close a single deal could have significant ramifications on earnings at the entire-firm level. In theory, it seemed easy enough to explain to investors the nature of a near miss—a customer was ill, or CA and the client were simply trying to nail down the final terms. However, in practice, analysts and investors reacted very negatively to such disappointments, so there was immense pressure to close contracts by quarter end.

Such near misses could have been devastating to CA's stock price had it not been for a practice that Richards and his sales team employed. "On the signature page of the contract, there's normally a company name, the name of the person signing, the title of the person signing, a signature block, and the date. We would fill everything out except the signature block, so all the customer had to do was open up the contract and sign their name. They didn't have to worry about filling in any of the other details. We did that all for them. We were trying to make the process as easy as we possibly could."

However, the date stamped onto the contract wasn't necessarily the date it was actually signed. Employees at CA would preprint a date near the end of the quarter. In this way, even if the customer didn't sign the contract until a day or two after the quarter ended, the contract would appear as though it had been signed a few days earlier. "From my perspective," Richards noted, "the preprinting of dates was nothing more than a subtle reinforcement to the customer that something needed to happen before a particular time." But in preprinting the dates, Richards and his colleagues at CA effectively eased the end-of-quarter rush by artificially extending the quarter to include several additional days.

As the practice grew over time, millions in revenues were attributed to earlier quarters. For Richards and other executives at CA, this practice allowed them to meet or even exceed earnings targets, which in turn helped propel CA's stock price upward. While these date adjustments violated GAAP, Richards tried to put this practice within the broader context of various illegitimate business practices. "This was simply a timing issue of a deal coming in and being recognized two or three days earlier as opposed to two or three days later," Richards explained. "This is nothing more than a timing issue. . . . I didn't feel that I was doing anything wrong."

IMAGINE YOURSELF IN Richards' position. Suppose you and your team have spent all winter negotiating a new $50 million contract. Analysts have heard rumors of the negotiation and expect its completion by quarter end. Your colleagues are looking to you to make sure the contract gets signed since their compensation, like yours, is dependent on getting the deal done. To your relief, on the evening of the final day of the quarter, March 31, you receive the call you've been waiting several weeks for. "The deal sounds good—we're in agreement with all the terms and conditions," says the client. "My flight is just boarding now, but I'll fax the signed papers to you as soon as I arrive."

Waiting at the office, you nervously track the flight. There's a tarmac problem that begins as a half-hour delay, then an hour, eventually growing to three hours before the plane finally takes off. When it finally touches down, the client immediately sends the contract over, but it's now well past midnight on April 1.

What are you going to do? Technically, the deal was executed after midnight. According to the accounting rules, the contract and its associated windfall of revenue belong in the new quarter. Are you prepared to tell your colleagues that they will not receive their bonuses this quarter because of this unexpected flight delay? Are you willing to risk your job if the stock drops precipitously for the same reason?

Many people looking at this dilemma would find it rather innocuous to say, incorrectly, that the contract was signed in the prior quarter. In many respects, such financial misconduct is the same behavior that Richards engaged in. But when investigators uncovered this behavior at CA, Richards and other members of CA's executive team would go to prison for deceptions that, in the words of the FBI assistant director-in-charge, amounted to "one of the largest corporate accounting fraud schemes on record."

Prosecutors and the media drew comparisons between the actions of executives at CA and those of executives at WorldCom, Adelphia, and Enron. Richards found these comparisons frustrating and tried to put what happened at CA in perspective. "These are not fabricated transactions," Richards argued. "These are not transactions that were reversed out two or three days later or cancelled. . . . These are legitimate pieces of business."

WHY REGULATORS PROHIBIT backdating contracts is quite clear. By obscuring investors' ability to accurately interpret the performance of a firm at the time the financial reports are prepared, adjusting the contract dates amounts to deception. Such actions undermine faith in reported earnings and can lower trust in financial markets. As a result, regulators punish executives who backdate contracts and manipulate earnings.

Consider the actions of another executive who similarly found himself short of expectations at quarter end. Instead of engaging in an illicit backdating practice as Richards had done, he could consider meeting market expectations by finding a different adjustment to make—one that didn't happen to violate any accounting rules. For example, his firm could accelerate or postpone a product release date to adjust the timing of revenue and expenses on its income statement. "A wide variety of practices exist and are utilized by virtually all of the larger companies. Reserve manipulation, product release dates, sales incentives, channel management, and shipping procedures are a few of the more common ones," explained Richards. "All of these are legal, but definitely cloud the ability of anyone to get a true picture of the health of an organization through their financial statements." The intent of this adjustment is precisely the same as that for Richards' prohibited backdating, but this executive's actions would be neither illicit nor punished. Such adjustments could be described as permissible earnings management.

It's not difficult to find evidence supporting Richards' argument that "the management of financial performance has become a science, one that is very widely practiced." Visually, we can get a sense of the ubiquity of earnings management by viewing a histogram of earnings per share for publicly traded firms in the United States. If firms were reporting earnings neutrally, this histogram ought to resemble a smooth bell-curve. However, in reality, there is a discontinuity around zero, with fewer firms than expected reporting very small losses and more firms than expected reporting small profits. These small profits, as opposed to small losses, can support higher stock prices and avoid various covenant violations. To achieve this nudge toward profitability, managers engage in a variety of earnings management techniques, some legal and some likely illegal. "Ultimately the lines between legal and illegal, as it relates to some of the practices above, become very blurry and are subject to individual interpretation," explained Richards. "The intention of all this behavior is to meet expectations."

Given that Richards was censured and later imprisoned because he sought to deceive investors by manipulating earnings, it's disconcerting that there exists a multitude of other well-accepted, even commonplace, ways to legally hit targets through managing earnings. The intent to deceive is the same, but one set of actions is illicit and others are ostensibly permitted.

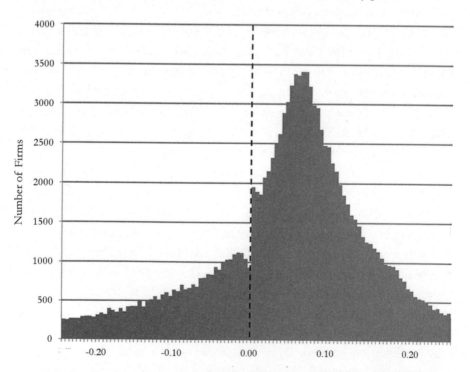

Figure 10.2: Histogram of earnings for publicly traded firms in the United States showing exceptionally few firms reporting very small losses.

To get a better sense of this quandary, consider another adjustment made by a different software firm around the same time. Like CA, this software firm faced the same pressures from clients and needed to hit its earnings target. Its executives were coming up short of expectations one quarter and considered backdating contracts and moving them into the current quarter, as CA had done. But one of the executives thought of an alternative that allowed the company to achieve the exact same effect without violating any accounting rules. The solution he proposed was quite simple: during the final week of the quarter, members of the sales staff who normally refunded customer orders were sent out for "training." Because these employees were "training," they were not available to cancel orders until the following week when a new quarter began.

In effect, the executives at this software firm temporarily lifted income for the quarter by postponing these cancellations, thereby allowing them to hit their earnings target. By engineering this scheme, the firm achieved the same effect as would have been accomplished by illicitly manipulating earnings by backdating contracts, but in a manner that would neither be detected by any outside investor nor be punished as a violation of GAAP.

This leads to the uncomfortable proposition that Richards and his colleagues were punished for simply not being clever enough. Had they come up with a more ingenious way of managing earnings to hit CA's earnings targets, they would not have faced any legal repercussions. Executives at the other software company who sent their staff for "training" reveled in their apparent cleverness, while Richards and his colleagues faced significant prison time. Like Richards, the executives at this second software company did not feel as though they had done anything wrong. On the contrary, by staying within the law, they believed it validated the propriety of their decision.

To outside observers, it's easy to condemn managing earnings. A common retort to such practices is that *any* deliberate action taken with the sole intention of hitting an earnings target to deceive investors ought to feel wrong, whether it's specifically prohibited by regulation or not. Often, there is some incongruity about why managers do not feel that these actions are harmful, since their harmfulness often seems obvious to outsiders with the benefit of hindsight.

But place yourself in the position of one of my business school students, whom I'll call Derek, who was troubled by some of his classmates' acceptance of legal, albeit manipulative, practices to hit earnings targets. Derek argued that he wouldn't engage in practices whose sole intent was to manage earnings. Such a choice would violate what he believed were appropriate standards of conduct and antithetical to what he thought was good business.

Derek eagerly looked forward to starting a position in the operations division of a major online retailer. Among his many responsibilities as an operations manager, Derek would need to place large orders at the end of each quarter to replace heavy equipment and parts to keep the distribution center operating efficiently and effectively.

A fellow student in Derek's class challenged him with a hypothetical dilemma: One afternoon near the end of a quarter, Derek receives an unexpected call from the company's CEO. After asking a few questions about how he's enjoying his position, the CEO makes a request. "Derek," he says, "I need you to hold off on placing that order for new equipment for a few days." Derek is a bit surprised, since maintaining the efficiency of the warehouse is considered crucial for the retailer's business and central to his duties. But Derek realizes that delaying the order by a few days wouldn't really affect anything from an operational standpoint, since these are routine equipment repairs and upgrades. But he is curious as to why he received this request, so he asks. The CEO replies: "Derek, it's been a difficult quarter in a couple of the divisions and it would be fantastic if you could hold off incurring any additional expenses this quarter to help us meet our guidance from analysts."

What would Derek do? Recall that he was adamant about not taking any action that would manipulate earnings. Would he tell the CEO of the firm, "No, we normally order this equipment every quarter so it's too bad that things are financially tough this quarter, but I'm still going to place this order"? Most individuals would view such an action as irresponsible, even absurd. It's pretty clear that Derek wouldn't last very long in any major organization with such a response. But if he delayed ordering equipment simply to help meet forecasts, isn't he doing the same thing that he condemned as being manipulative? More fundamentally, is the underlying intent of his conduct any different than Richards'?

To take this example even further, consider that there are few managers who would not choose to scale back on fixing buildings, reducing travel expenditures, and canceling holiday parties when faced with difficulties meeting expectations or financial targets. In most cases, such cutbacks would be called prudent management. In fact, *not* reducing expenditures when asked to do so by colleagues or during difficult economic times would generally be regarded as reckless behavior. Often, however, the only reason why these actions are undertaken is to help meet targets.

Herein lies the conundrum. Taking action with the intent to manage earnings is sometimes regarded as prudent management and at other times seen as improper manipulation. Sometimes it will land you in prison, while others times it will be celebrated. The trouble is, when the intent behind legal behavior and illegal behavior is the same, the illicit behavior is unlikely to engender a feeling of wrongdoing or creating harm. As Richards recalled, the possible harm to investors was "not even part of the thought process." In fact, backdating contracts could actually be viewed as having helped some CA's shareholders. By not conceding to large discounts on the final day of the quarter just to get the contract signed and waiting until Monday to sign at the full price, Richards ensured that the cash generated by the business would increase. Backdating is what allowed executives at CA to have the best of both worlds: booking revenue in the quarter when most of the negotiating was done, while also avoiding the need to provide unnecessary discounts to get a contract signed by quarter end.

Rather than feeling a sense of harm, executives committing such fraud can feel as though they are helping both the firm and its shareholders. "When you choose one or two quarters to look at when the stock moved down, it looks like the shareholders lost," Richards noted. "But you could have just as easily chosen another quarter where the revenue booked in that quarter inappropriately would have gone into another quarter and the value of the company would have increased because the company overbooked revenue that quarter."

Managing Within the Gray

In a murky world where earnings can be managed both legally and illegally, managers can readily find themselves engaging in acts on the wrong side of the law. "Unfortunately the world is not black and white," Richards lamented. "A senior manager spends most of their life in the gray regardless of their responsibility and that can be a dangerous and hard place to be."

This distinction was not lost on David Thatcher, former president of Critical Path. By 1999, electronic mail was taking off, and firms like Critical Path were focused on helping firms manage the growth of their internet communications. Under Thatcher's leadership, Critical Path grew to become the leading purveyor of e-mail management, essentially a precursor of the popular Gmails and Hotmails of today. *Forbes ASAP* magazine rated Critical Path with its highest score among fast-growing companies for the quality of its management, market opportunity, financing, and position. Critical Path was not, the author of the article noted, one of those companies "that are growing so fast that they spin out of control and crash." But by 2004, Thatcher would be sentenced to prison for his role in an accounting fraud to inflate Critical Path's revenues.

Much like Richards, Thatcher concluded that much of what managers do is operate within the gray. "You have 10 percent of transactions that are completely clean and no questions asked as far as revenue recognition," commented Thatcher. Of the remaining transactions, Thatcher went on, "you probably have 70 percent which are in the gray area. You're manipulating the accounting rules and still theoretically within the accounting rules, but it's in the gray area. And then you have a certain percent—say, 20 percent—that are absolutely outside the accounting rules."

"As an executive of a public company, you're not expected to stay in that 10 percent. You're expected to try—within the rules—to be as aggressive as you possibly can," explained Thatcher. This is ultimately where Thatcher encountered his own challenges and faced significant repercussions as a result. Late into one quarter, Critical Path was having trouble meeting the earnings estimates issued by analysts. On September 28, two days before quarter end, Thatcher managed to have one of Critical Path's customers buy out an existing royalty contract for $2.85 million and purchase an additional quarter of a million dollars' worth of software. In return, Thatcher agreed that Critical Path would buy approximately $4 million in software and services from the company, several million dollars more than Critical Path had agreed to acquire only a few days earlier. Under GAAP, such an arrangement would be considered a bartered exchange. "If you look at the strictest accounting rules," Thatcher noted, "they basically offset each other." However, if one views the deals as two separate transactions, one in which a client purchased some software from Critical Path and another where Critical Path bought some products from the client's firm, then Critical Path could recognize millions in much-needed revenue during the current quarter. Ultimately, Thatcher treated the deals as separate. Critical Path recognized over $3 million in revenue, which provided the vital boost it needed to beat consensus estimates. "From my viewpoint, no question it was revenue," Thatcher argued. "But if you look at that 10 percent [of accounting transactions without ambiguity], there's no room for two transactions between two companies, one where you're selling, one where you're buying."

This creates the potential for challenging dilemmas. "Virtually every corporate executive—every CEO, CFO—will venture into that gray area because they are almost mandated by their shareholders to do that. It's how far you venture into that gray area," Thatcher noted. "If you just purely lived within that 10 percent, it's almost impossible to get anything done. . . . It would be almost impossible to meet expectations."

An executive's success in meeting expectations and hitting targets can lead to the ends beginning to justify the means. As Richards pointed out, "The Wall Street number was pure. It was somebody else independent of me saying, 'Stephen, this is what you need to aim for this quarter.' I would judge my success on the ability to make that number. If we achieved that number, it was an endorsement that we were doing the right things. If we missed that number, then it was a reflection that we hadn't performed as well as we should have. My goal was just to get to or over that number— and if I did that, I succeeded."

During the time that executives are manipulating earnings, their firms appear stronger. With few investors, analysts, or other market participants unhappy with the firm's apparent success, executives can easily be lulled into feeling that their actions are not actually harmful. Shareholders appear to benefit and the executives reap the rewards of this supposed success. There's no uncomfortable dissonance.

"I had an incredibly good job and I was being paid very, very well. I had a lifestyle that few people ever had the opportunity to experience," sighed Richards. "I'd love to take the moral high ground—put my foot down, say absolutely not, smack my hand on the desk and say this has to stop. The reality is, given all the justifications I could come up with I don't think I'd rattle that chain."

11

You go from just being on top of the world

Insider Trading

"WHEN THE JUDGE sentenced me, he said ImClone, Enron, WorldCom. He said those three together," recalled Sam Waksal, the former CEO of ImClone Systems, of the moment he stood convicted of insider trading. "I thought to myself, 'Holy shit. Did someone really say that? Did someone really compare what I built for shareholders with them?'"

Waksal felt that the association between himself and other disgraced executives was totally unjustified. "It was a comparison to companies where thousands of people lost their jobs," Waksal lamented. "There was real fraud, cooking books, lying." Waksal understood that he wasn't innocent—he had pled guilty to engaging in insider trading and faced eighty-seven months in federal prison. Nevertheless, Waksal struggled to reconcile the egregious public perceptions of his actions with his own.

Until that point, Waksal had always considered himself extraordinarily fortunate. Along with his brother, he founded ImClone in the mid-1980s to search for new cancer treatments. In 1994, Waksal acquired the rights to a new molecule called Erbitux that had been discovered by a prominent researcher at the Sloan-Kettering Cancer Center. Some early lab tests showed Erbitux completely eliminating tumors in animals, but it was still an unproven product whose efficacy and safety had not been tested in humans.

Believing in its potential, Waksal began a small Erbitux trial on patients with head and neck cancer. Soon, preliminary data showed a promising shrinkage of tumors in several patients who had failed to respond to
other treatments. As Waksal began to raise additional capital and prepare
for a more ambitious clinical trial, ImClone provided Erbitux to a young
female patient named Shannon Kellum who had been diagnosed with colon cancer. After Kellum's chemotherapy failed, the cancer spread to her
liver and abdomen. Her doctors anticipated that she had less than a year
to live. At their behest, ImClone provided Erbitux to Kellum on a special
compassionate use basis.

Her doctors were astounded by what they observed next. Colon cancer
was not only one of the most common forms of cancer but also one of the
most deadly. Resistant to virtually all treatments, tens of thousands of
Americans died annually from the disease. But after treatment with Erbitux, Kellum's tumor shrank by 80 percent, and eight months later the
remaining cancer was surgically removed.

Bolstered by this outcome, Waksal decided to begin a clinical trial with
patients suffering from advanced-stage colon cancer who had failed to respond to other chemotherapies. It was an audacious and risky decision,
given the limited data on Erbitux's efficacy. But as the data came in the
following year, the results were impressive: over 20 percent of patients taking Erbitux witnessed their tumors shrink by 50 percent, an extraordinary
success for such sick patients. The drug also produced few of the debilitating side effects normally associated with powerful oncology treatments.

As news of the drug's success spread, ImClone's shares rose dramatically and the company began receiving hundreds of calls a day from patients desperately hoping to get Erbitux. The drug's promise placed it on
the FDA's fast-track to help expedite the approval process. The excitement around Erbitux culminated with an investment by Bristol Myers—
a major global pharmaceutical company—of more than $1 billion in
ImClone for partial ownership and the right to market the drug in September 2001. "I really felt like I'd gotten to a position both with the company and myself where we were going to have one of the major biotech
companies in the world," Waksal recalled.

But less than three months after the deal with Bristol Myers, rumors
began to circulate that something was amiss with Erbitux's approval with
the FDA. According to offline conversations between FDA officials and

representatives from Bristol Myers and ImClone, some FDA reviewers found ImClone's application to be inconclusive and questioned Erbitux's efficacy. In response, the FDA was considering a rare and unexpected "refuse-to-file" letter, essentially rejecting ImClone's application and forcing the firm to conduct new and costly trials. Waksal knew that investors would be stunned by such a major setback. Anticipation of Erbitux's success had already pushed ImClone's stock to extraordinary heights. In December 2001, ImClone had been included as one of the first biotechnology companies in the NASDAQ 100 index. No longer a fledging start-up, ImClone was now a $5 billion pharmaceutical enterprise. Waksal himself, as founder of ImClone, held shares worth more than $140 million.

At the same time that a *Los Angeles Times* article exclaimed how "Erbitux . . . is set to make one of the biggest splashes of 2002," Waksal frantically tried to figure out how to salvage Erbitux's application and ImClone's reputation. He decided to personally call officials at the FDA. Would FDA reviewers reconsider their stance? Could he temporarily pull the Erbitux application? Could the FDA at least extend the deadline so ImClone could send additional data? Although the FDA had yet to formally send the refuse-to-file letter, officials at the FDA seemed to have reached their decision, and Waksal's attempts to stall the outcome appeared futile. Officials indicated that a refuse-to-file letter was imminent.

Waksal phoned his daughter and told her to sell her $2.5 million in ImClone shares. "I didn't think about it," Waksal said. "I actually thought that I wasn't doing anything wrong because I thought that until I get the letter from the FDA and I know what's really happening, I'm not doing anything wrong."

Nevertheless, Waksal appreciated that his position within ImClone placed him in a privileged position. "I had an idea something was going on. I was looking at the world with eyes that were knowledgeable. Even though there were analysts out there that said there might be issues, I was looking at it through my eyes and I was the most knowledgeable person because I was CEO."

ImClone received the refuse-to-file letter on the afternoon of December 28, and executives publicly announced the FDA's decision later that evening. In response to the news, ImClone stock dropped from $55 to $46 a share. As more details about the refuse-to-file emerged and it became clear that there was substantial work ahead for ImClone to gain FDA approval, the stock continued to fall. By the end of January 2002, ImClone's stock was worth only $19 a share—a 65 percent decline in value in just one month.

Regulatory disclosures would soon reveal the well-timed stock sales by Waksal's daughter. Widespread public surprise and confusion about the failure of Erbitux, a drug that only a few months earlier had been heralded as a revolutionary cancer treatment, prompted a congressional inquiry. It soon became clear to securities regulators that Waksal had tipped his daughter to sell her shares in advance of the impending refuse-to-file letter. By providing this material nonpublic information to her in violation of his fiduciary duty to ImClone, Waksal had engaged in securities fraud. Soon, the case ensnared Waksal's friend and the popular lifestyle television host Martha Stewart, who had also sold her ImClone shares in advance of the FDA's letter. Stewart's involvement ignited even greater media coverage of the case.

"What I did is call my daughter, and that set off an explosion that changed my life. . . . I made a phone call that was stupid," Waksal said. "Within a year, I was out of the company and months after that would leave for prison. It's an amazing, unexpected turn in the world. . . . You go from just being on top of the world to then—you're gone, it's over."

The FDA would go on to approve Erbitux to combat colon cancer in 2004. ImClone's subsequent CEO would call it a "defining moment" for the company. Bolstered by the success of Erbitux, in 2008 Eli Lilly purchased ImClone for $6.5 billion. But Waksal would witness both of these events from the sidelines, as a convicted felon. "You're looking at your company as an outsider—something you built, something you feel that you've nourished."

"There are multitudes of ways that securities fraud takes place. This wasn't that," Waksal argued. "It was the drug that we always said it was. The clinical trial was correct. . . . Unlike schemes where you're trying to steal from the public, no shareholder of ImClone ever got hurt."

"WHAT'S SO BAD about insider trading?" asked the prominent legal scholar Henry Manne in 1967. Manne had just published a controversial book titled *Inside Trading and the Stock Market* that repudiated many of the common arguments against insider trading. "Prior to the year 1910, no one had ever publicly questioned the morality of corporate officers, directors, and employees trading in shares of corporations," he noted. The decidedly negative attitude toward insider trading that emerged during the early twentieth century struck Manne as poorly justified and even wrongheaded. "The tone of debate has remained essentially moralistic," Manne objected. "Logic has been totally lost to emotion."

Manne believed that the dramatic about-face in public sentiment toward insider trading arose from the growing stock market, which had fundamentally changed the relationship between insiders who ran firms and outsiders who invested in them. "In small enterprises social and psychological forces operate to maintain desirable interpersonal relationships, and individual policing is relatively easy and inexpensive. But these factors were missing in the large corporation with publicly traded shares," declared Manne. "No longer was it possible for each shareholder to demand in a personal and imperative way that his business associates deal with him fairly." Now, when a firm's director or officer purchased or sold shares from other shareholders on the basis of undisclosed news, this was viewed as an affront to other investors who saw such behavior as contrary to their interests.

After a careful two-hundred-plus-page analysis of the arguments for and against insider trading, Manne provocatively came out as its defender. By dissecting the costs and benefits of insider trading, he believed that others would be motivated to "make more appropriate moral judgments," implicitly lambasting both regulators' and the public's growing sense that insider trading was wrong. Manne even went so far as to suggest that the public anger in one recent insider trading case ought to be directed not at the directors who did the trading but, rather, at regulators themselves for doggedly pursuing regulation without the appropriate consideration of the economic consequences.

As might be expected, not everyone was receptive to Manne's argument. The head of the Securities and Exchange Commission was slated to review Manne's book but abruptly pulled out once he became aware of its thesis. Instead of being seen as a controversial issue worthy of discussion, insider trading was viewed by regulators as a clear and unabashedly harmful activity.

An astounding number of intelligent and well-paid executives are caught engaging in illicit trading each year. Between 2010 and 2014, regulators in the United States brought more than four hundred successful civil and criminal cases. The vigorous enforcement of prohibitions against insider trading is evidence that regulators view it differently from Manne. But compared with other white-collar crimes, the harm associated with insider trading is not as widely understood.

This chapter focuses on identifying the victims of illegal insider trading. As will become clear, the damage caused by executives who engage in illicit trading is abstract and the specific victims are not always readily identifiable. The harm tends to be psychologically distant, perhaps more so than with any other white-collar crime. This poses a challenge for executives since human intuition serves as a poor guide in sensing such harms and is likely to fail in the absence of competing norms.

To appreciate the complexity of the harm created by illicit insider trading, we need to understand the kinds of information that people have always relied on to legitimately trade in markets. It's only by appreciating the history of trading on inside information that we can begin to see what may—or, in some instances, may not—be so harmful about insider trading.

More Than You Know

People have always traded on privileged access to information. In the early nineteenth century, news traveled as fast as the gallop of a horse. When the Battle of Waterloo ended on Sunday, June 18, 1815, in present-day Belgium, it took days for the news to reach newspapers in London. However, one individual managed to get this news even sooner: Nathan Rothschild. The scion of the wealthy Rothschild banking family, he maintained his own private courier service across the vast expanse of northern Europe to speed his personal access to information.

Only hours after the battle was decided, agents employed by Rothschild acquired a copy of the *Gazette Extraordinary* in Brussels declaring the "bloody but brilliant" victory of British allied forces. The newspaper was immediately dispatched through the hands of one Rothschild agent after another until it reached one of his boats and crossed the English Channel. Once on British soil, the newspaper was taken by horse to London, where it arrived in Rothschild's hands by breakfast on Tuesday morning—nearly forty hours before the news reached the seat of the British government. News in hand, Rothschild headed to the financial markets where he began purchasing large numbers of British bonds from other investors who, unaware of the victorious outcome for the British, continued to sell them at a discount.

Rothschild had access to and traded on privileged information that others in the financial markets did not. Though few citizens in 1815 possessed Rothschild's resources to set up a private courier network, Rothschild's actions were not illegal then, nor would they be in any securities market today. Few would seek to censure Rothschild's actions because while he had gained access to privileged information, others could also have acquired this news.

Only a few months before Rothschild's profitable trades in London, another war, this one waged in America, had come to an end and news of its conclusion became a profitable asset. During the War of 1812, the British engineered a naval blockade that prevented many products from entering or leaving the United States. Unable to export valuable agricultural products like tobacco and cotton to their lucrative overseas markets, producers confronted depressed prices. On February 18, 1815, three New Orleans merchants learned from members of the British fleet that a peace treaty had been signed and that the blockade would soon be lifted. One of these merchants relayed the news to his brother, Hector Organ, a tobacco trader. This timing was especially fortuitous: Organ was in the midst of a negotiation that very day with Francis Girault, a commodities broker, to purchase a large amount of tobacco. Once news of the blockade's end was public, tobacco prices would significantly rise.

Wasting no time to act on the information, Organ returned to Girault at dawn the following day and agreed to purchase 111 hogsheads (approximately 60 tons) of tobacco, knowing that news of the end of the blockade would be public in a matter of hours. During the final negotiations, Girault asked Organ if there was any news expected to "enhance the price or value" of the tobacco that he was about to purchase. Organ conveniently ignored the question and the deal was completed.

Only a few hours later the rest of New Orleans heard the news, and the price of tobacco rose by upwards of 50 percent. Girault's firm was furious and refused to deliver the tobacco. Organ decided to bring suit, and the case eventually made its way to the Supreme Court. The verdict ultimately favored Organ—he was not required to tell another party what he knew—and Girault's firm was forced to deliver the tobacco at a loss.

Although Organ wasn't an insider himself, he received information from ostensible insiders through his brother. In this way, Organ knew to consummate his purchase quickly only because of his "insider" access to information. While this transaction was notable for the legal precedent it set, this certainly wasn't the first time that a businessman used his access to information for his own benefit and the disadvantage of another. Trading on privileged information has a long and contentious history.

According to a 1915 survey conducted by the *New York Times,* 90 percent of firm directors traded on information acquired from the firms they served. Such trading was legally permitted, and most directors expressed few qualms about using their firsthand knowledge of upcoming dividends, earnings, and other corporate events to profit in advance of other shareholders. One director who served on the boards of several prominent firms expressed the sentiment that

> if we were all Christian gentlemen with a very fine sense of honor, I suppose no Director would buy or sell stocks in his own company on information which comes to him as a Director. As a practical matter nearly all directors do. . . . If I see that earnings are improving, I feel that I have a right to buy or to sell if they are falling.

At the time, many directors viewed insider trading as a benefit associated with serving on a board—it was viewed simply as part of their compensation package. Daniel Drew, the eccentric railroad builder and financier, described in his autobiography the lucrative opportunities to trade once he became a board member. "They sent me word that I had been elected a member of the Board of Directors. I was at last on the inside," Drew wrote. "To be a director is something. It gives you Wall Street tips ahead of the people who are on the outside." Insider trading was not only permissible but, in some instances, even endorsed by executives and other business leaders.

FAST-FORWARDING A CENTURY, we find the global sentiment toward insider trading markedly changed. As of June 3, 2015, when the president of Uzbekistan signed a new securities law, every country with a public securities market—all 103—restricted insider trading. Although some countries enforce their prohibition criminally and others civilly, insider trading has become a globally recognized white-collar offense. "Insider trading law, and the actions of those charged with enforcing it," argued one American regulator, "can be seen as an expression of society's ambivalence toward the aggressive corporate culture it values."

Curiously, while insider trading is prohibited around the world, not all places do so by passing clearly defined laws. For instance, the most aggressive prosecutor of insider trading, the United States, does not have a law explicitly forbidding it. American regulators instead rely on administrative actions and judicial decisions to create an effective, albeit ever-evolving, prohibition. Other countries with major securities markets have specific laws that define illicit inside information and more clearly delineate what is appropriate and inappropriate trading. Yet these prohibitions, too, vary from place to place. The significant variation in these prohibitions has led to major differences in what constitutes illicit insider trading. Often, the types of insider trading actually prohibited by law—or, more significantly, not prohibited—counters conventional wisdom.

Consider the case of Mark Cuban. On June 28, 2004, Cuban received an urgent e-mail from the CEO of Mamma.com. Cuban was a major shareholder of Mamma.com after having acquired 600,000 shares, over 6 percent of the total company, several months earlier. Minutes after receiving the e-mail, Cuban called the CEO who told Cuban that Mamma.com was planning an upcoming private placement—a stock offering to a select group of investors—and that he wanted to gauge Cuban's interest. Cuban was furious. Private placements often lead to steep declines in a firm's stock price as ownership by current shareholders is diluted. Mamma.com planned to announce the offering after the stock market closed the following day.

Within hours of his call to the CEO, Cuban decided not only that he didn't want to participate in the offering but that he wanted to sell all his shares in the company to avoid dilution. Cuban called his broker and told him to immediately sell his shares. By the end of the following day, Cuban had gotten rid of all his 600,000 shares. That evening, after the markets closed, Mamma.com announced its private offering.

The stock opened the following day down, as expected, by nearly 10 percent. By the end of the week, it was down by 39 percent. By selling the stock in advance of the public announcement, Cuban had avoided this stock decline and saved nearly $750,000.

Cuban clearly traded on material, nonpublic information that he'd acquired from his privileged access to the CEO. However, was this illicit insider trading?

To many observers, the answer was a resounding "yes," since Cuban's actions readily comported with what they believed was illicit trading. Other stockholders of Mamma.com did not receive a private call from the CEO about the impending securities offering. Investors who bought shares from Cuban on June 29 certainly wouldn't have done so if they had gotten the e-mail and follow-on phone call that Cuban received.

It was exactly this sentiment—the belief that all investors trading on impersonal securities exchanges should have relatively equal access to material information—that motivated the passage of insider trading laws around the world. In countries like the United Kingdom, Australia, or Singapore, Cuban's actions would likely have violated the law. For example, when the billionaire hedge fund manager David Einhorn traded on advance news of a public offering after a conversation with a CEO in the United Kingdom, much in the same way as Cuban had done, Britain's Financial Services Authority fined him nearly £4 million for market abuse.

However, when the Securities and Exchange Commission sued Cuban for illicitly selling his Mamma.com shares, Cuban chose to bring the case to trial instead of pleading guilty. After a two-week trial, Cuban was acquitted by the jury as his actions were not illegal in the United States. In contrast to some other countries, illicit insider trading in the United States doesn't arise from simply trading securities based on material nonpublic information. It is also necessary that the acquisition of the information violate a fiduciary relationship—the duty of an individual to act solely in the interest of another party. Since Cuban gained his privileged information from the CEO of Mamma.com during a routine solicitation of capital, he didn't breach a duty he owed to Mamma.com. As we'll see, the specifics of how privileged information is acquired becomes critical for determining both what illicit insider is and who is harmed by this trading.

INSIDER TRADING HAS long held significant public interest thanks to movies like Oliver Stone's *Wall Street* or, more recently, Showtime's TV series *Billions.* Yet, the basic question of who is actually harmed is often overlooked. In most instances, identifying the victim of fraudulent activity is not especially difficult. With embezzlement, it's the individuals who lost property. With a Ponzi scheme, it's the individuals who deposited funds into a nonexistent investment program. But who are the victims of insider trading?

Some people say it's investors who unknowingly buy or sell shares from an insider. Others argue that it's the integrity of the market. Still others claim it's a victimless crime. Respected regulators, prosecutors, and judges cite each of these groups, but who is the actual victim?

To see why those who engage in insider trading may not intuitively see it as harmful, and why regulators and much of the public see it differently, it's necessary to identify its victims.

Harming What? Cheating Whom?

"The market is a victim," argued Preet Bharara, the district attorney behind many of the most prominent insider trading prosecutions. "Who's going to trade if they think the game is rigged?" asked Robert Khuzami, the former director of the SEC's Division of Enforcement.

The argument that the integrity of the market is the victim of insider trading follows a simple logic. If you thought that someone whom you were about to purchase shares from had significantly better information than you, you'd naturally have a greater reluctance to trade with him. If most investors had this same hesitation, liquidity in the marketplace would fall and the costs of transacting shares would increase. Multiplied over and over again, the costs of equity financing would rise and entrepreneurs would have more difficulty raising capital. Eventually innovation and economic growth could stall.

The argument that insider trading undermines the integrity of the securities markets has a scholarly sense to it, but the real question is whether this "steroid for traders," as Bharara once described it, actually creates these debilitating effects in any meaningful way. There is nothing unique about inside information: the presence of any investor who possesses significantly better information than others in the market can create these destabilizing effects. Taking the concern about information disparities to its extreme, some regulators have argued that all significant information disparities among traders are unfair and ought to be eliminated. But differences in the information possessed by traders are a pragmatic reality in any securities market.

Consider, for instance, that some investors can acquire public information more quickly than others. For several thousand dollars a month, an investor can subscribe to a direct Business Wire news feed that provides access to earnings news, government economic releases, and other data ahead of investors who rely on regular news services. Investors who pay for the news feed ostensibly acquire private information temporarily since this information is not simultaneously available to others. Those with access have the potential to make lucrative trades ahead of other investors.

Investors can also acquire additional data to help predict stock price movements. For a fee of $15,000 per month per stock, a company called iSentium provides investors a sentiment analysis of tweets that correlates with stock price momentum. Orbital Insight offers clients satellite images of parking lots of retailers like Walmart and Home Depot to help ascertain the growth of foot traffic into stores. Placed Inc. tracks the location of a half-million smartphone users to tabulate consumer traffic. And Genscape flies helicopters with infrared heat-seeking cameras over oil tankers to predict fuel supplies. In principle, all these data sources are available to all investors, so they are considered "public" from a regulatory standpoint. Yet, the extraordinary cost of such data means that only a very small number of investors actually possess this privileged information when trading.

While social media and helicopter data are at least hypothetically available to all investors, other information is exclusively available only to certain privileged individuals. Investors covet the opportunity to speak privately with a firm's senior management. Such offline conversations help investors better understand a firm's strategy and management's intentions for the future. However, these one-on-one meetings with CEOs are typically offered only to institutional investors with hundreds of millions or billions of dollars under management.

According to the law, all information discussed in these offline meetings is supposed to be immaterial—that is, not information "that a reasonable shareholder would consider . . . important in making an investment decision"—but it is unclear why an investor would be willing to fly across the country to meet privately with a CEO if he did not acquire ostensibly material information. Supporting this premise, in an empirical study that David Solomon and I published, we found that investors who meet privately with executives make more informed trading decisions than others—buying before the stock rises and selling before the stock falls.

All these different strategies suggest that there are many ways to effectively and legitimately become more informed than other investors in securities markets. And despite the fact that certain privileged investors have a significant information advantage over others, securities markets continue to thrive. Thus, befuddling the often-cited "market as victim" argument is the peculiar way that the law restricts certain kinds of insider trading and not others. In particular, whether informed trading is illegal or not often hinges on the source of that advantageous information. Yet, if perceived information disparities create a reluctance for investors to trade, then the source of information ought not matter.

To appreciate this perplexing distinction, consider a recent insider trading case against several senior data analysts at the credit card company Capital One. The analysts, Bonan and Nan Huang, hypothesized that there would be predictable correlations between purchases on Capital One credit cards and upcoming retail store earnings. The Huangs did hundreds of searches on the Capital One credit card sales database to figure out expected sales levels for different retailers. For instance, they searched for credit card purchases from Chipotle and found that Capital One credit card holders purchased large numbers of burritos and tacos during the summer of 2014. They surmised that Chipotle's overall revenues would be higher than anticipated. The Huangs purchased call options on 5,500 Chipotle shares the day before Chipotle announced its quarterly earnings, securities that would rise in value if they were correct. The next day, Chipotle revealed that its revenue was up over 28 percent, as the Huangs' analysis predicted, and the pair made over a quarter of a million dollars. Although their work closely resembled the sophisticated kind of quantitative research often done by hedge fund traders, the SEC sued these two analysts for employing Capital One's database to place their own highly profitable trades.

Suppose, however, that a savvy hedge fund trader realized the potential value of data-mining a credit card database and that Capital One opted to sell its database to him. Armed with this data, the hedge fund trader could have done the same analysis and placed the same informed trades as the Huangs. Like the Huangs, the hedge fund trader would have profited at the expense of investors who were willing to sell him shares or options. To the person selling shares, it would make little difference whether the trades were motivated by examining misappropriated data as with the Huangs or by purchasing an expensive credit card data set as with the hedge fund trader. Yet, only the trading by the Huangs would be considered illicit.

Even more bewildering is the fact that Capital One could itself legally trade on this data. Traders employed by Capital One and trading on the firm's behalf would unquestionably be engaging in the same sort of trading with nonpublic information, but it would be permissible since Capital One owned the data. From the standpoint of investors in securities markets who are concerned about potential information inequalities, it should matter very little whether it is Bonan Huang trading in his personal account, a hedge fund trader using a proprietary credit card database, or a corporate trader on behalf of Capital One using internal firm data. Ultimately, however, how the information was acquired acts as the crux for whether the trading was legal or illegal.

The victims of insider trading, as one prosecutor described it, are "all the honest people out there who are engaging in trading based on publicly available information, who are doing their research properly, who are not cheating, who are not taking the proverbial steroid of material nonpublic information." But what we find is that there are many ways for ostensibly material nonpublic information to be legitimately traded in securities markets.

While significant differences in investors' access to information are often viewed as unfair and detrimental to the market, they can also be seen as crucial to the maintenance of that market's efficiency. In fact, a well-functioning securities market is predicated on the basis that some investors have better information than others. If all investors held exactly the same information about a firm, there would be little reason for anyone to trade. As *Bloomberg* columnist Matt Levine once observed, "if you have no information to incorporate into the price, you're not doing anyone favors by trading. Least of all yourself: if you only have the same information as everyone else, how are you to make any money?"

In short, it is difficult to immediately characterize which and to what degree informational differences are actually detrimental to markets in practice. The integrity of the market may theoretically be harmed by illicit insider trading, but to the extent that all information differences between investors are viewed as detrimental, then the harm ascribed to illicit insider trading is likely small compared to that inflicted by everyday informed trading or nonillicit insider trading. In a sense, trading on privileged information that other investors do not have is simultaneously both detrimental and beneficial to securities markets. Consequently, to the extent that the market is victimized by illicit insider trading, it's a muddled target.

IN CONTRAST TO the difficulty of thinking about the abstract market as the victim of insider trading, individual investors potentially represent a more tangible casualty of illicit trading. Echoing this popular sentiment, the celebrated attorney Arthur Liman wrote that insider trading "is a most serious offense, a fraud on the trading public by which individual investors are invariably victimized." In a press release announcing the charges against several prominent hedge fund managers, Joseph Demarest, assistant director-in-charge for the FBI, noted: "Make no mistake—the twenty million dollars in illicit profits come at the expense of the average public investor." Substantiating the idea that there are specific definable victims harmed by illicit insider trading, regulators in United States have set up a website titled "Information for Harmed Investors" with materials on how to receive compensation from fines paid by executives who engaged in illicit insider trading.

One of the many funds created to compensate insider trading victims is known as the "Skowron Fair Fund." Dr. Chip Skowron was a successful portfolio manager at FrontPoint Partners who relied on his medical training from Harvard and Yale to trade health care stocks. In 2007, Skowron befriended a French doctor, Yves Benhamou, who led a clinical trial for a new hepatitis C treatment called Albuferon. The drug was initially heralded as a potentially breakthrough treatment that held considerable commercial promise for its developer, Human Genome Sciences. However, as the clinical results started coming in, Benhamou began observing significant setbacks to patients treated with the drug, including one who had died. After a number of friendly personal exchanges, Benhamou began calling Skowron with periodic updates about the deteriorating prospects of the more commercially promising dosage of Albuferon.

When Human Genome Sciences eventually announced several modifications to its trial for safety reasons, the stock plummeted by 44 percent. However, based on the information that Benhamou had previously provided to him, Skowron had already sold FrontPoint's shares in Human Genome Sciences. Skowron saved his portfolio from over $30 million in losses from the decline in Human Genome Sciences' share price. His trading was a clear instance of illicit insider trading, but should he have been able to intuitively identify the harm he was causing to specific people?

Each share that Skowron sold was purchased by an investor who presumably lacked the inside information that Skowron acquired. According to regulators and administrators of the distribution fund, these less-informed investors who purchased shares are the victims of Skowron's insider trading because they would not have bought shares of Human Genome Sciences had they possessed the same information as he did about the drug's prospects.

Although this argument is appealing on its surface, it's easy to see that it is also misguided. It isn't enough to say that these investors lost money on their trades. Rather, investors need to have lost money they wouldn't otherwise have. Specifically, Skowron's informed trading is detrimental to these investors only if it adversely influenced their investment decisions. The appropriate question to ask is not whether these investors would have purchased shares if they had the same information as Skowron but, rather, whether they still would have bought shares had Skowron not sold his shares.

When we consider the scenario in this way, it becomes less clear that these buyers were victimized by Skowron's selling. In all likelihood, these investors would still have purchased shares in Human Genome Sciences. Whether Skowron sold his shares or not, buyers would still not have had Showron's privileged information and their analysis would still have shown that Human Genome Sciences was worth purchasing at the price they purchased it. Instead of Skowron, it would simply have been a different investor selling his or her shares to these investors.

Fraud is predicated on the idea that an individual is doing something deceptive. But trading, even illicit insider trading, is rarely deceptive on a securities exchange. By seeking to sell shares, Skowron signaled his belief that Human Genome Sciences was overpriced and would fall in value in the future. Accordingly, it is difficult to argue that investors who purchased shares from him were deceived by his intentions. Beyond this, it was pure happenstance that any individual investor actually purchased shares from Skowron rather than from another seller. Securities exchanges are anonymous and impersonal. Investors do not know who they are trading with or exactly what information others possess. An investor's purchase order that was coincidentally matched by the exchange with one of Skowron's sell orders was made no worse off than another buyer who was matched with a different seller at that same time and at the same price. In a sense, the particular investor who purchased Skowron's shares, and is thereby supposedly harmed by his specific trading, is arbitrary on an anonymous exchange.

There is also the possibility that some investors who wanted to sell shares were crowded out because Skowron was selling. These investors who held onto their shares as the price fell are potentially the clearer victims of Skowron's trading. However, there is no way to identify sellers who would have sold their shares had Skowron not traded. Even if they could be identified, it would be impossible to definitively label these investors as victims since it is equally impossible to know with certainty if these individuals would actually have sold if Skowron had not been selling.

When the executives, like Skowron, I spoke with said that they didn't see specific people harmed by their insider trading, this reflected the inability of their intuitions to identify abstract victims harmed by their trading. Identifying these investors and the actual amount they lost is fraught with genuine difficulty. Many investors who are routinely deemed victims of illicit insider trading and collect restitution are actually not victims at all. And other investors, though victimized, can never be identified since we do not know who actually opted not to trade because of the insider trading. All of this is not to say that no investors are harmed by insider trading. However, the problem of identifying the specific people who actually would have been better off in the absence of an insider's trading remains an intractable challenge for which human intuition is of little help.

The complexity of identifying victims confounds the apparent simplicity of insider trading as a white-collar crime. Regulators often cite the commonsense belief that the reason to regulate illicit insider trading is to protect individual investors from being victimized. At the same time, the difficulty in clearly pinning down the specific victims seems to undermine

the motivation behind prohibiting certain kinds of insider trading and
not others.

AS DESCRIBED PREVIOUSLY, not all trading on material nonpublic information is illegal. There are many opportunities to engage in legitimate insider trading that, from the point of view of an investor trading with the
insider, have the same adverse impact as illicit insider trading. This puzzling distinction arises because illicit insider trading in the United States
doesn't simply occur whenever someone trades on material nonpublic information. Rather, illicit trading occurs when people trade on material
nonpublic information by breaching a duty of confidentiality they owe to
owners of that information. Several significant cases helped to clarify this
additional requirement.

In September 1982 the defense contractor Litton Industries decided to
expand its footprint in the electronics business. Litton's management enlisted the help of the investment bank Lehman Brothers to seek suitable
acquisition targets. By October 1982, executives at Litton had settled on
Itek Corporation, a specialty defense electronics firm. Following the advice of investment bankers at Lehman, Litton began purchasing stock in
Itek in preparation for the acquisition.

Lehman and Litton agreed that all employees at Lehman would keep
the acquisition strictly confidential. However, Ira Sokolow, a vice-
president in Lehman's Mergers and Acquisitions Department, passed this
information along to Dennis Levine, another employee at Lehman. Levine
agreed to purchase stock in Itek in anticipation of the merger and to share
the proceeds with Sokolow.

Levine called his broker, Bernhard Meier, and told him to invest his
entire account in Itek stock. The stock was only trading in the mid-$20s
and Levine could expect a significant premium once the deal was announced. Over the next month, Meier purchased 50,000 shares of Itek
stock for Levine.

Around this same time, Levine also called Robert Wilkis, a fellow investment banker at the prestigious firm Lazard Freres & Co. Levine and
Wilkis routinely shared information about pending deals with one another, and Wilkis soon purchased more than 5,000 shares in Itek based on
Levine's information.

Meanwhile, Meier noticed that every time Levine purchased shares, the stock soon rose. Meier and several colleagues thought it might be profitable to copy Levine's trades. They decided to piggyback on Levine's recent purchase and soon they, too, bought 5,000 shares in Itek stock for their own accounts.

Litton's board members spent a considerable amount of time debating the amount of premium that they needed to pay over the current market price to acquire Itek, a premium that kept growing as Itek's shares continued to rise. Eventually, in January 1983, Litton and Itek agreed on a price of $48 a share, a considerable premium over the $33 market price prevailing at the time. On the day of the announcement, Levine, Meier, Wilkis, and others sold their shares, realizing a million dollars in profit.

Levine had purchased shares long before this announcement for as low as $22. But the considerable trading by Levine and his associates helped raise the price of Itek shares. When Sokolow's indiscretions and the subsequent trading by others were revealed, Litton filed suit, arguing that it had significantly overpaid for Itek due to the run-up of the share price. Specifically, Litton argued that it overpaid by nearly $30 million because of the trading begun by Levine. An even higher price rise could have potentially endangered the entire deal. In effect, the trading by Levine, Wilkis, and Meier hurt the prospects of Litton Industries, which effectively owned the information.

The most direct harm inflicted by insider trading may not be on investors or the market but, rather, on companies with information to protect. It's not even necessary to actually take action to undermine a corporate strategy to potentially damage a firm, as the following example demonstrates. In the 1980s, R. Foster Winans wrote the popular "Heard on the Street" column for the *Wall Street Journal*. The prices of stocks that Winans discussed positively or negatively in his column often moved significantly soon after publication as investors bought or sold based on his arguments. In 1983, Winans began providing advance notice of the stocks he was writing about to his partner and stockbroker, who traded before his column hit newsstands. Over a four-month period, the group netted over $800,000 in profits.

There is no evidence that Winans undermined his journalistic integrity by altering the contents of his column to help this trading. But he did breach the *Wall Street Journal*'s confidentiality agreement by giving his column to others to trade on.

The *Journal*'s success as a newspaper critically hinged on its reputation and integrity. Winans did not have the right to misappropriate prepublication information from the newspaper—even something he himself wrote—for his own personal benefit. The reason is clear: Winans' trading could have jeopardized the *Journal*'s reputation. Accordingly, the court noted that only the *Wall Street Journal* had the right to make decisions that could undermine the integrity of the paper.

"Insider trading is not a complex crime," explained Charles Carberry, who ran the securities fraud unit at the Department of Justice. "It's theft. These guys are thieves. They steal information. . . . It's no different than if they were stealing ice skates."

If an employee steals a computer or other piece of equipment, it's easy to appreciate that someone has stolen a valuable asset. But instead of taking a physical item from the offices of the *Wall Street Journal*, Winans took something that was intangible—the contents of his own column. This intangible asset was just as valuable as cash in a securities market, where knowing how a stock will move ahead of time facilitates easy profits. In the United States, viewing insider trading as a crime akin to theft is consistent with the current regulatory regime. Although such an interpretation seems counter to much of the rhetoric around insider trading that focuses on "market fairness," the clearest victims of illicit insider trading are not investors who trade against those possessing privileged information but, rather, the firms whose information is stolen or misappropriated.

In 2015, an insider trading case reaffirmed that it's not simply trading with privileged information that's illegal, but where it comes from and under what pretense that matter. Sandy Goyal, a technology-stock analyst at the mutual fund company Neuberger Berman, regularly called an investor relations officer at Dell Computer named Rob Ray to get a better handle on Dell's business and performance. Goyal had previously worked in Dell's corporate planning division, and the two had kept in touch once Goyal left to pursue an investment management career. It was routine for Ray, as one of Dell's investor relations officers, to help people like Goyal understand the firm's business.

Figure 11.1: Information passing from Dell's investor relations department to a hedge fund portfolio manager.

In early May 2008, Ray spoke with Goyal for over an hour about Dell's preliminary expectations for Dell's upcoming quarter. From their conversation, Goyal began to appreciate that Dell was likely to exceed analysts' earnings predictions. Goyal decided to pass along what he learned from Ray to several people he knew, including an analyst at Diamondback Capital named Jesse Tortora.

As an analyst at Diamondback, Tortora had the task of conducting research and passing along trading ideas to Diamondback's investment managers. Tortora described what he'd been hearing about Dell from Goyal to Todd Newman, one of Diamondback's portfolio managers. Newman also thought that it sounded like Dell would do better than expected, and Newman decided to purchase a half-million shares in Dell for the fund he managed. When Dell announced earnings nearly two weeks later, Newman was delighted to see that Tortora's predictions had been correct. Dell reported earnings of $0.38 a share, beating the $0.34 a share expected by analysts. Newman's fund netted approximately a million-dollar profit from the trade.

The dialogue continued among these men throughout 2008. Goyal called Ray, who provided him insights into Dell's margins and revenues for upcoming quarters. When Goyal thought he had gained some valuable insights, he relayed what he learned to Tortora at Diamondback and, when the information seemed reliable, Tortora conveyed it to Newman. If

Tortora's insights seemed consistent with other analysis he'd been doing, Newman bought or sold Dell's stock.

Security regulators scrutinizing trading patterns observed the consistency of Newman's successful trades in Dell's stock. By January 2012, Todd Newman—along with Tortora and Goyal—were indicted for participating in an illicit insider trading ring and trafficking in confidential business information.

Newman found the charges baffling. It wasn't at all surprising to him that his trades in Dell were better than those of most other investors—it's one of the reasons he'd been paid more than $10 million since he started at Diamondback a few years earlier. "Professional investors spend eighty hours a week studying the business versus some retail guy who might spend an hour a week. It's impossible for professional and retail investors to have the same information and thoughts," Newman explained. He didn't see the information he got from Tortora, one of many inputs that helped him formulate his theses about which stocks to invest in, as being acquired illicitly. The fact that the information came from an investor relations officer at Dell seemed to support the sense that the information was appropriately acquired. As a portfolio manager who engaged in research to better inform his investment decisions, he considered speaking to executives—CEO, CFOs, investor relations officers—to be a quintessential part of what professional investors do. Executives were prohibited from providing certain kinds of explicit material information, but they still routinely provided clarity on models, affirmation about whether an investment thesis was on target, and additional detail to help investors like him better understand the firm.

"Investors call companies and talk about macro stuff," Newman explained. "For example, someone might say, 'I've heard this news about China, but I'm not really sure if it's true or not . . . maybe it's an isolated incident.' You'd see if you got a reaction so they don't have to discuss their individual businesses. If the firm says 'It's an isolated incident with that company,' you could take that to mean that China's okay for them. . . . Whether it ends up being the case or not, you have to wait and see. You never know, maybe they haven't seen it yet or maybe by the time they report numbers in a month, things will have changed by then. There's still risk."

The additional detail from management was on top of all the other publically available information that investors, like Newman, would acquire from firms. "Investors would call the company," Newman explained, "and say, 'Hey I'm working through my model, can you help me out? Some component costs are higher this quarter than last quarter and so I'm worried about your margins.' They'd say, refer to our last call or you're on the right track." Newman and his analyst would update their spreadsheets to incorporate this information. "Do they tell people exact numbers? No . . . but they can help your model."

The government's charges against Newman didn't allege that he had illicitly acquired confidential information himself. Instead, Newman, the government alleged, ought to have known that the data from his analyst, Tortora—who acquired this information from another analyst, who acquired this information from someone at Dell—was illicit inside information. Yet, since the source of the information was ultimately someone at Dell's investor relations department, Newman didn't see the impropriety of using it as an input in his investment decisions. "They have all these people working in IR—What do people think they do? Do people just think they put together the press release about recently reported earnings, the 10-K, 10-Q, and the annual report and that's it? There's ten to twenty people working there, there's more to their job. Their job is to take calls from people and answer questions."

Newman decided to bring his case to trial instead of taking a plea agreement. After hearing testimony from Goyal, Tortora, and members of Dell's investor relations team, the jury found Newman guilty in December 2012. "This was a stark crossing of the line, engaging in criminal conduct," noted Judge Richard Sullivan at his sentencing, "and that's just wrong." Newman was sentenced to fifty-four months in prison.

Newman vehemently disagreed with the judgment and decided to appeal his case. "When you call up a person in IR, they don't give you the numbers like the government thinks happens. But they do have to entertain questions. Investors can probably tell, if they call every quarter, when they sound a little better or worse than last," Newman explained. "It's just part of what happens. There's nothing wrong with it, it's just how people do research."

In 2015, the United States Court of Appeals overturned Newman's sentence and reversed his conviction. Specifically, the appeals court noted that

Newman's prosecution did not satisfy the conditions for illicit insider trading. There was no evidence that Newman knew that someone at Dell leaked confidential information and that the insider at Dell, Ray, did so for a personal benefit. Helping potential investors like Goyal understand the firm was explicitly Ray's job as an investor relations officer at Dell. Since Ray provided information in the course of professional employment and not as a personal favor to Goyal, Newman's eventual use of that information was not seen as illegal. Insider trading charges against Newman would be warranted only if he knew that individuals had stolen information from Dell for their own personal benefit.

To some observers, the reliance on the context that the information was acquired to determine whether there was illicit insider trading is disconcerting. This narrowing of what constitutes illicit trading allows some ostensibly undesirable conduct to continue. At the same time, it also prevents trading that would be widely viewed as benign from being deemed illicit. For instance, consider an analyst who after speaking with a CEO writes a report that contains some new material insights. The report is sent to a group of clients, some of whom trade on what they read. If simply trading on privileged information constituted illicit insider trading, any investor who read and traded after reading this report would have engaged in a crime. But the requirement that investors know that the information was conveyed to individuals in breach of their fiduciary duty helps avoid unexpectedly trapping investors in insider trading.

The additional criteria imposed on what constitutes illicit insider trading in the United States don't always comport with the public's—or even prosecutors'—perceptions of what trading ought to be prohibited. Newman recounted one experience from earlier in his career that made it especially clear that trading on information that others didn't have wasn't wrong, but rather what mattered was how that information was acquired. "I became friends with this one company after taking it public," Newman explained. "We were long the stock and I couldn't get the guy to call me back and I was like 'hum.' . . . I went to talk to the portfolio manager [PM] and told him that they usually call back within a day at most. The PM asked how long it's been. I said two days. The PM said to not worry about it, he's going to sell the stock just in case." The price of the stock soon plummeted. This taught Newman something that he would value later as a trader. "If someone breaks the chain in terms of what they normally do and does something different, it probably means that something changed. . . . He didn't call me back because he didn't want to talk to me." Ironically, Newman pointed out, this raises an obvious question. "Even though I never talked with him, is that insider trading? It's not information that anyone else got."

The government's prosecution of Newman sought to make trading on privileged information illegal. However, Newman's acquittal supports a more nuanced definition of what constitutes illicit insider trading. "The government presents it as black and white," Newman explained. "But there's so much stuff going on, little nuances and things you pick up over time just from the experience of being in the business and calling management and talking with people. That's just experience, it's not insider information."

Struggling to Feel Harm

Some people might assess the harms of insider trading differently than I have. Certainly, some cases may lend themselves to relatively greater harm to one group than another. If an investor, for example, knowingly traded against Newman, he might perceive himself as a victim. Although the way that insider trading prohibitions are enacted and enforced has an effect on who is perceived to be a victim, who is victimized ought not depend on the technicalities of how the law is written. We'd agree that someone held at knifepoint is victimized by his or her assailant regardless of how the law precisely defines assault. In this respect, the current regulation is both awkward and unsettling. Nevertheless, the objective here is to identify the harms under the current regulation rather than to question whether it is appropriately designed or not.

The challenge with identifying victims for insider trading is that less-informed investors—often precisely those cited as harmed by insider trading—are an inevitable and critical component to making markets function effectively. In most cases, there is little difference between a victim of illicit insider trading and someone else who simply traded with someone more informed than he was. Yet, the fact that some people trade in securities markets with individuals who are better informed than they are doesn't make them victims. The market is also not inevitably victimized by more informed traders: investors always know that there may be some investors who are better informed than they are. The source of the information advantage doesn't really matter from their perspective.

While insider trading is a common white-collar offense, for observers it is often difficult to agree on how to identify its victims. The most unequivocal victims—potential investors who are crowded out and firms that have information misappropriated—are groups that are not conventionally regarded as victims of insider trading. Moreover, the fact that they are abstract, even amorphous, entities does little to inspire our natural empathy for their losses. Given all this complexity, it's not surprising that insider traders themselves have trouble intuitively sensing and relating to the harm they cause.

SAM WAKSAL REMEMBERS one of the first conversations he had with his lawyer, Lewis Liman, after being indicted for committing securities fraud in conjunction with his insider trading. "I kept saying to him that I didn't really do anything wrong," Waksal recalls. "Lewis said to me, "Sam, would you have done the same thing if you were being filmed?" Waksal remembers pausing to think about the question and soon responded: "Probably not."

With the powerful tools at the disposal of regulators to monitor trades, it's difficult to imagine that people like Waksal couldn't appreciate that trades by family members were being carefully watched. Yet, Waksal never really felt that he was causing harm to anyone in particular. He never had that gut feeling telling him to stop.

"They wrote about me as if there was some giant byzantine idea that I was trying to perpetrate when in the end it was a phone call to my daughter that was an error in judgment," Waksal explained. "I don't know what I was thinking. . . . I wasn't, sadly."

12

I thought we were freakin' geniuses

Deceptive Financial Structures

I MAGINE IF I told you that I had a fantastic new business idea that was incredibly innovative, sure to disrupt a sluggish industry, and likely to be wildly profitable soon after its launch. Would you be interested? While you reflect on your luck at being offered to join such a fortuitous investment opportunity, you wonder: What's the catch? Oh yes, I reply, there's just one hitch—it's illegal.

At first blush, investing in such a venture may seem absurd to most law-abiding people. Yet, many of the most innovative businesses share the dubious distinction of being illegal, in part or in full, when first launched. Uber and Airbnb have faced years of significant and often acrimonious opposition from regulators. In some markets, these firms have had to curtail operations, modify their offerings, and even drop services altogether. In spite of these challenges, Uber and Airbnb are among the most lauded and valuable ventures to emerge at the start of the twenty-first century.

Not surprisingly, their founders and executives don't see them as operating illegally. Rather, it's all about how the regulation is interpreted. For instance, in New York, rules prohibit taxis from prearranging rides. Uber's customers use smartphones to order cars to predetermined locations, which makes it appear as though the firm's business model would conflict with regulation. However, Uber views itself as a technology platform, not a taxi company. "Prearrangement means it's basically on behalf of a base," argued Uber's founder Travis Kalanick. "We're not working with a base." Thus, Uber argues, much of the regulation around taxis and other ride-sharing services does not apply to its business.

But appealing to a creative interpretation of the law to assert a firm's compliance with regulation isn't always effective. In early 2016, Uber's French executives were put on trial for sidestepping France's transportation laws by enlisting drivers to work without appropriate licenses. In another example, the broadcaster Aereo sought to liberate viewers from their televisions by bringing local over-the-air broadcasts to computers through the Internet. Aereo employed thousands of tiny antennas, each individually assigned to a specific subscriber, to capture broadcasts. The company quickly gained eighty thousand subscribers in ten cities and was valued at $800 million. But despite its growing market presence, it was effectively shuttered by a Supreme Court ruling in 2014. While Aereo's attorneys argued that its service really only provided, in essence, a very long cable connecting an antenna to a subscriber's screen, the courts ruled that the service violated copyright laws by retransmitting signals of broadcast television networks.

The collision of business practices with regulation has an even longer history than the automobile, mobile phone, or the Internet. In the mid-nineteenth century, an entrepreneur named Lysander Spooner observed the high price of postage offered by the United States Post Office. Spooner decided to begin his own private delivery service called the American Letter Mail Company that took advantage of the burgeoning rail network to reduce the cost of mail delivery. Between January and July 1844, Spooner set up mail offices in New York, Philadelphia, Baltimore, and Boston, where the company sold stamps at nearly half the rate charged by government. Within a few months the American Letter Mail Company had captured much of the postage market along the northeastern seaboard.

Spooner's business seemed to be off to a promising start. However, according to the Private Express Statutes, the United States Postal Service has the exclusive right to deliver letters. The American Letter Mail Company operated in direct contravention of this law. Despite Spooner devising a mail delivery system that was both more efficient and more affordable, the federal government sued him and he was forced to close the American Letter Mail Company in 1844.

The apparent success of some firms, like Uber and Airbnb, that conflict with regulation and the failure of others, like the American Letter Mail Company and Aereo, raises an important question. How should executives respond when they encounter a prohibition that seems to prevent some business practice they wish to engage in?

One option would simply be to accept the regulation. When legislation spells out that some practice is forbidden or subject to heavy fines and penalties, entrepreneurs should just avoid doing it. But advising entrepreneurs to operate within the confines of the law presumes that the regulations in question are fundamentally well constructed and fair. However, these are many examples of regulation that seem to exist largely to protect the interests of a particular group at the expense of others. "Preventing harm" to one constituency might well be viewed as legalized entrenchment or protectionism by another.

Passengers may pay less for a ride with Uber than with a taxi, but taxi businesses, which buy or lease expensive licenses in exchange for regulated rates, have difficulty competing with Uber's prices and flexibility. Similarly, Airbnb argues that its business helps homeowners generate additional cash by letting them rent their homes when they are not in use, but regulators and critics see Airbnb as a service that creates unlicensed hotels, which boosts rent prices by reducing the housing stock. Whether Airbnb is viewed as beneficial or detrimental depends on whether you are an Airbnb customer (who now has more choices and better deals), a property owner (who can now make more money), or a local resident (who may incur higher rent and lose a sense of neighborhood because of the increased number of transient visitors).

For would-be entrepreneurs who view a particular regulation as a hindrance that needs to be overcome, the challenge is to figure out how to avoid a regulatory impediment in a way that is acceptable. Put more bluntly, how does one do something that is ostensibly illegal, but in a manner that is construed as legitimate? With some cleverness and ingenuity, managers can often engineer an alternative structuring of an arrangement or find a loophole in the regulation.

Consider the decision of how to most profitably recover valuable scrap metal from a retired container ship. The demolition of container ships is labor-intensive, dangerous, and time-consuming. When undertaken in high-wage locations like Europe, the process can become a major expense.

Not surprisingly, shipowners prefer to have this work done in a place like India or Bangladesh, where the same work can be completed at significantly lower cost.

Not everyone is ecstatic about disassembling ships on the coasts of South Asia, though. Much of this demolition work is done openly on the beaches, where chemicals can leach out from the ships. And the safety equipment employed by shipbreakers in South Asia is often limited. Responding to the perceived inadequate standards employed by these shipbreakers, the European Union passed a law banning European-registered ships from being dismantled in places that do not meet its standards.

Yet, shipowners have easily found a way around this law. Immediately before sailing a European vessel to demolition in India and Bangladesh, owners re-register their ship under the flag of a more accommodating country like Liberia, Comoros, Tuvalu, or St. Kitts. Now flying the flag of a non–European Union member, the ship can comfortably sail into Asian waters fully in compliance with regulation. Regulation avoided, problem "solved."

Some would applaud this rearrangement transaction as a clever way of managing costs, while others would deride it as irresponsible management. Shipowners reap the benefits of incurring fewer expenses, while shipbreaking employees and the environment pay the costs. However, not all regulatory avoidance schemes show such disinterest in the potential costs borne by others. Some managers undertaking such efforts genuinely believe that there are societal benefits associated with their efforts.

Wouldn't we all enjoy having grass that requires less mowing, less water to grow, and lower levels of pesticide to be kept pest-free? Scientists at Scotts Miracle-Gro created just such a genetically engineered product. Usually, the deliberate genetic modification of living organisms is regulated by several US government agencies, since material from bacteria is generally used to insert new DNA. However, researchers at Scotts found ways to introduce genes from other plants using a device called a "gene gun" instead of microorganisms. By doing so, they avoided nearly all the costly regulation created to oversee the commercial production of genetically modified products. "If you take genetic material from a plant and it's not considered a pest, and you don't use a transformation technology that would sort of violate the rules," argued Scotts CEO Jim Hagedorn in a conference call, "there's a bunch of stuff you can do that at least technically is unregulated." With some pride, Hagedorn explained that with the help of a research biologist Scotts had recruited, the company managed to create "a stunning array of products that are not regulated." To some observers, this sidestepping of regulation is a benefit that allows innovation to proceed more quickly. To others, genetic modification without any oversight is a disaster in the making.

DECEPTION, MAKING MISLEADING statements, and lying are all practices that regulation seeks to curtail. But since laws create specific rules regarding what people can and cannot do, it is often possible to follow the literal rule of law while simultaneously violating its underlying spirit against lying, cheating, or stealing. The exploitation of loopholes, as we saw above, isn't always undesirable or detrimental. Some of the most innovative businesses rely on aggressive interpretations of outdated regulation to provide better, lower-cost, or more efficient services. But well-intended practices can devolve into more nefarious behavior as perceived opportunities grow and boundaries become blurry. As the psychologists Francesca Gino and Dan Ariely have shown, creativity isn't always beneficial and can actually promote dishonesty. In a series of experiments, Gino and Ariely found that merely triggering people to use a more creative mindset increased their propensity to cheat by helping them find cleverer ways to justify their behavior.

Figuring out how aggressively to pursue loopholes is a difficult question without an easy answer. Sometimes exploiting loopholes is applauded as inventive, while at other times it's destructive. However, we can see what happens if every time a business encounters a law preventing it from moving forward, its executives see it as another hurdle to jump over, a problem to be solved.

This is Enron.

Too Clever for Their Own Good

It was one of the most remarkable success stories in the annals of business. In little more than a decade, a firm founded through a modestly successful merger of two oil pipeline companies transformed itself into the world's leading energy trader. Its chairman, Kenneth Lay, boasted that nearly half the firm's earnings in 1995 came from businesses that didn't exist a decade earlier. Continuing this spectacular growth, Enron's revenues grew from less than $10 billion in 1995 to over $100 billion in 2000, making it America's seventh-largest firm. *Fortune* magazine named Enron America's most innovative company for six consecutive years, and by 2001 its management was the second most admired of any large firm. When MIT's Sloan School of Management sought to determine which firm to name eBusiness of the Year in April 2001, an award for the company that "best demonstrates innovation, leadership, and social responsibility over the past year," it didn't have to look any further than Enron.

But only six months later, Enron's executives declared that their firm's financial statements were misstated by more than a half-billion dollars. By year end, Enron would file the largest corporate bankruptcy in US history. Questions and investigations ensued, and soon nearly a dozen executives would be called to account and indicted on criminal charges. As the firm liquidated, more than twenty thousand employees lost their jobs and over $60 billion in market value vanished.

Although much maligned in the press in the aftermath of its failure, Enron was no charade lacking in promise. If anything, the company could be faulted for having too many disparate ideas and operations that it sought to grow too rapidly. The essence of Enron's core business was a relatively straightforward proposition of better matching buyers and sellers of energy products. Among its first major innovations was the development of a gas bank where producers and consumers of gas products entered into long-term contracts with each other. By locking in prices, consumers hedged against the risk that natural gas prices would rise in the future and producers were protected from price declines. Interest in this business exploded, and Enron expanded this concept into other markets such as electricity, coal, and metals. It created additional markets in entirely new areas like Internet bandwidth, weather, and even air quality. Beyond its rapidly expanding intermediation business, Enron also managed a range of other energy-related businesses. It operated thirty-two thousand miles of gas pipeline, was the largest manufacturer of wind turbines in the world, and managed more than three dozen power plants in such places as India, the Philippines, Poland, and Turkey.

Enron's innovations extended beyond its energy products to the financial strategies it employed to fuel its development. Many of its projects required large initial capital outlays but were not expected to generate significant cash flows until much later. Although Enron's management believed that these projects would generate long-run value, undertaking them created immediate pressure on Enron's financial statements since cash inflows lagged behind cash outflows. This is where Enron's route into structured financing began.

"There was an overarching theme at Enron since its founding," described Andrew Fastow, Enron's chief financial officer. "You could use as much money as you wanted as long as you didn't use Enron's balance sheet." Avoiding types of financing that added debt to a firm's balance sheet through structured financial transactions was a well-honed practice in corporate finance known as "off-balance sheet financing." This practice allowed firms to avoid much of the dilutive or adverse credit effects associated with traditional financing. Successfully executed, structured finance lowered financing costs by transferring the risk off Enron's balance sheet to another party. In essence, it allowed Enron to do more with less.

Conservative—some at Enron would say outdated—financial regulation superficially limited much of the potential creativity with structured transactions. However, Enron's executives believed that by devising the right financial structure they could circumvent, overcome, or even avoid much of this regulation. Unbeknownst to many of Enron's indisputably brilliant executives, it was their prodigious efforts to see every problem as something that could be solved with greater financial ingenuity that sowed the seeds of the company's eventual collapse.

To UNDERSTAND THE benefits of employing a little financial ingenuity, it's illustrative to look at one particular Enron transaction known as RADR. In 1997, Enron had a problem. It wanted to divest itself from several wind farms in California to complete the acquisition of a utility company. Enron could divest either by selling the wind farms to another firm or by transferring them to a special purpose entity (SPE), which was a separate shell company that held assets. By placing assets in their own independent entity, SPEs were a popular tool that helped firms isolate risks and lower the cost of financing. With either option, the wind farms would be removed from Enron's balance sheet and no longer be under its control.

There was only one problem with selling the wind farms. The federal government provided a number of lucrative tax benefits to firms operating alternative energy sources and Enron's executives were loath to give these up. Ideally, they wanted to sell the wind farms and remove them from the company's balance sheet, but still effectively maintain control over them to continue reaping these tax benefits.

The challenge was that the rules governing the creation of SPEs were devised to prevent exactly this kind of arrangement. The general partner, the person who oversaw and controlled the legally separate SPE, couldn't be connected to Enron. The basic premise of having the general partner be an independent owner was that he would act in the interests of the SPE instead of the interests of the firm that had placed assets in the SPE. According to the regulation, the general partner couldn't be a "related party"— a board member, an employee of Enron, or a family member of an employee. From a legal standpoint, the general partner of the SPE had to be independent of Enron or else the wind farms would need to be consolidated back onto Enron's financial statements.

Luckily for the executives at Enron, there appeared to be an opportunity to overcome this requirement. "There was this anomaly, if you will, in the law," explained Andrew Fastow. One of the leaders in Fastow's structured finance group, Michael Kopper, was gay and had a longtime partner named William Dodson. But Enron was based in Texas, where same-sex relationships were not legally recognized. In effect, Dodson was not legally related to Kopper and therefore not a related party. "So notwithstanding they had a very similar relationship to a spousal relationship, technically, it worked under the law," remarked Fastow.

Enron listed Dodson as the general partner of the SPE, allowing Enron to divest but still effectively control the wind farms. It was a solution— employing a creative interpretation of a law to circumvent the underlying regulatory principle—that Enron would employ again and again to retain control over assets, while disavowing itself from the need to report those assets on its own financial statements. "At the time," explained Fastow, "we thought we were really clever with this solution."

MUCH OF ENRON'S use of structured financial transactions arose as "problems," or what executives came to call "opportunities," presented themselves. In March 1998, Enron invested $10 million in a burgeoning Internet service provider called Rhythms Netconnections at less than $2 a share. It was a fortuitous investment in the firm's growing venture portfolio. After going public a year later, the stock was worth $69 a share, and Enron's investment was worth a spectacular $300 million.

"By May 1999, we were getting worried that the stock would start declining in value and we'd be forced to reverse the gain in future quarters," Fastow explained. "The problem was that Enron was one of the initial investors in the company, so we were prohibited from selling the shares before the end of the year by a lock-up provision. The investment was mark-to-market, so if the price declined, Enron would be forced to take a write-down in the subsequent quarter. We wanted some way to lock in that gain now." The limited liquidity, large size of the position, and lack of similar securities in the market made it nearly impossible to hedge the Rhythms Netconnections position in the open market.

"In a complete coincidence, around the same time we discovered— and I really mean discovered—a special purpose entity that I didn't know existed," recalled Fastow. Earlier in Enron's history, its executives created a structure to offset the dilution arising from its employee stock option program. With the help of the investment bank UBS, this structure had been purchasing shares in Enron for years. With Enron's rapid rise in stock price, the value of Enron's stock in the structure significantly exceeded the value needed to hedge the employee stock option program. However, under Generally Accepted Accounting Principles, firms could not recognize increases in the value of their own stock. "There was a couple hundred million dollars in embedded Enron stock value locked in this structure," Fastow noted. "The problem was that if Enron just took the stock back, we wouldn't get to book any of those earnings since companies can't recognize increases in the value of its own stock as income. The accountants looked at it in all different ways and no one could figure out how to capture the appreciated value of the stock."

So Enron had two problems. For the Rhythms Netconnections investment, Enron wanted to avoid recognizing losses if the stock price fell, but it wasn't allowed to create such a hedge in the open market. Enron also wanted to recognize the appreciated value of its stock, but it couldn't do this under conventional accounting rules. "Eventually an idea popped up. What about if we married these two things—the RhythmsNet position and the embedded Enron stock—in a structure?" Fastow explained. "The value from the Enron stock could be used to hedge any declines in value of the RhythmsNet position. The appreciated value embedded in the UBS structure could be used to offset potential losses."

It was a clever solution that solved two "problems" at once. Enron effectively figured out how to capture the value of its own stock by hedging its venture investment in Rhythms Netconnections. The challenge was that executing such a transaction required an especially complex financial structure, as well as some additional outside capital. But Enron's leadership had an idea to make the transaction feasible: What if Fastow oversaw the transaction within Enron and as the general partner of the external firm that invested in the deal? "I had experience with complex structuring," described Fastow, "and I worked most often with the banks who were the most likely guys to go to get outside funding. To get this done in a month, it would take someone who had the relationship with the banks and private equity investors." Fastow also saw an opportunity to participate in this transaction himself in a way that he viewed as analogous to the participation of partners in investments at many financial and private equity firms. "It's common for investment banks to have funds that the executives run and also get to invest in. I wanted to bring that concept over to Enron. . . . The only real difference between myself and someone at a bank was that I was the CFO of a corporation."

It was an unconventional proposition. A corporate officer who essentially ran an investment fund that traded with his outside firm created an obvious potential for conflicts of interest. When Enron sought to sell an asset, Fastow could wind up essentially negotiating with himself as both the CFO of Enron and the general partner of the fund. Other executives at Enron and the board appreciated this cause for concern but saw Fastow's participation as necessary to expeditiously move the transaction forward. If approved, the structure would be mutually advantageous for both Enron and Fastow.

The idea for the structure, named "LJM" after Fastow's wife and kids, was brought to Enron's board. "The board loved the idea," Fastow recalled. "The only real concern raised was what was called the *Wall Street Journal* risk. Even if everything about the transaction was okay and approved by our attorneys and accountants, external lawyers, our auditors—even if we're right on all this, it's going to look nasty if the *Wall Street Journal* writes an article about it." Ultimately, however, the perceived benefits of creating LJM outweighed these concerns and the board approved the arrangement in June 28, 1999.

Fastow flew to London to meet with the other bankers participating in LJM. "We had multiple paths going on at the same time. Our accountant and attorneys were working on structuring the swap. They were talking to the accountants at Arthur Andersen, who were talking to their people at their head office in Chicago. I was working on getting all the paperwork in order with the banks. . . . It was exciting stress. You are working twenty-four hours a day on a deal. Everything we were doing was breakthrough, so no one quite counted on it until it happened."

Only two days after Enron's board approved LJM, the deal closed. "After we figured out how to solve the problem of the RhythmsNet stock with StockSub, everyone was ecstatic." Fastow and his team had managed to solve two problems—one that was not achievable in the market and the other ostensibly prevented by regulation—with a clever financial structure. "People were having parties and high-fiving," Fastow recalled with pride. "The business unit that got to book that $300 million, they were just walking around like peacocks."

ALTHOUGH MANY OF Enron's original structured transactions were employed to manage economic risks and events, over time its use of structured transactions began to evolve. The structures became more focused on managing Enron's financial statements to keep debt off the balance sheet, accelerate gains, and delay the recognition of losses. Enron's structures often complied with the technical letter of the disparate and complex rules but began to violate the fundamental spirit behind financial reporting. Enron's management appealed to rules in form rather than substance.

"Enron was extremely focused on hitting its earnings numbers. I remember that Skilling used to have a slide where he showed the number of companies in the United States that had so many years of 15 percent EPS growth, and there were only a handful like GE and Enron. He insisted that we continue to grow our EPS at 15 percent per annum. So the earnings targets were not based upon looking at an honest evaluation of the company's prospects and saying how much we could realistically expect to grow. Instead, it was really derived externally around this 15 percent target and then put back onto the operating units within the company," described Fastow.

"At the end of the third quarter 1999, the international group was having trouble hitting their numbers. To help them make their target, they wanted to sell a piece of Project Cuiaba." Enron, through its Brazilian subsidiary, held a 65 percent stake in a power plant and natural gas pipeline project in Cuiaba, Brazil. By September 1999, the construction on the project was still experiencing significant problems. Enron's management wanted to sell its stake in the project to another firm, but it found no willing takers. Enron, like most firms, would normally be forced to take a write-down to acknowledge the decline in the value of the project, but Enron had a structured finance alternative.

"We needed to get this done by the end of the quarter, but there was no way to find a buyer for such an asset in such a short period of time. Jeff asked if LJM had any firepower left to get such a deal done. Luckily, Credit Suisse (CSFB) and Natwest had originally put in $15 million in LJM so there was cash sitting there. So we said 'yeah, we'll take a look at it.'"

Using his LJM partnership, Fastow proposed a deal that met Enron's objectives, while also preserving his interests and those of the other LJM investors. "I didn't want to own a Brazilian power plant through LJM. CSFB and Natwest didn't want to own a Brazilian power plant, either. LJM could buy the asset, but Enron needed to continue marketing the asset to other buyers so we had some assurance that LJM wouldn't get stuck with it."

Enron and Fastow settled on an arrangement. LJM would purchase the Cuiaba project from Enron at an exploding yield or interest rate. "If Enron couldn't find a buyer by a certain point in time, the yield of the deal would jump from 13 percent to 25 percent," Fastow noted. While 13 percent might be competitive for such a deal, 25 percent would be very costly to Enron. "As a result, the business unit was very incentivized to find a buyer."

On the final day of the third quarter, September 30, 1999, LJM bought 13 percent of Enron's interest in Cuiaba for $11.3 million. Enron no longer needed to consolidate approximately $200 million in debt for the project on its balance sheet due to its reduced ownership in the project. At the same time, Enron recognized $65 million worth of mark-to-market natural gas contracts into its earnings from the sale. So although Project Cuiaba was a troubled endeavor that was declining in value, this financial structuring allowed Enron to book the project, at least temporarily, as a win.

The more creative and exotic the solution, the greater the accolades. Fastow would win the CFO of the Year award in 1999 for helping finance Enron's "amazing transformation," in the words of the presenters, "from pipelines to piping hot." According to one analyst from the investment bank Lehman Brothers at the time, "Thanks to Andy Fastow, Enron has been able to develop all these different businesses, which require huge amounts of capital, without diluting the stock price or deteriorating its credit quality—both of which actually have gone up. He has invented a groundbreaking strategy." Even Enron's analyst from the credit agency Standard & Poor's, who was charged with evaluating Enron's capacity to repay its debts, admired Fastow's ability to "think outside the box."

"It was very heady stuff," recalled Fastow. "This was rock star stuff in the corporate finance world. . . . As we got deals done, everyone in my group got very high levels of recognition. My group solved company problems."

"After we did the Cuiaba deal, Jeff saw how powerful a tool LJM could be for Enron. He wanted me to expand LJM, but we couldn't since it was originally structured specifically for the Rhythms hedge. Skilling suggested that we create another fund and start raising money for that. He just wanted to know how long it would take to raise and how big could I make it." Less than two weeks later, Fastow was back in front of the board proposing another investment partnership—this time, named LJM 2. "This was going to be a real private equity fund and much bigger," Fastow explained. "It was going to be structured like a traditional private equity partnership, but it was a fund that was going to be using its equity to facilitate highly structured transactions to benefit Enron."

On the one hand, Fastow found it awkward to be negotiating against the firm for which he served as chief financial officer. On the other, he felt that LJM 2 served the needs of Enron in an efficient manner. "We had people at LJM that would just field phone calls from business units at Enron. Negotiating was very odd, but all these deals were helping Enron. LJM 2 was only doing these deals because Enron asked us to. . . . It was mutually advantageous," Fastow explained. "Whenever the business unit heads couldn't quite hit their numbers, they could come to LJM 2 to help solve their problems."

One of the times a unit head came to Fastow was in late 1999. Enron owned three floating power plants off the coast of Nigeria. These barges were still under construction, but Enron wanted to sell a portion of them immediately. By successfully consummating the sale, Enron would get to recognize $12 million in earnings in the fourth quarter of 1999 and meet its earnings target.

Enron needed a buyer willing to pay millions for an asset that, in all likelihood, it didn't want to hold. At the very least, the most probable candidates to help facilitate such a purchase—investment banks—would be reluctant to lend millions of dollars to an exotic international project so quickly. Moreover, if Enron provided any explicit guarantee to purchase it back at a later point, the sale would not be considered legitimate and Enron wouldn't be able to recognize the associated earnings it desired. But once again Fastow had a solution.

"Merrill Lynch was willing to purchase the barges, but they said they didn't want to own them for more than six months and they wanted assurance of this. . . . The trick is that Enron couldn't guarantee to Merrill Lynch that they would be out of the barges in six months because then it wouldn't be considered a true sale. So I explicitly told them that Enron could not guarantee that the barges would be taken off their hands in six months. However, I told them that I happened to know of this private equity firm called LJM 2 that would, with a high degree of confidence, be interested in buying the barges in six months. Arthur Andersen had already made the determination that LJM was legally separate from Enron. So as long as I was clear, LJM 2 could offer assurances. Enron, on the other hand, couldn't offer these assurances." By contorting the underlying principles and creatively interpreting regulation, Fastow offered a solution that would allow Enron to temporarily sell the barges to Merrill Lynch.

"All of the Enron guys looked at each other after the meeting with the Merrill Lynch bankers, and we realized just how fantastic a tool LJM 2 was. We had LJM 2 available to give assurances to investors and that was really powerful," noted Fastow.

The deal closed on December 29, two days before the fiscal year end. Merrill Lynch's temporary purchase of the barges at the end of 1999 permitted Enron to recognize $12 million in earnings in the fourth quarter of 1999.

IN ENRON'S LATER years, many of its structured transactions had the perverse effect of accelerating good news but delaying the recognition of bad

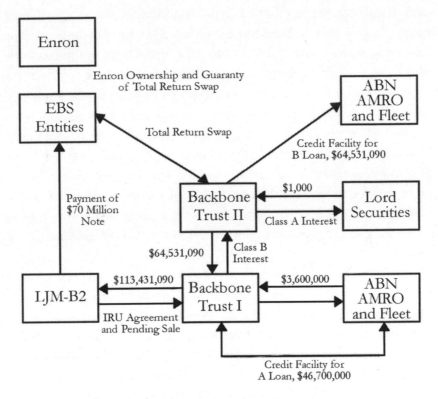

Figure 12.1: A depiction of one of Enron's structured
transactions, known as Backbone.

news. Rather than slow down and reexamine the strategy of a project that
didn't perform as desired, Enron managed to remove or temporarily obscure the loss with the help of financial structuring. In doing so, it burned
through much-needed cash managing the aesthetics of its financial statements rather than the business itself. "There was always a bit of a feeling
that there was some project in trouble, but we're inventing so many new
businesses—and the value of those are going to be so great," Fastow explained, that the underperforming business wouldn't matter in the end.
"But the reality is, if you have projects that are in trouble, you should report that and we didn't. We covered them up."

By 2000, Enron had over 1,300 partnerships and subsidiaries, many of
which arose from its various structured transactions. Simply listing the
names of all these entities took up 156 pages in its regulatory filings. With

such complexity, Enron created a set of financials that obscured how lever-aged and precarious the business had become. Even some of the firm's most senior executives couldn't understand the ramifications of the extraordi-nary amount of financial structuring artificially sustaining the company.

When Enron finally declared bankruptcy in late 2001, one lawsuit ar-gued that Enron's reported financials were ultimately a mirage: "Enron so engineered its reported financial position and results of operations that its financial statements bore little resemblance to its actual financial condi-tion and performance." Fastow appreciated how Enron often used struc-tured finance to manage the appearance of the firm's financials rather than the underlying economics. "Structured finance isn't always moving real risk," Fastow explained. "Sometimes it's just about moving the ac-counting risk."

"My intentions were good. I was trying to do what was best for Enron, but the way we as a company defined success was incorrect. We defined success by reported earnings and the stock price. We were not defining it as increasing economic value," Fastow described. "There may have been a belief at points that we were doing both, but I think as time passed we de-ceived ourselves into confusing reported financial results with economic substance." Enron's bankruptcy examiner noted that six accounting tech-niques produced 96 percent of Enron's reported net income in 2000. Sim-ilarly, these maneuvers enabled Enron to report only $10.2 billion in debt as opposed to $22.1 billion.

"We tried to do it by technically following the rules," Fastow admitted. And, he asked, "couldn't you say that if all transactions and accounts are technically correct, then whatever the outcome, they are not misleading?"

Defense attorneys often employ a strategy that illuminates the perverse effects of focusing on technical details at the expense of the bigger picture. When a defendant is accused of committing a serious crime, the attorney sometimes tries to convince jurors that his client's behavior was little more than "mere preparation." To do this, the attorney describes his client's ac-tions as thousands of minuscule steps—each seemingly innocuous on its own. The attorney will then explain how the first couple steps do not estab-lish an attempt to commit a criminal act. Beyond that, each additional step is so trivial that it's hard to discern which specific step made his actions go from "mere preparation" to actual engagement in criminal activity.

Although each step appears guiltless on its own, when all of the steps are put together the outcome may appear far more mischievous. In the same way, individual parts of a structured transaction may appear acceptable on their own, but when they are combined the outcome can be deceptive and misleading. It's just difficult to see what particular part is "wrong" when transactions are broken down into numerous pieces. In many instances, Enron may have been "technically following the rules by disclosing everything that was required to be disclosed," as Fastow noted, but this didn't mean the end result wasn't misleading.

Fastow would eventually plead guilty to conspiring to mislead shareholders about the true financial position of Enron and serve five years in federal prison. "I was doing exactly what I was incentivized to do. We wouldn't have gone through all this trouble if we just wanted to cheat. We were finding ways to get around the rules but going through a complex process to find the loopholes to allow us to do it. . . . I cheated fair and square."

"People always asked me whether transactions followed the law. No one ever asked me about the intent of what I was doing," Fastow explained. "It was precisely the innovative and aggressive structuring that I was getting awards for. People thought this stuff was frickin' brilliant."

"It's Intoxicating to Come Up with This Stuff"

In a much-cited 1947 court opinion, Judge Learned Hand wrote that "over and over again courts have said that there is nothing sinister in so arranging one's affairs as to keep taxes as low as possible. Everyone does so, rich or poor, and all do right, for nobody owes any public duty to pay more than the law demands." Around the world, judges have echoed similar sentiments—taxpayers have no obligation to pay more tax than that required by law.

Taxpayers have long engaged in planning exercises to minimize their tax burden. In 1696, when England passed a law taxing the number of windows within each inhabited residence, homeowners—so as to avoid the tax—soon began boarding or even bricking up windows when assessors came to inspect. In seventeenth-century Tsarist Russia, taxes were assessed on each household regardless of how many individuals lived there. To mitigate the tax, households would squeeze as many members as possible into each residence.

Today, tax rates vary according to the type of taxpayer and the category of asset. These differences create opportunities and incentives to strategically organize affairs to reduce or stave off payments. Tax professionals who study the United States tax code—which, as of 2014, was 74,608 pages long—often find ways of restructuring an individual or firm's affairs to lower tax liabilities. By rearranging activities, they can often construct a way of conducting a transaction that lowers the tax burden while still satisfying the tax rules.

Consider an example, described by University of Pennsylvania legal scholar Leo Katz, that captures much of the spirit of these tax-reducing transactions. A shoemaker supports his lazy son by giving him $1,000 in cash each year as a gift. His earnings are taxed at a considerably higher rate than his son because of the considerable income he earns as a successful shoemaker. Ideally, the shoemaker thinks it would be nice to take a $1,000 deduction to lower his tax burden for providing this gift. However, since the shoemaker earned the income, it is he who must cover the burden of the taxes and the law does not allow tax deductions for gifts to family. After some further thought, the shoemaker comes up with a clever idea to get around this obstacle.

The following year, the shoemaker decides to give his son a gift of $10,000. After making the gift, the shoemaker immediately asks his son for a loan of $10,000, ostensibly to run his business. The shoemaker offers to pay his son a generous 10 percent interest rate, or $1,000 a year, on the $10,000 loan. His son happily agrees.

By engaging in this engineered transaction, the shoemaker continues giving his son $1,000 a year (taxable to his son, but at his lower rate) and the shoemaker now gets to deduct $1,000 in interest expense from his income. The shoemaker has his $10,000 back in his account and the son continues to receive payments from his father just as before. The only party adversely affected by this transaction is the government, which now receives less tax revenue. There is little economic or business purpose for the shoemaker's rigmarole other than lowering his tax liabilities. It is an aggressive, albeit simple, tax shelter.

Although there is no universally agreed-upon definition of what constitutes a tax shelter, it is usually characterized by shifting, exempting, or deferring income to effectively lower an individual's tax burden. Some forms of sheltering create an "investment" that produces greater tax savings than the associated economic loss. Others produce losses that can be used to offset gains from other unrelated sources of income. Achieving these results is contrary to the desires of regulators and tax collectors and often requires considerable ingenuity and creativity. It's why Yale Law School professor Michael Graetz has colorfully described a tax shelter as "a deal done by very smart people that, absent tax consideration, would be very stupid."

Tax structuring allows individuals with similar incomes to face different liabilities. Beyond issues of equity and fairness, critics grumble that even legal tax planning and sheltering produce little or even negative social benefit. Illicit structures go even further by expropriating revenues that are expected to maintain the state. "Tax planning . . . produces nothing of value," wrote University of Chicago Law School professor David Weisbach. "Nothing is gained by finding new ways to turn ordinary income into capital gain, to push a gain offshore, or to generate losses. No new medicines are found, computer chips designed, or homeless housed through tax planning. At a minimum, defenders of tax planning must justify why we should care about a nonproductive activity."

MARK WATSON NEVER saw himself becoming a structured-products professional. An accountant by training, Watson joined KPMG in 1992 and focused on tax planning in the firm's personal financial planning group. Recognizing his aptitude and talent, KPMG quickly promoted Watson through its ranks to partner in its prestigious Washington National Tax office, the firm's "think tank." There he worked on a variety of issues related to individual taxation, especially gifts and estates.

"Most people don't like to pay taxes and certainly don't want to pay any more taxes than they have to. So there is always pressure put on tax professionals—or incentives if you want to look at it from that angle—to come up with strategies to reduce taxpayers' tax bills," explained Watson. "That's just inherent in our system."

Like other accounting firms, KPMG began to dramatically increase the range of tax services it began offering to individuals during the 1990s. This was a new line of work for accounting firms, which historically were viewed as conservative organizations better known for their restraint than for financial creativity. But partners at places like KPMG realized that

they were ideally suited to capitalize on the enormous fees from more innovative tax products by building on the relationships they had already
developed with their clients.

"Executives at Schering-Plough, Pfizer, and Microsoft are getting ready
to do an exit and are sitting with their M&A and tax people structuring
the deal, and then at some point they are going to say, 'what about me?
I'm going to get $300 million out of this deal and who's going to take care
of my problem?' They are going to say that Goldman has a solution for
me, Merrill has a solution, Solomon has a solution—what can you offer
me?" explained Bob Jones, another executive who frequently interacted
with Watson and his colleagues at KPMG.

"What the accounting firms said is 'hey, wait a second, we have a much
better relationship with these executives than the bankers. I mean, the relationship between the corporates and the bankers is only as good as their
last transaction, but people don't usually change accountants every
year. . . . We can give our clients a better solution than what the banks can
offer them. All we need to do is apply the corporate tax code to partnerships' . . . and that's how this whole set of tax minimization techniques to
individuals started," explained Jones.

Once accounting firms decided to begin marketing tax products, the
packaged-shelters business took off. It was a lucrative area that attracted
many savvy professionals. Inside of KPMG's Washington, DC, tax headquarters, several partners created a group informally dubbed the "skunk
works." The group drew its name from a secret World War II research lab
that focused on developing stealth planes to defeat the Axis powers. Yet,
instead of working on weapons to defeat a hostile adversary, KPMG's
skunk works focused on devising innovative tax strategies that could
eliminate large tax liabilities for wealthy US taxpayers. The group sought
sleek "turn-key" strategies that could readily be sold to high-net-worth
clients.

"Historically, it was one-off situations," Watson said. Tax lawyers or
accountants "would run across a situation where they tried to figure out
how to solve a problem for a client. But this was different. This was coming
up with a strategy and then going out and finding a client with that problem." But this fit with KPMG's new business strategy, described by one internal memo as "the simple concept of investing in the development of a

portfolio of elegant, high-value tax products" that could easily be sold through the firm's marketing and distribution network.

Watson co-led the Innovative Strategies Group. As part of this role, it was his responsibility to ensure that products sold to KPMG's high-net-worth clients complied with applicable tax laws. Not long after assuming the position, Watson was confronted with a new structure devised by several members of KPMG's tax team and their outside advisors called BLIPS: Bond Linked Issue Premium Structure. The basic idea was that the client would form a single-member limited liability corporation (LLC) and, through this LLC, borrow money from a bank at an above-market interest rate. After a complex set of partnerships, swaps, and foreign currency transactions, the loan would be repaid, thereby incurring an early repayment penalty. This penalty would serve as a paper loss that clients could use to shelter other income from taxes. There was a lot of excitement around the product within KPMG. John Lanning, KPMG's vice-chairman of tax services, e-mailed Watson hoping that the product could be approved in a "dramatically accelerated time frame" due to the significant "market potential" of the product.

Drawing on a host of highly specialized subfields from partnership to international taxation, BLIPS stood too far outside Watson's area of expertise for him to be comfortable penning an opinion on the structure's validity as a legitimate investment. Watson decided to enlist the outside opinion of others, especially on the critical issue of whether the structure had so-called economic substance. For BLIPS to be legal in the eyes of tax authorities, investors had to enter the transactions with a reasonable expectation that they could make a profit. BLIPS was designed to offer a large tax loss without the investor needing to risk anything economically, so Watson told colleagues he wasn't sure if it would be able to adequately satisfy this criterion.

Transactions with some business or commercial purpose can also have large tax benefits. For example, firms that manufacture goods domestically in the United States can qualify for special tax deductions. If executives have data suggesting that sales will rise if their products have "Made in the USA" on the labels and they decide to shift operations back to the United States to sell more products, the firm can enjoy greater sales and also lower its taxes. But suppose, as in the case of BLIPS, that a transaction was primarily designed to achieve some tax benefit, and the potential economic benefits were just tacked on. Would the transaction still be legal? In particular, how much "business purpose" is needed to create a legitimate transaction?

The issue of economic substance was punted among various leaders at KPMG, including the head of the professional practice group and the head of its Washington tax center. A financial market quant named Amir Makov was brought in from Presidio Advisors, one of the firms helping execute the complex securities transactions, to explain the supposed economic substance. If any of the currencies were devalued during the investment period, Makov explained, investors were poised to make significant returns. Although such a profit was remote, Makov demonstrated that it was mathematically possible through a case study. While some of the partners found Makov's analysis compelling, others considered the speculative nature of the potential profit as reason why tax authorities might not view BLIPS as legitimate.

Each client who viewed the documents describing BLIPS was asked to sign a confidentiality agreement. Executives from KPMG further made sure to never leave these documents behind to avoid details leaking to competitors or the IRS. Although the transaction was structured to last seven years, the documents spelled out how the investor would reap the much-desired tax shield by exiting the transaction after only two months.

As months went by and the structure still hadn't been approved, many in KPMG's leadership became increasingly frustrated. As Watson continued to insist that BLIPS lacked economic substance and that KPMG might be penalized if the company pressed ahead with the product, several other high-level executives at the firm began cutting him out of the loop and discussing the structure outside his presence. At one point, John Lanning, KPMG's vice-chairman of tax services, e-mailed colleagues in the tax group, saying that "I would have thought that Mark would have been involved in the ground floor of this process, especially on an issue as critical as profit motive. What gives? This appears to be the antithesis of speed to market." Philip Wiesner, KPMG's partner-in-charge of its Washington National Tax office, wrote that "the time has come to shit and get off the pot." In response, Jeffrey Stein, deputy chairman of KPMG, responded: "It's shit OR get off the pot. I vote for shit."

Watson was still not enthusiastic about BLIPS. But his superiors at the firm deferred to his judgment, placing him in a difficult position. Either he could approve a product he feared the IRS would challenge or he could be responsible for single-handedly undermining months of work by dozens of people and sacrificing millions in future profits. "I don't like this product and would prefer not to be associated with it," Watson wrote in one e-mail. But, he added, if the letter included some modified language, then "I can reluctantly live with a more-likely-than-not opinion being issued for the product."

Members of KPMG's tax team continued to push ahead with the structure. Richard Smith, one of KPMG's top tax experts, showed Watson an e-mail drafted by KPMG's partner-in-charge of its Washington National Tax office with his assessment that a court would maintain that BLIPS had economic substance. Later that day, Watson sent an e-mail to the group saying that he was "ready to proceed." After six months of back and forth the transaction was finally ready to move forward, and KPMG began marketing BLIPS in the summer of 1999. "Ultimately, I capitulated," sighed Watson. "I did so because I really didn't want to believe that my partners at a Big Four accounting firm would get into something that would be illegal."

The next year, however, the IRS began to investigate KPMG's tax practice. By the middle of 2002, the Justice Department had gotten involved. Many of KPMG's senior partners were hauled in front of the Senate Permanent Subcommittee on Investigations and forced to explain their own sales materials, which seemed to clearly market BLIPS as an illicit tax shelter. In 2005, nineteen people were criminally indicted. In addition to KPMG employees, the indictments included R. J. Ruble, a lawyer at the prestigious firm Sidley Austin, who provided clients' opinion letters supporting the validity of the transaction, and three people at the outside advisory office of Presidio. Jones was among those indicted. So too was Watson, even though he had warned colleagues about BLIPS for months and even testified about his doubts before the Senate committee.

THE DEPARTMENT OF Justice estimated that $1.28 billion in government revenue was lost to BLIPS. "Crimes like terrorism or murder or fraud or embezzlement produce instant recognition of the immorality involved," began Senator Carl Levin at the inquiry. "But abusive tax shelters are MEGOs—that means 'my eyes glaze over.' Those who cook up these concoctions count on their complexity to escape scrutiny and public ire." A broader congressional investigation of tax shelters was launched to understand how accounting firms, historically seen as custodians of corporate accountability, had instead become creators of products that undermined responsibility.

R. J. Ruble gained prominence as a tax attorney for arguing that the tax system is an adversarial process: tax attorney versus the government. "You're supposed to be an advocate for your client. You're not an advocate for the government," argued Ruble. "I do not believe that these rules mandate an overriding duty to the tax system."

But David Weisbach of the University of Chicago argues that there is a need to consider the consequences of tax sheltering to the overall well-being of the tax system. He asks people to consider a hypothetical new tax product called the "backflip shelter." The structure is simple: if a taxpayer successfully completes a backflip, the shelter reduces the taxpayer's liability by 10 percent. Given the low cost of doing a backflip, many taxpayers will be incentivized to give one a try.

If government spending is maintained at the same level and every taxpayer performs a backflip, people will be in the same position as before. Taxpayers end up paying the same amount as before since the government is forced to raise tax rates, but each taxpayer is now stuck performing a useless backflip, too.

We'd expect some taxpayers to be unaware of the backflip shelter and its associated tax savings. Those who do not perform the tax gymnastics will be stuck paying higher taxes. But why would individuals who perform the pointless act of employing a backflip shelter be more deserving of a tax break than those who do not? Imposing additional costs, in the form of a higher tax burden, on those who do not perform backflips is an inefficient distortion within the tax system. In this regard, structuring seems to be an inane but lucrative activity.

Those designing tax structures tend not to focus on the larger macroeconomic consequences of their actions. Designing an effective structure is just another profitable investment to pursue. "I looked at the world to see whether there was a mispricing among securities: Is there an opportunity out there to arbitrage the market or change the risk-return on a structure?" explained Jones. "You apply the same tools to the tax code. The only difference is that instead of working off basis points, you're working off percentages. The amount of excess value that you could make by applying this solution to a tax or accounting problem far exceeds the two or three basis points you could get on an investment portfolio."

Such prodigious effects might seem vacuous and with little merit to outsiders, but to the many professionals working in the tax structuring area, designing these products actually offered significant intellectual attraction. Ruble described how tax structuring was "very much like figuring out a very complex puzzle." For Watson, "it was very intellectually interesting, it was challenging, it was kind of fun to be able to sit there and think about how can we make these pieces work to get the result we're after."

By viewing financial structuring problems as complex puzzles or difficult riddles to be solved, many executives avoided confronting the harm they had done to government coffers and the well-being of other taxpayers. Others, like Jones, saw nothing wrong or unethical in the aggressive structures they sought to create. "I was in a good career making a couple million a year," recalled Jones, "so it's not that I'm going to risk everything to go do something shady or illegal. . . . There's not a single point where I could say, you know something, I would have done something different over here, or this would have been a red flag, or, you know, I did something wrong."

After being criminally prosecuted, Jones reflected on what he believed happened. "My true crime is that I democratized the tax code. These products were always available to the ultra, ultra-rich—those that make a half-billion or a billion a year. What happened in the BLIPS years is that suddenly people who only made $50 million or $20 million a year had a solution." There would be humor in hearing someone say he helped democratize tax products by serving people who "only" make $50 million a year—if only he didn't genuinely believe this sentiment.

"If you asked me, 'what was your mistake, what would you have done differently, what do you think you guys did wrong?'" Jones continued, "I think it has to do with the mass marketing of the products. As long as this thing was kept so you did only five or ten big deals, I don't think you would have had this kind of uproar."

Jones' only real regret is that he got caught.

The Ubiquitous Loophole

Apple has been named the world's most-admired company by *Fortune* magazine every year since 2008. Customers anxiously await its newer and sleeker designs of iPhones, MacBooks, and iPads. Investors have been rewarded with stock returns of over 1,500 percent during the past decade as Apple became the first American company to have a market capitalization greater than $700 billion.

But Apple's rise to become the world's most profitable technology company is not without a more pernicious side. In a series of articles that would go on to win the Pulitzer Prize, journalists at the *New York Times* described how Apple employed financial engineering to avoid billions in taxes. Apple shifted intellectual property rights abroad, for example, and created offshore subsidiaries with tens of billions of dollars in income, but essentially no employees and no residence for tax purposes. Although an Apple spokesperson defended the company by saying that "Apple has conducted all of its business with the highest of ethical standards, complying with applicable laws and accounting rules" and a later congressional inquiry did not find any laws broken, leading lawmakers were aghast at the extraordinary lengths to which Apple's executives went to avoid taxes. In Senate subcommittee hearings with Apple's senior executives, Senator Carl Levin began:

> The offshore tax avoidance tactics spotlighted by the Subcommittee do real harm. They disadvantage domestic U.S. companies that aren't in a position to reduce their tax bills using offshore tax gimmicks. They offload Apple's tax burden onto other taxpayers. . . . The lost tax revenue feeds a budget deficit that has reached troubling proportions, and has helped lead to round after round of budget slashing and the ill-advised sequestration now threatening our economic recovery. Because of those cuts, children across the country won't get early education from Head Start. Needy seniors will

go without meals. Fighter jets sit idle on tarmacs because our military lacks the funding to keep pilots trained.

Andrew Fastow regards Apple's tax maneuvers as analogous to the financial structuring "accomplishments" at Enron. "What we were doing in finance is no different than what Apple or any other firm does to lower its taxes," Fastow explained. "When Congress passes a new law about a tax rate they don't really pass the law and say but if you figure out a way to set up a subsidiary in the Cayman Islands that ostensibly manufactures bamboo drink umbrellas you can use that as a tax shelter. But there are guys who figure that out. . . . It's just finding loopholes."

Fastow offered a hypothetical to explain how a loophole can appear to be clever, even ingenious, on its surface, but can nonetheless lead to perverse outcomes. Suppose as a teenager you were invited to a friend's house. Your parents said you could drive to the party under the one condition that you wouldn't drink any alcohol. You agree and when a friend offers you a beer when you arrive, you decline the drink in deference to your parents' rules.

A little later during the party, another friend comes over to you to offer you something new—a beer pill. The tablet offers the exact same intoxicating effect as a beer, but it's a pill, not a drink. Technically, consuming the beer tablet wouldn't violate your promise. Your parents asked only that you not drink any alcohol. You swallow the pill, delighted that you get to partake in alcohol consumption with your friends without disobeying your parents' rules.

Much like the teenager in this example, executives at Enron mistook drinking, rather than alcohol consumption, as the act the parents were seeking to prevent. While rules provide prohibitions, they are often not complete. Finding an ingenious or unexpected workaround doesn't necessarily reduce or prevent harm. Synthetic drugs known as "bath salts" exploit minor changes to their chemical composition to avoid being illicit, but they still cause extraordinary harm to those who ingest them. Likewise, the delirious consequences of excessive alcohol are the same whether the alcohol is consumed in liquid or pill form.

Exploiting loopholes distances executives from the underlying harm by making it seem more acceptable. If you figure that you're not breaking a rule, then it's easier to feel that you are not harming anyone and are therefore not subject to any adverse consequences. Consider, for instance, Burmese Buddhists, who loathe killing any creature whether human or animal. Those who violate this prohibition will have a miserable existence in future lives. But, as described by the nineteenth-century anthropologist Adolf Bastian, some Burmese fishermen found a way to escape this damnation by avoiding the literal act of killing. The fishermen reasoned that the fish they caught "are merely put out on the bank to dry after their long soaking in the river," explained Bastian, "and if they are foolish and ill-judged enough to die while undergoing the process, it is their own fault." By believing that they sidestepped the explicit act of killing the fish, these fishermen felt comforted that they avoided the terrible consequences.

Executives seek loopholes to improve the profitability of their firms rather than the quality of their souls, but the superficiality of reasoning that something is acceptable if it "technically" doesn't violate a prohibition is similar. In 2007 Lehman Brothers' balance sheet was looking increasingly risky to investors, and it was on the verge of a credit rating downgrade. Executives at Lehman sought to reduce the appearance of risk by employing something known as "Repo 105."

With Repo 105, just a few days before the end of the quarter Lehman would sell assets and use those proceeds to pay down its liabilities. By transferring tens of billions of dollars off its balance sheet, the firm became less leveraged and looked less risky to investors. Yet this transfer was only temporary. Immediately at the start of the new quarter—literally just long enough for the firm to produce its quarterly financial statement—Lehman would unwind the transaction and shift all the assets and liabilities back onto its balance sheet. Yet, since these billions of dollars in liabilities were not on its balance sheet at quarter end, executives at Lehman didn't need to disclose their existence to investors.

In internal e-mails, several senior members of Lehman's finance group questioned this dubious gimmick to make the firm appear less risky.

> Vallecillo: So what's up with repo 105? Why are we doing less next quarter end?
>
> McGarvey: It's basically window-dressing. We are calling repos true sales based on legal technicalities. The exec committee wanted

the number cut in half.

Vallecillo: I see . . . so it's legally do-able but doesn't look good when we actually do it? Does the rest of the street do it? Also is that why we have so much BS [balance sheet] to Rates Europe?

McGarvey: Yes, No and yes. :)

According to Martin Kelley, Lehman's global financial controller, "there was no substance to the transactions." The Repo 105 deals were simply done to improve the appearance of the publicly reported financial statements. Lehman's executives couldn't find a law firm in the United States willing to sign off on Repo 105 transactions, either. They eventually found a British law firm, Linklaters, that was willing to give its assurances on the use of Repo 105 under English law—but only if the transactions were executed in the UK. Lehman's executives figured out how to manage this requirement, too. To the extent that a US-based Lehman division sought to do Repo 105 transactions, executives could simply transfer the assets temporarily to a UK-based Lehman subsidiary, which could undertake the transaction itself.

Such creative efforts to sidestep regulation is consistent with what University of Chicago accounting Professor Roman Weil has called the "show me where it says I can't" approach to financial management. Weil argues that it has become common for managers to say, "detailed accounting rules cover so many transactions and none of them covers the current issue so we can devise accounting of our own choosing." A manager might infer that a transaction is acceptable and appropriate because he cannot find an explicit rule forbidding it. But relying on this logic leads to the calamitous and incorrect notion that regulation has managed to restrain all adverse conduct.

Fastow looks back on his career at Enron and wonders what he could have done differently. "If I had the character I should have had, I would have said time out . . . but I didn't," he explained. "But the reality is, if at any point in my career I said 'time out, this is bullshit, I can't do it' . . . they would have just found another CFO, but that doesn't excuse it. It would be like saying it's OK to murder someone because if I didn't do it someone else would have."

What makes fields like structured finance and tax challenging is that those who succeed often do so by being focused on rules rather than on principles. Individuals who are clever and figure out more creative solutions to "problems" are quickly rewarded.

"Everyone thinks these structured finance deals are reprehensible, but guys who find loopholes are sometimes celebrated," Fastow said wistfully. "The person who found the Apple tax loophole that's saved them literally tens of billions of dollars of income, I'm sure he's as well compensated as the guy who invented the iPad . . . that is, until someone in the government says maybe that is tax evasion instead of tax avoidance."

13

You couldn't stop because you would wreck everything

The Ponzi Scheme

NONE OF THE former executives I spoke with saw himself as a fraud. Some, of course, clearly recognized that they had committed a crime, but the person they saw in the mirror was successful, entrepreneurial, and ambitious. They didn't see themselves as the kind of people who would create fraudulent enterprises and swindle others.

Most victims of deception are easy to spot—the investors whose savings disappear, the employees who lose their jobs, the members of the public who feel betrayed by a person they once admired. But as I saw it, the individuals perpetrating these schemes were also victims of a sort—victims of their own self-deception.

It's difficult for most of us to comprehend how someone can create a fraud that causes losses in the hundreds of millions or even billions of dollars. When revealed, the magnitude of the deceit is so extraordinary and overwhelming that it's difficult to believe that anyone managing such an operation could ever have meant well. Yet, some of these frauds began as legitimate businesses.

What starts as a small problem, or an obstacle to surmount, grows. Unresolved, it escalates one small step at a time. The problem looks much like it did before to the person overseeing the firm. The problem's growing magnitude isn't readily perceptible. He's convinced that the issue can be overcome with a little more time, a change in market conditions, or just a bit more luck on the next deal. Far beyond the point where the fraud might be rectified by legitimate means, he still has trouble seeing exactly what he has created. After years of lying to himself, it can be difficult to see the truth even when it's clearly pointed out by others.

One particularly insidious type of deceptive enterprise is the Ponzi scheme. The operator of a Ponzi outwardly promises investors a healthy— even fantastic—return on their investment. But rather than invest these assets in legitimate profit-making activities, the manager uses the proceeds from new investors to pay what he promised earlier ones. A Ponzi scheme is fundamentally built on a lie and can be sustained only as long as enough new money is found to pay off prior obligations. The scheme seems so obviously fraudulent that it's hard to imagine the person behind such a scheme persuading himself otherwise.

"We are creative narrators of stories that tend to allow us to do what we want and that justify what we have done," explained psychologists Ann Tenbrunsel and David Messick. "We believe our stories and thus believe that we are objective about ourselves." But these stories may often be little more than fiction. Through both their use of language and their actions, the three men described in this chapter—Marc Dreier, Steven Hoffenberg, and Robert Allen Stanford—tried to hide what they were doing as much from themselves as from others. They deceived investors, employees, and the public, but each just as successfully deceived himself.

Surrendering to Ambition

"I was following a conventional path to success, from Yale College to Harvard Law School to a New York law firm. . . . Success seemed preordained," explained Marc Dreier, the founder and former head of Dreier LLP. "I didn't think too much about what success actually meant. I was simply comfortable with the expectation that if I continued down that path, I would be rewarded, sooner rather than later, with whatever it was that we were all striving towards. . . . I was just looking forward to being somebody. To being important. That was everything to me. And I thought it was my destiny."

By age fifty, Dreier thought he had achieved that destiny by creating an innovative law firm with over 250 attorneys. Dreier's firm succeeded in luring away entire departments of attorneys from competitors and acquiring a diverse base of clients in finance, real estate, fashion, and technology.

But in the fall of 2008, Dreier would find himself standing in the Canadian office of the Ontario Teachers Pension Fund impersonating another attorney in a desperate attempt to sell a fraudulent $50 million note to a hedge fund in order to keep Dreier LLP afloat. For all his ambitions and pretenses to success, Dreier had ended up creating a Ponzi scheme that relied on hundreds of millions of dollars of fraudulent promissory notes.

"This is not just a story about someone who engaged in a significant crime," Dreier pointed out to the writer Bryan Burrough soon after his arrest, "but the less dramatic point . . . is people who are following a certain path, who go to the right schools, who do the right things, you can still lose your way."

"Even a good person can lose their way."

DREIER APPRECIATED THAT he had a privileged upbringing. In high school he was voted "Most Likely to Succeed," and he excelled academically at Yale. Those around him were charmed by his personality and Dreier developed the self-assurance that he could accomplish whatever he set out to do. "I was ambitious and hard-working. . . . I was very confident in my apparent strengths and oblivious to my weaknesses." It was this sort of drive that sent Dreier on to Harvard Law School. "We were not at Harvard because we had weaknesses," he recalled of himself and his classmates.

After encountering little but success in his pre-professional life, Dreier had his first taste of a significant setback. Wachtell Lipton, a law firm that would later become the most prestigious and profitable in the country, had recruited Dreier for a summer internship after his second year at Harvard. Dreier enthusiastically looked forward to working under one of its senior litigation partners. Unfortunately, before Dreier arrived, the partner left Wachtell Lipton to serve as counsel for the Watergate committee. With that partner away, Dreier spent most of his summer assisting with corporate and tax-related work. "I made the very poor decision to pout most of the summer and give half an effort," Dreier lamented. He was bitterly disappointed when Wachtell Lipton did not extend him the customary post-graduation employment offer.

With this black mark on his résumé, Dreier found it more difficult to gain an offer from another top-tier New York law firm following graduation. The experience was sobering. "I realized for the first time that success might not come as easily as I assumed," Dreier recalled. "Recognition seemed more difficult to attain. It seemed to require not only talent but also some good luck and good choices."

Dreier eventually found work at Rosenman & Colin, a firm that had a distinguished litigation practice. He devoted himself to its practice and made partner. A decade later, in 1989, Dreier was offered the opportunity to join Fulbright & Jaworski, one of the larger and more prominent law firms in the country, to lead its litigation practice in New York. It was the chance at leadership that Dreier had long sought in his legal career, and he soon found a career-defining case. On behalf of the investment firm Wertheim Schroder & Company, Dreier began a complex securities suit against the global consumer-products manufacturer Avon about the redemption price of its preferred stock. After a judge permitted Dreier to represent all preferred stock holders in the case, Dreier saw damages potentially running into the hundreds of millions of dollars and his own reward in the tens of millions if he won the case.

In the midst of the litigation, Dreier's client, Wertheim, was acquired by a British investment bank that decided against continuing the costly suit against Avon. After spending many hours on the case and believing that there was much value in continuing the suit for other plaintiffs, Dreier objected. Rather than acquiescing to the wishes of the management committee, which sought to appease the client, Dreier made the surprising move to leave the firm. "I felt I could no longer work for or with people that I didn't find agreeable," Dreier recounted. "Although I had been a partner, I was still answering to senior partners whom I didn't very much respect and I was tired of it. . . . I knew that if I didn't try to do something soon to change my circumstances, they would never change."

"DURING MOST OF my years practicing law, I had never thought about starting a business or even being 'in business,'" Dreier explained. "I liked to think of myself instead as having a profession and being part of the community of large and established law firms that were not 'just' a business."

"I believed that I was a very talented litigator, but did not obtain the level of financial success or recognition that litigation partners were realizing at some other firms. . . . I was earning considerably less money and seemingly enjoying less prestige," Dreier recalled. "This became a source of considerable frustration."

Dreier also thought that starting a firm might satiate his own growing entrepreneurial stirrings. "I was becoming jealous of clients. Not just jealous of all the money they seemed to be making, but jealous of the businesses they were building, the tangible things they seemed to be accomplishing, and the satisfaction they seemed to obtain from that," Dreier explained. "I was very much drawn to the new challenge of being not just a lawyer, but starting and managing a business that would have my own imprint and would succeed or fail according to my own efforts and my own rules."

After more than two decades of practicing law, Dreier decided to create his own legal practice—one not only that he would lead but that would overcome what he saw as many of the impediments faced by the legal profession. He believed he could create a new type of firm that would be different from and superior to the prevailing models. "It was my impression that there was widespread dissatisfaction among attorneys working at large firms. They felt undervalued, unrespected, and underpaid, especially relative to their counterparts in the financial sector and many of the clients they were representing." Dreier said. "I started my firm with the very ambitious goal of reinventing the business model for law firms."

Individual attorneys were going to be given far greater autonomy at Dreier LLP. He wanted his partners to spend less time on mundane administrative matters and more time attracting lucrative clients. He'd eliminate the elements—lack of freedom, time, and support—that often hampered attorneys in creating their own individualized practice at other firms. Attorneys would receive a business development allowance that they would use to market and showcase their individual talents. Instead of relying on the firm's reputation as the means to generate new business, individual attorneys would nurture and grow their individual brands.

Dreier was also not wedded to the hourly-fee arrangement that was the bread and butter of the legal profession. He felt it was outdated and often poorly suited for attorneys. "'Successful' people—rich people—were not paid by the hour," Dreier remarked. "They were paid for results or expertise. Even doctors were not paid by the hour. Only lawyers. And this convention, more than anything else, was holding back law firms and frustrating their financial ambitions." Dreier encouraged his attorneys to devise new fee arrangements that better suited the particulars of each client. Dreier attorneys could charge a traditional hourly fee, but they were also free to consider result-driven, flat, or contingency-based fees.

Perhaps most radically, Dreier planned to overturn the usual way attorneys were themselves compensated. At most large firms, remuneration was mainly driven by seniority and the firm's overall performance. Dreier wanted to shift away from this model and instead tie each partner's compensation much more closely to what they generated.

Dreier's proposals were unquestionably innovative. But attorneys, especially those who already had established practices, were a risk-averse group. Without the name recognition or prestige of other top New York firms, Dreier needed to figure out how to make his upstart venture attractive. He immediately looked at the significant financial outlay that most law firms expected of their partners. "Under the conventional business model for law firms, the partners underwrote the expenses of the firm by making contributions to the firm's capital upon joining the partnership." The contribution was a major financial sacrifice—often hundreds of thousands of dollars—and it would be returned only when an attorney retired or left the firm. Dreier decided to forgo the capital contribution as a financial inducement. "They could leave their old firm and pocket their capital contribution rather than reinvest it." But Dreier decided to go even further to attract what he felt was the best legal talent. When a new attorney joined the firm, Dreier offered an attractive level of guaranteed base compensation projected by the fees that the lawyer was expected to generate.

All of these changes were devised to make Dreier LLP a lucrative and liberating environment for the attorneys it attracted. But for Dreier to succeed, he still needed to convince prospective attorneys that this model was tenable. "A business model in which a single partner—me—bears all the firm's expenses posed two large problems," Dreier explained. "First, I had to convince prospective parties that I could readily carry these expenses before they were prepared to join the firm. And secondly, I had to actually be able to do so once they did join. Neither was easy."

As with almost any entrepreneurial venture seeking to rapidly grow and expand, some financial strain was expected, and Dreier LLP was no exception. Successful contingency-based deals could take years to pay off, and in the interim Dreier was expected to bear all the expenses of the firm and his attorneys' guaranteed base compensation. Running the business frugally was one option to help the firm manage costs while it grew. But the attorneys Dreier sought to attract wanted demonstrated success, in Dreier's opinion, rather than simply the prospect of success and stability in the future. To project this success, even in its earliest days, Dreier spent lavishly on office space and on acquiring the trappings associated with a top legal practice.

To fund the firm's growth to recruit new attorneys, Dreier initially borrowed heavily at high interest rates. As the firm grew and developed economies of scale, he reasoned that these costs would become more manageable. It wasn't long before he appreciated that just the opposite seemed to be occurring. "I had badly underestimated the operating expenses of the firm—and as the firm grew, the expense got entirely out of control." Costs grew exponentially with the firm's expansion, while revenue growth was modest by comparison.

"It was this dilemma—my need to service this ever-increasing debt and to bear the ever-increasing expenses of the law firm, while at the same time not appear to be financially needy in any way which would undermine the appeal of the firm to prospective partners and clients—which ultimately drove me to my Ponzi scheme."

DREIER SAW THAT he wouldn't be able to fund his firm entirely by legal means. "It was late in 2001 that I first thought of the notes as a vehicle to misappropriate money and I began to do so not long thereafter, in early 2002," Dreier recalled.

Dreier decided to acquire much-needed additional capital by selling debt to hedge funds under the pretense that it was from Solow Realty. Dreier had previously represented Sheldon Solow, the billionaire real estate mogul and owner of Solow Realty, in several contentious lawsuits, so investors naturally assumed that Dreier spoke on Solow's behalf. Solow's significant wealth also meant that few investors would question the creditworthiness of the notes. "Solow was known as a very unorthodox, but successful, real estate developer, which allowed me to convince investors that the notes were genuine," Dreier explained. Hedge funds represented an appealing target for Dreier's deception. "They had relatively young and inexperienced people in a position to commit a lot of money without too much oversight," Dreier pointed out. "They were greedy and found the premium return irresistible, even if it might seem too good to be true."

The obvious challenge of selling debt notes ostensibly backed by Solow's realty business was that Dreier needed documentation of its financial condition. Fortunately, Solow's business was privately held, so little information was public. While this meant Dreier had to concoct a set of plausible financial statements from scratch, it also had the advantage that investors wouldn't be able to readily check the information Dreier produced. "I was a litigator, not a corporate lawyer, but I had enough familiarity with such documents to use various models that my firm had prepared on other matters and to work off form documents that were often provided by the hedge fund investors," Dreier explained. Using some publicly available statements, "I managed to mimic and extrapolate from the financials."

Dreier's first pitch was to a large Connecticut-based hedge fund called Amaranth. He explained that Solow Realty needed $20 million in additional capital to expand its real estate operations. Backed by documents that Dreier provided, the deal soon went through with little resistance. After selling that first note, Dreier recalled, "I felt relief, not so much that I was worried it would not work, but more that I would now be able to get out from under my debt and start to operate the firm more ambitiously. . . . I was feeling that this first note was sort of giving me a new start, which added to my sense of relief and even optimism."

Dreier used the funds to expand the number of attorneys at his firm and renovate the office space to the lavish standards of other top New York law firms. But these represented immense financial outlays that quickly consumed the proceeds generated by selling the note. "The initial misappropriation proved to be inadequate to make the firm what I wanted," Dreier said, " . . . so I did it again." Dreier sold another $40 million note, then a $60 million note.

At the same time that Dreier was expanding his law firm from the proceeds of the notes, his personal spending rose dramatically. "I had to be the most important reflection of the firm's success. . . . I had to cultivate a financial reputation as someone who was reaping the rewards of my new law firm model to such an extent that there was no doubt about my financial wherewithal to continue to grow and bankroll the firm," Dreier explained. "I attempted to do that by frequently entertaining clients and attorneys on my yacht, in my glamorous apartment, at my Hamptons beach house, and even the upscale restaurant that I bought in LA for the very purpose of showing off there. . . . This of course only added to my financial burden, but was indispensable to maintaining the image of success that was necessary to succeed."

Dreier believed the firm would eventually earn enough money that he could pay off the fraudulent loans and extricate himself from his crimes in such a way that his firm would survive and even thrive. "The firm was making money," he insisted. "Fees were exceeding normal operating expenses and margin was growing. There was also the prospect of big payoffs down the road from ongoing contingency cases." Some aspects of Dreier's model for his firm were, at least in theory, working as he had hoped. At the same time, however, "revenues were certainly growing significantly each year, but my capital expenses and operating expenses were growing even more quickly. I never let the revenue catch up to the costs because I felt compelled to keep investing in the firm so that it could have the type of impact, in terms of the lawyers and clients it would attract, that would position it eventually for sustained success." Dreier summed it up: "My ambitions outstripped my finances."

Fortunately for Dreier, when notes came due, many investors simply rolled them over and renewed them for another year. They asked few questions and were content with Dreier's explanation that Solow was too busy to discuss deals in person. Dreier avoided the uncomfortable—and impossible—position of returning the funds he borrowed.

"While I became more proficient technically at falsifying documents, after the first year or two it become more and more difficult to find funds that would take my notes," Dreier recalled. He began to slowly increase the rate of interest offered by the notes—from 8 percent, to 9 percent, then 10 percent.

But the balance that Dreier managed to construct rapidly dissolved in the financial crises of 2008. "As the credit markets tightened, those that were interested were demanding more specificity in the financial information and bigger returns," Dreier explained. He began offering investors a 12 percent interest rate and shorter maturities. This still wasn't enough, so he presented investors the opportunity to purchase preexisting notes—notes supposedly issued previously to other investors, both at attractive interest rates and at a discount to their face value. "Initially," Dreier re-counted, "the discounts were only a few percent, but ultimately I sold notes for as much as 30 percent off the principal amount." But by the fall of 2008, with the failure of multiple financial institutions looming, Dreier couldn't satisfy the needs of hedge fund investors by offering attractive rates. The hedge funds had their own redemptions to manage and were demanding their money back when their notes came due. Dreier saw what was ahead: $48 million due in September 2008, $15 million in November, and another $100 million in December. In January 2009, he'd need still $100 million more. It was an extraordinary amount of cash to return to investors.

The situation grew even worse when one of his attorneys called Dreier to say that he required almost $40 million from one of Dreier LLP's es-crow accounts to pay creditors. But less than half that amount was still in the account: Dreier had already used it to pay back principal on a note that had come due. Just in time, Dreier found an investor willing to pur-chase a sufficient amount of notes by offering very attractive terms to make it through to the end of the year. But during Thanksgiving week, the hedge fund unexpectedly backed away. Panicking, Dreier desperately sought to avoid a collapse. "By the end of 2008, I had run out of hedge funds interested in Solow notes."

Dreier tried one more trick. "If I could find a different 'borrower' with similar credentials," he realized, "some funds might still be interested." One of the largest purchasers of Dreier's fraudulent Solow notes, Fortress Investment Group, already had more than $100 million outstanding Solow notes. Dreier thought he had a solution. "The Ontario Teachers Pension Fund was a client of mine at the law firm. They seemed like a good possibility as a substitute for Solow because they managed a great deal of pension money and were widely perceived as very creditworthy," Dreier explained. He fabricated a note from the Ontario Teachers Pension Fund and offered it to Fortress.

As Dreier hoped, Fortress was interested. The fund agreed to purchase a $50 million note backed by Ontario Teachers the following week. There was just one condition: "Fortress insisted on an in-person execution of the Ontario Teachers note. They insisted that the note be signed in their presence as compared to all the prior notes where the hedge funds had accepted e-mailed signatures of the borrower which I could therefore forge." Dreier realized that getting this deal closed was going to be far more difficult. "That money had to be presented in court the following day. So, it was a different and even more urgent need to obtain new money than in the past."

Dreier concluded that there was only one possible solution: "I had to impersonate an officer of the Ontario Fund at the signing."

He flew to Toronto to act as the attorney from the Ontario Teachers Pension Fund. "Because I had succeeded with some impersonations and brazen acts before, I entertained the possibility that I could somehow do it again, even though this particular impersonation was far riskier and even more ridiculous," Dreier recalled. "As strange as it sounds, not getting caught just wasn't my main priority. My priority was still to find some way, even if it was far-fetched, to keep the debt current and keep the firm alive and keep my reputation."

It was an audacious idea that collapsed when the representative from Fortress with knowledge of people at the Ontario Teachers Pension Fund didn't recognize Dreier. "After I went through with the impersonation in Toronto, I knew that the representative of the hedge fund at the signing had been suspicious. I left for the airport where my chartered plane was waiting, but at the airport I received a call from the head of the fund telling me that they thought something was wrong," Dreier explained. "At that point I could have boarded the plane and fled," Dreier recalled, thinking of the alternative options that were available but not taken. "Instead, I went back to the office of the Teachers Fund, thinking I could possibly still talk my way out of it."

After seven years and nearly $800 million in fabricated notes, though, Dreier was finally cornered. Canadian police arrested him in the Ontario Teachers' offices. A United States court would sentence Dreier to twenty years in prison.

"It's a slippery slope once you surrender to ambition," Dreier commented. "I did not set out to steal hundreds of millions of dollars, but ended up doing so incrementally after crossing a line I could not retreat from. . . . Once I started, there seemed to be no way out other than to continue."

Like Dreier, Charles Ponzi, the businessman for whom the Ponzi scheme was named, believed he had an idea for a lucrative business. In the early twentieth century, a consortium of governments created a system of International Reply Coupons designed to make it easier for individuals to send the cost of return postage to a correspondent in another country. These coupons could be purchased at post offices around the world and sent in the envelope along with a letter. The recipient could redeem the coupon for local stamps to send a letter back.

After World War I, the exchange rates between currencies fluctuated dramatically, a circumstance that the creators of the International Reply Coupons had not anticipated. Ponzi realized that this situation had created the potential for significant profit. A person could buy reply coupons in countries where the currency was severely devalued, like Spain or Italy, and mail them to the United States to be redeemed at much higher prices. Pleased by the results of experiments using a few coupons from friends in Europe, Ponzi set out to attract investors with promises of 50 percent returns on their capital in ninety days. Soon enough, hundreds of people poured tens of thousands of dollars into his Securities Exchange Company.

Even with millions of coupons, however, there was no way Ponzi could fulfill his promises of profits on that scale. Even if he acquired the extraordinary number of coupons needed to fuel the business, a doubtful proposition in itself, the costs of physically moving and exchanging them would make the operation unsustainable. Ponzi's ambitions outstripped his financial reality. He began using capital from new investors to pay back prior investors' contributions. But even as his situation grew out of control, Ponzi remained optimistic that he could get out of the scheme he created. "I was getting accustomed to chasing rainbows," Ponzi later wrote. "As one would fade away, I would pursue another. For a dreamer, I certainly was persevering. I never was a quitter." Dreier was not a quitter, either. He believed that if Dreier LLP had "survived just another year or two," his strategy of investing in contingency legal work would have paid off very handsomely.

Optimism is a characteristic that serves human beings well in many circumstances. It spurs determination during difficult times and encourages tenacity when the odds of success look bleak. For entrepreneurs, optimism is a critical prerequisite to taking the risks that inevitably arise in building a new venture. While advantageous at times, optimism can also mask reality by creating the false hope that things will be different in the future. Dreier believed he was destined to create something successful and failed to appreciate the waywardness of his approach as he sought that greatness. "I overestimated myself," Dreier now concedes.

"For six-plus years I did manage to pay everyone everything that was owed to them, plus a very nice profit for them. I did this, of course, by victimizing new lenders who, inevitably, would suffer the loss, but I continued to believe that somehow I would turn the firm into such a money-maker that I would be able to cover all the debt," Dreier explained. "I also believed, even if very irrationally, that I would not end up hurting people, because, in the end, everyone would be paid."

Dreier was respected by his employees and valued by his clients. This made it easier for him, even rewarding in a way, to continue the scheme. "I was keeping lots and lots of people employed at the firm and . . . they were in a way unwittingly benefiting from my perpetuating the scheme," Dreier explained. "I tried to rationalize that the potential harm was offset by the current good and just hoped that it would somehow all work out."

Inside a Ponzi

What is it like to manage a Ponzi scheme? What ramifications does running a fraud have on the rest of a person's life? How does an executive proceed with "normal" business, knowing that their enterprise will eventually fail? During my conversation with Steven Hoffenberg, the chairman and CEO of Towers Financial Corporation, he described in blunt terms what it was like to create one of the largest Ponzi schemes in history.

In the 1980s, Hoffenberg helped pioneer a new kind of financing for health care providers known as factoring. Towers purchased, at a 5 percent discount, outstanding bills that insurance companies owed to hospitals, nursing homes, and other medical facilities. Towers would pay the hospital half the original amount in cash and then the remaining 45 percent once it had collected the receivables. It was an appealing arrangement for cash-strapped hospital administrators and lucrative for Towers. The receivables could often be collected in as little as a month or two, generating annual returns as high as 30 to 40 percent if all went according to plan.

The business took off. Within five years, Towers provided financing for 250 different health care providers. The *Wall Street Journal* lauded Towers as the "leading hospital-bill factoring firm." Employees at Towers were well compensated, and Hoffenberg provided perks, such as daily breakfast for all seven hundred employees, to help motivate and retain them.

Towers financed these medical receivables by issuing promissory notes to investors. Many investors found these notes attractive since the offering documents indicated that the amount of collateral underlying the notes was greater than the principal. Thus, even if Towers was unable to collect some of the debt from an insurer or health provider, investors could still anticipate seeing a return on their capital. The attractive risk-return profile enticed not only individual investors but also major institutional accounts like the pension fund of the city of Detroit and even the Roman Catholic Church. Over 2,800 investors from across the country invested in Towers' notes.

Hoffenberg's zeal propelled him to expand his business even more rapidly. Towers moved into other areas of debt collection and into new business areas entirely. The firm quickly acquired large amounts of receivables, but in its haste, many of these turned out to be of dubious quality. Losses piled up as Towers paid more for bundles of receivables than it was ultimately able to collect. Still, Towers was expected to pay the generous rates of return it promised investors on its notes. If Towers didn't fulfill its obligations on its promissory notes, it would default. Yet, Hoffenberg saw that the only way that Towers would have sufficient cash to pay back these investors was to issue more notes. The business model was working, Hoffenberg felt, but he just needed more time.

Further complicating matters was Hoffenberg's realization that it would be difficult to sell additional notes if Towers exposed its existing losses. Towers' investors sought stable returns backed by the promise of reliable collateral. To satisfy investors' expectations, Hoffenberg and his employees decided to make a variety of "adjustments" to the firm's accounting to bolster the firm's financials. When they began collecting receivables, Towers showed the anticipated amount of collectables immediately as income, even before the collections process began. When Towers was simply acting as a collections agent for a fee, rather than as the owner of the receivables, Towers' financial records would show it

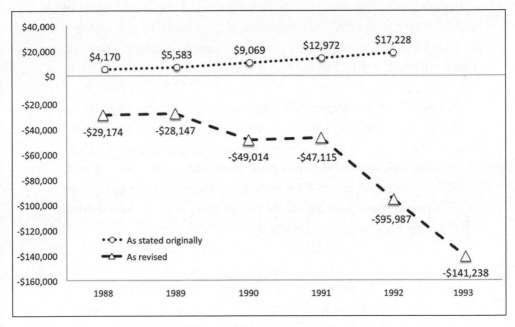

Figure 13.1: Towers income as reported to investors
and as later restated by the bankruptcy trustee.

owning the receivables anyway. And when uncollected receivables were past due and were therefore unlikely to be collected, employees at Towers "refreshed" the dates so the receivables appeared to be new. These adjustments transformed the income statement of Towers from heavily loss-making to dazzlingly profitable.

In 1993, only a year after the *Wall Street Journal* extolled Towers for its innovative business, the firm collapsed. Strikingly, what had begun as a potentially prosperous idea, one that even the bankruptcy trustee described as a "terrific business," devolved into a business that sustained itself only by selling new notes to pay off earlier notes—a Ponzi scheme. Hoffenberg was sentenced to twenty years in prison, and a judge imposed on him an extraordinary restitution of $475,157,340 for losses associated with the fraud.

Did Hoffenberg feel reluctant, guilty, or afraid as his firm unwound? Did he understand the problem was growing and would inevitably lead to collapse? During our conversations, Hoffenberg shared his perspective of a chief executive running a Ponzi scheme. Excerpts from this dialogue illustrate how Hoffenberg viewed running a deceptive enterprise as a pragmatic issue rather than a moral one.

> Soltes: How did the amount of fraudulent notes grow so rapidly?
> Hoffenberg: Once you start a Ponzi scheme and go into the cash register, you can't get out. You eat up so much money going into the cash register that you need more and more money to feed it—so you're stuck. They were throwing money at me and the more business we did, the more losses we had. . . . You couldn't stop because you would wreck everything.

> Soltes: Weren't you apprehensive about the consequences?
> Hoffenberg: Morals go out the window when the pressure is on. When the responsibility is there and you have to meet budgetary numbers, you can forget about morals. Circumstances overrule morals.

> Soltes: How did sustaining this fraud affect your life?
> Hoffenberg: When you're a CEO doing a Ponzi, you have to put your life into different boxes. You don't have a choice. You have to put your family life into one box, your business in a box, your emotions in another. You've got no choice. That's the way it had to work or you can't function. If you put things in boxes, you'll be able to slide through and pull it off.

As Hoffenberg revealed during our conversations, he viewed the Ponzi at Towers as simply another business problem to manage. Although as chairman and CEO he appreciated at some abstract level that he had responsibility for the consequences of the fraud, the magnitude of the problem never resonated with him emotionally. He didn't see himself as personally selling notes to investors. He wasn't the Towers accountant who created the adjustments in the financial records. He didn't physically print the financial statements depicting the false numbers. It's as though he feels that he didn't perpetrate the fraud and instead was a bystander to his own decisions.

Soltes: Did you ever feel guilty about selling these notes to investors and sustaining this fraud?

Hoffenberg: I never sold securities. I'm a salesman and creator of innovative products. I'm on the road or on an airplane. I had nothing to do with selling the Ponzi and I didn't do the accounting. I'm culpable, but I'm not the one doing it.

Soltes: As CEO of Towers, shouldn't preventing such a fraud have been your responsibility?

Hoffenberg: You just didn't have the time. The CEO is either a salesman or an accountant. You can't be both. There is not enough hours in the day. When you run a large company and you're CEO, you're faced with decisions all the time. Nobody can tell you that every decision they reach is right. This one was a bad call that hurt everything. It's that simple.

Soltes: What would you change if you had a chance to do it all over again?

Hoffenberg: Nothing . . . the model was perfect. It operated on eight cylinders and if not for the income-recognition wrong call, the company would have been a Fortune 1000 company. Keep in mind that Towers wasn't really a Ponzi. What the word "Ponzi" means is that you're taking new money to pay old money. That's not what Towers did. Towers invested this money and actually made a fortune on it, but we couldn't make the fortune quick enough and we turned left instead of right on some offering documents.

Hoffenberg had a deep sense of optimism about himself and even his firm despite the worsening of the deception. By seeing the fraud as separate from everything else in his life, he maintained an illusion of success that was bolstered by public recognition in places like the *Wall Street Journal*. Even amidst the fraud, he saw himself as running an accomplished—even thriving—business that simply had some "income-recognition" problems.

While Hoffenberg readily admitted that he ran a Ponzi scheme, he also felt that it was not truly a Ponzi. A Ponzi scheme, in essence, utilizes proceeds from issuing new notes to pay earlier notes that have come due. The only "business" in a pure Ponzi scheme is the ruse itself, making its collapse inevitable once the operator runs out of new investors to recruit. Yet, Hoffenberg considered Towers to be making investments in a myriad of businesses with the proceeds from the notes. Although the more he invested, the greater the losses, the proceeds from investors were not being strictly recycled from one investor to another. "We're not Bernie Madoff at all," he insisted to me. "He never invested anything, we invested everything."

This raises a question: At what point does a legitimate business become a Ponzi scheme? Many businesses sustain losses during their initial years, but their executives continue raising money. For example, the much-touted online grocery service Webvan, which collapsed in 2001, raised hundreds of millions in financing without ever being able to anticipate turning a profit. "We expect to continue to have operating losses and negative cash flow on a quarterly and annual basis for the foreseeable future," the company told investors when it prepared for its initial public offering. Yet, despite the highly speculative nature of the business model, which struck many as destined to fail, the entrepreneurs leading Webvan certainly did not regard themselves as sustaining a deceptive enterprise when they sought additional funding.

Whenever new capital is raised to pay off prior obligations to investors for a faltering enterprise, the company begins to slowly take on the characteristics of an illusionary scheme. The question is, when does a business go from legitimate but unsustainable to being a Ponzi? And should the intentions of the executives matter in making this determination?

At a bank run by Sir Allen Stanford, just this question is at issue.

Anticipating a Ponzi

In 2008 Stanford sat comfortably at number 205 on the Forbes List of the richest Americans, with an estimated net worth of $2.2 billion. He was the most prominent private benefactor on the small island nation of Antigua, where his firm, Stanford Financial Group, was based. Many knew him by the honorific "Sir Allen" after he was knighted by Antigua's governor-general in November 2006.

Stanford's bank offered clients the opportunity to purchase certificates of deposit (CDs). In the United States, CDs are generally viewed as conservative investments that provide more attractive returns than savings accounts. Stanford bested American banks by offering 2 percent, or sometimes even more, for CDs at his bank. The better rates that he offered helped his bank prosper, and the deposits grew from half a billion dollars in 1999 to over $8 billion in 2008—a growth rate of over 30 percent a year. By the start of 2009, Stanford boasted that the bank had over 30,000 depositors from 131 countries.

But in February 2009, officials from the United States raided Stanford's bank and abruptly shut down his operations. The SEC called his business "a fraud of shocking magnitude that has spread its tentacles throughout the world." Prosecutors alleged that Stanford misrepresented his offerings to investors and misappropriated billions in investor money for his own personal consumption and investment. According to the charges, Stanford's bank had some limited investments but was at its very essence a Ponzi scheme that issued new CDs to pay off redemptions of earlier CDs. Stanford pled not guilty to the charges against him, but he would be found guilty at trial. In 2012, he was sentenced to 110 years in prison for orchestrating the fraud.

"I am sure your 'real' opinion of me, like 99% of the world, is I am a rotten piece of shit who stole from widows and orphans and got what I deserve," Stanford wrote in one of his early letters to me. "However, there really is another side to the Stanford story, and it is 180 degrees different than what is currently in the public domain."

Stanford wanted to show me how he saw his business.

ONE FACT BEYOND dispute was that Stanford's empire was expansive. His firm consisted of approximately 150 legal entities, with 128 physical offices in 14 different countries. Stanford was Board Chairman of the 12 largest affiliates. For others, sister companies as he liked to call them, he delegated responsibility and sought to maintain the "the view from 41,000 feet" with reports from regional representatives.

At the center of this empire was the Stanford International Bank (SIB), which issued CDs to investors at attractive interest rates. In early 2009, SIB offered a one-year CD for 4.5 percent, while the average at US banks was 2 percent. Stanford responded to claims that his rates seemed too generous: "Although SID CD rates were consistently higher by 2 percent, these rates were neither unusual nor extraordinarily high when compared to our non–US bank foreign competitors."

Stanford contended that his bank offered higher rates for several reasons. "SIB had several operational advantages over US domestic banks," he explained, "but SIB's greatest advantage that resulted in the bank's depositors earning a higher return than paid by US banks was SIB's 'operating philosophy.'"

Stanford explained to me the four operating advantages that he believed allowed SIB to offer these more generous rates to clients. First, the bank operated in a jurisdiction that left profits untaxed. Second, because it was privately owned, SIB could return money to depositors without worrying about investors. Third, it offered relatively few products, and these were "easy to administer, low risk, and generally all profitable." Finally, since SIB had only its headquarters in Antigua ("a state of the art physical plant of nearly 40,000 sq ft.," Stanford noted) and one small office in Montreal, it could channel the savings on overhead to its customers.

To bring in new deposits to the bank, Stanford relied on affiliate companies domiciled in each country to market CDs to prospective clients. When an investor purchased a CD, SIB would pay the affiliate a referral fee of 1 percent to 3 percent of the CD's face value. By having affiliates sell CDs, rather than the bank itself, Stanford explained, "SIB did not have the costs associated with a physical presence in that country and only paid for business that was generated as a result of the introduction of a new client to SIB in Antigua."

Stanford described to me how the bank invested the money once it arrived in the bank. "Although the Stanford business empire was large and diverse, we were never involved in exotic or difficult-to-understand investments or businesses. The Stanford Board had a fifteen-minute rule, which meant if we could not fully understand an investment or business, and all the risks associated with it in fifteen minutes, we never touched it." It was reminiscent of the rule of thumb often suggested by Warren Buffett, one of the savviest investors in recent history: invest only in businesses that can be readily understood and fall within one's circle of competence.

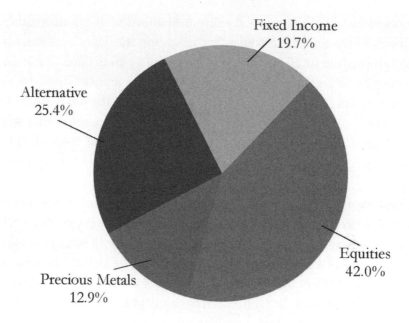

Figure 13.2: The portfolio of Stanford International Bank
according to its 2007 annual report.

Stanford explained how country-based affiliates helped pick many of the specific investment ideas. "Due to having our finger for years on the pulse of the investment opportunities in the affiliates' home countries," Stanford explained, "it provided many ground-floor investment opportunities for SIB in these markets. For example, in Ecuador, SIB was able to get in on the ground floor of a pharmaceutical company IPO that yielded SIB a 28 percent return on investment."

A 2008 brochure described the bank's investments as "a well-diversified portfolio of highly marketable securities issued by stable governments, strong multinational companies, and major international banks." A simple pie chart provided in the firm's annual report depicted the proportion of investment in various areas. For instance, the 2007 report depicted the investment categorization breakdown between fixed income and alternative investments.

The business, as Stanford saw it, was both simple and successful. Far from floundering or fraudulent when it was taken over by American regulators, he argued, the firm was thriving. "Why go after a solvent, vibrant, honest, global empire I had poured thirty years of my life into?"

GOVERNMENT PROSECUTORS CHARGED Stanford with misrepresenting the bank's investments, fraudulently overstating the value of assets, and misappropriating funds between affiliate firms he controlled. "First and foremost, he lied about what happened to depositor money," argued prosecutor William Stellmach in his closing statements to the jury. "He said it was going into safe, conservative, highly marketable securities that were highly liquid. And the truth was that he sank billions to keep afloat his companies down in the Caribbean and those businesses of his were money pits."

The allegation that investors were misled about the nature and risk of the bank's assets made Stanford furious. "Stanford was a hugely successful global company with none of the securitized subprime toxic shit—that was being peddled as safe and liquid—on our balance sheet," Stanford argued. He pointed out that, before the 2008 crisis, many of the leading financial institutions in the United States had held hundreds of billions of dollars in mortgage-backed securities rated as safe AAA. Yet, by 2010, over 90 percent of these securities were reduced to junk status. "Stanford did not invest in any of the securitized debt, sub-prime crap . . . not one dollar. . . . We stayed clear of the explosive derivatives markets altogether." It didn't make any sense to Stanford that prosecutors argued that he had mischaracterized the risks of his bank's assets if American banks were allowed to depict their subprime mortgage holdings as safe and liquid. To regulators, Stanford complained, "it didn't make a flying shit that Stanford never participated in any of this CDO-subprime toxic disaster. Not one dollar."

Even if investors were properly informed about the risks, could SIB repay depositors? The court-appointed receiver placed in charge of Stanford's bank said that the bank held less than $500 million in securities at the end of 2008—less than 7 percent of the bank's total obligation in CDs. Including the diverse set of other assets—real estate, aircraft, and other investments—the receiver argued that the combined value was less than $1 billion, suggesting that SIB was insolvent by more than $6 billion. Accordingly, the government alleged that the bank's liabilities so greatly exceeded its assets that Stanford's business was unsustainable.

Stanford rejected this estimate as biased. "Even though we were also affected in our investment portfolios and holdings [by the financial crises], the Stanford Financial Group of companies worldwide still had $3 billion more in assets than liabilities," he contended. He said there was much more cash and securities in other foreign accounts that simply had not been examined by the receiver. "What about the other 211 bank accounts and the billions of dollars they held and the other 220 investment accounts and the billions they held," he asked. "What happened to all that money that everyone seems to have forgotten about?" In addition to the cash and other liquid securities held by SIB, a significant portion of the bank's assets—upwards of 80 percent—was put into a diverse set of private equity and real estate investments that were not readily valued on any exchange.

The value of one project in particular—a luxury-club development in Antigua—became a major point of contention in Stanford's trial. As described by prosecutors, his bank purchased approximately 1,500 acres of land to build a resort for ultra-high-net-worth individuals for $64.5 million. This land was transferred to another Stanford entity, and a year later it was transferred back to the bank with a revised value of $3.2 billion. While prosecutors alleged that the increased value was unsubstantiated, to Stanford the revised valuation reflected the value of comparable per-acre values at other resort developments. The use of a per-acre value of $2 million, even lower than some other properties that sold for upwards of $5 million an acre, suggested that the Stanford property was valued at $3.2 billion. In Stanford's view, he was simply lucky to acquire the land at such a reasonable price. Thus, prosecutors alleged that the land was wildly overvalued, while Stanford claimed that using comparables to assess value, a method permitted under accounting rules, suggested that the same land was appropriately— even conservatively—valued. So, what was the fair value of this land?

Calculating the fair value of unique illiquid assets is subjective. How should we assess the market value, for instance, of a painting that's never been sold? Such values are subject to interpretation and to variation over time depending on what people are willing to pay. Appropriate assessments of fair value rely heavily on the assessor's or auditor's due diligence and expertise to verify that the estimate accurately reflects the market value of the asset.

The accountant for SIB was an Antiguan firm called Hewlett & Co., which employed fourteen people. I asked Stanford whether Hewlett might have been ill-suited to evaluate a global enterprise as complex as his. "Hewlett and Company had been the external auditors of all the Antigua-based companies for years," he wrote back in response. "They knew our operation and business model well, met all the stringent requirements to audit a group of companies of our size and complexity, and SIB's board was very confident and comfortable with the integrity and quality of the firm." When asked whether a well-known international auditor would have provided more assurance and a stronger defense when these valuations were questioned, Stanford replied: "The name of a US-based Big 4 accounting firm on SIB's financials would have meant nothing to the government and their panic-driven and greed-driven and career-driven agenda."

AFTER FEBRUARY 2009, regulators placed the SIB in the hands of a receiver because they saw the business as an unsustainable operation subsisting only on the inflows from additional CDs. Unlike most alleged Ponzi schemes, which are placed under the supervision of regulators only after collapsing, Stanford's bank was taken over in advance of such a failure, to "protect investors and to halt this fraudulent scheme," in the words of regulators.

"The bank's claims are improbable," noted regulators about the SIB's investment strategy, in their court request to take control of the firm. The question is how improbable must a bank's future be in order for regulators to shut it down and appoint a receiver. If there's a 50 percent probability of failure, regulators may be protecting additional investors from being duped, but they would just as likely be unjustly shuttering a sustainable business and harming current holders. If the business has a 75 percent likelihood of being insolvent, should it be shuttered? 90 percent? 95 percent? It's only once the business has failed that there is 100 percent certainty that closing the bank would have been in the best interest of all investors, but by then it is too late.

During the financial crisis of 2008, numerous large financial institutions found their own solvency dubious as the value of their assets sank. "It's difficult in the middle of a run or a panic to determine whether something is insolvent because you don't know how to value the assets," noted Harvard Law School professor Hal Scott. "At the end of the day, it's an art, not science. . . . [How to] determine whether an institution is, or isn't, solvent has been one of the most difficult problems for a very long time."

As Stanford saw it, American banks unrealistically described their subprime investments as safe assets based on full market prices, and when those assessments turned out to be wildly optimistic, the same banks were bailed out. Meanwhile, his bank made it through the crisis without financial assistance, and he was prosecuted simply because he was an easy scapegoat as a billionaire running an offshore bank. "No one in these Too Big to Fail institutions gets even a slap on the wrist," Stanford argued. "All these 'incompetent' employees of these huge Ponzi scheme institutions had to do to avoid any criminal prosecution for their clearly criminal actions was simply pay hundreds of billions of dollars in 'fines' to settle with the Department of Justice."

Stanford saw the major American financial institutions as the real fraudulent enterprises, whose executives merely paid their way out of facing serious punishment. Stanford continued: banks "didn't pay a nickel of these 'fines' themselves as these 'fines' were all paid for out of taxpayer bailout money, shareholders' money, or they simply told regulators they needed to raise some capital and issue some new debt or equity offering and get the same tax-paying public to fund a new round of capital infusion money to pay off these 'incompetent' greedy buffoon thieves criminal shenanigans."

Stanford often referred to regulators' prior inspections of his firm that found no evidence of wrongdoing. "No one lost a dime until the government took over Stanford's US operations . . . not one complaint. No one ever lost one dollar, ever." In a June 2005 meeting with colleagues, Jeffrey Cohen, the SEC's assistant director of enforcement, concluded that Stanford's business was operating appropriately. The minutes of the meeting reported Cohen's thoughts: "disclosure very cleverly crafted—impeccable for most part[.] Investors well off, enjoying returns—no concrete evidence of Ponzi." This sentiment was further echoed by others at the SEC. As noted by one of the SEC's attorneys, "unlike a lot of Ponzi schemes that have collapsed when you've got investors calling you and . . . they can't get their money out or there's clear misrepresentation . . . we just didn't have that."

Perhaps Stanford's bank could have represented its investment risks in a more transparent way. Maybe the investments were riskier and less liquid than described in its marketing documents. But what if Stanford's business was shuttered simply because it had the potential to fail? Could Stanford be right, and could regulators have shuttered a viable, solvent business?

IF STANFORD'S BUSINESS was as strong, stable, and legitimate as he argued, it's difficult to understand why there are so many contradictions.

For instance, Stanford prided himself on the employees he attracted to work at his companies. "I would stack the entire Stanford domestic and international talent pool up against any of our much larger competitors anywhere in the world," Stanford explained. "I can look back with pride at the rock-solid quality of human talent that allowed Stanford to achieve our consistent growth and success." Yet, it was several of Stanford's most senior executives who admitted to and later described in detail the alleged fraud at his firm.

One of the most important was James Davis, Stanford's chief financial officer. Davis was Stanford's college roommate at Baylor University. "Davis was . . . a solid, nose-to-the-grindstone, ultraconservative, straight-laced, well-grounded, commonsense-thinking, mature and ethical individual," Stanford recalled thinking when he hired him. Davis would later admit to government prosecutors that the Stanford bank was unsustainable and had reverse-engineered its financial reports to consistently show profits. Davis would also admit to tax evasion and misappropriating tens of thousands of dollars from his wife's life insurance policy, meant for his children, for his own use. "We made the worst choice imaginable in selecting Jim Davis," Stanford explained with the benefit of hindsight.

What puzzled me was that, in one e-mail, Stanford would defend Davis as having a "good analytical mind" who could adequately manage the complexities of leading the bank. Then in another e-mail, Stanford would call him a "spineless liar." It was difficult to reconcile how Davis could at once be sufficiently competent to manage a multibillion-dollar enterprise while personally compromised in so many ways.

To Stanford's own financial advisors, those tasked with selling CDs to investors, it was a mystery how the bank consistently generated its attractive returns. For instance, in March 2008, Scot Thigpen, a vice-president and financial advisor, e-mailed Neal Clement, another advisor, to ask how

SIB CDs could be viewed as so safe and reliable, given they were not backed by FDIC insurance as CDs are in the United States.

> Neal,
>
> Accredited Investors are pretty savvy investors lots of times. How do you show them these available CD rates and not have the info about the investment performance of the portfolio you can discuss with them. If the CD is backed by the portfolio, seems like we could show the portfolio returns. Nobody ever needs to see a report on FDIC insurance because the perception of that strength is already there. How do we get assurance that this portfolio/product is guaranteed and only have a "I have been told it is a strong portfolio" rationale to share. Make sense?
>
> This is an incredible time to be sharing this with accredited investors but it just seems that we need to be well equipped for the presentation.
>
> HELP!!!
>
> Scot

Less than twenty minutes later, Clement responded:

> Scot,
>
> I never talk about the SIB portfolio to any of my clients. I mention that the portfolio is managed by a large number of managers with large minimum (50M or more). I sell the CD just like a AAA bond. . . . If I have a client that has to see the portfolio, the SIB is not for them!!!!! . . .
>
> Neal Clement

If the investments were as successful as Stanford claimed, one wonders why the bank would be so reluctant to be more transparent about its strategy. It's also perplexing that neither the chief investment officer nor the chief financial officer—really, anyone beyond Stanford—understood the values of all the firm's assets.

No individual item proves with certainty that SIB was impossible to sustain. Even now, years after it was taken over by a receiver, the global complexity of the business makes a final reckoning about the bank difficult. Nevertheless, it's easy to see that Stanford's business was both less secure and more poorly managed than the one depicted in the glossy brochures that enticed many of the bank's clients. There was deception at the Stanford International Bank. The only question is how pervasive it had become, how long it had been going on, and whether it would inevitably have led to the bank's demise.

STANFORD AND I spent nine months exchanging messages during his appeal. He patiently addressed my questions about the operations, business, and management of his bank as I raised them. As 2015 came to a close, Stanford finally sent me an e-mail seeking my opinion. It read:

> I would like to know your honest and blunt opinion of the irrefutable facts that you have been presented with . . . and please Eugene, don't disrespect me by dancing around the question with a "politically correct" answer . . . in your own mind with all you know, am I guilty as convicted? . . . or was this all a huge charade of deflection, cover up and theft of unimaginable proportions all orchestrated by the SEC and supported and covered up by the DOJ and the courts? There truly is no other conclusion Eugene . . . it is black or white, not grey. I look forward to your quick and 100% honest no bullshit answer. And regardless of what your true feelings are we will always remain friends.
>
> Allen

I wasn't sure how to provide an honest opinion when clearly, in his mind, there was only one conclusion. I responded that it wasn't my place to play judge and jury, but there were also too many contradictions that I couldn't satisfactorily resolve with the data in front of me. If he wanted validation for his view of Stanford International, I couldn't provide it. "Your opinion is your opinion," Stanford replied diplomatically. "Even though I am extremely disappointed it does not change our relationship. . . . Only my walking out the front door of this shit hole will prove my innocence and even then not to all."

STANFORD DOESN'T FEEL shame or guilt for the losses incurred by the tens of thousands of investors at his bank because he sees the failure as resting with regulators. "The illegal and unconstitutional actions by the US government caused this implosion and thefts around the world," Stanford continued to insist. He also believes it is now impossible to recover many of the assets of his bank since they have fallen into the hands of corrupt legislators and bankers. "It is all part of the biggest theft caused by a US government agency in US history," Stanford maintained. "The end result is all this money and all the other assets are now lost, stolen, or national-ized, and were then sold or given away to politically connected people in the countries where Stanford had offices and where the US had no jurisdiction."

Ultimately, Stanford sees the world through a particular lens. He takes little responsibility for anything fraudulent discovered within his firm. He created a financial empire and believes that history will show that his firm achieved everything it claimed. "I will win this war," Stanford wrote me. "Make no mistake Eugene, I am going to win."

14

When I look back, it wasn't as if I couldn't have said no

Bernie Madoff

"I REALLY HAVE NOT been able to figure out how I let myself do this," Bernard Madoff expressed in frustration after serving two years of his 150-year sentence. "Is there a flaw in me?"

It was a serious question. Madoff often contemplated that perhaps the easiest and most sensible explanation for his behavior was to concede that he is an aberrant individual. The magnitude of the scheme he perpetrated—one that lasted decades and created tens of billions in fraudulent profits—baffles even him. "I don't expect your students to understand," Madoff went on. "It's hard for my own family to understand because the numbers were so goddamn large."

After being chronicled in a half-dozen books and a television mini-series, Bernie Madoff's career is well-known. He began as a trader in over-the-counter securities and grew into a leading broker of NASDAQ and off-exchange NYSE-listed securities. Less visibly, he ran a large investment advisory business offering stable and desirable returns. Unbeknownst to his many investment clients, however, this investment advisory business was a massive Ponzi scheme. When Madoff finally confessed that his investment advisory business was a fraud in 2008, billions in fictitious profits immediately vanished. Eventually, more than $20 billion in capital would be found to have been misappropriated among his many investors.

The effects of this fraud were extraordinary. Charities, schools, and the Jewish community were all deeply affected by the losses. Thousands of investors were left scrambling to ascertain what they lost and what they might be able to recover. The financial statements that Madoff's firm had been sending them for years were completely fictitious. Under the intensity of the ensuing scrutiny, Madoff's eldest son committed suicide. Instead of enjoying a comfortable retirement after a constructive and prosperous career in the securities industry, Madoff will die in a federal prison.

These are the descriptive facts about a man's career and the cataclysmic effects of his actions on those who once trusted him. But why it happened—why Madoff would create the largest Ponzi scheme in history—cannot be understood by simply examining this narrative.

"There is a difference between the two examples of wrongdoing," Madoff once reflected. The first, Madoff went on, is "where someone starts out deciding to do wrong." The entrepreneur who creates an operation with no pretense of legitimacy falls neatly into this group. The second type of wrongdoing arises when an executive "finds himself trapped in a business situation and makes the tragic mistake that he believes will eventually work itself out." This is someone who intended to create a worthwhile and sustainable enterprise but, when pressed under difficult circumstances, chooses to engage in duplicity rather than see his business slow or fail. Both are failures with adverse consequences, but the origins of the duplicity are different.

Given the duration of Madoff's fraud, many are quick to place Madoff in the first category, as someone whose objectives were nefarious from the very beginning. But such an interpretation gives him too much credit. Madoff's scheme lasted longer and was more "successful" than anyone could ever have planned. Further complicating this explanation is that Madoff did have considerable professional success outside his fraudulent investment advisory business. In fact, numerous important—and profitable—innovations can be traced to advances heralded by his firm. Among these, Madoff introduced new technology that improved efficiency and reduced the costs of trading securities. His efforts to divert trading away from the NYSE floor helped democratize securities markets. Together, these innovations helped propel Madoff's firm to handle 10 percent of all NYSE-listed stock trading by the early 1990s. As one group of finance scholars put it at the time, "The successful securities market of the future will not imitate the New York Stock Exchange; it will imitate the entrepreneurial spirit of the likes of the Madoff brothers." In light of the professional accolades Madoff accumulated from his market-making activities, his failure was not inevitable from the start.

Still, Madoff's fraud is far too large to be viewed as an isolated error in judgment. Time and time again, Madoff had the opportunity to avoid fraudulent activity, curtail its escalation, and prevent further damage. "When I look back, it wasn't as if I couldn't have said no," Madoff acknowledged. "It wasn't like I was being blackmailed into doing something." He had the opportunity to prevent the catastrophe that he created, but chose not to. His decision was all the more significant because of his position of leadership. "I know the rules and regulations better than most people because I drafted most of them," Madoff explained to regulators two years before confessing his fraudulent investment advisory business. "The bad news is if I violated them, I can't say I didn't know, I was ignorant. I know what the rules are."

It would be convenient if wrongdoing could easily be ascribed either to poor intentions or to challenging circumstances combined with shortsighted choices. However, this distinction falsely simplifies matters because choices are a reflection of both innate dispositional factors and environmental influences.

Much of the emphasis in prior chapters has been on how the particular circumstances faced by executives facilitated their ability to overlook the harm of their actions. Like some of these cases, Madoff's victims praised, even celebrated, him while he was defrauding them. It was only later, once his deception was revealed, that his investors would react as victims. This difference in timing helped Madoff avoid the need to directly confront the harm of his actions while he was perpetrating his fraud.

Yet, Madoff's fraud is distinctly different from many other prominent cases of executive malfeasance. It wasn't that his victims were distant unknown individuals whom he could not relate with. Madoff intimately knew many of the people who would later call themselves his victims. And even after his fraud was exposed and the devastation became evident, the harm still didn't deeply resonate with Madoff.

Madoff's failure is a tragic amalgamation of character and circumstance. It is only by understanding how these factors work in concert that we can come to appreciate the origins of the largest Ponzi scheme in history.

MADOFF'S UNASSUMING ENTRANCE into the securities market began in 1960. Lacking the pedigree or personal connections to join one of the prestigious firms in New York, Madoff initially set up shop at an empty desk in his father-in-law's accounting firm, far from the glamour of Wall Street. With savings accumulated from work during college and some gifts from his recent wedding, Madoff began trading over-the-counter (OTC) securities that didn't meet the stringent requirements for trading on one of the larger regional or national exchanges. The thinly traded and weakly regulated nature of the OTC exchange made it the "wild west" of securities markets, where significant amounts of money could be quickly made or lost.

Madoff joked that "people always said, 'show me a businessman who doesn't take risk and I'll show you a businessman who's unsuccessful.'" Volatile as the OTC market was, trading OTC stocks provided a pathway for entrepreneurial types like Madoff to seek their fortune on Wall Street. Among its benefits, the OTC market lacked the steep membership fees that were required on the more established exchanges. "I clearly was an outsider of the establishment, not coming from money or even a connected family," Madoff explained. But starting his own firm—Bernard L. Madoff Investment Securities—was empowering. "All of sudden I had the mindset where I felt that I could accomplish anything."

One of the most daunting challenges for any investor seeking to buy one of the thousands of OTC stocks was getting reliable price information. There was neither a physical floor exchange where traders convened to transact nor an automated system providing timely data. Instead, the most authoritative source available was a legal-size directory printed on pink paper that showed quotes for different stocks. Available by subscription, the directory—known as the "pink sheets"—provided the dealers' names, phone numbers, and offering prices for thousands of securities.

An inescapable challenge of relying on this directory was that the information it contained was already outdated by the time it arrived on Madoff's desk. Overnight news and further trading during the day influenced investors' willingness to transact stocks. To get a sense of the prices at which brokers were offering to buy and sell, Madoff, like other traders, would call around to get up-to-date information. Each time Madoff placed a trade, it was manually logged into his trading ledger, often with the assistance of his wife, Ruth. Madoff would then wait for the delivery of the physical stock certificates, hoping each time that the counterparty wouldn't renege on the trade.

Besides trading in his own account, Madoff purchased stocks for his modest base of clients. In 1962, he purchased several promising new ventures trading on the OTC market. His prediction turned out to be wildly optimistic. The firms soon failed, virtually wiping out the accounts of his clients. "I took a risk which I didn't really understand," Madoff later recalled. "Then I felt guilty about it." In hopes of keeping the investors from fleeing after incurring such losses, Madoff decided to buy these largely worthless securities back from his clients. It was a costly decision that erased most of the profits he had made thus far, but it preserved his reputation. "After that," Madoff explained, "I wanted to limit the risk I took, which is why I got involved in arbitrage." With the limited capital he still had remaining, Madoff decided to focus on less speculative forms of trading.

Market makers, like Madoff, were stockbrokers who offered to buy or sell a stock whenever a client called. For each security they were active in, market makers set a "bid" price equal to the price they would be willing to buy the stock at and an "ask" price for which they'd be willing to sell the stock. In the OTC markets, where there was little price transparency, the gulf between what traders were willing to buy and sell a stock at was large—often as much as 20 or 30 percent. By persistently calling around to different brokers, Madoff often found pricing discrepancies between what different dealers were offering to buy and sell a stock at. This created an arbitrage opportunity whereby Madoff could purchase a stock from one broker and then quickly resell it to another at a profit.

Amidst larger and better-known dealers, Madoff found it difficult to distinguish himself. It was an intensely competitive business in which relationships often trumped performance. Madoff wanted to stand out by offering better quotations than other dealers, but there were few ways to let other brokers know these prices. Traders continued to pass over his small outfit for more established firms.

Luckily for Madoff, in 1963 the SEC published a study urging significant changes in the securities markets. Among the suggestions made by regulators was the need for more transparent pricing in the OTC market. Spurred on by recent computing innovations, regulators envisaged a system that would display the best "bid" and "ask" price from dealers throughout the day. By providing visibility to whichever market maker offered the most competitive quotes, the system would give eager upstarts like Madoff the opportunity to compete against even the largest firms. Not surprisingly, Madoff—along with his brother Peter, who joined his firm—enthusiastically embraced this technological push and joined the working group to create the system. By investing early, they were well poised to benefit from the launch of the first automated national securities market, the NASDAQ, in 1971.

Appreciating the advantages that technology offered their firm, Madoff and his brother sought other ways to attract orders by processing them electronically. Madoff initially focused on OTC stocks, but the far more liquid NYSE-traded stocks offered more lucrative and less risky trading opportunities. Madoff's firm was not a member of the NYSE, so he could not trade on the floor of the exchange. But Madoff realized there was an opportunity to turn this restriction onto itself. NYSE members had the exclusive right to trade on the floor of the exchange, but its members were barred from trading NYSE securities off the exchange floor. Not bound by this restriction, Madoff decided to create an off-exchange market for NYSE securities. Although others had done this before for large institutional accounts, Madoff realized that by streamlining the process electronically he could process massive volumes of retail orders through his firm at a lower cost than the NYSE.

Madoff's timing was fortunate since regulators also wanted to see the monopolistic grip of the NYSE loosened. Other firms soon joined Madoff in trying to attract trades off the NYSE floor. In an attempt to stand out, Madoff advertised in newspapers and began guaranteeing execution that was at least equal to, but often better than that on the NYSE. Seeking to further distinguish himself, Madoff decided to introduce an innovation that would court significant controversy among exchange members. He borrowed a practice that had long been used by dealers in OTC securities: Madoff would offer financial incentives to brokers who traded with his firm. Thus, instead of charging a commission to trade like most firms, he'd actually pay brokerages a penny a share to send their trades to his firm. Madoff's profitability would rely entirely on his ability to capture the spread, or difference between the "bid" and "ask" price, when trading securities.

Not surprisingly, Madoff's offer to pay for trading volume turned out to be highly alluring. Madoff began gaining prestigious clients including

FOR BROKERS/ DEALERS ONLY

NET MARKETS
(Inside Consolidated Quote)
On All Telephone Issues

American Tel & Tel

American Tel & Tel
When Issued

American Infor Tech Ameritech
When Issued

Bell Atlantic Corp
When Issued

Bell South Corp
When Issued

NYNEX Corp
When Issued

Pacific Telesis Corp
When Issued

Southwestern Bell Corp
When Issued

US West Inc
When Issued

 Bernard L. Madoff
INVESTMENT SECURITIES
Established 1960
110 Wall Street, N.Y, NY 10005
(800) 221-2242
(212) 825-3900
Member SIPC

Figure 14.1: An advertisement for Madoff's market-making business
in the December 6, 1983, issue of the *Wall Street Journal.*

Charles Schwab and Co., A. G. Edwards & Co., and Fidelity. As he gained greater order flow, Madoff cut transaction costs and bested the NYSE in speed of execution. One analysis showed that Madoff's system could process trades in less than half the time as the NYSE. *Forbes* magazine would write that "this much is clear: the established stock exchanges can ignore the Madoffs of the world only at their peril." Trading volume through Madoff's firm grew rapidly, and it would eventually command a significant portion—upwards of 10 percent—of all trading in NYSE-listed securities.

These innovations garnered Madoff considerable respect and admiration in the securities industry. In 1986, Madoff was profiled as one of the highest-paid executives on Wall Street. Three years later, he was presented with the OTC Man of the Year award. "More than any single individual," noted the article introducing Madoff as the award recipient, "he is responsible for bridging the gap between the listed markets, whose stocks his firm trades off the exchanges, and the OTC markets." Madoff would go on to hold numerous leadership positions including chairman of the NASDAQ and chairman of the National Association of Securities Dealers. Government agencies like the SEC would regularly seek his guidance when considering new regulations. Madoff, as one reporter put it, "was considered a leader in the stock trading business."

ALTHOUGH MADOFF BEGAN receiving more accolades publicly, privately he began to see problems emerging in his business. Security dealers, like Madoff, inevitably exposed themselves to risks when creating markets. If Madoff agreed to purchase stock from another dealer and the price subsequently fell, he incurred a loss. Similarly, when he sold stock and the price rose, Madoff missed out on that profit. The spread between a stock's "bid" and "ask" compensated market makers for taking on this uncertainty with fulfilling orders, but profitability was hardly assured. "You can't be a trader or market maker without being a risk taker," Madoff explained. "I mean, it's just impossible."

Madoff could eliminate much of this risk by pairing each buy order with a corresponding sell order. His computer systems sought to find these matches, but the needs of clients meant that purchase and sell orders often didn't match. Even when it was not possible to pair orders against each other, Madoff pointed out that "you were obligated to fill bids and offers when they came to you to be competitive to your client." Fulfilling orders without having an immediate match created obvious risks. But the willingness of market makers to buy stock without knowing exactly when or to whom they would be able to sell it to next was their job and was crucial to well-functioning markets. "It was typical for our trading inventory to close the day with a net long or short position of 500 million to 1 billion dollars," Madoff recalled.

In some cases, investors sought to purchase a stock that market makers, like Madoff, wouldn't have available in their own portfolio. Nonetheless, as a bona fide market maker, Madoff needed to provide a price at which he'd be willing to sell it to them. If a client accepted the price and proceeded to buy a stock that currently was not in his possession, Madoff would sell it to them in something known as a "naked short." After shorting the stock, Madoff was then expected to soon find the security from another broker. If the stock price declined in the interim, Madoff, like other market makers, benefited by acquiring that stock at a lower price. This practice, while controversial in some circles, was viewed by regulators as not only legitimate but actually crucial to ensure the efficiency and liquidity of markets "I made a lot of money in the 1970s going short as a market maker," Madoff explained." So I had confidence in myself in being short." This subtle but euphemistic expression—"shorting" to clients—would set the foundation for Madoff's audacious fraud, which would emerge from his second major line of business.

In addition to his market-making operations, Madoff managed assets for individual and institutional investors. Rather than charging fees based on the amount of assets under his purview, as with most mutual or hedge funds, Madoff ran this investment advisory business as an extension of his market-making operations. Clients were assessed fees for trading a set of proprietary investment strategies he offered. Many of these were arbitrage-based strategies, while others tried to capture price momentum in equity markets.

The investment advisory business began as a closely held partnership primarily of family and friends. But this grew over time as some of Madoff's acquaintances, satisfied with their returns, encouraged him to take in additional capital. Several individuals offered to create feeder funds that would direct capital to Madoff for his firm to manage, allowing him to avoid needing to campaign and personally market his strategies to investors. The historically attractive and stable returns Madoff offered were sufficiently enticing to draw in new clients.

While the 1980s had generally been a period of rapid growth for Madoff's market-making operations, his investment advisory business struggled. Profitable arbitrage strategies that Madoff had once employed were no longer viable due to changing market conditions and increased competition. Other once-profitable investment strategies were no longer possible given the enormous amount of money under his care. On top of this, the markets experienced a precipitous decline in 1987 that left Madoff reeling from losses he sustained while unwinding strategies he had employed with several prominent clients. With strategies he historically relied upon to generate profits no longer feasible and losses mounting, Madoff's investment advisory business became increasingly untenable.

At first, Madoff tried to adjust how he invested clients' money to accommodate the increasing amount of funds he needed to deploy. "We tried different variants. We started to not invest 100 percent in the market, we would invest 75 percent or, say, 50 percent in the market and put the rest of the money in Treasury bills. So investors had a portfolio that was 50 percent Treasuries and 50 percent in the strategy."

"That's what we were doing for a while," he explained, "but I became more and more desperate. . . . This approach limited the upside since the Treasuries might only yield 4 or 5 percent in those days if you went out long term." Madoff's investment advisory business began to buckle, as promises to investors clashed with the difficulty of delivering on those expectations.

"Although I could have admitted failure and returned the money, I knew I would never get another chance with these funds after losing my credibility. In hindsight, this would have been the smart thing to do."

Madoff's clients, whether investing directly with him or through one of the closely tied feeder funds, never noticed the transition from actual to fictitious trading in their accounts. "The disclosure always stayed the same. When I was doing a strategy—whether it was with convertible bonds, covered options, or the split-strike conversion—I was disclosing exactly what I was doing," Madoff said. "What I did not disclose was the point that I wasn't doing the strategy anymore—I was just shorting the strategy to them and not actually doing the physical trading."

From his perspective, Madoff was simply selling—in his parlance, "shorting"—the investment strategy to his clients. As a market maker Madoff was in the position, under certain circumstances, to sell securities to clients without actually holding them. "Selling short was an everyday occurrence with me, so when I started going short the strategy, it wasn't something that I looked at as being particularly unreasonable. There was no violation in shorting to customers—market makers do it every day. It's part of the business."

"The only thing that I did do that wasn't legal was when I shorted I did not put it on my books as a short sale. So I would have had a 'books and records' violation," Madoff explained. He viewed what happened as something closer to oversight than to recklessness. He continued, "Everything on the customer side was being reflected properly." In particular, as Madoff explained, the trades shown on clients' statements were the trades he wanted his clients to take to generate the desired level of return. The clients thought Madoff was placing their trades in the open market, but in reality they were only "trading" with him.

"My problem wasn't going short to clients—that wasn't a violation. It was the nondisclosure of the size of my short position on my financial reports. . . . Clearly the way I did it was improper, but if I had shown the short positions, then I would have been all right."

Euphemistic labeling has long been used to mitigate the uncomfortable feeling people experience when engaging in harmful conduct. For instance, military pilots describe bombing missions as "serving the target" and civilians killed are called "collateral damage." Using terminology that routinizes an uncomfortable activity makes it easier to proceed without dissonance. The fact that Madoff regularly shorted stocks to clients in his legitimate market-making business helped him feel that it was also reasonable to do so in his investment advisory activities. In the process, legitimate and illegitimate practices blurred. He hijacked the parlance used by market makers and applied it inappropriately to investment management. "I deluded myself into thinking this was business as usual. It was no big deal. The dealer side of the community always traded from the short side of the market—it was not unusual for anyone to go short stock to clients when taking the other side of the trade."

Rather than quitting the investment advisory business as losses mounted, Madoff continued to take in even more capital from investors. "I figured that eventually things would change and then I'll get to actually start doing the model trades. As I took in more money to work with, I'd recover. I saw this as an opportunity to earn my way out of the hole."

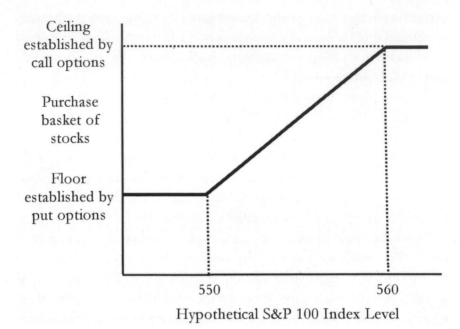

Figure 14.2: Madoff's split-strike conversion strategy that investors
believed they were purchasing.

As Madoff continued the fraud, his problems compounded far beyond
what he described as merely a "disclosure problem." "When you keep
generating profits for the clients, but you take the net losses—you're eating your capital. Whatever the customer is making, you're losing." By
providing statements to clients showing returns of 10 percent annually
but earning only 4 percent or 5 percent on the capital they invested, Madoff would inevitably face a reckoning.

Madoff didn't immediately appreciate the depth of his problem because of his peculiar way of seeing his investment advisory business as an
extension of his market-making business. The main strategy offered to his
investment advisory clients was something known as the "split-strike conversion." The strategy entailed investors purchasing both stocks linked to
the S&P 100 index and a put option that would be profitable if the value of
those stocks fell below a certain level. Simultaneously, the investor would
sell a call option, which would cancel out gains from those stocks if they
reached a certain price. Selling this call option reduced the cost of running
the strategy. By investing in this set of securities the investor had the

opportunity to profit from short-term gains in stock price, but in a manner that limited their potential losses. From Madoff's perspective as a market maker, the strategy simply entailed clients entering three different transactions with him as a market maker: "The strategy was I would short them the stock, short them the put, and buy from them the call."

"You could net the positions against each other as long as it was bona fide arbitrage," Madoff explained. "You're short a common stock, but the customer is long the call to you so it doesn't come out to that much. . . . They were basically limiting my potential of loss." That is, shorting this strategy to a customer didn't appear that costly to Madoff at any given moment, because what customers were buying from him and what he was selling to them appeared to largely—but certainly not completely—offset each other if prices moved significantly. It's this unconventional—and artificial—mental accounting that Madoff relied on to shield himself from fully realizing the magnitude of the eventual losses. These accounting gymnastics made the losses appear relatively modest for any individual account at any given point in time. "But of course I kept on doing it time and time and time again, so eventually it caught up with me. . . . It became a capital problem after enough time went by." By viewing these transactions from the standpoint of a market maker trading with clients whose only problem was one related to "books and records," Madoff lulled himself into not seeing the obvious.

"It's like a comedy of errors," Madoff explained. "To cover the losses, I decided to take in money from hedge funds. And in order for me to do that, I had to commit to a long-term strategy that I wouldn't send the money back. I kept taking in more money, figuring that once the market allows me to do the strategy I will be able to fix it. . . . I allowed myself—and I really have to say 'allowed,' since no one put a gun to my head—to keep taking in more money. I kept on waiting for the environment to change and of course it never did. . . . It turned into a total fiasco."

As time passed, Madoff inevitably realized the truth: he would never really be able to make up the losses from "shorting" the strategy to clients over the prior years.

"By 1994 or 1995, I basically stopped doing the split strike entirely. I just had the money housed in treasuries," Madoff admitted. "When I realized I wasn't going to be able to get out of it, I don't know what the hell I was waiting for. I just didn't have the courage to unwind it."

ONCE MADOFF STOPPED trading the strategy for his investment advisory clients, it was only a matter of time until the business unraveled. "It's still amazing to me," Madoff reflected. "How could I have actually as late as the mid-2000s been shopping for new and larger office space for my London office? I even considered purchasing the old post office building on Lexington Avenue to move our N.Y. office into in 2005. Talk about not being capable of facing reality."

Instead of facing greater pressure from investors, however, Madoff saw the amount of money flowing into his funds grow more quickly than ever. From his perspective, this gave the false impression that his investment advisory business was somehow flourishing. "The hedge fund's money just grew exponentially. The money just kept pouring in from these people. I wasn't accepting the fact myself, foolishly, that the more money I took in, the more difficult it was going to be."

"Clearly there was a time that I realized that I'm never going to dig myself out of this hole and cover the shorts by actually going out to legitimately buy the stock. . . . When you're in that deep and you realize what the potential problem is—you can't deal with it, you can't face it."

"How did I live?" Madoff asked himself. "How did I exist?"

Madoff wasn't alone in perpetrating this fraud. Frank DiPascali, Madoff's longtime lieutenant and financial officer, was his closest confidant in managing the investment advisory business. Together, they fabricated much of the paperwork needed to maintain the appearance of trading once it had stopped. Despite all the effort needed to continue the fraud, they avoided appraising the purpose of sustaining a scheme that would surely come to an end. "I didn't want to discuss it with him," Madoff explained. "I never wanted to discuss the real problem since it was not something I could do anything about." They avoided conversation about the inevitable.

At one point, Madoff considered leaving the problem behind. "Why didn't I just run away? I mean, I certainly knew that I had problems and I knew I wasn't going to be able to recover from this. I had the ability to stash money overseas in banks because I had all these banking connections. I could have done that. I could have just disappeared." But he felt that he couldn't just leave the firm he had built, despite the fact that his investment business was now little more than a fraud.

In 2006, in response to a tip, officials at the SEC began investigating Madoff. The informant's allegations against Madoff ranged broadly: he acted as an unregistered investment advisory, he misled investors about the nature of his investment strategies, and the investment management business itself was a Ponzi. As part of the investigation, officials brought Madoff in for a deposition. During this conversation, officials asked Madoff detailed questions about his business, including where the vast holdings of securities that supported the investment management business were kept. Madoff responded to these questions with specifics, even providing the number for his account at the Depository Trust Company (DTC), where, he said, billions of dollars of securities were housed.

"When I left that afternoon, I thought it was all over. I assumed that in the morning they were going to call up the depository and check to see if I had them there." Madoff held less than $24 million worth of S&P 100 securities in the account on the day of his testimony. At the same time, a single hedge fund investing with Madoff reported $2.5 billion of S&P 100 stock on its statement.

Officials at the SEC made a perfunctory call to the DTC, but they didn't verify Madoff's statements by explicitly requesting or checking records. "The biggest blunder that they did was not checking the depositories, which is where I said the securities were housed," Madoff marvels. "Why they didn't do that is beyond me."

Madoff often reflected on how he managed to so narrowly escape getting caught. "The bank custodians were very hesitant to give out information even to regulators. There were all sorts of Chinese walls established with giving that information out, since they didn't want to give out the positions of firms." Despite these hurdles, regulators had a variety of options at their disposal to acquire the needed information to expose Madoff. "What they could have said to me—'we want to see your copy of the depositary trust agreement.' What they normally do is have the depositary trust send it directly to the SEC. They could have done that, but they didn't do that."

Given Madoff's prominence in the securities industry, the most damning allegation—that Madoff was running a Ponzi—apparently seemed too preposterous to investigate carefully. SEC staff described the investigation as a "fishing expedition." By January 2008, the SEC officially ended the investigation, with the internal report concluding that "the staff found no evidence of fraud." Madoff registered as an investment advisory, as officials requested, and the investigation closed uneventfully without any action being taken against him.

While Madoff understood that it was mere luck that he didn't get caught in 2006 by regulators, his Ponzi could not last indefinitely. "You know it's strange. I actually at one point was hoping that the world would come to an end," Madoff said. He saw many other firms devastated when their records were destroyed during the World Trade Center attacks in September 2001. In several cases, vaults containing security records were obliterated. He fantasized that if this happened again, the ensuing confusion could wipe away his fraud. "If there was another 9/11 where everybody's records blew up and the depositories got melted down, no one would have been able to piece the whole thing back together again." It was a terrifying vision. "In my mind, I said I don't want my grandchildren to die, I don't want my family to get wiped out, but if the world is coming to an end—it's coming to an end."

WHILE THE FRAUD was ongoing, Madoff seemed oblivious to the eventual harm he was going to cause his investors. "I sort of rationalized that what I was doing was okay—you know, that it wasn't going to hurt anybody." His myopia was driven in part by the fact that investors were praising him, often clamoring to give him more money to manage, even as he was defrauding them.

In Madoff's opinion, his deceitful behavior was not so exceptional. Rather, it simply reflected the prevailing norms on Wall Street. "Find me an owner in the manufacturing field that didn't cheat on his inventory counts or his taxes and I will be willing to change my opinion. . . . Find me an individual who has not written off personal expenses on his tax returns as business expenses. Find me a person that has not padded or filed false insurance claims. I acknowledge there are different degrees of these activities and I am not suggesting that all are acceptable. My point is simply to state that I believe that this is the reality of life, and those that don't accept this are either delusional or less than honest." Madoff saw his own failing as emblematic of the perverseness of misconduct in the financial industry. As evidence of the ubiquity of this misconduct, he pointed to one study cited by the *New York Times* showing that more than a third of people making more than a half-million dollars annually had witnessed wrongdoing in the workplace.

Madoff even saw the behavior of his own clients as contributing to his views on the pervasiveness of wayward conduct. "The same people are crying and whining to me now, these same people at every level—I'd say that 80 percent of my clients, they were basically legitimate people and respected businesses—were involved in cheating in one form or another method that they could have gone to jail for if caught."

When regulators were investigating Madoff's business practices in 2006, several of his investors suspected that he might be using his market-making business to illicitly front-run trades in his investment advisory business. Front-running is the practice of trading securities in advance of a client's order to gain a better price. "They [Madoff's investors] seemed to take comfort in this explanation," Madoff recalled. "If this practice was ever stopped by regulators, all that would result was a fine and the end of my performance followed by the withdrawal of their capital." In this regard, Madoff argued that investors took little interest in how profits were earned. "I have never met an investor who cared whether his profit was made by questionable happenstance as long as he was not going to get in trouble. . . . Front-running, while completely illegal, did not bother these clients." The truth of Madoff's business would ultimately be far more troubling to these investors. "Of course, the reality was that there obviously was no front-running because I was not doing any actual trading."

Madoff sees his own dishonesty—while larger in magnitude—as not so different from that of many others in financial services. "There is a mentality in Wall Street that everything is so complicated that the existing rules are incapable of taking the realities of their business into consideration. Therefore, they adapt the rules and regulations to suit their needs of getting the trade done." Madoff also points to the same attitude in politics and government. "As an example, look at the present state of Social Security and the government debt worldwide. Talk about a Ponzi scheme. All they do is keep printing money to pay off the existing bond holders and creditors. Please explain to me what the difference is."

There's something odd about hearing Madoff describe the troubling pervasiveness of misconduct, given his own behavior. Some of his observations reflect his particular perception of business conduct more broadly. For instance, Madoff sees tax evasion as rife among virtually all those who've achieved some degree of success. "I have certainly not come across any European businessman who didn't have an account in a tax haven. . . .

They would go to any length to not pay taxes. Forget Warren Buffett. He is the biggest bag of wind there is."

While Madoff's views about the business world may exaggerate the pervasiveness of dishonesty, they nonetheless reveal how he judged the world around him. We see Madoff's conduct as an aberration, but he views his own conduct as just reflecting the prevailing norms in the financial industry.

MANY OF THE executives I spoke with did not perceive the harm associated with their choices at the time they were making them. It's only with the benefit of hindsight that the detrimental effects of their conduct became clear to them. Madoff similarly failed to appreciate the harm while his Ponzi was ongoing, but more exceptionally, he continued to largely overlook it following the collapse of his business. In the more than five years I spent speaking and corresponding with Madoff, he never expressed a genuine sense of remorse or contrition for his fraud.

To many, Madoff's fraud seemed especially deceitful because of the damage it inflicted on members of the Jewish community as well as on university endowments and charities. Madoff clearly acknowledges that his actions were deceptive: "Look, I do understand the terrible feeling of betrayal, and nobody wants to lose what they assumed they had." Yet, even now, Madoff denies causing the immense damage often depicted by his victims and the media.

Madoff interprets the losses from his Ponzi in many instances as a matter of unwinding gains that investors received from earlier investments with him. For example, he argues that the significant damage to some charities was not actually so serious when one considers the returns he previously "earned" for these clients:

> The only accounts I took on were the nonprofit accounts that were funded by the profits of existing accounts and also composed of profits previously generated by me. . . . All of the Picower, Shapiro, Chais, and Levy nonprofit donations and foundations were 100 percent examples of the above. It really upset me that [a reporter for the *New York Times*] mentioned to me that the Levy daughter had lost her foundation money and that was a terrible loss. The fact

was that her entire foundation came from profits I earned for her father as well as her.

Madoff also views much of the financial distress of his former investors as an exaggeration. Often, he even takes comfort in seeing his investors, rather than himself, as the irresponsible party.

It's not like going into a bank with a gun and saying "give me your money" and running out. All I did was make rich people richer and I made some rich people poorer, but not poor. This whole charade that's been going on with clients claiming that I wiped them out, I ruined them . . . there's not one client that I had that was not already a wealthy person by anyone's standard. . . . When I was generating all these profits, a lot of these clients were throwing caution to the wind.

It doesn't mean what I did was correct—I'm not using this as a defense. But I sit here and look at these people sitting there like poor souls saying "he wiped me out, he cheated." Yeah, I cheated them. I betrayed their trust—there's no question about that. But these are all people that signed statements that said they were worth at least $2 million. They all had income of at least $250,000 net. These are wealthy people.

A lot of them, their mothers, fathers, and grandparents, lived off the profits for years and then just left them money in accounts— and now that disappeared. Quite frankly, those monies weren't their money. It was money that was earned by me. If it wasn't for me, if their parents didn't have accounts with me over the years, they never would have lived as well as they did and they wouldn't have been able to leave them money. The whole thing just doesn't make sense.

There was a callousness in the way Madoff saw the financial losses and hardship incurred by his former clients. It was the investors, he argued, who placed money into his fund near the end of his Ponzi who should bear the fault for naïvely investing in something they didn't fully understand.

"The clients that did come in late—they knew what they were doing at that stage in the game," Madoff explained. "There were so many stories going around about that there must have been something wrong. People just didn't care. It was the old greed factor."

IT IS EASY to believe that understanding the difference between right and wrong is sufficient to steer people to act in the appropriate way. But Madoff illustrates that this is not enough—that something more is needed. Madoff knew that what he was doing was deceitful and illicit. He was aware that there was no way for his business to recover. He understood that his actions would make people who trusted him worse off, and that the longer he continued the worse off they would become. So why didn't he stop?

Madoff is quick-witted, clever, even brilliant in some regards—talents he applied to further a fraudulent investment scheme rather than build constructive wealth. At the same time, he distinctly lacks the ability to relate emotionally to the havoc he created. In several of our conversations, I tried to offer evidence that some individuals were genuinely harmed by his actions, but he remained impassive.

Beyond investors, Madoff's family was deeply impacted by his actions. In 2010, two years after his arrest, Madoff's son Mark hanged himself in his family's living room. Madoff did not speak often about the event, but the first time he mentioned it, in late 2011, was both illuminating and harrowing.

Madoff and I were discussing accusations that he never traded for his investment advisory clients. Madoff described how he wished he had taken his case to trial, rather than pleading guilty, to set the record straight. He said that he didn't know if his family had the grit to endure the public criticism of a trial, and that he pled guilty to make it easier for everyone. He then cavalierly remarked: "The reality of it is my son couldn't stand up amongst the pressure *anyhow,* so he took his own life." In the many hours of conversations I had with Madoff, this statement stood out for its callousness. A father couldn't understand the impact that his actions had on his own son.

Individuals differ in their capacity to empathize. Most people are attuned to the basic feelings and emotions of others. These empathic feelings help people understand what others value and foster socialization.

However, some people have a far weaker capacity to appreciate the emotional state of others. Madoff falls into this latter group.

Madoff remains dispassionate even about circumstances that are of the greatest significance. In September 2014, a colleague e-mailed me news that Madoff's second son, Andrew, had just died of cancer. As I was beginning to read the article, my office phone rang. I picked it up and was surprised to hear Madoff on the line. He had heard the news of his second son's death on the radio and asked if I could read the obituary to him.

Shaken by the fact that a father had called me to convey news of his son's death, I turned my attention to describing the news in the most compassionate way I could. I wasn't a professor or researcher at that moment— just one person speaking to another. I read him a Reuters article about his son's death. When I reached the end, I was at a loss to know what to say. Instinctively, as we often do when hearing of a death, I asked him how he was doing. Madoff responded: "I'm fine, I'm fine." After a brief pause, he said that he had a question for me. I thought he might want me to send a copy of the obituary to him or deliver a message on his behalf to someone. It wasn't that. Instead, he asked me whether I'd had the chance to look at the LIBOR rates we discussed in a prior conversation.

This particular phone call with Madoff stuck with me more than any other. Shortly after finding out his son had died, Madoff wanted to discuss interest rates. He didn't lose a beat in the ensuing conversation, continuing to carry on an entirely fluent discussion on the arcane determinants of yields. It didn't seem as though he wanted to switch topics because he was struggling to compose himself. And it didn't seem as though he was avoiding expressing emotion because the news was so overwhelming. In some way, it almost seemed as though I was more personally moved by the death of Andrew in those moments than his father.

To a psychiatrist, Madoff displays many symptoms associated with psychopathy. His lack of remorse, failure to take responsibility, inability to plan ahead, and persistent deceitfulness all contribute to such a designation. While labels themselves are of little use, viewing Madoff through this lens helps place his prior actions and current rationalization of that behavior into context. Madoff interprets and responds to emotion differently from most people. Regardless of how close he got to investors, his personal limitations enabled him to continue his fraud without remorse or guilt.

WHILE MADOFF WAS perpetuating the fraud, he was celebrated by investors and lived a privileged life. He held leadership positions and was respected by peers. In its own artificial way, his business appeared to be thriving. Because he felt little need to take into account the effects of his fraud on investors, family, or friends, there was little reason for him to voluntarily confess. He—albeit no one else—was better off continuing.

The prompt to end a fraudulent scheme arises only when the feelings and reactions of others are taken into consideration. It comes from a sense of not wanting to accept more money from investors who would not be repaid—from a desire to stop perpetuating a fraud that would only cause more harm to others. But Madoff has an inability to empathize with his investors. Without this nagging sensation, he never experienced the gut feeling that he needed to stop.

Although Madoff is not especially moved by the suffering of others, he was not inevitably destined to become the architect of a massive Ponzi scheme. "Everyone thinks I had this master plan and they give me credit for being this master thief. That was not the situation," he once remarked. Madoff's fraud emerged from challenges that are not uncommon in business. But rather than curtailing his operations, changing his business strategies, and realizing that what he was doing was not viable, Madoff proceeded as he always had. In decision after decision, he acted myopically without regard for the longer-term ramifications of his choices. Ultimately, Madoff's Ponzi scheme arose because he made decisions under pressure without consideration of how they influenced others. He managed to create extraordinary suffering for his investors, his friends—even his family—while experiencing little emotional turmoil himself.

Even Madoff realized it didn't need to be this way. More than two years before confessing that his investment advisory business was fraudulent, he offered some useful business advice during testimony to regulators. "There's plenty of ways you can make money in the business doing the right thing," he explained. "You don't have to look to do the wrong thing."

CONCLUSION

Toward Greater Humility

ISTORICALLY, "BUSINESS WAS simple—it was individual—it was done only in a limited area," began Owen Young, the charismatic chairman of General Electric, in his dedicatory address for the Harvard Business School on June 4, 1927. Young continued:

> Any infraction of the rules of the law, or of the church, or of the principles of business were quickly recognized and generally known. The community could and did, in those days, discipline the individual man of business effectively. No one could maintain his good will and profess one thing in church on Sundays and practice another thing in his business on week days.

Young offered the example of the wealthy Boston merchant Robert Keayne. In 1639, a court fined Keayne £200—an enormous sum at the time—for selling buttons, nails, and thread at excessively high prices, a crime known as oppression in colonial New England. Over and above Keayne's censure in court, he was berated and nearly excommunicated by his church. In an attempt to redeem himself, Keayne, once one of the wealthiest and most prominent merchants in all of New England, was forced to stand in front of his congregation and "with tears acknowledge and bewail his covetous and corrupt heart." For selling products at a 50–100 percent profit—not an atypical margin for a successful modern manufacturer like Apple—Keayne faced an admonishment that would weigh heavily on him for the rest of his life.

By the time of Young's speech, such public denunciations were far less effective. Businessmen were no longer limited to operating within a single small community surrounded by family and friends. Enterprising businessmen could reach new geographic areas far away from their humble origins. While such prospects created extraordinary opportunities for economic growth, they also dismantled a social process that supported accountability. Young anticipated the consequences of this widening reach of business:

> A man could not sell a spavined horse as sound in his own community without penalty, but he could sell a spavined motor as sound in some other community, perhaps indeed halfway around the world, without being quickly discovered at home. Even if discovered, the penalty was not so great. The sale of a spavined horse to one of his own community may have been a moral delinquency. The sale of a spavined motor to people quite unknown may have been regarded locally as a clever piece of business. . . . The widening area of business and the highly specialized character of the good outstripped all local sanctions and tended to leave the individual free from restraints.

Although Young spoke almost a century ago, he identified a sentiment held by many of the executives described in these pages: what might be morally disapproved of in one community might actually be applauded in another. Without any immediate reckoning, executives can feel a sense of pride in their actions and, in some cases, even be exalted by members of their insular business communities.

TODAY, MUCH EFFORT is spent reducing the consequences of corporate misconduct. While the aggregate costs are difficult to assess precisely, one estimate placed the annual cost of financial fraud in the United States at nearly $400 billion. With such significant consequences, it is not surprising that a diverse consortium of interested parties—including business schools, trade groups, corporations, and regulators—has sought to curtail this damage.

Teaching "business ethics" is one common means of trying to address this problem. It would be difficult to find a business school that lacks an ethics curriculum. Most corporations routinely mandate that employees undergo ethics seminars and training programs. And trade associations increasingly require members to take courses on appropriate professional conduct. The aim of all these efforts is to create managers who not only comply with the law but also steer away from its murky boundaries.

People participating in such programs are often given exercises of dilemmas requiring trade-offs. For example, the discussion might explore short-term boosts to profitability at the expense of long-term sustainable development or greater personal consumption at the cost of public well-being. Participants spend time discussing their views of an appropriate resolution that balances their legal, ethical, and economic objectives. The decisions made by many of the executives in this book could be discussed in this manner—and indeed they have been in classrooms around the world. The objective of such exercises is to help participants enhance their decision-making skills to become better leaders.

Yet such training, though well-intended, is often ineffective. Ethics cases are convenient tools for teaching and debate because they succinctly isolate trade-offs that have to be made. The problem is that the consequential decisions that can unwind a career are usually not so neatly isolated from the thousands of other decisions a person makes. By bringing a specific dilemma into focus for a discussion, it changes how we both think about and seek to resolve that dilemma. There is an implicit—and flawed—assumption that participants would employ the same decision-making process they used in the classroom if they faced the same predicament at some point in their own future.

To appreciate this disparity between thinking and doing, consider the decision of Rajat Gupta, McKinsey's former managing director, to provide inside information to the hedge fund manager Raj Rajaratnam. During a Goldman Sachs board meeting, Gupta learned about an upcoming quarterly earnings loss that the investment bank planned to announce. Only twenty-three seconds after the meeting ended, Gupta called Rajaratnam and divulged this news. Rajaratnam sold his position in Goldman the following day before the news was public and avoided almost $3 million in losses.

Viewed neatly in isolation, Gupta made an extraordinarily foolish decision. Participants in a classroom discussion would invariably agree that they would not similarly divulge this information if they were in Gupta's position. But Gupta, someone widely lauded for his thoughtful leadership and deep strategic mind, obviously made a different decision. In the short time before the call, he didn't undertake some elaborate calculation during which he reasoned that the benefits of providing this information to Rajaratnam outweighed the expected costs. Instead, Gupta proceeded with the call as guided by his imperfect intuition.

With the benefit of hindsight, it's easy to see decisions that deserved more attention. But the consequential nature of our decisions is not always clear at the time they are being made. In fact, when decisions are made intuitively, it's easy to largely ignore or even entirely overlook their possible consequences. The cues that tell us to slow down and think more deeply about the potential effects of a choice are often absent. It's only later, when the effects are revealed, that we appreciate that some decisions should not have been made so quickly.

In business ethics discussions, many of the most significant challenges associated with decision making have already been vastly simplified or even eliminated by identifying the salient issues and trade-offs for participants. Who are the parties affected? What are the likely consequences? Are our commitments toward others being upheld? What are the potential reputational effects? The very act of asking and seeking answers to these kinds of questions forces participants to engage in more deliberative reasoning. But in practice many, if not most, decisions are resolved intuitively. As a result, the judgments reached during a classroom discussion of an ethical dilemma often reflect a decision-making process that differs from how participants encounter and resolve such dilemmas if similarly faced with one in their own day-to-day life.

This discrepancy is one that Dennis Gioia appreciates. Gioia is now a management professor at Penn State, but in the 1970s he was the vehicle recall coordinator at Ford Motor Company. While Gioia was at Ford, the company confronted recurring instances of the popular Pinto car bursting into flames and incinerating passengers when the car was rear-ended.

As the coordinator of recalls, Gioia had the ability to pull the poorly designed vehicle from the road. "I now argue and teach that Ford had an ethical obligation to recall," Gioia explained. "But, while I was there, I perceived no strong obligation to recall and I remember no strong ethical overtones to the case whatsoever." In fact, even when Gioia viewed photos of the charred remains of one Pinto inside which several people had died, what followed was merely a short lapse in proceeding as usual. "After the usual round of discussion about criteria and justification for recall, everyone voted against recommending recall—including me. It did not fit the pattern of recallable standards; the evidence was not overwhelming that the car was defective in some way, so the case was actually fairly straightforward. It was a good business decision, even if people might be dying."

Another way in which classroom dilemmas differ from real life is that they're resolved through argumentation among people with different opinions and viewpoints. Being exposed to varying and conflicting ways of seeing problems provides an opportunity to reason about, and revise, one's initial intuitive judgment. However, there are often fewer dissenting viewpoints in actual settings where decisions are made. In day-to-day life, people tend to rely on their initial and often unsatisfactory intuitive judgments.

The differences between discussing decisions in theory and making decisions in practice suggest that individuals may successfully resolve ethical dilemmas during, say, a company-mandated tutorial, yet fail to do so later when facing them in reality. Worse, the confidence created when individuals easily resolve ethical issues "on paper" can give them greater faith in their ability to successfully resolve dilemmas in real life. Perversely overconfident in their capabilities after such training, they may pay even less attention to their decisions out of the mistaken belief that they will be able to successfully resolve them in the future. These "blinds spots," as described by psychologists Max Bazerman and Ann Tenbrunsel, often contribute to people's tendency to act far less ethically in practice than they anticipate.

"What we all think is, when the big moral challenge comes, I will rise to the occasion," argued Steven Garfinkel, the former chief financial officer of DVI. Garfinkel believed that he would successfully handle difficult and complex situations when they came his way as an executive. But now, with the benefit of hindsight, he sees how this confidence was misplaced. "There's not actually that many of us that will actually rise to the occasion," lamented Garfinkel. "I didn't realize I would be a felon."

SUPPOSE THE FORMER executives described in this book viewed their fateful decisions at the time through the lens of an outsider. Would Sam Waksal have called his daughter and provided her inside information about the pending failure of a drug? Would Andrew Fastow have created elaborate illicit structured transactions to meet quarterly expectations? Would Marc Dreier have impersonated a client to create a fictitious note? If these executives had been yanked out of their offices at those moments and exposed to alternative perspectives and a careful consideration of the consequences, I suspect they would have made different choices. Their failure was one of relying on faulty intuitions rather than engaging in poor deliberative reasoning.

Framed differently, few if any of the enterprising young students sitting in elite business schools anticipate graduating, ascending the ranks of their firm, and becoming wealthy by designing an elaborate ruse. Similarly, no student graduates with a plan to become successful and then, later, to engage in some fraudulent behavior that could lead to prison and professional ruin. Yet, even at my own institution, Harvard Business School, where every student has the intellectual capacity to successfully resolve and avoid decisions that could lead to prison, there have been more than two dozen graduates who've engaged in white-collar crime.

While individuals can have the intelligence to effectively resolve dilemmas when they are explicitly presented "on paper," when these same people face dilemmas in their day-to-day life, they often make different—and decidedly worse—decisions. Several factors contribute to this discrepancy: relying on faulty intuition, not engaging in deliberative reasoning, and lacking exposure to differing viewpoints. The question is how to design mechanisms that bring some of the more attractive elements that arise within an organized classroom discussion to the settings in which actual decisions are made.

By understanding the particular ways misconduct arises, we can endeavor to anticipate these mistakes and design ways to preempt them. In particular, how can busy executives and other individuals become more likely to identify consequential decisions when they may be relying on faulty intuitions? How can they be encouraged to spend the necessary time engaged in deliberative reasoning? How can they be exposed to more contrasting and conflicting viewpoints during the decision-making process? Addressing the issue of why successful resolution of ethics dilemmas often seems easy in the classroom but hard in practice is crucial to averting the types of failures described in this book.

The Need for Uncomfortable Dissonance

Recall the last time you were driving along a freeway. You may have been listening to the radio or talking with friends. If the car in front of you got too close, you switched lanes. You whizzed alongside other cars as you comfortably and uneventfully made it to your destination.

At some point during this journey, you may have glanced down and seen your speedometer reading 75 mph. You probably returned to humming along with the music or chatting with your companion and gave little thought to the fact that you were above the posted limit of 65 mph. Your speed raised little cause for alarm since the cars around you were going just as fast and you were simply keeping up. The fact that you were doing something illegal—speeding—probably never entered your mind. There was no instinctive feeling that you were doing anything potentially harmful to yourself or others.

There are a variety of influences that might cause you to slow down and drive at—or at least closer to—the posted speed limit. Your spouse might implore you to drive more carefully because it is getting dark or raining. You might slow down upon witnessing an accident ahead of you, thinking that moments earlier it could have been your car. And you would quickly decelerate if you saw a police car ahead. It takes some kind of uncomfortable dissonance, an external influence or event that conflicts with your intuition, to motivate a behavioral change.

Executives, like drivers along a freeway, also need to experience some dissonance to stimulate a reevaluation of their initial intuitive judgments. Dennis Kozlowski, the former CEO of Tyco, described how infrequently he experienced such dissonance as chief executive. "When the CEO is in the room, directors—even independent directors—tend to want to try and please him," Kozlowski explained. "The board would give me anything I wanted. Anything." Not surprisingly for Kozlowski, this created a feeling of entitlement. "We believed our own press. . . . With myself and others—even the board—you become consumed a little bit by your own arrogance and you really think you can do anything."

With little resistance from others at Tyco, Kozlowski rarely felt the need to double-check the appropriateness of his actions. Though one of the highest-paid CEOs in the country, he would later be convicted for embezzling nearly a hundred million dollars by inappropriately forgiving loans owed to Tyco. "I wasn't paying attention to the approvals and non-approvals," Kozlowski noted. "What I really needed to do was to get a piece of paper and have the board sign off personally for me on every bonus—and make a big issue of it," Kozlowski explained with the benefit of hindsight. "It's something you don't think about, going through the course of building the company. You think about where's your P&L? What's working with your 260,000 employees? I mean, we were doing $250–350 million in sales a day. Those are staggering numbers and you're not sitting around thinking about what are the mechanics of the approval of your bonuses."

Kozlowski's expenditures included $6,000 for a shower curtain, $15,000 for a dog-shaped umbrella stand, and $1 million for his wife's Roman-themed birthday party in Sardinia. The disclosure of a $20 million payment—$10 million in cash and another $10 million to charity—to one of the board members for helping arrange an acquisition eventually served as the impetus for conflict between Kozlowski and Tyco's board of directors. After hearing about the payment during a cocktail party in Boca Raton, other board members were outraged that Kozlowski would proceed with such a transaction without their consultation.

Executives, like other individuals in positions of power, can neglect to take into account or imagine the sentiments of those around them. The $20 million discretionary payment to a single board member and the use of a million dollars of company funds for a family member's birthday party illustrate this lack of awareness that can accompany power in its most pernicious form. Inattentive to the opinions and judgments of others, executives can continue to make myopic decisions until they are eventually detected and contested. However, such latent after-the-fact exposure is too late to stave off the harmful effects of such decisions.

To the extent that intuitions fail to motivate more lawful behavior in business settings, executives would benefit from experiencing more uncomfortable dissonance at the time that decisions are being made, so as to avoid the most detrimental choices. This dissonance would force a slowing down, a consideration of alternative perspectives, and a change in course when the situation merits such attention. The challenge is figuring out how the opportunities to create this discomfort can realistically arise.

Seeking Disagreement

In the fall of 1989, a biochemist named Mark Whitacre joined Archer Daniels Midland (ADM), one of the largest agricultural companies in the world. At ADM, which marketed itself as "Supermarket to the World," Whitacre held the prestigious position of president of the BioProducts division—a rapidly growing part of the company that manufactured amino acids like lysine, an important component of animal feed.

Whitacre's success at the BioProducts division led to a quick promotion to corporate vice-president at ADM, and with this advancement came numerous perks, including corporate-jet use and a sizable salary increase. It also entailed a new responsibility. By 1991, Whitacre would join the team of ADM executives negotiating with the company's Korean and Japanese competitors to rig the global markets for lysine and citric acid. Meeting in hotel suites and country-club golf courses, the executives negotiated how much of each product their companies would individually and collectively sell, raising global prices and pocketing higher profits at the expense of consumers.

One evening in November 1992, Whitacre spoke with his wife Ginger about his experience at ADM: "She asked several direct questions. . . . I explained how we were getting together with our competitors and fixing the prices of several key ingredients." Whitacre told his wife that "on our expense reports we had to put that we met with people other than who we're really meeting with because we wanted to hide the paper trail of who we were really meeting with."

"She was appalled," Whitacre remembers clearly. She said that "it was all deception." Ginger told Whitacre that he needed to confess to authorities. "It was a way for me to separate from a culture that I had fallen into. . . . She felt like she was losing me." Soon, Whitacre found himself describing the price-fixing to the FBI. In the process, he not only revealed one of the most significant corporate conspiracies in US history but became the most senior executive of any large firm ever to become a whistleblower. Over the next two years, Whitacre wore a microphone and tape recorder for the FBI, collecting many hours of incriminating—and embarrassing—material for the prosecution.

FBI agents and prosecutors long wondered why Whitacre turned into an informant. He was making a significant amount of money from his salary at ADM, and few would have suspected these misdeeds. Meanwhile, he was also putting himself at enormous risk, since he was simultaneously embezzling millions of dollars from the company—a crime for which he eventually spent over eight years in prison. To Whitacre, his change in sentiment didn't arise from simply reflecting on his own conduct but, rather, from conversations with his wife. "If it was not for a thirty-four-year-old stay-at-home mom raising three young children at the time, the largest price fixing scheme in U.S. history never would have been exposed," Whitacre admitted.

Whitacre's experience speaks to a way in which people revise their intuitive judgments. Ginger was someone Whitacre deeply respected, and she was outside his day-to-day work life. She provided Whitacre starkly different views of what defines appropriate conduct and gave him the conflicting viewpoint needed to motivate a change in his behavior.

IN POPULAR MYTHOLOGY, we have little angels and demons hovering over our shoulders providing advice. The angel is our conscience guiding us to behave ethically, while the demon nudges us toward mischief. The two entities offer conflicting advice, each prodding our emotions in an effort to prevail.

Such figures are obviously fictitious, but so too are the deliberation and struggle that are envisioned to emerge during decision making. Instead, choices are often made in isolation or while we are surrounded by people with similar tendencies and incentives. Unlike the battle between the mythical angel and demon, there frequently is no genuine debate between opposing viewpoints. What might appear to be—and even feel like—reasoning might be nothing more than reflection to support a judgment that was already reached intuitively. Reasoning, as was pointed out by the psychologist Jonathan Haidt, is often much more like a lawyer defending a client than a scientist seeking the truth.

Some decisions that seem intuitively acceptable are masks for illicit practices that reflect emerging or prevailing norms within a particular subculture or industry. The options-backdating scandal in 2006 that en-gulfed hundreds of firms, many of them technology- and Internet-focused, reflected just such a norm. Ben Horowitz, one of the most prominent venture capitalists in Silicon Valley, described how he would have become complicit in the backdating scheme had it not been for a discussion with an outsider.

In 2002, Horowitz hired a talented chief financial officer named Shar-lene Abrams for Opsware, an enterprise software company he had founded. Horowitz was impressed by Abrams' early efforts to revamp Opsware's processes and procedures. One issue that Abrams brought to Horowitz's attention was a concern that the stock option incentives were not opti-mized to provide maximum benefit for its executives. Horowitz explained:

> One area where she thought we were less than competitive was our stock option granting process. She reported that her previous com-pany's practice of setting the stock option price at the low during the month it was granted yielded a far more favorable result for em-ployees than ours. She also said that since it had been designed by the company's outside legal counsel and approved by their audi-tors, it was fully compliant with the law. . . . It all sounded great: better incentives for employees at no additional cost or risk.

Before implementing the new plan, Horowitz decided to discuss it with someone else. "I told [Abrams] that a better stock granting process sounded great, but I needed Jordan Breslow, my General Counsel, to re-view it before making a decision. . . . [Abrams] was surprised, as her previ-ous company had run this practice for years with full approval from PricewaterhouseCoopers, its accounting firm."

Breslow came back to Horowitz with his opinion. "I've gone over the law six times and there's no way that this practice is strictly within the bounds of the law. I'm not sure how PwC [PricewaterhouseCoopers] jus-tified it, but I recommend against it." As a result, Horowitz soon decided against implementing the more competitive options dating plan suggested by Abrams.

Two years later, regulators began investigating the practice of backdat-ing options. Abrams was implicated for incorrectly recording the date that she and other executives received their options during her prior employment. Eventually, she would serve nearly four months in prison for tax evasion related to the fraudulent backdating and be barred from serving as an officer or director of a public company. Horowitz reflects on the experience as one in which he considered himself quite fortunate for avoiding more serious consequences himself. "The only thing that kept me out of jail," Horowitz explained, "was some good luck and an outstanding General Counsel, and the right organizational design."

Horowitz had certain routine procedures in place that led him to consult with an outsider he trusted before reaching a decision—especially on an arcane accounting topic that lay outside his own expertise. He set up a system that prepared him to deliberate. Notably, it wasn't because Horowitz had any exceptional values or principles as a leader that he avoided prison. In fact, Horowitz's initial intuitions suggested approving the options scheme. It was only through discussing dilemmas with people on the outside, a spouse in the case of Whitacre and an attorney-confidant for Horowitz, that both of these men revised their initial judgments.

Since morally questionable decisions are often made in relative isolation with few outsiders expressing opposing viewpoints or judgments, some firms have created hotlines that employees can call to discuss dilemmas they encounter. For instance, at a call center set up by the Institute of Chartered Accountants in England and Wales, one member called the hotline after finding out that staff purchases of goods manufactured by the company were being used to fund the firm's Christmas party. These purchases were not being logged in the firm's financial system, as would be expected by the accounting rules. The caller sought external advice from someone unconnected with the firm who might be able to offer advice on how to respond.

Although ethics hotlines can provide helpful guidance for those who call, they also presume that individuals are capable of identifying the dilemmas that require additional discussion and contemplation. However, many of the people who would benefit most from such discussion don't call because they don't identify the moral dilemma in the first place. Once individuals become more senior within an organization, they tend to be more susceptible to overconfidence and trust their own ability to successfully navigate challenges when they arise. In the process they become even less likely to encourage external viewpoints that can encourage dissonance.

IF ANY OF the former executives discussed in this book imagined the younger version of himself peering into the future to observe his later conduct, he would likely be surprised to see the person he had become. But "nobody is ever the villain in their own narrative," noted the behavioral finance scholar David Solomon. "So if someone takes actions that threaten to paint them as a bad person, they are more likely to change their opinion of what's right and wrong, rather than change their opinion of themselves. It's like a frog in a pot of water that dies by being slowly brought to a boil. People can make poor decisions by getting gradually worse without realizing how far they've shifted."

People naturally try to disavow and dismiss information that contradicts their worldview. They often continue as if nothing is wrong even when something is seriously amiss. This continues until eventually "they come across a piece of evidence too fascinating to ignore, too clear to misperceive, too painful to deny . . . forcing them to alter and surrender the worldview they have so meticulously constructed," explained sociologist Diane Vaughan.

As uncomfortable as it is to have our beliefs questioned, the process of defending a viewpoint can often lead us to reevaluate and improve our judgments. We need this confrontation if we are to surrender and reevaluate our worldview. Constructive argumentation engages the reasoning process and improves the quality of reasoning itself. It's when beliefs go unchallenged because they are shared among like-minded individuals that judgments are most likely to reflect naïve or ill-suited intuitions—as many of the former executives discussed in this book would attest.

Just imagine these executives trying to persuasively defend their conduct at the time they were making their decisions. How successful would they have been in making a compelling case? I suspect that many would have found it very difficult to reasonably defend their choice of action and would ultimately have decided on another course.

All people, even those most senior within an organization, need other people who can probe their judgments and advise caution when they see trouble approaching. These warnings might come from a spouse, a friend, or a trusted colleague outside their immediate circle. Knowing who these other people are and having them in place can foster more effective leadership. Put more simply: poorly adapted intuitions need not be the final arbitrator of decisions. Overriding our initial impressions requires the opportunity to engage with contradictory viewpoints. Unfortunately, executives all too often surround themselves with sycophants who do not seek to deeply challenge them. The opportunities for dissent do not exist.

Ineffectual Compliance

The best way to reduce the incidence of white-collar crime—argue many prosecutors, judges, and scholars—is through vigorous enforcement. Through the imposition of lengthy prison sentences and large fines, according to this theory, executives ought to be dissuaded from engaging in illicit conduct. An important survey by scholars at Yale Law School found that judges agree, viewing deterrence as the most important goal of white-collar sentencing. Although there is much enthusiasm about the supposed deterrent effect of imprisoning executives who commit wrongdoing, evidence demonstrating the efficacy of this approach is far more elusive.

To appreciate why vigorous enforcement is not always effective in creating lasting deterrence, consider the consequences of greater policing on speeding behavior. With the cooperation of a police department, researchers posted police cars on a set of highways to observe how drivers responded to seeing additional police presence. As expected, drivers slowed down upon seeing the police. However, once the drivers managed to get a little physical distance between themselves and the police, the drivers accelerated. In fact, their speed rose exponentially in proportion to their distance away from the police car. Enforcement had an effect, but it was localized.

To investigate whether increased police enforcement had a lasting behavioral impact on drivers, the researchers tracked the license plates of cars over subsequent days to see how long the reductions in drivers' average speed lasted. The researchers found that, after seeing a police cruiser for the first time, drivers would return to their old ways within three days. When the police car was posted on the same stretch of highway for five consecutive days, drivers slowed down for a longer period, but this reduction, too, would vanish within six days. Ultimately, greater enforcement did not cause lasting changes in driving habits since speeding continued to feel like the appropriate norm for most drivers.

It's not that lasting deterrence is impossible to achieve, it's just more difficult than many people expect. For deterrence to directly impact behavior, the aversion to engaging in particular conduct needs to become so salient that individuals are overtly concerned. In 1974, Sweden established random roadblocks across the country that stopped drivers and screened them with a breathalyzer to assess their blood alcohol level. Those who exceeded the limit were immediately charged with driving under the influence and hauled into the police station for additional blood testing. The costly and intrusive program was effective in reducing drunk driving, but within a few months after this ambitious enforcement effort ended, drivers returned to their prior habits, having figured out that the likelihood of being caught was no longer so high. Thus, even very expensive enforcement efforts, like this one in Sweden, are not effective in maintaining lasting deterrence. The effect lasts only as long as people are consciously aware of the threat.

The difficulty of effectively deterring criminal acts, including those committed by executives, through greater regulatory sanctions and enforcement leads to a disconcerting conclusion: from an economic perspective, the "optimal" frequency of corporate malfeasance may not actually be zero. To be clear, this doesn't mean that misconduct is desirable. Naturally, the eradication of fraud from the financial system would be beneficial for consumers, shareholders, and investors. However, as the University of Chicago accounting professor Ray Ball pointed out, it's costly to deter fraudulent activity, and at some point it simply becomes uneconomical to create further deterrence and enforcement mechanisms. Imagine an economy with multiple auditors for every firm and redundant regulators to check each transaction that every executive has made. Although a system with double and triple checks would render fraud largely detectable and thus untenable, the negative externalities and associated costs of such a regulatory regime would be so onerous that more harm than good would be done.

This does not mean that we ought to simply resign ourselves to accepting the status quo of white-collar criminality; rather, my point is that fraudulent activity cannot be eliminated by solely relying on regulatory deterrence or enforcement efforts. Creating the type of provisions that would make the deterrent effect salient might be so intrusive that doing so would not be socially optimal. China once doled out the death penalty for white-collar convicts, but even with this ultimate punishment looming, executives continued to engage in corporate mischief.

Sanctions, even when incredibly severe, are often just too far removed and remote to become relevant to executives in their everyday decision making. It is only when the sanctions begin to influence everyday norms that avoiding certain types of undesirable conduct becomes ingrained within business culture. For example, regulators can endeavor to make penalties seem more relevant by widely publicizing cases of corporate misconduct and the resulting sanctions. However, instead of viewing this publicity as explicitly deterring future executive misconduct—a claim that relies on executives making their criminal decisions through an analytical process—it would be more appropriate to view these announcements as efforts to improve and strengthen business norms. Such efforts can slowly inculcate better values and nudge intuitions toward improved legal compliance by helping people better appreciate the undesirable and detrimental nature of certain actions.

It is possible that by helping to enforce particular values, individuals improve their conformity to those norms themselves. For example, when a member of the Orthodox Jewish community is sanctioned by a rabbinical court, the sanctions are enforced not only by a regulatory body but, more critically, by other members of the Orthodox community. In particular, members are asked to avoid socially interacting with or even supporting the business of the offender. By calling on the entire community to act, these norms are reinforced within members of the community while simultaneously punishing the offender.

In contrast to this rather stringent and public disciplining of norm violators in some Orthodox communities, white-collar offenders often face a starkly different—and notably weaker—set of sanctions by peers. Executives engaging in misconduct may be castigated by the press, but they often receive far less criticism within their own social communities. Letters sent on behalf of former executives by other distinguished individuals during sentencing frequently suggest more communal support than condemnation. It appears that, with the exception of some egregious cases of malfeasance, executives are often not deeply shamed by their immediate community. George Bernard Shaw once eloquently drew a similar distinction by comparing the treatment of common "street thieves" to elite offenders who steal during the course of business:

> The thief who is in prison is not necessarily more dishonest than his fellows at large, but mostly one who, through ignorance or stupidity, steals in a way that is not customary. He snatches a loaf of bread from the baker's counter and is promptly run into jail. Another man snatches bread from the table of hundreds of widows and orphans and similar credulous souls who do not know the ways of company promoters; and, as likely as not, he is run into Parliament.

Although there is "no soul to be damned and no body to be kicked," corporations can be held criminally responsible for the misconduct of their employees in the United States and several other countries. Corporate offenders can be fined—in some cases, very heavily—for their misdeeds, but unlike people, they do not face incarceration or many of the life-long effects of being a felon. For instance, the day after settling criminal charges with federal prosecutors for helping wealthy individuals evade taxes, executives at Credit Suisse held a conference call to reassure analysts that the criminal conviction would have "no impact on our bank licenses nor any material impact on our operational or business capabilities." And, ironically, fines levied on offending firms are ultimately paid by shareholders rather than by the executives or employees who actually engaged in the misconduct. Without the specter of the full justice system hanging over them as is the case with individual defendants, labeling firms as criminal often has surprisingly weak, or even misdirected, effects.

When a plane crashes, a team from the aerospace firm that built it is immediately dispatched to investigate and to work alongside governmental investigators and regulators. There's a genuine desire by aerospace executives and employees to understand the root causes of the failure and, if equipment is found to be at fault, to make appropriate changes to prevent future catastrophes. But unlike an aerospace firm trying to understand the failure of one of its planes, many industrial and financial executives have little interest in understanding the causes of destructive behavior within their own firms. Instead, it seems as though they would prefer to quietly pay fines, move on, and, in many cases, carry on business much as before. Given this disinterest in understanding the root causes of malfeasance and making genuine changes in response, it's not surprising that firms that are found liable or enter deferred prosecution agreements are often reoffenders in the future.

When regulators in the United Kingdom questioned Douglas Flint, chairman of HSBC, about the aiding of tax avoidance in his firm's private banking operations, he argued that: "I don't feel that proximate to what was happening in the private bank." But when the chairman who oversees a firm doesn't deeply relate to his firm's problems, who will seek to instill different norms? If the potential for criminal sanctions do not make senior leaders feel sufficiently proximate to take action to prevent failures, we must consider other ways to bring the firm's failings to the forefront of their attention.

While there are sensible reasons to avoid permanently impairing firms based on mistakes made by individual employees, offending firms should also not enjoy all of the same benefits as nonoffending firms. Companies that cultivate better norms of conduct and whose employees avoid malfeasance ought to have some advantages compared to those that do not. One path to consider in creating such advantages is through the firms' ability to attract and recruit the best talent.

Suppose that firms convicted of recent criminal offenses—firms that are felons in the eyes of the law—were not permitted to recruit on university campuses. Such a prohibition could be voluntarily implemented by individual schools and enforced during the time that the firms are implementing better systems. While this might appear to be a small penalty, temporarily banning these firms from campuses—a choice instituted by schools, not regulators—could instill an urgency to better address the roots of misconduct that might exceed even the largest fines.

Recruitment by criminal organizations on university campuses is not merely a hypothetical, either. During the 2015–2016 academic year, ten firms recruiting at Harvard were found to have had a criminal conviction or a deferred prosecution agreement in the previous year. Several firms were even on court-ordered probation—the closest they can get to "doing time"—while recruiting on campus.

In the case of firms that rely heavily on recruiting from university campuses, inhibiting their ability to attract new talent could have a profound impact on their competitiveness. Creating this impediment to attracting the kind of employee firms seek to hire would also motivate boards of directors to take greater accountability for the actions of all employees. To the extent that some firms are sanctioned for not consistently upholding the values that are cherished by institutions of higher learning, these firms would temporarily lose their license to use school resources to recruit for their organizations. Capturing the attention of students on campus would no longer be a preordained right but, rather, would represent a privilege that firms earn.

In some of the most lauded and valuable organizations in the world, deviance has seemingly become normalized. The remarkable frequency of such conduct isn't a state that we should accept. Endeavoring to create better norms shouldn't be something simply discussed as an ideal in classrooms or textbooks. Instead, it ought to be practiced through the policies that institutions create.

A Humble Conclusion

With ever-growing psychological distance separating people engaged in commerce, our antiquated moral intuitions are not well designed for the modern business world. And, unfortunately, there are no courses or preparatory materials that can immediately update and adapt intuitions for all the challenges that managers may confront during their careers. Even forty or fifty hours of training to cultivate stronger intuitions would be little more than a blip in time compared to all the other influences one is surrounded by in just a few weeks in any profession.

Even at places like McKinsey, KMPG, and Deloitte, which genuinely endeavor to promote a set of principled norms, some senior leaders have engaged in practices that are in direct opposition to their firms' values. Such deviations underscore the fact that newly created norms are neither natural nor permanent. Practicing and even "living" these values for decades within one of these firm cultures is insufficient to avoid the corrupting influence of encountering new and different norms. Maintaining new intuitions requires continual renewal and reinforcement. For these moral intuitions, there is no such thing as permanence.

THERE'S A FINE distinction between being confident and displaying hubris. The successful financiers Lloyd Blankfein of Goldman Sachs and Bill Ackman of Pershing Square Capital have both expressed how they believe their firms are doing "God's work." Even if stated in jest, this belief in the righteousness of their ambitions and the lack of any sense of fallibility is precisely the sentiment formerly held by many executives prior to faltering.

Nitin Nohria, dean of Harvard Business School, described an assignment he gives to new CEOs to complete during a training program for senior leaders. The CEOs are asked to rank a list of ten responsibilities— setting their firm's strategy, getting a new management team, and working with the board of directors, among others—from the item they feel most to least prepared to take on as they begin leading a multibillion-dollar organization.

Invariably, new CEOs rank "setting the right moral tone" as one of the easiest aspects of management. "They all feel deeply secure in their own moral compass," Nohria explained. "They have a sense that they are a people of extraordinary moral character and that it is very unlikely that they are going to do anything in their organization to lead either the organization astray or do something that will get them in the front pages of the newspapers." Yet, as Nohria pointed out, it is exactly many of these same leaders who later appear on the front pages of newspapers for engaging in precisely the egregious conduct that they once insisted they would never do.

The simple fact is, most of us think that we are better and more moral than we actually are. No one, especially those who have achieved success, believes that they are likely to stumble and err. It is this sense of invincibility that has felled leaders across a range of fields—including the cyclist Lance Armstrong, the writer Jonah Lehrer, and the NBC news anchor Brian Williams. It's only after faltering that people humbly ask, as observed by the psychologist Max Bazerman, "How could that have happened? and Why didn't I see that coming?"

One of the things that I've found especially fascinating during my conversations with the former executives discussed in this book is how strongly people hold on to the notion that it wasn't really their actions that were all that deceitful or destructive. Their actions are not that bad, they argue, when compared with what others have done. According to the executives who committed insider trading, it's the ones who committed financial fraud who really damaged the integrity of financial markets. According to those who engaged in financial fraud, it's the executives who built Ponzi schemes that lacked an underlying business who are the real culprits. And for those who created pyramid schemes, it's the investment bankers who went unpunished during the financial crises who are the real villains. Virtually every one of the former executives I spoke with pointed out, even complained, that it was not he who was the true villain—it was always someone else.

Beneath the irony of this defense, there is an interesting truth. We all confidently believe that we would have behaved differently if placed in the shoes of an executive engaging in malfeasance. However, this confidence is artificial.

We don't get to reevaluate executives' decisions using our current beliefs, the norms we're instilled with now, or our current perspectives on what matters most. Likewise, we don't get to bring along any finely tuned intuitions that we've acquired in our own lives to avoid this kind of behavior when we place ourselves in these executives' shoes. Instead, we have to imagine ourselves surrounded by their norms and immersed in their culture—not just in the present but in the past as well. We have to see ourselves as being shaped by the experiences they faced throughout their careers, not by those we face in our own.

If we see ourselves as experiencing the world as many of these former executives did, I don't believe we can actually know how we would act if placed in their shoes. If anything, maybe we ought to humbly recognize that we might have behaved as they did. Yet, we can still hope, wish, and believe that we would act differently. Frankly, however, we just can't know.

Perhaps Marc Dreier, the former graduate of Harvard and Yale who engineered a Ponzi scheme, actually had it right when he reflected on this conundrum. "It is easy to say you would never cross the line, but the line is presented to very, very few people," Dreier explained. "How many could say for sure that they would never do what I did if they had the opportunity and thought they wouldn't get caught?"

Appreciating our lack of invincibility—our inherent weakness and frailty—offers us the best chance of designing the appropriate mechanisms to help manage these limitations. If we learn to be more suspicious of our gut feelings when placed in new or difficult situations, we can acknowledge the need to create more opportunities for reflection and to bring in the viewpoints of others to question us. If we humbly recognize that we might not always even notice the choices that will lead us astray, we are more likely to develop ways to identify and control those decisions. But it's only when we realize that our ability to err is much greater than we often think it is that we'll begin to take the necessary steps to change and improve.

ACKNOWLEDGMENTS

I've long been a voracious reader and a prolific collector of books, but writing one of my own has given me a new respect for the stacks and stacks of texts that fill my home. The writing, editing, and rewriting to convey what one wants in an inch-thick pile of paper helped me appreciate that the author on the cover who gets the credit is just a part of a much broader effort.

As the prologue of the book makes clear, this project was one that grew uniquely out of my experience after joining the Harvard Business School. I don't think there is another institution in the world that would have given me the resources, time, and—most critically—the encouragement to embark on the journey that became this book. I fondly recall my first meeting with Nitin Nohria after he became dean of the Business School. Knowing that he had an interest in business ethics, I showed him a copy of my case "A Letter from Prison." His questions and curiosity helped me realize that the problems discussed by the case were not narrow ones contained within a single academic discipline. Dean Nohria saw that my approach was worthy of a book long before I realized it myself, and I've been incredibly appreciative of his support ever since.

At HBS, I've been especially lucky to be around two people—Max Bazerman and Francesca Gino—who not only served as inspiration because of their academic work on the psychology of ethical decision making, but whose encouragement and outright enthusiasm made me want to tackle this question in the broadest possible way. Max and Francesca were kind enough to help me better understand their work over the years I labored on this project, and if not for them this book would reflect a far narrower and ultimately less compelling inquiry. They know how to make research feel genuinely fun and I feel so fortunate that this project gave me an opportunity to spend time with them.

My colleagues in the accounting and management unit at HBS provide the kind of environment that makes coming into school each day a rewarding intellectual experience in all the best ways. From the debates in teaching group, to the hallway conversations, to feedback on presentations, it's been a wonderful home over the last seven years. Without these interactions, the initial letters from several former executives I received would simply have yellowed in their envelopes. Luckily, Krishna Palepu nudged me to write the case during my first semester at HBS. Bob Simons, always one to provide a unique and clever perspective, offered me just the advice I needed to turn a letter into a case that would resonate with others. David Hawkins offered me the privilege of making "A Letter From Prison" the final case taught in our course's cuirriculum. Paul Healy helped me think more deeply about approaching some of the challenges that one inevitably confronts while exploring such a challenging topic. Suraj Srinivasan has been a mentor since I was a graduate student and he's always given me just the right kind of advice. Bob Kaplan gave me the opportunity to discuss the project in his fantastic risk management executive education course, where he pointed out several connections with other areas that I previously hadn't considered.

My day-to-day discussions with Ian Gow, Jonas Heese, VG Narayanan, Karthik Ramanna, Tatiana Sandino, and Gwen Yu made writing this book feel like anything but a solo exercise. Srikant Datar attended the first time I taught the case, when I still had my case method training wheels on, but he still managed to see a spark in what I was doing. Dennis Campbell, along with delivering thoughtful advice, taught me about the wonders of coffee from exotic locales, which was often exactly what I needed in the final stages of book writing.

This project genuinely grew from my experience in the classroom. No one has made me think harder and helped me more in this way than Mike

Tushman, who leads the executive education course "Program for Leadership Development" that I now teach in. He offered me the encouragement—and latitude—to push this project further and consider more deeply about how to make it resonate with others. Although I'm the one standing in the front of the room, I've learned so much from the many participants in this program. Hearing them share their experiences has been incredibly enlightening and I deeply appreciate all the PLDers who've contributed to this book, both inside and outside the classroom. Teaching in PLD over the last three years has been one of the highlights of my professional career.

Throughout the years of working on this book, I've been extremely fortunate to have the help of several extraordinary people who've done everything from rummaging through the library for obscure documents to badgering courts for "lost" filings. Over the last five years, I've been especially lucky to have Sara Hess's energy and talent to help bring this project to fruition in innumerable ways. More recently, I'm grateful for David Singerman's exacting eye as he carefully picked through every chapter with a fine-toothed comb and used his talents to spot inconsistences and improve the clarity of the text. Curating the hundreds and hundreds of references and notes to make this text come together was a major undertaking for which I am indebted to the skillful hand of Natasha Dodge. All this could not have been done without the enthusiastic support of my research director at HBS, Teresa Amabile. Beyond helping me get the financial support needed to work on the project, Teresa helped me carefully think about how to tackle some of the more challenging aspects of this kind of field-based work.

The topic of corporate misconduct, even beyond that covered in the book, is one that I've explored in other papers, cases, and projects. I've benefited from the insight and research of Jonas Akins, Nanette Byrnes, Stephanie Havens, Courtney Hooton, Nik Kalyanpur, Sharon Kim, Alastair Su, Elizabeth Watkins, and Hilary White in exploring this topic in all its possible forms. In Baker Library, Meghan Dolan and Barbara Esty helped dig up some of the more interesting and elusive facts for the book. Laura Linard, director of the historical collections at HBS, manages to offer a new fascinating area to explore each time we meet. My sister, Eileen, endlessly supports all my endeavors and always manages to broaden my world with the unique references she sends me.

My longtime co-author and close friend David Solomon was generous enough to read each chapter (and some twice!) and give the kind of constructive—and colorful—feedback that one could only dream of while working on a project of this scope. Max Bazerman, Derek Haas, and Paul Healy took considerable amounts of their time to offer comments on the book's earlier and rougher forms. The effort to provide feedback on a 400-page draft is truly generous. Chris Costa, beyond offering fantastic ideas and pointing me in the direction of new, interesting sources while working on this project, read a copy of the proof and made numerous valuable suggestions. Sometimes it was the informal conversations that proved to be most valuable while I worked through some of the arguments. I have Chester Lee, Eric Powell, and Thales Teixeira to thank for their provocative discussions.

Although the methodological approach I employed for this project differed from the one that I was taught as a doctoral student, I still see the University of Chicago Booth School of Business as my intellectual home. It's here that I learned to think about problems more deeply and rigorously—tools central to any careful inquiry. I'm grateful to my advisors, Christian Leuz, Doug Skinner, and Abbie Smith, for helping nurture this skill in me during my time in the program. It was during a fortuitous springtime conversation that Ray Ball introduced me to what research accountants do and inspired me to go in the direction that I've found intellectually fulfilling ever since. Few conversations have been more pivotal and I'm so appreciative for Ray's patience in exploring these ideas with me from the ground up.

The Leadership and Corporate Accountability Group at Harvard Business School, the accounting department at the University of Chicago, members of the PCAOB, and economists at the Federal Reserve Bank of New York were all kind enough to give me the chance to present some of the material in the book, and the comments I received were immensely useful. Luigi Zingales, a scholar I admire for his own breadth in research, was generous with his time in discussing not only ideas but also how to approach writing one's first book. Baruch Lev taught an amazing seminar at NYU and gave me the opportunity to speak about some of these ideas with his class. During the more than two years I spent writing the book, conversations with Joe Badaracco, Clay Christensen, John Coates, Patty

Dechow, Leo Katz, Andrew Lo, Anette Mikes, Malcolm Salter, Stanley Sporkin, and Linda Thomsen all influenced its arguments. In the fall of 2014, I had the great pleasure of sitting in the white-collar crime seminar led by John Coffee and Judge Rakoff at Columbia Law School. It was a fascinating experience, and had I taken such a course fifteen years earlier I might have found myself pursuing law as a profession.

An early conversation with Steven Pinker, a scholar I've admired since I was in grade school, put me in touch with my agent Max Brockman, who helped me turn an idea into a compelling book proposal. John Mahaney at PublicAffairs exceeded all my expectations for an editor. He read chapters again and again (and sometimes again) not only to make the material more accessible but also to structure arguments so that they were stronger and sharper. Going from Word document to finished book requires a fantastic team with a range of skills from production management to copyediting. I was lucky to have Melissa Veronesi and Christine Arden as part of that team. Throughout my time at HBS, David Porter has made my life a whole lot more organized. Yet Dave's done far more than just this. I work a lot, but each day in the office is better because of Dave's energy and positive outlook that always lead to a good laugh.

My parents have been endlessly supportive of me throughout my many years in school. In so many ways, I'm a product of all their efforts. They've guided me to be a better person, and now that I'm a parent myself, they set an inspiring example of what great parents do. When they read this book, I hope they feel a measure of pride for the person they've helped create.

While I was writing this book, my wife, Jennifer, and I were extraordinarily lucky to have our first daughter, Aria-Belle. "Books and babies" was always our inside joke to describe what we were creating while she was pregnant. It turned out that it took me a lot longer to write a book, and AB really only knew me as that person who went back and forth to the office while I wrote night and day for her first year. Thanks to my beautiful wife for joining me for weekend meals at the office, always offering different ways to view matters in the world, and reading, then re-reading chapters. I know I spend a lot of time in my little bubble working and I can't tell you how appreciative I am that you let me indulge in my intellectual curiosities.

The arguments in this book are my own, but the success of this project very much relied on the former executives who spent considerable amounts of time speaking with and writing to me. I know it wasn't always easy for them to discuss their experiences or to respond to my questioning. Many might have found it easier to move past their prior errors and not speak with me at all. I sincerely appreciate their willingness to engage with me for this project. Beyond the book's contribution to the business community, I hope that in some small way it also offers a way for these men to more deeply understand themselves.

ILLUSTRATION CREDITS

Prologue.1   Letter from Richards: Eugene Soltes, "A Letter From Prison," HBS No. 110-059 (Boston: Harvard Business School Publishing, 2011).

1.1   Scott London in parking lot: United States Department of Justice.

1.2   Executive behind bars: Bob Gomel, *Life* Picture Collection, February 1, 1961.

2.1   Corporate Crime Comic: By Permission of Denis Kitchen of Kitchen Sink Press. Illustrated by Peter Poplaski.

3.1   Comparing man to animal: Giovanni Battista della Porta, "De humana physiognomonia libri IIII," (1593), courtesy of the Francis A. Countway Library of Medicine at Harvard Medical School.

3.2   Hooton's depiction of a fraudster: By Permission of Harvard University Press. Originally in E. A. Hooton, 1939, "Old American Criminals: Mosaic of Excess Metric and Morphological Features, Independent of Age and State Sampling: Forgers and Frauds," *Crime and the Man*, Cambridge, MA: Harvard University Press, p. 73. Copyright renewed 1967 by Mary C. Hooton.

4.1   Rice Krispies box: Photograph of cereal box courtesy of Baker Library at Harvard Business School.

5.1   White-collar crime cartoon: By Permission of Sage Stossel, *The Atlantic* ('Street Justice,' September 10, 2015).

5.2   Ranking of moral judgment: Illustration design by Elizabeth Watkins. Moral development by profession is measured by the p-index in the defining issues test (DIT). The DIT was designed as an easy to deploy "paper and pencil" alternative to Kohlberg's interview, but scholars later found several differences emerge given the differences in measurement (Thoma and Dong 2014). Studies assessing moral development by profession noted in the figure include—Junior high school students: Rest (1982); Pharmaceutical sales representatives: Shank (2005); Accounting firm partners: Ponemon (1992); Corporate board members: Brower and Shrader (2000); CFOs: Uddin and Gillett (2002); Middle management at manufacturing firms: Elm and Nichols (1993); Navy enlisted men: Rest (1982); Attorneys: Scofield (1997); Journalists: Coleman and Wilkins (2004); Doctors: Rest (1982); Moral philosophers: Rest (1982)..

7.1 Trolley switch dilemma: Illustration design by Alyssa Steiner.

7.2 Trolley footbridge dilemma: Illustration design by Alyssa Steiner.

7.3 Annual Report: Scan courtesy of Baker Library at the Harvard Business School.

8.1 ABACUS term sheet: ABACUS 2007-AC1 Final Term Sheet, available at the Financial Crisis Inquiry Commission at Stanford Law School.

8.2 Running from courthouse: Carlo Allegri, November 26, 2014. Reprinted with permission of Reuters Pictures.

10.1 Razmilovic wanted poster: US Postal Inspection Service.

10.2 Earnings management histogram: Calculation courtesy of Jihwon Park. For methodology underlying histogram, see endnote Figure 10.2 on page 376.

11.1 Insider communication: Illustration design by Alyssa Steiner.

12.1 Enron structured deal: Enron Backbone Transaction as described on page 6 in Appendix M to the Second Interim Report of Neal Batson, Court-Appointed Examiner (Case No. 01-16034).

13.1 Towers income: Illustration design by Elizabeth Watkins. Data is reported in the bankruptcy trustee's lawsuit (filed January 28, 1994) as reported in "The Amazing Towers Financial Affair" by Hilary Rosenberg in *Institutional Investor* (June 1994).

13.2 Stanford bank portfolio: Illustration design by Elizabeth Watkins. Data is reported the 2007 Stanford International Bank Annual Report, p. 20.

14.1 Madoff advertisement: Advertisement shown in the December 6, 1983, issue of the *Wall Street Journal* on page 45.

14.2 Split-strike conversion: Illustration design by Elizabeth Watkins. Strategy shown in a Fairfield Sentry Limited Presentation (October 2007) by the Fairfield Greenwich Group on slide 13.

Endnote.1 Tyco earnings: Illustration design by Elizabeth Watkins. Calculation courtesy of Jihwon Park.

NOTES

Prologue

1   **"It is hard to understand . . . "**: Peter Lattman, "Former Hedge Fund Trader Sentenced in Insider Case," *New York Times*, May 2, 2013.

1   **"You never really understand . . . "**: Lee (1960), p. 36.

1   **"to learn from . . . "**: Neff and Citrin (1999), p. 27.

1   **"We are confident . . . "**: Neff and Citrin (1999), p. 16.

1   **Convicted and headed to prison:** Ebbers was sentenced to twenty-five years in prison. Kozlowski was sentenced for between eight years and four months to twenty-five years. In 2006, Lay was found guilty of six counts of fraud and conspiracy; he faced between twenty and thirty years in prison but suffered a heart attack and died prior to sentencing.

2   **Collectively fined:** Michael Dell was fined $4 million (US Securities and Exchange Commission, Litigation Release No. 21599, July 22, 2010), and Hank Greenberg was fined $15 million (US Securities and Exchange Commission, Litigation Release No. 21170, August 6, 2009). Frank Raines agreed to forgo $24.7 million in compensation and to pay $2 million in penalties ("OFHEO Issues Consent Orders Regarding Former Fannie Mae Executives," Office of Federal Housing Enterprise Oversight press release, April 18, 2008). Both Dell and Greenberg consented to settle the SEC's charges without admitting or denying the charges. The firms of numerous other leaders named in *Lessons from the Top* (e.g., Computer Associates, GE) also faced charges related to fraud, but in those instances the executives named in the book were not charged.

2   **Gupta convicted of insider trading:** Gupta was convicted of insider trading in connection with Galleon Group (see "Former Chairman of Consulting Firm and Board Director, Rajat Gupta, Sentenced in Manhattan Federal Court to Two Years in Prison for Insider Trading," The United States Attorney's Office, Southern District of New York, October 24, 2012).

2   **"the Jeffrey Skilling I knew . . . "**: Christensen, Allworth, and Dillon (2012), p. 3.

2   **Offenders whose motivations were puzzling:** The scholarly literature in account-
        ing and finance has made significant strides in predicting the types of firms likely to
        engage in misconduct (e.g., Dechow et al. 2011; Hobson, Mayew, and Venkatacha-
        lam 2012), but predicting is different from understanding the motivation of execu-
        tives to engage in illicit conduct. One paper within this literature that does focus on
        understanding executives' incentives is Schrand and Zechman (2012) on executive
        overconfidence.

3   **Stephen Richards' letter:** Eugene Soltes, "A Letter from Prison," HBS No. 110–059
        (Boston: Harvard Business School Publishing, 2011). In his original letter, Richards
        refers in the singular to "a senior manager" but later uses the plural pronoun "their."
        Senior managers, rather than "a senior manager," is noted for consistency.

4   **Diversity of explanations for executives' misconduct:** Zahra, Priem, and Rasheed
        (2007) and Prentice (2007). In a reflection of the range of explanations, one police
        chief quoted in Hagan (2010) said: "We have looked at the causation of crime from
        perspectives ranging from economic factors and phases of the moon to biological
        phenomena. . . . Do we know what we need to know? Are we asking the right ques-
        tions? I am afraid at the present time we are not" (p. 14).

4   **Little understood about choices that led to their downfall:** Joe Queenan of the *Wall
        Street Journal* argues that there is even more to learn from failure than from success:
        "Give Commencement Podiums to Losers," *Wall Street Journal,* May 25, 2013. For a
        discussion of the motives of white-collar offenders: Bucy et al. (2008).

4   **Definition of white-collar criminal:** Some scholars and organizations argue that a
        white-collar criminal is anyone who commits an offense that employs deceit without
        a threat of violence—such as passing a bad check. Others contend that a white-collar
        criminal is anyone of high socioeconomic standing who commits a crime, even if
        that offense—for example, solicitation—is unconnected to their business (Podgor and
        Dervan 2016). Rather than relying on either of these categorizations, I used what I
        believed was the most natural interpretation of the term "white-collar crime" in de-
        ciding who to interview and where to focus my attention—namely, that white-collar
        criminals are people of high social standing who commit offenses while conduct-
        ing business. Although I appreciate that there are more expansive ways of defining
        white-collar criminals and white-collar crimes, it was the downfall of privileged ex-
        ecutives who seemed to have so much to lose and so little to gain from engaging in
        misconduct that originally created my interest. Likewise, it was the privilege enjoyed
        by these executives that created the impetus for much of the public furor against their
        conduct.

6   **Laws themselves may also be changing:** Silverglate (2009) and Fischel (1995).

8   **Role of character in causing white-collar crime:** Some people have a higher procliv-
        ity to engage in wrongdoing due to the nature of their character, which some might
        describe as a psychological aberration. For instance, in Chapter 14, I'll discuss Ber-
        nard Madoff, who exhibits a lower capacity to empathize than many other executives.
        I'll explore in Chapter 3 why such differences in character are likely to contribute to
        differences in behavior, but since these executives were not necessarily destined to
        commit crime, it's not accurate to ascribe their white-collar crimes to innate biologi-
        cal anomalies.

8   **Former executives and how they reflect on their actions:** Throughout this book,
        I largely focus on the malfeasances committed by the senior-most executives who
        hold leadership positions in a firm. Other researchers, however, have explored uneth-
        ical and/or fraudulent behaviors committed by people lower within organizations—
        behaviors that occur far more routinely. Factors contributing to fraud within middle/

lower management: Badaracco and Webb (1995), Milgram (1963), and Milgram (1974). "Ordinary" unethical behavior: Gino (2015). Fraud and limitations of the marketplace: Akerlof and Shiller (2015).

9   **Learn from the mistakes they made:** As the psychologist Roy Baumeister wrote, "It is a mistake to let moral condemnation interfere with trying to understand—but it would be a bigger mistake to let that understanding, once it has been attained, interfere with moral condemnation" (Baumeister 1999, p. 387). Explaining versus understanding evil: Waller (2007) and Miller, Gordon, and Buddie (1999).

9   **Prosecutorial overreach:** Readers may at times be concerned about what they perceive as prosecutorial overreach in seeking criminal sanctions for some executives in question. The desire to seek such significant penalties in these instances can remind one of a game once played by prosecutors, as described by Tim Wu: "At the federal prosecutor's office in the Southern District of New York, the staff, over beer and pretzels, used to play a darkly humorous game. Junior and senior prosecutors would sit around, and someone would name a random celebrity—say, Mother Theresa or John Lennon. It would then be up to the junior prosecutors to figure out a plausible crime for which to indict him or her. The crimes were not usually rape, murder, or other crimes you'd see on *Law & Order* but rather the incredibly broad yet obscure crimes that populate the U.S. Code like a kind of jurisprudential minefield: Crimes like 'false statements' (a felony, up to five years), 'obstructing the mails' (five years), or 'false pretenses on the high seas' (also five years). The trick and the skill lay in finding the more obscure offenses that fit the character of the celebrity and carried the toughest sentences. The, result, however, was inevitable: 'prison time'" (Tim Wu, "American Lawbreaking," *Slate,* October 14, 2007).

9   **All susceptible to making same mistakes as these former executives:** What accounts for this disconnect is the "fundamental attribution error," a bias whereby people believe that others' decisions are made on the basis of internal characteristics and personality whereas their own decisions are based on the external characteristics of the situation they confront. For more information on the fundamental attribution error, see Ross (1977) and Ross and Nisbett (1991).

9   **Less time pondering what might undermine these accomplishments:** A notable exception to the trend of focusing on managerial success has been recent work by psychologists studying behavioral ethics who have made progress in understanding the different biases that can lead us to become "sidetracked"; in particular, see Gino (2013), Bazerman and Tenbrunsel (2011), and Ariely (2012).

Chapter 1: Pillars of the Community

15   **Deckers trade:** This trade never actually took place but, rather, was created as part of the FBI investigation into London's activities.

16   **"The general policy was not to indict . . . ":** Victor Navasky, "A Famous Prosecutor Talks About Crime," *New York Times,* February 15, 1970. By the late 1960s, Morgenthau had decided to break this unwritten code and indict his first set of executives—partners at a major accounting firm. The executives were soon found guilty of fraudulently altering statements at trial and potentially faced years in prison. "We received an awful lot of criticism from the accounting profession and from some lawyers saying that we were being too harsh in holding these people responsible in a criminal case," Morgenthau recalled. However, "we just felt that when accountants break the law and they do it knowingly and they certify a commercial balance sheet,

they should be held responsible in a criminal case just the way somebody is who robs a bank or steals a car."

17   **"misleading and incorrect":** Sutherland (1940), p. 2.

17   **Examples of much earlier cases of financial misconduct and fraud:** Although incarcerating business leaders was rare prior to the mid-twentieth century, some prominent executives were criminally sanctioned before this time. Richard Whitney, vice-president and later president of the New York Stock Exchange during the Great Depression, was convicted of embezzlement and sentenced to more than five years in prison (MacKay 2013, Galbraith 1954). America's first treasury secretary, Robert Morris, spent over three years in debtor's prison (Rappleye 2010). And James Landis, the second commissioner of the Securities and Exchange Commission and later dean of Harvard Law School, served time for tax evasion (Ritchie 1980). Partnoy (2009) Taylor (2013), Wilson (2014), Crane, Raiswell, and Reeves (2004), Klaus (2014), and Thornton (2015).

17   **Origins of Sutherland coining "white-collar crime":** In 1926, a piece in *The Literary Digest* alluded to several of the themes later described by Sutherland, specifically calling these individuals "white-collar bandits" ("War on the White-Collar Bandits," *The Literary Digest,* March 6, 1926). Muckraker journalism: Braithwaite (1985), Newman (1958a), and Pettegree (2014).

17   **"heaved scores of sociological textbooks . . . ":** "Poverty Belittled as Crime Factor," *Philadelphia Inquirer,* December 28, 1939.

17   **"which discarded accepted conceptions . . . ":** "Hits Criminality in White Collars," *New York Times,* December 28, 1939.

17   **"the financial cost . . . ":** Ibid.

18   **"ambulance chasers . . . ":** Sutherland (1940), p. 4. Europeans also have expressions for white-collar economic crimes that precede Sutherland's remarks (see Kellens 1968).

18   **"legitimate rackets":** Sutherland (1940), p. 3.

18   **"White-collar crime . . . ":** Sutherland (1940), p. 5.

18   **"the most admirable . . . ":** Calkins (1928), p. 293.

18   **"most influential man . . . ":** Edna Lonigan, "Wanted: A New Criticism of Business," *The New Republic,* June 26, 1929, p. 144. Also see Calkins (1928), p. 232.

18   **Era of prosperity with executives who enjoyed admiration and respect:** Regarding this "era of prosperity," see Seligman (2003), p. 2. However, such optimism was not universal. In June 1929, a writer for *The New Republic* disapprovingly noted "how little modern business has been exposed to realistic criticism" (Edna Lonigan, "Wanted: A New Criticism of Business," *The New Republic,* June 26, 1929, p. 142).

19   **S&P Composite Index value:** The return of S&P's Composite Index is computed from Center for Research in Security Prices (CRSP) data on the S&P's stock index.

19   **Change in perceptions of business:** Galambos (1975) and Mayo and Nohria (2005).

19   **"ideal modern bank executive":** Carlton Shively, *New York Sun,* May 1929, as cited in "Damnation of Mitchell," *Time,* March 6, 1933, p. 53.

19   **"responsible for this stock crash":** "Damnation of Mitchell," *Time,* March 6, 1933, p. 53.

19   **Sutherland developed interest in corporate malfeasance:** Sutherland began collecting materials as early as 1928; for further details, see preface to Sutherland (1983, p. xvii) and Cohen, Lindesmith, and Schuessler (1956).

19   **"I would do it again . . . ":** Philip Kinsley, "Insull: I Would Do It Again," *Chicago Daily Tribune,* November 3, 1934. Also see Eugene Speck, "Samuel Insull Still Sees Self as a Great Man," *Chicago Daily Tribune,* March 18, 1934.

19   **Sutherland's reaction to Insull:** Geis and Goff (1986), p. 5.

19   **"by flagitious practices . . . ":** Ross (1907), p. 48.

19   **"But since they are not culpable . . . ":** Ibid.

19   **"murders with an adulterant . . . ":** Ross (1907), p. 7.

20   **"these white-collar criminaloids . . . ":** Sutherland (1934), p. 32.

20   **Sutherland's presidential address:** In a 1932 article titled "Social Process in Behavior Problems," in *Publications of the American Sociological Society,* Sutherland hastily noted for the first time that prior theory of criminal behavior "does not explain the financial crimes of the white-collar classes." Two years later, Sutherland briefly alluded to the concept of white-collar crime in his popular textbook *Principles of Criminology* (1934). But it was not until 1939 that Sutherland finally presented his ambitious assessment of the white-collar crime problem in his speech to the American Sociological Society. In 1959, the organization switched its name to the American Sociological Association.

20   **Growth of consumer protection laws:** Nadel (1971), Mayer (1989), Winerman (2003), and Daemmrich and Radin (2007).

20   **"financial pirates . . . ":** Keller and Gehlmann (1988), p. 331, with emphasis on "but" in the original. Keller and Gehlmann, citing others, note that variations of this quote can be found in numerous sources.

20   **Legislators did not want to lose licensing fees:** Reflecting on the weakness of blue-sky laws, Seligman (2003) notes that "as early as 1915, the Investment Bankers Association had reported to its members that they could 'ignore' all blue-sky laws by making offerings across state lines through the mails" (p. 45).

20   **Rein in corporate conduct at the federal level and Sherman Act:** Of the 438 actions favorably pursued by the Department of Justice for Violations of the Sherman Act between 1890 and 1929, only 27 percent were criminal prosecutions against firms (Sutherland 1945). Also see Cahill (1952).

20   **Early-twentieth-century economic regulation:** Seligman (2003). Limits of self-regulation: Balleisen (2009).

21   **Roosevelt proposed regulation to control "privileged princes":** In his Democratic National Address on June 27, 1936, Franklin Roosevelt was particularly vocal about some of the problems posed by business claiming that "privileged princes of . . . new economic dynasties" threatened the freedom of the American people by controlling labor conditions, hours worked, and wages earned—and by gambling with individuals' savings. He went on to say that "through new uses of corporations, banks and securities, new machinery of industry and agriculture, of labor and capital—all undreamed of by the Fathers—the whole structure of modern life was impressed into this royal service." His speech ultimately called for an increased governmental role in protecting "equal opportunity in the market place" from business interests.

21   **"bankers high & low . . . ":** "Damnation of Mitchell," *Time,* March 6, 1933.

21   **Executives usually avoided criminal prosecution:** See Yoder (1978) for a discussion of why corporate punishments are not more severe. Yoder contends that the leniency of such sanctions is a consequence of the "problem of moral neutrality," for, he argues, "there is no clear correlation between what is commercially acceptable vs. legally acceptable behavior" (p. 41).

21   **"the crimes of the lower class . . . ":** Sutherland (1940), p. 8.

21   **"how the criminal law":** Sutherland (1940), p. 8. In 1904, George Alger alluded to some of the same challenges that Sutherland associated with criminalizing actions of people of high social status. "As a people," Alger (1904) argued, "we have a curious

dislike to punish severely criminals of good social standing who have respectable friends."

22 **SEC's seeking of criminal charges by referral:** Rabin (1972) and Matthews (1971). Zimring and Hawkins (1973) argue that it is the punishment, rather than the crime itself, that is considered disgraceful.

22 **"white-collar criminals are segregated . . . ":** Sutherland (1940), p. 8.

22 **Executives compared to the clergy:** Sutherland (1940), p. 9.

22 **Criminal activity seemed to be restricted to street crimes:** In 1930, the Federal Bureau of Investigation began to report and record national crime statistics as part of its Uniform Crime Reports (UCR) program. The UCR covered statistics on violent crimes such as murder, rape, robbery, and assault as well as property crimes such as burglary, larceny, and vehicular theft.

22 **Documented crime:** Sutherland (1940), p. 1.

22 **"since crime is concentrated . . . ":** Sutherland (1940), p. 1. For a discussion of feeble-mindedness and crime, see Zeleny (1933).

22 **"businessmen are generally not poor . . . ":** Sutherland (1948), p. 79.

22 **Erroneous approach by criminologists:** Sutherland (1949), p. 9.

23 **Sutherland preaching theory:** Geis and Goff (1986).

23 **Sutherland's methods:** Sutherland (1983), p. xiv.

23 **Sutherland recorded actions against firms:** In this study, Sutherland defined violations of law as the following: "restraint of trade; misrepresentation in advertising, infringement of patent, trademarks, and copyrights; 'unfair labor practices' as defined by the National Labor Relations Board and a few decisions under other labor laws; rebates; financial fraud and violation of trust; violations of war regulations; and some miscellaneous offences." See chapter 2 in Sutherland (1983) for additional data on violations.

23 **Sutherland's findings:** Sutherland (1949), p. 18.

23 **"the ideal businessman . . . ":** Sutherland (1968), p. 69.

23 **Perception of business in the 1940s:** Mayo and Nohria (2005).

23 **"daring to call . . . ":** Bacon (1950), p. 309.

23 **"an unlawful act . . . ":** Sutherland (1949), p. 35.

23 **Press concerns about Sutherland's assertions:** Geis and Goff (1983), p. x. Also see Geis and Goff (1986). Documents suggest that, rather than considering white-collar crime solely as an academic interest, Sutherland personally believed that companies should be condemned for their immoral actions. In 1942, he sent a letter to the manager of the Hoosier Motor Club in which he wrote: "I feel the government is entirely justified in sending the FBI to investigate you. They may find that your action is directed from Berlin or they may find that it is merely selfish interest in your own welfare; the effects are the same" (Geis and Goff 1983, p. xv).

23 **University concerns about donors:** Geis and Goff (1983), p. x.

24 **Sutherland removing names from book:** Geis and Goff (1983) describe Sutherland's angst over removing this content (pp. x–xi), but later Geis and Goff (1986) wrote that Sutherland had "readily agreed to have the names of the corporations deleted" (p. 20). After removing the names, though, Sutherland sent relevant court cases to individuals who requested the names of the corporations, but he did not release the firms' names themselves (Geis and Goff 1983, p. xi). A later revised and uncut version of the book, published in 1983, provides firm names.

24 **Academic reviewers recognized that Sutherland's contribution:** Hermann Mannheim, a prominent criminologist, called the book a "milestone," and Robert Sorenson wrote in the *Journal of Criminal Law and Criminology* that it deserved "excited

promotion rather than mere reviewing" (Mannheim 1949, p. 244; Sorenson 1950, p. 82). However, Sutherland's book also drew criticism for extending several arguments beyond his data. The most prominent criticisms focused on arguments by Sutherland that blurred the distinction between criminal prosecutions and civil charges, anthropomorphized corporations, and extended analyses to people despite looking only at data on corporations. Further discussion of criticism of Sutherland's work: Tappan (1947), Cressey (1951a), Newman (1958b), Caldwell (1958), Geis (1962), and Bell (1960).

24 **Undesirable activities occurring at the highest echelons of society:** Others had mentioned the idea behind white-collar crime earlier, but with less force and empirical clarity (e.g., Morris 1935).

24 **Scholarship after Sutherland:** Clinard (1952), Cressey (1953), and Hartung (1950). Geis (1992) noted that white-collar crime as a scholarly pursuit was largely abandoned in the 1960s.

24 **"institutional crimes can never . . . ":** "Books in Brief: White Collar Crime by Edwin H. Sutherland," *Harper's Magazine, 199,* 1949, p. 110.

24 **"Most of the studies . . . ":** Geis and Goff (1986), p. 25.

24 **Survey on attitudes about crime in 1950s:** Rettig and Pasamanick (1959).

24 **Media and corporate malfeasance in the 1960s:** Hodges (1963).

25 **Journalists' limitations:** Yoder (1978), p. 48. Modern criticism of the business press and corporate malfeasance: Schiffrin (2002), Sherman (2002), Starkman (2008), and Geis and Goff (1983).

25 **"The cultural, spiritual, social, moral . . . ":** Theodore Levitt, "Are Advertising and Marketing Corrupting Society? It's Not Your Worry," *Advertising Age,* October 6, 1958, p. 89. Levitt went on to write that "as a business man I suggest you serve business and yourself. That is your only function. Savings souls, promoting or preserving spiritual values, elevating taste, cultivating human dignity and consumer self-respect—these high-priority objectives are other people's business if that is what they want to do. The businessman's job is to do the things that are the pure, undiluted objectives of business—to satisfy the materialistic and related ego objectives of those who run it" (p. 92).

25 **"Here were the classic elements . . . ":** Anthony Lewis, "Trust Case Raises Big Questions," *New York Times,* February 12, 1961.

25 **Electrical equipment price-fixing conspiracy:** Herling (1962) and Fuller (1962).

26 **Price-conspiracy market shares:** Fuller (1962), p. 34.

26 **Judge Ganey's findings:** Richard Austin Smith, "The Incredible Electrical Conspiracy," *Fortune,* April 1961, p. 133.

26 **"tiny $2 insulators . . . ":** Ibid.

26 **Media attention unrivaled in the history of journalism:** Dershowitz (1961) argues that although this was the largest and most-publicized antitrust prosecution in history, the vast majority of the attention was focused on the executives being sentenced rather than on the firms (p. 289).

26 **"In the past 30 years . . . ":** Robert F. Kennedy, "Robert Kennedy Examines the Electric Company Scandals: This Case Is a Reflection on All of Us," *Life,* February 24, 1961, p. 31. Supporting Kennedy's comment, Cahill (1952) notes that "no businessman has ever gone to jail for violation of the Sherman Act" (p. 46).

27 **"where the small businessman . . . ":** Robert F. Kennedy, "Robert Kennedy Examines the Electric Company Scandals: This Case Is a Reflection on All of Us," *Life,* February 24, 1961, p. 32.

27 **"cold-blooded ":** Geis (1977), p. 117.

27   **"fine man . . . ":** "Robert Kennedy Examines the Electric Company Scandals," *Life,*
      February 24, 1961, p. 31. Defendants' attorneys' responses are also described in "7
      Electrical Officials Get Jail Terms in Trust Case," *New York Times,* February 7, 1961.

27   **Coverage and discussion of trial:** Richard Austin Smith, "The Incredible Electrical
      Conspiracy," *Fortune,* April 1961; Richard Austin Smith, "The Incredible Electrical
      Conspiracy—Part II," *Fortune,* May 1961; Herling (1962); Fuller (1962); Geis (1977);
      Fisse and Braithwaite (1983); Baker and Faulkner (1993); and Sonnenfeld and Law-
      rence (1978).

27   **"There goes my whole life . . . ":** Richard Austin Smith, "The Incredible Electrical
      Conspiracy," *Fortune,* April 1961, p. 134.

28   **Kennedy suggested it would be worthwhile if the business community could de-
      velop standards:** The Presidential News Conference was held on February 8, 1961. At
      the conference, Kennedy commented: "I am hopeful that the Department of Justice,
      the Antitrust Division which was very effectively led in recent months, and other
      agencies of the Government . . . —and the Congress—will concern itself about the
      problem of conflicts of interest and monopolistic practices, as well as even more il-
      licit practices conducted in the American business community. And I hope that the
      business community itself will consider what steps it could take in order to lift this
      shadow from its shoulders" (John F. Kennedy, Presidential News Conference, Febru-
      ary 8, 1961).

28   **Ethics advisory council:** Members of the clergy were regularly involved in discus-
      sions of business ethics in the 1960s. In fact, one of the most well-known studies of
      corporate ethics early in this decade, published in the *Harvard Business Review,* was
      completed by Reverend Raymond Baumhart (see Baumhart 1961).

28   **Starkly unfavorable response from businessmen in attendance:** This cold reception
      reflected the growing antagonism between the business community and the presi-
      dent. After President Kennedy helped union steel workers negotiate a wage increase,
      U.S. Steel unexpectedly raised its prices. In response, Kennedy responded that "all
      business men were sons-of-bitches, but I never believed it till now." The quote, cap-
      tured by journalists, placed Kennedy in an awkward situation.

28   **"Two or three people . . . ":** Hodges (1963), pp. 28–29.

28   **"not something we can forget . . . ":** Robert F. Kennedy, "Robert Kennedy Examines
      the Electric Company Scandals," *Life,* February 24, 1961, p. 32. However, Jack Katz,
      a sociologist from UCLA, observed of the 1960s that "these were isolated events. No
      patterned expansion of general movement in law enforcement sprang from them"
      (Katz 1980, p. 162).

29   **"If he fixes . . . ":** Fisse and Braithwaite (1983), p. 187. The commentary originally
      appeared in *Value Line Survey,* March 13, 1961.

29   **Economic regulation and enforcement:** Kadish (1962) and Green (1997).

29   **Debate about what specific behavior ought to be prohibited by regulation:** Cahill
      (1952) notes that "it does seem clear that Congress never intended that individuals be
      criminally prosecuted for non-racketeering violations" (pp. 45–46). Also see Jackson
      and Dumbauld (1938).

29   **"Without moral wrongfulness . . . ":** Green (1997), p. 1569.

29   **"Sure, collusion was illegal . . . ":** Quoted in Richard Austin Smith, "The Incredible
      Electrical Conspiracy," *Fortune,* April 1961, p. 135.

29   **"these men did not act . . . ":** "WE Officials to Keep Posts," *The Herald,* February 6,
      1961, pp. 1–2. The legal response to corporate misconduct is discussed more broadly
      in Geis (1977) and Coffee (1977).

29   **Convicted executives continuing their careers:** Herling (1962).

30 **Ginn's career post-indictment:** Obituary of William Ginn, *Daily Gazette*, February 4, 1993.

30 **Lewis Burger accolades:** Upon his death, Burger also received commendation by the State of Illinois in a Senate Resolution (States of Illinois 91st General Assembly, SR0323).

30 **Attitudes toward the indicted executives:** Herling (1962).

30 **Price-fixing cost to the public:** Commission on Law Enforcement and Administration of Justice (1967), p. 24.

30 **"The public tends . . . ":** Commission on Law Enforcement and Administration of Justice (1967), p. 158. Despite the limited attention paid to business crime in its report, the commission does acknowledge the significance of white-collar crime. In the report's introduction, the commission states that "the price fixing by 29 electrical equipment companies alone probably cost utilities, and therefore the public, more money than is reported as stolen by burglars in a year" (p. 48).

Several years later, a survey of college students still found widespread ambivalence and even ignorance about white-collar criminality. Of the more than three hundred students surveyed, only 32 percent could reasonably define a white-collar offense. When asked what, if anything, they feared about white-collar crime, 60 percent of the students answered that they were unsure about their feelings regarding the consequences of such crime, or even about how they would feel as victims of a white-collar crime (Reed and Reed 1975).

30 **"It is essential . . . ":** Commission on Law Enforcement and Administration of Justice (1967), p. 159. Competing evidence suggests that, in at least some limited contexts, people view white-collar crime more seriously: Braithwaite (1982), Newman (1957), and Frankel (2006).

31 **"Forces in the criminal justice system . . . ":** Ogren (1973), p. 968.

31 **Society without laws against fraud:** Ogren (1973), p. 988.

Chapter 2: Creating the White-Collar Criminal

33 **Corporate bribery:** Louis M. Kohlmeier, "The Bribe Busters," *New York Times*, September 26, 1976; Sporkin (2004).

33 **"What bothered me . . . ":** Sporkin, interviewed by Irving Pollack (2003).

33 **"How did . . . ":** Sporkin (2004), p. 15.

33 **"discovered that . . . ":** Sporkin (2004), p. 3.

33 **Eli Black jumped from the 44th floor:** The specific floor is subject to some dispute. Kohlmeier ("The Bribe Busters," *New York Times*, September 26, 1976) cites the 44th floor, Ferrara (interviewed by Kenneth Durr, 2008) cites the 90th floor, and Noonan (1984) cites the 22nd floor. As the building has only 59 floors and Black's office was on the 44th floor, it seems that the 44th floor is most likely.

34 **"Ralph . . . ":** Ferrara, interviewed by Kenneth Durr (2008), p. 12. Typographic errors in the original quotation were revised after a conversation between Ferrara and myself in June 2016.

34 **Black committed suicide after depositing funds into Swiss bank account:** United Brands agreed to pay President López a total of $2.5 million in two installments. Black committed suicide before the second installment was paid. He sent a letter to shareholders in August 1974 claiming that United Brands had reached "an understanding" with the Honduran government in regard to banana export taxes. See "Buying Favor," *The Wall Street Journal*, April 9, 1975.

34   **United Brands' bribery:** Tracy (1976); Douglas Martin, "Oswaldo López Arellano, 88, Two-Time Honduran President," *New York Times,* May 18, 2010.

34   **Lockheed Martin's bribes:** Noonan (1984) and Kotchian (1976).

34   **Foreign bribery:** Michael Jensen, "U.S. Company Payoffs a Way of Life Overseas," *New York Times,* May 5, 1975.

34   **United Brands' bribery:** "Buying Favor," *Wall Street Journal,* April 9, 1975.

35   **Castle & Cooke payments:** Castle & Cooke was accused of paying police and military officials to ensure the safety of employees working in dangerous locations. See Walter Guzzardi, Jr., "An Unscandalized Views of Those 'Bribes' Abroad," *Fortune,* July 1976.

35   **"lawless behavior . . . ":** Fischel and Sykes (1996), p. 339.

35   **Increased incidence of corporate criminality in the 1970s:** Nader (1965), Nader (1973), Clinard and Yeager (1980), Cullen, Maakestad, and Cavender (1987), Mayer (1989), Johnson and Douglas (1978), Comer (1977), and Simon and Eitzen (1990). **History of environmental and consumer protection:** Vogel (1981).

35   **Car manufacturer's decision to leave faulty fuel tank in place, to a chemical company discharging pesticides into waterways:** This is in reference to the Ford Motor Company's Pinto automobile scandal and Allied Chemicals' release of pesticides into Virginia waterways. For further discussion, see Fisse and Braithwaite (1983).

35   **"the business pages . . . ":** Coffee (1977), p. 1101.

35   **"crime in the executive suite . . . ":** Irwin Ross, "How Lawless Are Big Companies?" *Fortune,* December 1980.

35   *Corporate Crime Comics: Corporate Crime Comics* was short-lived, with only two issues printed with limited print runs. However, people were initially optimistic about its potential ("Who Says Comics Are Just for Children?," *St. Petersburg Independent,* April 19, 1980, p. 5-D).

35   **Only 19 percent of survey respondents:** Another discussion of the growth in corporate criminality in the 1970s can be found in "High Rating Is Given to Doctors," *New York Times,* August 22, 1976. Also see Cullen, Link, and Polanzi (1982) and Cullen et al. (1985).

37   **Social movement against business:** Katz (1980), Vogel (1979), McCraw (1981), and Poveda (1992).

37   **"out of step . . . ":** Selwyn Raab, "U.S. Attorney Calls F.B.I. Out of Step," *New York Times,* July 4, 1976.

37   **FBI's greater enforcement of white-collar crime:** Simon and Swart (1984), Rowan and Mazie (1980), and Obermaier and Morillo (1990).

37   **"Attorneys employed . . . ":** Genego (1988).

37   **Department of Justice made white-collar crime a top priority:** Not everyone agreed with this focus. Wilson (1975) wrote that "predatory street crime is a far more serious matter than consumer fraud, antitrust violations, prostitution, or gambling, because predatory street crime . . . makes difficult or impossible the maintenance of meaningful human communities" (p. xix). Also see Genego (1988).

37   **Foreign Corrupt Practices Act and deductibility:** Noonan (1984), Coffee (1977), and Chu and Magraw (1978).

37   **Executives responsible for conduct outside of their direct supervision:** *United States of America v. John R. Park,* 421 U.S. 658, U.S. Supreme Court, June 9, 1975.

38   **"are thinking about . . . ":** "The Law Closes In on Managers," *Business Week,* May 10, 1976, p. 112.

38   **"At 10:30 a.m. yesterday . . . ":** James B. Stewart and Daniel Hertzber, "Insider Trading: The Scandal Spreads—Street Bombshell: Inside-Trading Scandal Implicates High Aides at Goldman, Kidder—Chiefs of Arbitrage Arrested, Along with Third Man in

the Widening Fraud—Traders Watch a Handcuffing," *Wall Street Journal,* February 13, 1987.

38   **Rudolph Giuliani:** Kirtzman (2000).

38   **Perp walk:** "Interview with Rudolph Giuliani, United States Attorney for the Southern District of New York," *Corporate Crime Reporter,* April 1987.

38   **Intimidation by Rudolph Giuliani in white-collar cases:** Fischel (1995).

39   **Employing RICO to yield prosecutions:** Formally, the legislation is Title IX of the Organized Crime Control Act of 1970.

39   **Giuliani, RICO, and financial crimes:** Thomas E. Ricks, "Giuliani Would Use Racketeering Law If Warranted in Wall Street Inquiries," *Wall Street Journal,* January 25, 1988.

39   **"to drop . . . ":** Fischel (1995), p. 123.

39   **Applying RICO to financial crimes:** L. Gordon Crovitz, "The SEC Overstepped When It Made Insider Trading a Crime," *Wall Street Journal,* December 1990; Baird and Vinson (1990); Blakey et al. (1990); and Fischel (1995). The breadth of RICO's application continued to be a subject of debate; see, for example, Stigall (1995).

39   **Charges against Ivan Boesky:** Not everyone agreed that Giuliani's prosecutions were consistent with perceived notions of justice; see Fischel (1995) and Silverglate (2009).

39   **"long probationary periods . . . ":** Herling (1962), p. 196.

40   **"the time has come . . . ":** James Sterngold, "Boeskey Sentenced to 3 Years," *New York Times,* December 19, 1987.

40   **White-collar crime prosecution under Thornburgh:** Thornburgh (2003).

40   **"The rules apply . . . ":** Rubin (2000).

40   **Three impediments for Sutherland:** In December 1944, on the fifth anniversary of his 1939 presidential address, Sutherland planned to give another presentation on white-collar criminality that laid out these criteria. The address was canceled owing to fuel rationing regulation during wartime, but a subsequent publication ("Is 'White Collar Crime' Crime?" *American Sociological Review, 10,* 1945, 132–139) laid out its arguments.

41   **Convictions in United States:** Corporate Fraud Task Force (2008).

41   **Status and wealth prove to be a vulnerability:** Some have argued that the television personality Martha Stewart, for instance, would not have been criminally prosecuted had it not been for her celebrity status. Stewart's lawyer, questioning her prosecution, asked: "Is it for publicity purposes because Martha Stewart is a celebrity?" (Kurt Eichenwald, "Prosecuting Martha Stewart: The Government; Prosecutors Have Reasons for Stalking Celebrities," *New York Times,* June 5, 2003).

For discussions of the gradual social movement against white-collar crime, see Katz (1980), Cullen, Link, and Polanzi (1982), Cullen et al. (1983), Kramer (1989), Poveda (1992), and Cullen, Hartman, and Jonson (2009). Other scholars argue that regulators became less vigilant in the early 1980s; see, for example, Hagan (2010).

41   **"He had the money . . . ":** Ian Mount, "Spain Toughens Up on Financial Criminals," *Fortune,* October 25, 2014.

41   **"in consideration . . . ":** "Guilty Hyundai Boss Escapes Jail," *BBC News,* September 6, 2007.

41   **"are so important . . . ":** "Is Korea Soft on White-Collar Crime?" *Korea Herald,* March 6, 2012.

41   **International white-collar crime:** "Omani CEO Jailed for 23 Years in Graft Case: Court," *Reuters,* February 27, 2014.

41	**Six years in prison:** The study referenced is Karpoff, Lee, and Martin (2008). Penalties for fraud in the United States: Karpoff, Lee, and Martin (2008), Srinivasan (2004), and Bowman (2004).

41	**"The number . . . ":** "Mendelsohn Says Criminal Bribery Prosecutions Doubled in 2007," *Corporate Crime Reporter, 36,* September 16, 2008.

42	**Article about how to adjust going to prison:** "Going to Jail," *Wealth (Financial Times* quarterly), Autumn 2014; also see Rochelle Toplensky, "How to Ease Yourself into the Prison Experience," *Financial Times,* September 19, 2014.

42	**Programs to prepare executives for incarceration:** Wall Street Prison Consultants, Executive Prison Consultants, and Prison Consultants (in the United Kingdom) are examples of these services. Another resource that provides background material on serving time in prison is *Federal Prison: A Comprehensive Survival Guide* (Richards 2012).

42	**Quintupling of penalties:** See *United States of American v. Rajat K. Gupta,* 11 Cr. 907 (JSR), Sentencing Memorandum and Order, United States District Court Southern District of New York (October 24, 2012). For a discussion of the sentence length post-passage of the Sarbanes-Oxley Act, see Podgor (2007a), Podgor (2007b), Bowman (2004), and "Go Directly to Jail: White Collar Sentencing After the Sarbanes-Oxley Act," *Harvard Law Review, 122,* 1728–1749.

42	**"there may never . . . ":** Shawn Young and Peter Grant, "Executives on Trial: More Pinstripes to Get Prison Stripes," *Wall Street Journal,* June 20, 2005. Examples of changes in white-collar sentencing: Bowman (2004), p. 428.

42	**Occupy Wall Street:** Bill Chappell, "Occupy Wall Street: From a Blog Post to a Movement," National Public Radio, October 20, 2011; and Josh Fjelstad, "The 50 Best Signs from #OccupyWallStreet," *BuzzFeed,* October 7, 2011.

43	**"economic crimes . . . ":** Supreme Court of the United States, Syllabus, *Skilling v. United States,* 561 U.S. 358, October 2009.

43	**"Obscene Deal":** Joachim Jahn, "Obszöner Deal," *Frankfurter Allgemeine Zeitung,* August 5, 2014.

43	**"This is something . . . ":** John F. Burns, "Formula One Chief Bernie Ecclestone Settles Bribery Case for $100 Million," *New York Times,* August 5, 2014.

43	**Outrage at the lack of individual prosecutions:** Expressing such criticism, Senator Elizabeth Warren remarked: "If you're caught with an ounce of cocaine, the chances are good you're going to go to jail. If it happens repeatedly you may go to jail for the rest of your life. But evidently, if you launder nearly a billion dollars for drug cartels and violate our international sanctions, your company pays a fine and you go home and sleep in your own bed at night. Every single individual associated with this. I just, I think that's fundamentally wrong" (Mokhiber, "Top 100 Corporate Criminals of the Decade," *Corporate Crime Reporter,* 2013). The reasons for this lack of prosecution are examined in Jessie Eisinger, "The Rise of Corporate Impunity," *ProPublica,* April 30, 2014. For a discussion of the role played by accusation in corporate wrongdoing, see Faulkner (2011). Laufer (2014) argues that "firms, as a wrongdoer, are not worthy of moral indignation" (p. 30); rather, genuine moral indignation over corporate crime tends to arise from focusing on the individuals involved.

43	**"The failure . . . ":** Rakoff (2014), p. 18.

43	**"that stuff . . . ":** News Conference by President Barack Obama, October 6, 2011.

43	**Criticism of extraterritorial laws:** Podgor (2003).

Chapter 3: Bad People Making Bad Decisions

47   **"At the sight . . . ":** Lombroso (1911), p. xiv–xv.

47   **Pythagoras and appearances:** Riedweg (2005).

47   **"there was never . . . ":** Aristotle (1984), p. 1237.

47   **Giovanni Battista della Porta:** McPhee and Orenstein (2011) and Baltrušaitis (1989).

48   **Lavater and early physiognomy in popular culture:** Graham (1960), Graham (1979), Tytler (1982), Hartley (2001), Fara (2003), and Rafter (2008).

48   **Lavater and facial features:** Although Lavater's ideas were well respected at the time, there was little evidence and even less scientific theory to support what a particular bump on the head or the flushness of the cheeks meant with regard to behavior. Phrenology was fraught with even greater disagreements in interpretation, ultimately leading to its demise.

48   **Further discussion of phrenology:** Lavater (1817), Rafter (2008), Young (1970), and Gall (1835).

48   **Usage of physiognomy:** "Additions and Corrections in Former Obituaries," *The Gentleman's Magazine, 71*, February 1802, p. 184.

48   **Lombroso's tools and methods:** Horn (2003).

48   **"All these characteristics . . . ":** Lombroso (1911), pp. 7–8.

49   **Lombroso and criminal anthropology:** Lombroso (1895–1896).

49   **"Born criminal" terminology:** The term "born criminal" was coined by Lombroso's close disciple, Enrico Ferri (Sellin 1958, p. 482).

49   **Premise that some people are "born criminal" and caveat by Lombroso:** Beginning as early as the second edition of *The Criminal Man,* Lombroso began to incorporate environmental factors that included atmospheric and climactic inferences, imitation, density of population, and education level.

49   **"there are some bad apples":** George W. Bush, "Exchange with Reporters in Orlando, Florida," in *Public Papers of the Presidents of the United States: George W. Bush, 2002, Book I—January 1 to July 31, 2002* (June 21, 2002), p. 1037.

49   **"simply 'rotten apples' . . . ":** Chamber of Commerce of the United States of America (1974), p. 55.

49   **"represent a deeply flawed individual":** *United States of America v. Bernard L. Madoff,* 09 Cr. 213 (DC), United States District Court for the Southern District of New York (June 29, 2009).

49   **"bad eggs":** "Wharton Grads Respond to Rajaratnam Conviction," *Fortune,* May 17, 2011.

49   **"because the public . . . ":** Simpson (2013), p. 320. The meaning of the proverb pertaining to "a few bad apples" has undergone many changes over time. The history of these changes is described in Geoff Nunberg, "Bad Apple Proverbs: There's One in Every Bunch," National Public Radio, May 9, 2011.

49   *Mens rea* **and crime:** Levitt (1922) and Wilson and Herrnstein (1998). Some white-collar statutes do not have a *mens rea* requirement and are strict liability—for example, section 13 of the Rivers and Harbors Act. See Greensberg and Brotman 2014 for additional discussion.

50   **"it is better . . . ":** *Buck v. Bell,* 274 U.S. 200, Supreme Court of the United States (May 2, 1927).

50   **State eugenics laws and sterilization:** Largent (2008), Cohen (2016), Robitscher (1973), Haller (1984), and Rafter (1997).

50   **"Criminals are organically . . . ":** Hooton (1939b), p. 309.

50   **Lombroso work and celebrity:** One respected physician wrote, "It is to Lombroso that the honour of founding the scientific study of the criminal must ever chiefly belong" (Ellis 1914, p. 43). Over time, Lombroso modified and expanded upon the circumstances associated with different types of criminal activity. Backing away from pure biological origins for deviant behavior, he commented that criminals who commit fraud and other financial crimes are not necessarily born criminal (Lombroso 1911, p. 261).

50   **"father of modern criminology":** Wolfgang (1961), p. 361.

51   **"this anthropological monster . . . ":** Goring (1913), p. 370.

51   **Goring saw criminals differently than Lombroso:** Lombroso had inconspicuously exaggerated the physical differences between criminals and noncriminals by not taking into account noncriminal correlated variables like age, height, and race.

51   **"devastating critique":** Cohen (1966), p. 50. Many criminologists took his study as a resounding refutation of Lombroso's "born criminal" theory.

51   **Physical differences between criminals and non-criminals and inferiority:** Incidentally, Goring (1913) noted that criminals "technically convicted of fraud" do not actually show differences in stature and body weight relative to the general population (p. 137).

51   **Goring replaced with another inferior person:** Ironically, as adamantly as some criminologists adopted Goring's analysis as a complete refutation of Lombroso's "born criminal" theory, others viewed the study as a vindication of Lombroso's notion of the biologically inferior criminal. It all depended on how the reader wanted to interpret Goring's conflicting analysis.

51   **"disgust[ed] with . . . ":** Hooton (1939b), p. 371.

51   **Hooton the anthropologist:** "He was a great, inspiring teacher; under him Harvard became the center of training in physical anthropology and his students also became leaders in the field." (Krogman 1976, p. 9).

51   **Goring and Lombroso:** Hooton (1939b), p. 371.

52   **"almost justify . . . ":** Hooton (1939b), p. 98.

52   **"You may say . . . ":** Hooton (1939b), p. 130.

52   **Doubts that bodily measurements could be connected to criminal behavior:** Hooton understood that some would be reluctant to accept his interpretation. In the opening of his book, Hooton wrote that "the anthropologist who obtrudes himself into the study of crime is an obvious ugly duckling and is likely to be greeted by the lords of the criminological dug-hull with cries of 'Quack! Quack! Quack!'" (Hooton 1939b, p. 3). Still, Hooton probably underestimated exactly how ferocious the response to his study would be.

53   **"inherently inferior . . . ":** Hooton (1939b), pp. 388, 397.

53   **"the funniest . . . ":** Reuter (1939), p. 125. Hooton and criminality research: Krogman (1939), Tucker (1940), Merton and Ashley-Montagu (1940), and Shapiro (1954).

53   **By the 1950s, broad interest in physical differences declined:** Hooton brought W. H. Sheldon to Harvard to continue this study. Sheldon's morph classification was initially heralded as having great promise, and a writer at *Life* exclaimed that he succeeded in "what Hippocrates tried to do 2,500 years ago; he has shown that character and physique are closely related" (Robert Coughlan, "What Manner of Morph Are You?" *Life,* June 1951, p. 68). Sheldon and somatotyping: Sheldon and Tucker (1938), Sheldon, Stevens, and Tucker (1940), Sheldon (1949), Sheldon (1954), Hersey (1996), and Aldous Huxley, "Who Are You?" *Harper's Magazine,* November 1944. Appreciation of Sheldon's methods was hardly universal, though; his analysis came under strong criticism by several prominent academics (see Sutherland 1951; Andrews 1941; Sheldon

1954; Glueck and Glueck 1956; and Ron Rosenbaum, "The Great Ivy League Nude Posture Photo Scandal," *New York Times,* January 15, 1995).

53 **"except for Professor Hooton . . . ":** Vold (1951), p. 157. Hooton also influenced Sheldon Glueck, who dedicated his book to Hooton, saying that he "long ago directed our attention to the possible role of body build in human behavior" (Glueck and Glueck 1956, p. v).

53 **Société Générale:** Francois Brochet, "Société Générale (A): The Jérome Kerviel Affair," HBS No. 110–029 (Boston: Harvard Business School Publishing, 2010).

54 **Low self-control caused by poor parenting, while others argued that it was due to heredity:** Gottfredson and Hirschi focused on social factors that they believed could inhibit self-control and foster criminality. In their view, low self-control was specifically caused by "ineffective child rearing" (Gottfredson and Hirschi 1990, p. 97). According to their theory, good parents closely supervise their children. When problems arise, attentive parents squelch the behavior by punishing their children, thereby fostering self-control in the future. More recent research, however, has countered the idea that self-control is primarily determined by parenting.

54 **Genetic and other factors contributing to self-control:** Unnever, Cullen, and Pratt (2003), Wright and Beaver (2005), Beaver et al. (2010), and Pinker (2011).

54 **"marshmallow test":** Mischel, Ebbesen, and Zeiss (1972), Metcalfe and Mischel (1999), Mischel et al. (2011), and Mischel (2014). Some evidence suggests a degree of malleability of self-control, see: Piquero, Jennings, and Farrington (2010). Ability to wait as it relates to criminal behavior: Åkerlund et al. (2014).

54 **Managerial misconduct and personal deficiency:** Gottfredson and Hirschi deny that "people are born criminals, inherit a gene for criminality, or anything of the sort" (Gottfredson and Hirschi 1990, p. 96). However, their theory suggests that individuals who are poorly reared can maintain this deficiency throughout life. Following their argument, the social mechanism must have led to some biological conditioning; otherwise it's unclear how this trait could be stable over time. In addition, there is a greater genetic component to self-control than originally acknowledged by Gottfredson and Hirschi. Thus I interpret their theory of self-control as biologically rooted, originating at birth or in early childhood, despite the fact that Gottfredson and Hirschi did not originally conceive of it as such.

55 **People with low self-control are more likely to engage in deviant behavior:** According to Gottfredson and Hirschi (1990), a lack of self-control explains not just white-collar crime but "all crime, at all times" (p. 117). One specific situation that seems to obviously violate their theory is the decision to have an abortion prior to its legalization in 1973. As noted by Geis (2000), "Surely, it would be stretching matters greatly to maintain that the actions of women who opted for illegal abortions could be understood in terms of an absence of sufficient self-control"(p. 40).

55 **Jonathan Burrows:** Jenny Anderson, "Fund Manager in London Who Dodged Train Fare Is Barred from Financial Jobs," *International New York Times,* December 15, 2014.

55 **Non-white-collar offenses committed by white-collar criminals:** Davidson, Dey, and Smith (2015), Davidson, Dey, and Smith (2014), Benson and Moore (1992), and Weisburd et al. (1991). Gottfredson and Hirschi's hypothesis would predict that the absolute, rather than relative, percentage of executives convicted of white-collar offenses ought to be high. According to their theory, there ought to be relatively little difference between the records of white-collar and non-white-collar offenders other than those that arise from differences in the incidence of detection and conviction.

Specialization by criminals: Benson and Moore (1992) and Wright, Logie, and Decker (1995).

55   **Could expect number of CEOs convicted of malfeasance to be higher:** An alternative explanation is that executives convicted of fraud could simply be particularly talented at evading detection of their other criminal endeavors. This could explain the attenuated detection rate of non-white-collar offenses. But the detection rate of "street offenses" tends to be significantly higher than for cases of fraud, so it seems unlikely that the only offense ever detected was the one that happened to also be the most difficult to detect.

55   **"there's nothing . . . ":** *United States of America v. W. Scott Harkonen,* CR 08-164 MHP, United States District Court for the Northern District of California (April 13, 2011), p. 156.

56   **self-control as a "muscle":** see Muraven and Baumeister (2000), Muraven, Tice, and Baumeister (1998), Tangney, Baumeister, and Boone (2004), Hagger et al. (2010), and Myrseth and Fishbach (2009). Self-control and dishonesty: Mead et al. (2009) and Gino et al. (2011).

56   **"absence of self-control . . . ":** Geis (2000), p. 43. Akers (1991) describes Gottfredson and Hirschi's attempt to avert a tautological argument.

57   **All crime caused by the same biological aberrations:** Andrea Glenn and Adrian Raine note in a 2014 review that "most studies define antisocial behavior and crime broadly, without distinguishing between violent and non-violent offenders" (Glenn and Raine 2014, p. 54). Other instances of this lack of differentiating can be attributed to naïve or overly general characterizing of crimes. Gottfredson and Hirschi, for instance, broadly describe crime as being easy, thrilling, and offering few benefits. For other scholars, investigating the causes of violent street crime isn't the primary interest of the investigation. If white-collar crime isn't dismissed outright as being less important, it becomes incorporated as an afterthought to maintaining the allure of an elegant theory that can explain crime as a whole.

57   **Explore, not minimize, differences to explain criminality:** A number of important questions pertaining to race and criminal activity—issues widely debated in the criminological literature—are also not necessarily as relevant for explaining white-collar crime; see Adler, Mueller, and Laufer (2013).

57   **"I do believe . . . ":** Raine (2013), p. 13.

57   **Violence and brain imaging:** Raine (1993) and Lee, Chan, and Raine (2008).

57   **"constitutionally different than other men":** Raine (2013), p. 86.

58   **"Rather than . . . ":** Raine et al. (2012), p. 2933.

58   **"white-collar criminals . . . ":** Ibid. Raine and his co-authors were careful to qualify their findings by noting that their sample did not include individuals convicted of especially significant white-collar crimes such as securities fraud. They also focused on the structure, rather than function, of the white-collar brain. With these qualifications in mind, Raine's study offered a scientifically sophisticated attempt to describe a biological basis for white-collar criminality.

58   **Humans and chimpanzees:** King and Wilson (1975).

58   **Genes and personality:** Bouchard and McGue (2003), Bouchard and Loehlin (2001), Tellegen et al. (1988), and Miller, Lynam, and Leukefeld (2003).

58   **Identical twins reared apart:** Grove et al. (1990) and Christiansen (1977).

59   **Antisocial behavior and genetics:** Glenn and Raine (2014), Ferguson (2010), Rhee and Waldman (2002), and Wasserman and Wachbroit (2001).

59   **Testosterone and personality:** Sellers, Mehl, and Josephs (2007) and Newman and Josephs (2009).

59 **Genetic influence and testosterone:** Bogaert et al. (2008), Ohlsson et al. (2011), Panizzon et al. (2013), and Harden et al. (2014). Testosterone and aggressiveness: Archer (1991) and Book, Starzyk, and Quinsey (2001). Testosterone and risk-taking: Apicella, Carré, and Dreber (2015).

59 **Facial structure and cheating:** Haselhuhn and Wong (2012) and Stirrat and Perrett (2010).

59 **Facial structure, aggressive behavior, and testosterone:** Lefevre et al. (2013), Carré and McCormick (2008), Carré, McCormick, and Mondloch (2009), and Weston, Friday, and Lio (2007).

59 **Testosterone and misreporting:** Jia, van Lent, and Zeng (2014) and Lee et al. (2015). Effects of testosterone and cortisol on financial market stability: Cueva et al. (2015).

60 **Biological cause for corporate misconduct:** Relying on biologically rooted explanations to entirely explain corporate misconduct inevitably runs into a fundamental roadblock having to do with the fact that the laws defining conduct are created by regulators and politicians and thus are fluid and subject to change over time. Many of the prosecutions over the past two decades are the result of the recent passage and enforcement of insider-trading laws. Before 1990, only thirty-four countries in the world had prohibitions against insider trading. So it would be impossible for those convicted to have been biologically destined to violate an insider-trading regulation that had not yet existed at their birth or even later childhood. In short, the violation of a standard created by social institutions cannot be entirely caused by some biological phenomenon.

60 **"is a person . . . ":** Kofi Annan, letter to Judge Rakoff, September 21, 2012.

60 **"many millions of people . . . ":** Bill Gates, letter to Judge Rakoff, July 24, 2012.

60 **"never encountered . . . ":** *United States of American v. Rajat K. Gupta,* 11 Cr. 907 (JSR), Sentencing Memorandum and Order, United States District Court Southern District of New York (October 24, 2012), p. 11. Heroic leaders and white-collar crime: Arnulf and Gottschalk (2013).

60 **Blank-slate theory:** Pinker (2002) and Pinker (2004). Biosocial interaction and epigenetics: Raine, Brennan, and Mednick (1994), Raine (2002), Walsh and Beaver (2009), and Carey (2012).

61 **Variations in level of empathy:** Baron-Cohen (2011) and Schouten and Silver (2012). Testing of psychopathy in managers: Babiak and Hare (2006), Babiak, Neumann, and Hare (2010), and Board and Fritzon (2005). Dark personalities: Paulhus (2014). Relation between narcissism in executives and fraud: Rijsenbilt and Commandeur (2013).

61 **Effectiveness of psychopathy in professional settings:** Babiak, Neumann, and Hare (2010), Gao and Raine (2010), Babiak (1995), Babiak and Hare (2006), and Blair (1995). Another antisocial behavior that has been examined in the context of malfeasance is Asperger's disorder; see Kibbie (2012) and Haskins and Silva (2006).

61 **Exploring the relationship between deviance, empathy, and business:** Blickle et al. (2006), Hogan and Hogan (2001), and Kets de Vries and Miller (1985). In a recent piece of research investigating the neurobiological basis for corporate misconduct, Eskenazi, Hartmann, and Rietdijk (2016) propose that higher empathy might actually lead to a greater propensity to engage in misconduct in some instances. Specifically, they explore how social sensitivity could incline individuals to yield to managerial pressure by overly aligning interests within a firm.

62 **Genetic versus environmental factors:** Cloninger et al. (1982). Biosocial interaction: Raine (2002) and Walsh and Beaver (2009).

62 **Role played by context and the surrounding culture:** Strictly speaking, biology in its broadest sense must explain all conduct, since all human action is a result of physical

operations that arise within the body. Speaking of biology and behavior in this sense obscures understanding its contribution toward differences in human behavior, though. Consequently, "biology" in this chapter, like most discussions of "biology and behavior," focuses on understanding its contribution at a higher level of characteristics rather than at some molecular level.

62   **"This is a deepening mystery . . . ":** *United States of America v. Kareem Serageldin,* 12 Cr. 90, United States District Court Southern District of New York (November 21, 2013).

Chapter 4: A Press Release with Consequences

65   **Preliminary study of gamma interferon and IPF:** Ziesche et al. (1999).

66   **Off-label medicine:** Radley, Finkelstein, and Stafford (2006) and Conti et al. (2013).

66   **Thalomid sales:** Thalomid sales in 2003 totaled $224 million, with 90 percent of prescriptions from off-label oncology usage. See C. E. Unterberg, Towbin Company Report on Celgene Corporation (August 20, 2004), by Matthew Osborne.

69   **Idiopathic thrombocytopenic purpura:** UpToDate, "Immune Thromboctopenia," by James Bussel (current as of April 2016).

71   **"Intermune Announces . . . ":** "Intermune Announces Phase III Data Demonstrating Survival Benefit of Actimmune in IPF" (news release), August 28, 2002.

71   **Sell-side analyst interpretations:** Martin Auster and Kelly Stoehs, "InterMune, Inc.," SunTrust Robinson Humphrey, August 29, 2002, p. 1; and Caroline Copithorne, M. Ian Sornaiya, Steven Boscoe, and Sujata Patel, "InterMune Hits a Double," Morgan Stanley, August 29, 2002. In the original analyst note, the author employed the singular "was" and stated that "results from a Phase III study of Actimmune was mixed."

71   **Dissemination of clinical trial results:** Fleming (2010).

71   **"I was stunned by the misrepresentation . . . ":** Letter from Thomas R. Fleming, September 5, 2002.

72   **Interpretation of p-value:** The lower the p-value, the more likely that Actimmune had the desired treatment effect on patients suffering from IPF. The financial trader and statistician Chester Lee offered a useful example to illustrate the meaning of p-value: "Suppose you pulled one card out of a deck and it was Queen of Diamonds, and your friend guessed it correctly as 'Red.' You're probably not impressed, since he could've just made a guess and he would be correct about half the time (i.e., p-value is about 50 percent). On the other hand, if your friend guessed it correctly as 'Queen of Diamonds,' you are probably impressed, because the probability that he guesses the card and gets it correct is very low (i.e., p-value is less than 2 percent). This card trick example illustrates the meaning of p-value and statistical significance; when the probability of something happening due to random chance is low, it's probably not due to random chance."

72   **Arbitrary level of .05:** Wasserstein and Lazar (2016). Statistical significance in medical research: Lee (2011), Katz (2004), and Food and Drug Administration, *Guidance for Industry: Providing Clinical Evidence of Effectiveness for Human Drug and Biological Products,* May 1998.

72   **Statistical validity of tests ex-post:** The testing of different sub-groups after examining data—known as "p-hacking"— is a widespread practice that confounds the interpretation of the p-value. One colleague, after reading a draft of this chapter, sent me a note saying that "the kind of thing [Harkonen] almost went to prison for is absolutely routine and par for the course in academia." Several recent meta-analyses confirm

the pervasiveness of researchers engaging in additional sub-analyses until they find a statistically significant effect. For more on p-hacking, see Head et al. (2015) and Simmons, Nelson, and Simonsohn (2011).

72 **Fleming's assessment of Fabrazyme:** *United States of America v. W. Scott Harkonen,* Declaration of Donald B. Rubin Ph.D., in Support of Defendant W. Scott Harkonen's Sentencing Memorandum (November 15, 2010), p. 10.

74 **"Mr. Harkonen lied . . . ":** US Attorney's Office, Northern District of California, "W. Scott Harkonen, Former Biotech CEO, Convicted of Wire Fraud" (news release), September 29, 2009.

74 **"All lies . . . ":** Carson (2010), p. 17.

75 **Esso oil company:** Esso would later become Exxon. "Put a Tiger in your tank" advertisement: Ash (1969).

75 **"Vague statements . . . ":** Hoffman (2006), p. 1406, defines puffery.

75 **Puffery and materiality:** Padfield (2008) and O'Hare (1998).

75 **"is exceeding . . . ":** Padfield (2008), p. 367.

75 **Tellabs case:** *Makor Issues & Rights, Ltd. v. Tellabs, Inc.,* 437 F. 3d 588, 7th Cir. (January 25, 2006); Ben Klaymen, "Tellabs Cuts Q1 Earns, Sales Guidance a Second Time," *Reuters,* April 6, 2001; Reuters News, "Tellabs Cuts First-Quarter Outlook," *Reuters,* March 7, 2001; and Jonathan Burns, "Tellabs: Environment Very Different Than a Few Weeks Ago," *Dow Jones Newswires,* April 18, 2001.

76 **"essentially . . . meaningless":** *Makor Issues & Rights, Ltd. v. Tellabs, Inc.,* 437 F.3d 588, 7th Cir. (January 25, 2006), pp. 597–598.

76 **Puffery and perceptions:** Olson and Dover (1978), Rotfeld and Rotzoll (1980), and Haan and Berkey (2002).

76 **Kellogg's immunity-boost claim:** Federal Trade Commission, "FTC Investigation of Ad Claims that Rice Krispies Benefits Children's Immunity Leads to Stronger Order Against Kellogg," June 3, 2010.

76 **"it is not the lie . . . ":** Bacon, edited by Montague (1825), p. 4.

76 **Deceptive product promotions:** Craswell (1985) and Preston (1998).

78 **Rubin's assessment of the clinical trial:** *United States of America v. W. Scott Harkonen,* Declaration of Donald B. Rubin Ph.D., in Support of Defendant W. Scott Harkonen's Sentencing Memorandum (November 15, 2010).

78 **Not a failure, not a success:** As accurately noted by Donald Rubin, "the formal statement for a p-value that is 'not significant' is that the test 'failed to reject the null hypothesis,' not that the p-value suggests that we should 'accept the null hypothesis as true'" (ibid., p. 7).

78 **No known treatment for IPF:** As of 2016, the prognosis for people diagnosed with IPF is poor. Only 20 to 30 percent of patients are alive five years after their diagnosis (see UpToDate, Talmadge E. King Jr.'s literature review, which is current as of February 2016).

78 **"We can't even figure out . . . ":** *United States of America v. W. Scott Harkonen,* CR 08-164 MHP, United States District Court for the Northern District of California, Transcript of Sentencing Proceedings (April 13, 2011), p. 158. In the judge's comments, "real" was recorded as "really."

Chapter 5: The Triumph of Reason

81 **GSK and bribe reimbursement:** Patti Waldmeir and Andrew Ward, "GSK Salesmen Want 'Bribes' Reimbursed," *Financial Times,* May 28, 2014. I appreciate the help of

Ms. Waldmeir for putting me in contact with one of GSK's managers who lodged this complaint.

82   **The laws of imitation:** Tarde (1962). Tarde's background and influence: Tarde (1962), Davis (1906), Candea (2010), and Beirne (1993). Kedia, Koh, and Rajgopal (2015) provide empirical support of earnings management contagion (a potentially fraudulent but not necessarily criminal offense) at the firm level.

82   **Scholars picked up on Tarde's work:** Edwin Sutherland, the most prominent scholar to build and further refine Tarde's initial theory, argued that criminal behavior is learned by associating with people who favor criminal behavior. According to Sutherland's theory of differential association, the ratio of contact an individual has with people who view criminal actions favorably, as opposed to unfavorably, determines the likelihood that an individual will decide to engage in criminal conduct. Differential association: Sutherland (1934), Sutherland (1940), and Adler, Mueller, and Laufer (2013). In support of Sutherland's theory of differential association, Dimmock, Gerken, and Graham (2015) investigate how investment advisors are more likely to engage in fraud if they interact with co-workers, encountered via a merger, who also engaged in fraud. Dechow and Tan (2016) show how the practice of backdating options spread through managerial connections to parrticular law firms. Sutherland maintained that influence is a function of frequency, duration, priority, and intensity (see Bernard, Snipes, and Gerould 2010).

82   **Exposure or illicit or immoral conduct in business:** Toffler (1986), Waters, Bird, and Chant (1986), Badaracco and Webb (1995), and Heath (2008). Financial services: Santoro and Strauss (2013) and Peter Eavis, "Regulators Size Up Wall Street," *New York Times*, March 12, 2014. Early survey on unethical conduct: Baumhart (1961). Capitalist system and ethical behavior: Coleman (1987), Coleman (2002), Braithwaite (1989), Lane (1953), Wang, Zhong, and Murnighan (2011), Wang, Malhotra, and Murnighan (2011), Sutherland (1983), and Cressey (1986). Experimental evidence supporting social transmission of deviant behavior: Mann et al. (2014) and Gino and Galinsky (2012). Survey evidence of compromised principles: Posner and Schmidt (1987).

82   **Some people heavily exposed to illicit practices behave otherwise:** One important issue concerning the idea that corporate misconduct arises from learned behavior is that it's easy to imagine how the second, third, and fourth executive could learn about and take part in an illegal scheme. Yet this doesn't explain why someone would conceive the scheme in the first place, or who that someone would be. In one speech, Sutherland did point his finger at one group who he thought were the "inventive geniuses" responsible for creating most white-collar crimes: lawyers. He wasn't clear, however, as to where lawyers themselves learned this criminal behavior. Without a compelling explanation for the origin of their deviance, these criminal schemes seemingly appeared out of thin air and then were imitated by others.

82   **Cressey focused his attention on one group of offenders:** Cressey sought to reexamine several limitations of Sutherland's work on differential association, focusing in particular on one crucial flaw in Sutherland's analysis: Sutherland studied corporations, not people, and thus remained disconnected from the question of why individuals commit offenses. Cressey saw an opportunity to address this shortcoming by focusing on professionals who actually engage in white-collar crimes. He also questioned the often-held belief that embezzlement arises simply from a low level of willpower or a lack of moral fiber. In Cressey's opinion, such hidden weaknesses could be generically applied to any sort of deviant behavior. Such character flaws become

evident only "after the fact" and therefore offer little in the way of explaining and possibly preventing criminal behavior.

82 **Interviewing in prisons:** Newman (1958a).

82 **"There are very few people . . . ":** Cressey (1953), p. 47.

83 **Non-shareable problem could be solved secretly:** Many of the embezzlers Cressey spoke with described the urgency needed to solve the financial problem. But Cressey found other people with similarly urgent nonshareable financial problems who did not resort to embezzlement. The urgency of a particular setback contributed to its perceived severity, but it was not the cause of the criminal offense. This recognition that urgency does not necessarily result in criminality is what led to Cressey's second condition.

83 **"I learned all of it in school . . . ":** Cressey (1953), p. 82.

84 **"In the real estate business . . . ":** Cressey (1953), p. 104.

84 **"If he cannot do this . . . ":** Cressey (1965), p. 15. Excuses and rationalizations: Gellerman (1986), Snyder, Higgins, and Stucky (1983), Cressey (1951), and Cressey (1965).

84 **"It demonstrates . . . ":** Schuessler (1954), p. 604.

84 **"ponderous and pedantic":** Cressey (1973), p. v. As evidence of Cressey's difficulty in pleasing everyone, one reviewer lamented how "early pages labor away at somewhat tiring length" on certain details, while another said that Cressey's language needed greater precision to be properly described as scientific writing. For reviews of Cressey's work, Clinard (1954), Cannon (1956), Lindesmith (1954), and Schuessler (1954).

84 **Pressure, opportunity, and rationalization:** Albrecht and his colleagues (1982) called these factors "red flags." The three factors the authors identified were situational pressures, opportunities to commit fraud, and personal integrity. In his subsequent writing (e.g., Albrecht 1991), these three factors were transformed into the three elements in the modern fraud triangle.

84 **Development of the fraud triangle:** Albrecht et al. (1982), Albrecht (1991), and Albrecht (2014).

84 **Extending the fraud triangle:** Wolfe and Hermanson (2004), Ramamoorti (2008), Dorminey et al. (2010), Dorminey et al. (2012), Kassem and Higson (2012), Ramamoorti et al. (2013), Cohen et al. (2010), and Murphy and Dacin (2011). Sentencing and the fraud triangle: Haugh (2014). For a clever test utilizing the framework underlying the fraud triangle to explore cheating among taxi drivers, see Rajgopal and White (2015).

84 **Regulations pertaining to the fraud triangle:** AU-P section 316, *Consideration of Fraud in a Financial Statement Audit* (AICPA, *PCAOB Standards and Related Rules,* Interim Standards), and SAS No. 99 and No. 113, *Consideration of Fraud in a Financial Statement Audit* (AICPA, *Professional Standards,* vol. 1, AU section 316).

84 **Textbooks and the fraud triangle:** Wells (2011).

85 **Limitations of fraud triangle:** There are several important limitations to the fraud triangle. Experimental evidence supports the validity of some individual components of the triangle, such as how rationalizing behavior can allow individuals to feel moral while engaging in deviant conduct (Shalvi et al. 2015, Trompeter et al. 2014). But the entire model has never been subject to rigorous testing. For this reason, the fraud triangle has not gained acceptance within the legal community. In one appellate court brief, it was explicitly noted that the fraud triangle "had never been adopted as a reliable scientific method in any court of law" (*Robert Haupt v. David O. Heaps,* Court of Appeals of Utah, Case No. 20040296-CA October 14, 2005).

85   **Managerial decision making and trade-offs:** Hammond, Keeney, and Raiffa (1999) and Bazerman and Moore (2013).

86   **"illegal acts which are characterized by . . . ":** United States Federal Bureau of Investigation (1989).

86   **Additional biographical details on Kohlberg:** Rest, Power, and Brabeck (1988) and Kohlberg (1991).

87   **Kohlberg's foundational work:** Kohlberg (1958), Kohlberg (1969), and Colby and Kohlberg (1987). **Criticism of Kohlberg:** Simpson (1974), Gilligan (1982), and Bloom (2013).

87   **Desirability of higher stages of development:** Kohlberg (1981).

87   **Kolhberg and schools:** Power, Higgins, and Kohlberg (1989) and Blatt and Kohlberg (1975).

87   **Cognitive moral development and business:** Trevino and Youngblood (1990), Ponemon (1992), Weber (1990), Elm and Nichols (1993), Armstrong (1987), Colby and Kohlberg (1987), and Forte (2004). Ethical training in professional schools and business: McMahon (1975), Pamental (1988), Rest (1988), Khurana (2007), and Warren, Gaspar, and Laufer (2014). Using cognitive moral development theory to educate: Trevino (1992, p. 454), Schwitzgebel (2009, p. 713), Boyd (1981), Goldman and Arbuthnot (1979), Penn and Collier (1985), and Power, Higgins, and Kohlberg (1989). Regression in moral growth in business: Armstrong (1987). Moral development and business ethics: Piper, Gentile, and Parks (1993).

88   **Growth of cognitive moral development research:** Rest (1983).

88   **Use of the defining-issues test to evaluate cognitive moral development:** Rest (1983), Rest (1986), and Elm and Weber (1994).

89   **Behavior of ethicists:** Schwitzgebel (2009) and Schwitzgebel and Rust (2014).

89   **Discrepancy between moral development scores and actual behavior:** The aggregate data on moral cognition and moral action are mixed, with some studies showing evidence in favor of a connection between reasoning and behavior and others not (for reviews, see Blasi 1980, Rest 1983, Thoma 1985, and Schwitzgebel 2009). In contrast to some rather more optimistic interpretations of the data, I believe the correlation (.3) between moral judgment and behavior provides rather weak evidence of a meaningful relationship. Often, however, researchers simply assumed that a meaningful relationship existed. For example, Weber (1990) writes that "it can be inferred that managers reasoning at stage 3 or stage 4 will exhibit behavior that is consistent with the descriptions of these stages" (p. 696).

89   **How moral judgments are made:** Kohlberg (1969). A similar normative approach is often taken with corporate codes of ethics; see Adams et al. (2001).

89   **Decision making and perspective/situational factors:** March (1994), Tenbrunsel and Messick (1999), Ross and Nisbett (1991), and Dorris (2002). Honesty and situational factors: Hartshorne and May (1928).

89   **Good Samaritan experiment:** Darley and Batson (1973).

89   **Failed to recognize the moral dilemma:** Rest (1986) describes this failure in steps 1 and 4 of his model.

89   **Series of steps necessary to behave ethically:** As Rest (1986) explained, "When a person is behaving morally, what must we suppose has happened psychologically to produce that behavior? Our answer to that question (still somewhat tentative) is to postulate that four main kinds of psychological processes have occurred in order for moral behavior to occur" (p. 3). Component model of moral decision making: Rest (1983), Rest (1986), Jones (1991), and Tenbrunsel and Smith-Crowe (2008).

90 **"Any financial exposure . . . ":** E-mail from Gregg W. Ritchie to Jeffery N. Stein, OPIS Tax Shelter Registration, May 26, 1998. Among the sanctions that Ritchie ultimately faced was the loss of his CPA license in April 2012 for committing fraud in the practice of public accountancy, failing to observe professional standards, and knowingly disseminating materially misleading information (Case No. AC-2010-10, decision effective April 28, 2012). In the e-mail, Ritchie misspells "exposure" as "esposure."

91 **Anything distinctive about "moral" decisions:** Researchers like to envision choices as being framed in ways particular to their discipline. For example, those who examine ethical decisions tend to see judgments as employing a particular framework about the "right" thing to do, and those studying legal decisions focus on how individuals decide to stay within the bounds of law.

   Each frame of reference (moral, economic, legal, personal, environmental, etc.) draws a particular set of issues into focus (Jones 1991, Tenbrunsel and Messick 1999, and Tenbrunsel and Smith-Crowe 2008). Few economic decisions are bereft of legal and moral content. And many environmental decisions also have economic, legal, and moral implications. Depending on the circumstances, one frame may naturally be given greater primacy, but it's actually hard to find business decisions that are framed by only one set of issues. Nonetheless, as shown by Tenbrunsel and Messick (1999), it's possible to shift the frame of reference, thereby leading people to focus more on some elements involved in the decision than on others.

91 **"Fugitive on the run . . . ":** Larry King, "A Legacy of Questions: Banker's Disappearance Causes Family to Ask Why," *St. Petersburg Times,* May 12, 1987.

91 **Messer's story:** Larry King, "Banker on Run from Tampa Arrested in Ga.," *St. Petersburg Times,* September 2, 1987.

91 **"Unlike the tempestuous and murderous spouse . . . ":** Ralph Nader and Mark Green, "What to Do About Corporate Corruption," *Wall Street Journal,* March 12, 1976.

92 **"My way is to divide half a sheet of paper . . . ":** Franklin, edited by Bigelow (1887).

92 **Weighing costs and benefits:** Franklin, edited by Labaree and Bell (1956).

92 **Becker and optimality of deterring all crime:** Becker argued that the economically optimal level of deterrence does not necessarily lead to deterring all crime. In fact, it was quite unlikely to do so since the enforcement costs would at some point become overwhelmingly expensive. Instead, Becker simply argued that would-be offenders internalize the potential cost of offending. In an emergency, for instance, it might make sense to speed to the hospital since the expected benefit would exceed even the highest traffic violation fees. As he once stated in an interview, "to get people upset, I like to say that there's an optimal amount of crime" (Mahmoud Bahrani, "The Economics of Crime with Gary Becker," *The Chicago Maroon,* May 25, 2012).

92 **Harsh punishments in eighteenth-century Europe:** Radzinowicz (1948).

93 **Bentham's theory:** Bentham (1830).

93 **Maximizing well-being through Bentham's rational calculation:** Bentham (1789) explicitly argued that individuals calculate: "Men calculate, some with less exactness, indeed some with more: but all men calculate. I would not say that even a madman does not calculate."

93 **Bentham's list of pleasures and pains:** Bentham (1789).

93 **"govern us in all we do . . . ":** Bentham (1789), p. 125.

93 **Descriptions of Bentham:** Mitchell (1918), Stigler (1950), Lucas and Sheeran (2006), and Adler, Mueller, and Laufer (2013).

93 **Gary Becker and Bentham:** Becker (1968), Michael and Becker (1973), Becker (1976), and Hurtado (2008).

93 **Criticism of non-economic approach:** In a line that would cause scholars in other fields to criticize the economic approach to understanding crime, Becker wrote: "I cannot pause to discuss the many general implications of this approach, except to remark that criminal behavior becomes part of a much more general theory and does not require ad hoc concepts of differential association, anomie, and the like" (Becker 1968). Additional critiques of non-economics-based research: Hirshleifer (1985) and Dilulio (1996).

93 **Becker on crime:** Becker (1968), Becker (1993), and Becker (1995).

94 **Crime and economics:** Pyle (1983) and Heineke (1978).

94 **Rational choice approach outside of economics:** Akers (1990), Piquero, Exum, and Simpson (2005), Paternoster and Simpson (1993), Hechter and Kanazawa (1997), Piquero and Tibbetts (2002), and Friedrichs (2010).

94 **"the most complete and coherent account . . . ":** Ulen (1998).

94 **"Economists have stripped morality . . . ":** Richard Horton on Twitter, December 31, 2012. Response by Parkin, Apples, and Maynard (2013).

94 **"Individuals maximize welfare . . . ":** Becker (1993), p. 386.

94 **Incorporation of identity and morality into economic models:** Akerlof and Kranton (2005), Akerlof and Kranton (2000), and Levitt and List (2007).

96 **Friedman and the "as if" assumption:** Friedman and Savage (1948) and Friedman (1953).

96 **Described the psychological decision-making process:** Throughout the later twentieth century, researchers sought to clarify the discussion around economic models by pointing out that rational choice was a normative, rather than exclusively positive, model. Cost-benefit and rational choice as a normative theory: Larrick, Nisbett, and Morgan (1993) and Thaler (1980).

96 **"all men calculate":** Bentham (1789).

96. **"individuals consciously and deliberately . . . ":** Klein (2010). Crime described as calculated choice: Cornish and Clarke (1986), Shover and Hochstetler (2006), Coleman (2002), and Baer (2008).

96 **"executives contemplating . . . ":** "Tailoring Punishment to White-Collar Crime," *Business Week,* October 28, 1985, p. 20; also cited in Becker and Becker (1997), p. 140. Scholars in fields outside of economics also noted that the economic model of choice did not imply reasoning; see McCarthy (2002) and Posner (2011).

97 **"are highly skilled . . . ":** James Stewart, "In a New Era of Insider Trading, It's Risk vs. Reward Squared," *New York Times,* December 7, 2012.

97 **"Ultimately, the convictions . . . ":** "U.S. Attorney Preet Bharara on Cleaning Up Wall Street and the Thin Line Between Confidence and Arrogance," *Knowledge@Wharton,* October 12, 2011.

97 **Penalties for white-collar crime:** Hearings before the Subcommittee on Crime and Drugs, United States Senate, 107th Congress, Second Session, June 19, July 10, and July 24, 2002 (Serial No. J-107–87).

97 **"know the available punishments . . . ":** "Go Directly to Jail: White-Collar Sentencing After the Sarbanes-Oxley Act," *Harvard Law Review, 122* (2009).

97 **"one of the principal objections . . . ":** Ogren (1973), p. 974. Notably, Ogren expressed skepticism of this widely held notion. Referring to Bentham's notion of human behavior, he wrote that "it is doubtful that white-collar criminals are indeed uniformly well-trained, highly rational human calculators" (p. 974).

Chapter 6: Intuitive Decisions

100 **"While I am perplexed . . . ":** "London Mayor Guilty of Fraud and Forgery: Former Liberal MP Tried to Have Taxpayers Cover Cost of Son's Wedding," *Toronto Star,* June 14, 2014. This is not to deny that it would be possible to create a cost-benefit model for even the most extreme cases. By taking into account time preferences (e.g., hyperbolic discounting), information collection, and processing costs, one could mathematically represent all these cases. This, however, would be a mathematical model of behavior rather than a psychological model. An extensive literature in behavioral economics addresses some of the challenges of viewing behavior as purely rational, as was initially envisioned in the economic literature (e.g., Thaler 2000, Kahneman and Thaler 2006, Loewenstein and Thaler 1989, Rabin and Thaler 2001, Frank 1990).

101 **Estimates about amount of information we process:** Several different estimates place the amount of conscious information flow between only a few bits a second to upwards of 40 bits a second. Whether the estimate is on the higher or lower end of this range, Zimmerman (1989) aptly summarizes that "What we perceive at any moment, therefore, is limited to an extremely small compartment in the stream of information about our surroundings flowing in from the sense organs" (p. 172). See also Nørretranders (1998).

101 **"The economic approach . . . ":** Becker (1976), p. 7. As noted in Chapter 5, formal economic models did not describe the economic approach as a psychological model of decision making. However, as this theory became popularized and entered the legal and public domains, it became commonly interpreted as a psychological model. More recently some economists have sought to bring in more psychology to the model. For instance, Shah and Ludwig (2016) explore the idea of the accessibility of different options in conjunction with the model. In this regard, some options never really "come to mind" depending on a person's past experiences and how he sees a situation.

102 **"It just dawned on me . . . ":** Maier (1931).

104 **"moral dumbfounding":** Haidt, Bjorklund, and Murphy (2000) and Haidt (2006).

104 **Assessing right and wrong:** Nisbett and Wilson (1977).

104 **"Most of a person's everyday life . . . ":** Bargh and Chartrand (1999), p. 462.

104 **Unconscious decision making:** Wegner (2002).

104 **Decision-making processes:** Evans (2003), Evans (2008), Evans and Stanovich (2013), Lieberman (2000), Lieberman (2007), and Kahneman (2011).

104 **Bounded by the capacity of working memory:** The bounded capacity of the human mind was eloquently described by Herbert Simon in his pioneering work on economics and psychology (e.g., Simon 1956a, Simon 1956b).

105 **Bat and ball study:** Frederick (2005).

105 **Optimizing behavior and neuroeconomics:** Camerer, Loewenstein, and Prelec (2005). Employing greater mental activity does not mean that the brain is working harder in the sense of consuming more calories. Mental effort and energy consumption: Van den Berg (1986), Gibson (2007), Gibson and Green (2002), and Lennie (2003).

105 **Become habitual and second nature:** The human body is constantly finding ways to facilitate more efficient decision making to reduce the effortful cognitive burden. One dramatic example comes from a study that examined people playing the computer game Tetris. When they began playing, many different parts of their brains were extremely active. But as they continued playing over several weeks, their brain activity

reduced considerably to the point where only a few localized parts of their brains exhibited significant arousal (Haier et al. 1992).

105 **Popular interpretation of cost-benefit:** One could argue that humans have adapted intuitive responses that reflect the judgments that would result from successful cost-benefit decisions (e.g., Gladwell 2005, Klein 2013). It is more accurate to describe these intuitive decisions as evolved or learned responses than as the rapid cost-benefit decisions envisioned by economists.

106 **Phineas Gage:** Harlow (1869), Damasio (1994), and Sam Kean, "Phineas Gage, Neuroscience's Most Famous Patient," *Slate,* May 6, 2014.

107 **"I found myself . . . ":** Damasio (1994), p. 44.

107 **"We might summarize . . . ":** Damasio (1994), p. 45.

108 **"We do not just see . . . ":** Zajonc (1980), p. 154.

108 **Unconscious emotion:** Winkielman and Berridge (2004). Marketing executives have long known about—and even tried to use—these unconscious affective evaluations. In the mid-twentieth century, researchers tested whether signals presented unconsciously to individuals influenced perceptions. In one experiment, random shapes were shown to subjects for a mere 1/1000th of a second. This exposure was so brief that subjects lacked the ability to consciously recognize the shape. Surprisingly, people exposed to shapes flashed more frequently ended up expressing a greater liking for those shapes despite not knowing what the shapes were or why they liked them.

108 **Exposure effect and automatic evaluation:** Kunst-Wilson and Zajonc (1980), Zajonc (2001), Zajonc (1968), Harrison (1977), Chen and Bargh (1999), Duckworth et al. (2002), and Ladd et al. (2014). The ability of unconscious information to influence perceptions led to concern that this practice might be adapted and abused by advertisers. Television networks, state legislatures, and even some professional bodies responded by preemptively banning "subliminal advertising" (Schwarzkopf 2005).

108 **Physical changes that influence behavior:** For an excellent discussion of the physiology of risk-taking, see Coates (2012).

108 **Fear response:** LeDoux (1996), LeDoux (2000), and Damasio and Carvalho (2013).

108 **Functions of emotion:** Levenson (1999) and Levenson (1992).

108 **Danger detector and automatic evaluation:** LeDoux (1996), Margolis (1987), Ferguson and Zayas (2009), and Ito and Cacioppo (2000).

109 **Somatic marker hypothesis:** Damasio (1994), Bechara and Damasio (2005), Reimann and Bechara (2010), and Dunn, Dalgleish and Lawrence (2006). Biological signals and financial risk: Lo and Repin (2002), Coates and Herbert (2008), and Smith et al. (2014).

109 **Iowa Gambling Task:** Bechara et al. (1994), Fernie and Tunney (2006), and Buelow and Suhr (2009).

109 **"When the bad outcome . . . ":** Damasio (1994), p. 173.

110 **"may 'say' the right thing . . . ":** Bechara and Damasio (2005), p. 372. Iowa Gambling Task and vmPFC damage: Bechara et al. (1997) and Bechara et al. (1994).

110 **Importance of gut feelings:** As Tim Cook, the CEO of Apple, once pointed out, "The most important things in life, whether they're personal or professional, are decided on intuition. . . . You can do a lot of analysis. You can do lots of things that are quantitative in nature. But at the end of it, the things that are most important are always gut calls" (quoted in Josh Tyrangiel, "Tim Cook's Freshman Year," *Bloomberg Businessweek,* December 6, 2012).

110 **Characteristics of human nature:** Waller (2007), de Waal (1996), de Waal (2006), Wright (1994), Williams (1989), Pinker (2011), Oakley (2007), Wilson (1978), Wilson (2014), and Pfaff (2015).

111 **"this interpretation . . . ":** de Waal (1996), p. 14. Genes and behavior: Dawkins (1976) and de Waal (1996).

111 **Genes and the brain:** Marcus (2004).

111 **Kin altruism:** Hamilton (1964). Kin by association: Johnson et al. (1986).

111 **Reciprocal altruism:** Trivers (1971).

111 **Altruism in nonhumans:** Wilson (1975), Preston and de Waal (2002), de Waal (2012), Flack and de Waal (2002). Selfish genes: Dawkins (1976), Sober (1988), and Darwin (1871), p. 105: "The difference in mind between man and the higher animals, great as it is, certainly is one of degree and not of kind." Other theories of altruism: Simon (1990) and Batson (1990).

111 **Moral and social interaction:** Woodward and Allman (2007).

112 **Autism as a socio-affective disorder:** Williams et al. (2001).

112 **Emotions influencing social/moral behavior:** Keltner, Haidt, and Shiota (2006), Haidt and Joseph (2004), Woodward and Allman (2007), Nesse (1990), Frijda and Mesquita (1994), Parkinson, Fischer, and Manstead (2005), and Steven Pinker, "The Moral Instinct," *New York Times,* January 13, 2008. Commitment devices: Frank (1988).

112 **Development of cooperation:** Axelrod (1984), Axelrod and Hamilton (1981), and Tooby and Cosmides (1989). For more detailed discussions of the social role played by emotions, see Keltner, Haidt, and Shiota (2006), Nesse (1990), and Keltner and Lerner (2010).

112 **Perceptions of and reactions to emotions:** Preston and de Waal (2002) and Wicker et al. (2003).

112 **Emotional contagion:** Hatfield, Cacioppo, and Rapson (1993) and Hatfield, Rapson, and Le (2011). Altruism/empathy: Batson et al. (2002), Hoffman (1981), Eisenberg, Valiente, and Champion (2004), and Batson and Shaw (1991).

112 **"Distress at the sight . . . ":** de Waal (2006), p. 51. Mindreading: Goldman and Sripada (2005) and Goldman (2006).

112 **Origins of empathy:** Darwin (1871), Flack and de Waal (2000), and Preston and de Waal (2002).

112 **Altruism in monkeys:** Masserman, Wechkin, and Terris (1964).

112 **Aversion to simulated harmful action:** Cushman et al. (2012).

113 **Morality and language:** Mikhail (2007), Mikhail (2011), Hauser (2006), and de Waal (2006), pp. 166–167. Another theory supporting the innate functioning of morality is modularity; see Pinker (1997), Haidt and Joseph (2007), and Kurzban (2010).

113 **Endowed with sense to behave less adversely to one another:** By observing children's behavior, we can find further evidence of the human tendency to avert causing harm and assist those in need. Development of altruism in youth: Bloom (2013), Hamlin, Wynn, and Bloom (2007), Warneken and Tomasello (2009), Hamlin, Wynn, and Bloom (2010), Over and Carpenter (2009), McDonald and Messinger (2011), Decety, Michalska, and Kinzler (2011), Hay and Cook (2007), and Shweder, Turiel, and Much (1981). Influences of culture: Henrich et al. (2010). Similarities in morality around the world: Haidt and Joseph (2007) and Steven Pinker, "The Moral Instinct," *New York Times,* January 13, 2008. Human universals: Brown (2004) and Brown (1991).

113 **"Humans evolved . . . ":** Shermer (2004), p. 71.

113 **Fragility of morality:** de Waal (2006).

114 **Hunter-gatherers and evolution:** Marlowe (2005). Modern skulls and the stone-age mind: Cosmides and Tooby (1997) and Cosmides and Tooby (1989).

114 **Decline in face-to-face communication:** Turkle (2015).

114 **Intuitive responses in familiar and unfamiliar contexts:** Sunstein (2005), Wilson (1998), and Ornstein and Ehrlich (1989).

114 **Subordinating morality:** Wilson (1993) and de Waal (1996). For an example of subordinating morality in the Ik tribe, see Turnbull (1972).

Chapter 7: The Ease of Overlooking Harm

115 **China earthquake in 2008:** Jake Hooker and Jim Yardley, "Powerful Quake Ravages China, Killing Thousands," *New York Times,* May 18, 2008; also see United States Geological Service, Earthquake Hazard Program.

115 **"Let us suppose . . . ":** Smith (1761), p. 211–212. Smith and the China disaster: Roberts (2014).

116 **"He would, I imagine . . . ":** Smith (1761), p. 212.

116 **"And when all this fine philosophy . . . ":** Smith (1761), p. 212.

116 **"seems plainly an object . . . ":** Smith (1761), p. 212.

116 **Trolley dilemma survey:** Hauser (2006) and Hauser et al. (2007).

117 **Surgeon killing healthy patient:** This example is described in Thomson (1985). The question of expediting the death of one patient to save others has arisen in practice; see Jesse McKinley, "Surgeon Accused of Speeding a Death to Get Organs," *New York Times,* February 27, 2009.

118 **Further discussion of the trolley dilemma:** Foot (1967), Thomson (1986), and Edmonds (2014).

119 **Aversion to intimate harming others:** As the psychologist Joshua Greene (2013) has explained, "experimental trolleyology indicates that there is something like an automated antiviolence system in our brain"(p. 227).

119 **Trolley dilemma and fMRI results:** Greene et al. (2001) and Greene (2013).

119 **Firing-rate statistics:** Grossman (2009), Marshall (1947), and Spiller (1988). Grossman (2009, pp. 254–257) describes how new training methods that more closely simulate actually killing another person help condition soldiers to overcome this aversion.

120 **Distance harms differed from intimate harms:** The rise of drone warfare raises similar challenges. Soldiers have less engagement with targets when using drones than in conventional warfare where they physically engage. See Corey Mead, "A Rare Look Inside the Air Force's Drone Training Classroom," *The Atlantic,* June 4, 2014.

120 **Scott Hirth:** The case was settled with the SEC without Hirth "admitting or denying the allegations." See *Securities and Exchange Commission v. Scott Hirth, and ProQuest Company, now known as Voyager Learning Company,* 08 CV 13139, United States District Court Eastern District of Michigan (July 22, 2008).

120 **Separating losses from fraud from underperformance:** It is often difficult to isolate the negative employment consequences associated with fraud from the impact of a poorly performing business. In some instances, employees might appear to lose their jobs because of a fraud, but in fact the fraud kept the business afloat longer—and therefore maintained the employees' jobs longer—than if there had been no fraud. One could say that at least some employees benefited in part from the crime (i.e., those who would have been fired earlier due to firm underperformance had it not been for the fraud) in such cases. However, there may be other negative externalities associated with employment during a fraud that could offset any apparent benefits for these employees.

120 **"I know how awful . . . ":** *Skilling v. United States of America,* 2009 WL 4825147 (Joint Appendix), Declaration of Philip K. Anthony, Ph.D., in Support of Defendant Jeffrey Skilling's Motion to Transfer Venue, November 8, 2004, p. 162.

121 **"The emotions . . . ":** Baumeister (1999), p. 9.

121 **Intensity of feelings/salience of situation:** Jones (1991), Loewenstein (1996), and Milgram (1974).

121 **"Corporations were rare . . . ":** Porter (1992), p. 9.

121 **By the sixteenth century:** This statement is not meant to imply that, prior to this time, individuals did not seek to trade commercially at a distance (e.g., for evidence of considerable trade along the "Silk Road," see Frankopan 2015). There is also evidence of earlier firms resembling joint-stock companies (e.g., Walker 1931, Schmitthoff 1939). The sixteenth century witnessed more frequent formalizing of larger nongovernmental fundraising arrangements and a dramatic increase in their use (e.g., Micklethwait and Wooldridge 2003).

122 **Businesses in early New England:** Bailyn (1955).

122 **Early shareholders in New York:** Hilt (2008), Rousseau and Sylla (2005), and Sylla (1998). The usage of currency provided even earlier opportunities to separate these personal ties. Mihm (2007) offers a fascinating description of the usage of counterfeit currency in the early United States.

122 **Number of stockholders:** The number of Americans who owned stock rose from 4.4 million to 14.4 million—5 percent of the population—between 1900 and 1922 (Hochfelder 2006). Separation of ownership and control at AT&T: Lipartito and Morii (2010), Berle and Means (1932), and Temporary National Economic Committee (1940).

123 **"if I look . . . ":** Slovic (2007), p. 80. This quotation appears to have evolved over time from a longer statement made by Mother Teresa when she was being interviewed for the documentary film *Work of Love;* the version printed here was subsequently published in Mother Teresa's *Words to Love By* (Notre Dame, Ind.: Ave Maria Press, 1983, p. 79).

124 **Identifiable-victim effect:** Slovic (2007), Slovic and Västfjäll (2010), and Small, Loewenstein and Slovic (2007).

124 **"Some call it . . . ":** Robert Lindsey, "Kotchian Calls Himself the Scapegoat," *New York Times,* July 3, 1977. Kotchian (1978) provides his own account of the payments.

124 **Lucarelli insider trading case:** *United States of America v. Michael A. Lucarelli,* 14 Civ. 6933 (NRB), United States District Court Southern District of New York (August 24, 2014), and Peter Henning, "Questions for the Government in an Insider Trading Case," *New York Times,* September 2, 2014.

125 **Government desire to improve chances of conviction:** In Chapter 11, I examine the identification of victims in cases of insider trading like this one involving Lucarelli.

125 **Garfinkel:** Garfinkel's account is described in *Dennis J. Buckley v. Deloitte & Touche USA LLP,* No. 06 Civ. 3291, filed August 15, 2012.

125 **Harm as a by-product of white-collar crime:** Coleman (1987).

126 **Volkswagen's high emissions and mortality:** Barrett et al. (2015).

127 **WorldCom fraud:** Markham (2006).

128 **CFO awards:** Jayne O'Donnell, "A Couple of Bad Apples Spoiled 'CFO' Award; Magazine Scrapped Honor After Deceit," *USA Today,* May 6, 2004.

129 **"Throwing a switch . . . ":** Singer (2005), p. 348. "Old" versus "new" killing methods: Singer (2011). Emotion and the trolley dilemma: Greene et al. (2001) and Greene (2013).

129 **Psychological distance arising from the situation as compared with distance created by an individual's disposition toward others:** For executives like Bernard

Madoff who know their victims and seem to have a lower ability to understand the harm they cause (as described in Chapter 14), their own psychology distances potential victims more than the nature of the business transactions. In this regard, it's not the arm's-length business transactions that distance them from their victims. Rather, their innate character and psychology play a much stronger role in creating psychological distance and fostering their inability to relate to the harm they cause.

Chapter 8: The Difficulty of Being Good

131   **The Difficulty of Being Good:** The title of the chapter was inspired by Das (2009), who explores the concept of morality within the *Mahabharata.*

131   **Avoid killing:** The fact that a majority of people are unlikely to commit murder even if there is no prohibition doesn't mean that we ought to "legalize murder." Laws against murder are effective in reducing its incidence by incapacitating individuals who have normalized to engaging in murder (e.g., gang members, serial killers) and in deterring those who might engage in it on the margin (e.g., by trying to recruit an individual to kill someone). Arrest rates and crime: Levitt (1998). Coercion and the law: Schauer (2015).

131   **9 percent of the adult population:** This estimate also includes psychotherapist medications repurposed for recreational use. Aggregate drug usage in the United States: "DrugFacts: Nationwide Trends," National Institute on Drug Abuse, National Institutes of Health, US Department of Health and Human Services (revised in June 2015).

131   **Drug use and the certainty/severity of legal recourse:** MacCoun (1993), Paternoster (1987), Paternoster et al. (1983), and Paternoster and Iovanni (1986). For evidence that suggests a stronger deterrence effect in other settings, see Levitt (2002).

132   **Obeying the law:** Tyler (2006), Tyler and Darley (1999), Robinson and Darley (1995), and Ostas (2007). Tyler (1990) provides a compelling model showing the relative weight of each factor with morality dominating respect for the law and the likelihood of being caught. Specifically, the relative beta weights when all factors are examined simultaneously in the model: will you be caught? (.02), do you respect the law? (.11), and are the rules moral? (.33). Role of morality in legal compliance: Tyler (1990), Tyler (1997b), Grasmick and Green (1980), Grasmick and Bursik (1990), Christensen and Eining (1991), and Paternoster and Simpson (1996).

132   **Prohibitions consistent with individuals' moral intuitions:** Legal prohibitions can also be effective when citizens face essentially perfect enforcement. For instance, few citizens of North Korea would openly dissent against the regime because they know that doing so would immediately result in harsh and certain punishment. Even those North Koreans who privately hold different moral intuitions tend to comply. In this way, they respect the law's legitimacy, even though the law itself may not resonate with them. Tyler (2006) has also found that legitimacy of the law—the sense that people believe they ought to obey it—contributes to compliance.

132   **"If you show them . . . ":** Jim Cramer, "Cramer Interviews US Attorney Preet Bharara," *Mad Money,* CNBC (July 18, 2012).

132   **Most executives remain honest:** In many jurisdictions with little to no enforcement of its "white-collar laws," this hypothetical is actually pretty close to reality even today. Many executives operate in jurisdictions in which there is essentially no enforcement of securities rules—and they still choose not to violate those rules.

133 **Parking violations by diplomats:** Fisman and Miguel (2007). Diplomatic immunity for New York parking violations was revoked in November 2002.

134 **Organizational culture:** Schein (2010), Kotter and Heskett (1992), Deal and Kennedy (1982), and Louis (1986).

134 **"the way we do things around here":** Bower (1966), p. 22. Graham et al. (2015) explore the process of creating corporate culture and how this contributes to a firm's value.

135 **Prevalence of fraudulent business practices:** "Overcoming Compliance Fatigue," 13th Global Fraud Survey, EY. I appreciate the assistance of Chris Costa for numerous helpful conversations and for providing country-level data. Andrighetto et al. (2016) explore variations in tax compliance in Italy and Sweden to understand different styles in dishonesty by country.

135 **Financial advisors and commission:** See "Fact Sheet: Middle Class Economics: Strengthening Retirement Security by Cracking Down on Conflicts of Interest in Retirement Savings," The White House, Office of Press Secretary, April 6, 2016.

135 **"Customers first" in retirement savings:** "Press Briefing by Press Secretary Josh Earnest, 4/6/2016," The White House, Office of Press Secretary, April 6, 2016.

136 **Use of firm resources for personal use:** In contrast to the scenario suggested by this example, much of culture is gained through nonconscious and often nonverbal means. See discussion in Fiske (1999).

136 **Practice becomes an organizational norm:** Not only do violations of such norms feel wrong to oneself, but witnessing another member of one's subculture violating a norm produces a feeling of consternation and disapproval. Norms and organizations: Cialdini and Trost (1998) and Bettenhausen and Murnighan (1985). Designing norms and mechanisms of learning: Cialidini et al. (2006) and Seligman 1970. Hogarth (2001) describes several factors that influence the proclivity to create intuitions including predisposition as well as internal and external motivation.

136 **Deep-seated norms that operate automatically:** When a norm begins operating at this deep affective level, it creates a somatic marker—the biological "gut feeling" associated with a particular action, as described in Chapter 5. Once such a marker is acquired toward a deviant opportunity (in which negative ramifications are observed), this option is linked with a negative gut feeling. With little deliberate consideration, people can reject that option in favor of one without such a negative association that is more amenable to success. In a sense, our brains effectively train themselves. People do not need to experience the negative repercussions of a choice in order to feel repulsed by or attracted to it.

136 **Employing managers who possess intuitions that run contrary to the law:** From the viewpoint of those employed by a firm, developing consistency between intuitions and regulation is also pragmatic since the firm will struggle for its continued existence if its employees continually make decisions that conflict with the law. However, to the extent that some firms are perceived as "too big to fail," they may be able to continue acting in opposition to the law for a considerable period of time. However, continued illicit behavior seems untenable when there is sufficient regulatory and public accountability.

136 **Corporate values:** Badaracco (2013), Weaver, Trevino, and Cochran (1999), Paine (1994), and Simons (2010). Integrity and corporate reputation: Macey (2013). Exploring when norms are internalized: Minoura (1992) and Harris (1995).

137 **"Tourre handed . . . ":** *Securities and Exchange Commission v. Fabrice Tourre,* 10 Civ. 3229 (KBF), United States District Court Southern District of New York, Opinion and Order, Katherine B. Forrest District Judge (June 4, 2013), p. 4.

138 **"contained incomplete information":** US Securities and Exchange Commission, "Goldman Sachs to Pay Record $550 Million to Settle SEC Charges Related to Subprime Mortgage CDO" (press release), July 15, 2010.

138 **"If there was something wrong . . . ":** Justin Baer, "Tourre Interviews: Case Will 'Stay With Me Forever,'" *Wall Street Journal,* August 1, 2013.

138 **Banking culture:** Hill and Painter (2015).

138 **"we are dedicated . . . ":** "Business Principles and Standards," Goldman Sachs Business Principles, n.d.

138 **"the vast majority . . . ":** United States District Court Southern District of New York, In re Goldman Sachs Group, Inc. Securities Litigation, Defendants' Memorandum of Law in Support of Their Motion to Dismiss the Consolidated Complaint (October 6, 2011).

138 **Judge's response to Goldman Sachs:** Judge Paul Crotty, who oversaw the case, was rather perturbed by this admission. In more colorful language than is typical in judicial opinions, Judge Crotty wrote: "Goldman's arguments in this respect are Orwellian. Words such as 'honesty,' 'integrity,' and 'fair dealing' apparently do not mean what they say; they do not set standards; they are mere shibboleths. If Goldman's claim of 'honesty' and 'integrity' are simple puffery, the world of finance may be in more trouble than we recognize" (*Ilene Richman v. Goldman Sachs Group,* 10 Civ. 3461 [PAC], United States District Court Southern District of New York, Opinion of Judge Paul A. Crotty, June 21, 2012, p. 7).

139 **"We have an indoctrination program":** Marvin Bower, "Meeting of Members, McKinsey & Company," p. 3, Corporate Archives, McKinsey & Company, January 13, 1945, as cited by McKenna (2006), p. 205.

140 **McKinsey and professionalism:** Bower (1966) and McKenna (2006).

140 **Gupta, Kumar, and McKinsey:** McDonald (2013), Raghavan (2013), and Deb (2013).

140 **McKinsey and outside activities:** Michael Stewart, a McKinsey partner and director of communications, stated to *Bloomberg News* in 2011 that "it has always been a clear violation of our values and professional standards for any firm member to provide consulting or advisory services outside of McKinsey for personal monetary gain." However, the McKinsey and Company "Firm Policies," a document that summarizes the expectations of its consultants and that McKinsey partners sign, did not state any such prohibition explicitly as of May 15, 2008.

144 **"It is astonishing . . . ":** See Anil Kumar's testimony in *United States of America v. Raj Rajaratnam,* 11Cr. 907 (JSR), United States District Court Southern District of New York (March 14, 2011).

144 **"I just wanted to . . . ":** Ibid.

145 **Affective persuasion:** Edwards (1990), Edwards and von Hippel (1995), and Shavitt (1990). An interesting analogy may be seen in the efforts being made to convince parents to vaccinate their children. Conveying evidence of the vaccines' effectiveness often does not change views, which are affectively driven. See Nyhan et al. (2014), Kahan (2013), and Kahan (2014).

146 **Social comparison:** Festinger (1954). Hornstein, Fisch, and Holmes (1968) created a clever experiment to show how our judgments are influenced by those we identify with. The researchers placed in various locations in Manhattan several dozen wallets containing cash, owner identification, and other personal effects. The wallets were identical except for an enclosed letter whose contents varied in describing how the wallet had already been lost and was being returned. Those who picked up the wallet and read the letter were meant to infer that the wallet was lost by the person trying to return the wallet. The "writer" also explained in the note how satisfying or challenging they had found the task of returning the wallet to its rightful owner.

Researchers then added a twist by varying the identity of the writer. Some of the letters were written by locals while others were from foreigners visiting New York. The researchers expected their subjects, mostly New Yorkers, to follow the lead of the letter writer when the writer was more like themselves, but not when the identity of the writer was dissimilar. It turned out that subjects were twice as likely to return the wallet when the letter was written by a conscientious American than when it was written by a responsible, albeit dissimilar foreigner. In addition, when the American letter writer remarked on the inconvenience of returning the wallet, subjects were less likely to return it a second time.

146 **GE and earnings management:** The fraudulent accounting practices by GE deemed illicit by the SEC were for a period soon after Welch had departed GE. This discussion of GE's earnings management under Welch's tenure is not meant to imply that practices were illicit during this time. However, to the extent that executives at other firms believed that GE was "successfully" managing earnings through illicit practices, they were inclined to adopt those practices themselves. (Description of GE in Stice and Stice (2014)).

146 **"relative obscurity":** Jonathan Laing, "Tyco's Titan," *Barron's,* April 12, 1999.

147 **Tyco and cyclicality:** Cynthia A. Montgomery et al., "Tyco International," Harvard Business School Case 798–061, March 1998 (revised in May 2007).

147 **"I envied GE . . . ":** Many assets on the financial statements were held at their historical cost. By going "mark-to-market," the firm could reassess their value based on prevailing market prices. To the extent that there was no liquid market price, firms could assess the value based on modeled values. In some cases, this practice provides firms considerable latitude in assessing the value of assets on their financial statements, leading to significant gains or losses on the firms' income statements. For a discussion of fair values, see Pozen (2009).

147 **"When a new CEO took over...":** Year-over-year change in net income is computed using data from WRDS. Tom Brakke (@researchpuzzler) circulated a similar figure on social media in October 2012.

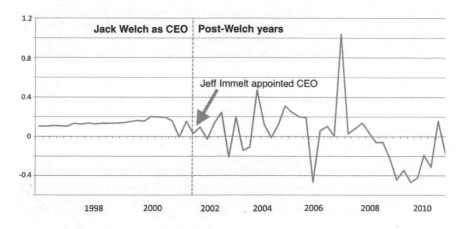

147 **"Even though . . . ":** Welch (2001), p. 225.

148 **"certain production . . . ":** "How General Electric Damps Fluctuations in Its Annual Earnings," *Wall Street Journal,* November 3, 1994.

148 **Earnings management at GE:** Ibid.

148   **"In the zeal . . . ":** Arthur Levitt, "The 'Numbers Game,'" Remarks by Chairman Arthur Levitt, Securities and Exchange Commission, NYU Center for Law and Business, September 28, 1998.

148   **"GE bent the accounting rules . . . ":** US Securities and Exchange Commission, "SEC Charges General Electric with Accounting Fraud" (press release), August 4, 2009. The fraudulent accounting practices alleged by the SEC took place after Welch departed GE.

149   **Charges against Kozlowski:** Neal (2014).

149   **Making moral judgments:** In an elegant framework known as the "social intuitionist model," the social psychologist Jonathan Haidt depicts how moral judgments are made (Haidt 2001 and Haidt 2012). In a similar spirit, I describe in this chapter how intuitions are often influenced and altered by those around us who exert their influence. Reasoning can also play a role in moral decision making; however, this is a weaker and less pervasive mechanism.

149   **Death penalty:** Lord, Ross, and Lepper (1979).

150   **Motivated reasoning and fMRI:** Westen et al. (2006).

150   **"You should take a look . . . ":** Fabrice Tourres, "Re: Fw: ft—friday," message to Marine Serres (e-mail), January 23, 2007. In the text of this e-mail, "monstrosities" was misspelled as "monstruosities" and portions were translated from the original in French.

151   **"I will look . . . ":** Lord Molson, as cited in Tavris and Aronson (2007).

151   **Time and reasoning:** Paxton, Ungar, and Greene (2011) and Paxton and Greene (2010). According to the economic theory of cost-benefit analysis, every decision is fully calculated, so further reflection shouldn't lead to a change in judgment. Camerer, Loewenstein, and Prelec (2005) describe this as "deliberative equilibrium." Additional reflection is not always effective in corrective biases, however (Schwitzgebel and Cushman 2015).

152   **"Given time . . . ":** Greenspan (2013), p. 34.

152   **"activities are characterized . . . ":** Mintzberg (1989), p. 10.

153   **Time usage by managers:** Mintzberg (1973), Mintzberg (1975), and Chugh (2004). Academics have similarly been known to overlook their own actions. Philip Zimbardo, the Stanford psychology professor who ran the much-cited Stanford Prison Experiment, recalls the "slap in my face, the wake-up call" when he was directly confronted about the problematic nature of his experiment (Zimbardo 2007, p. 170).

153   **Mindlessness:** Langer, Blank, and Chanowitz (1978), Langer (1989a), and Langer (1989b).

153   **"We may sum up . . . ":** Solomons and Stein (1896), pp. 508–509. See also Stein (1898).

154   **Mindlessness communication experiment:** Langer, Blank, and Chanowitz (1978).

155   **"as punishment . . . ":** Russell Wasendorf, suicide note, July 9, 2012.

155   **Cognitive dissonance:** Festinger (1957).

155   **"I have to say . . . ":** Russell Wasendorf, suicide note, July 9, 2012.

156   **Sarbanes-Oxley and singing financial statements:** Another interpretation for the signature line is that it was not meant to instigate greater reflection by executives, but simply to provide accountability to executives who erred. Signing financial statements and honesty: Shu et al. (2012).

Part III: The Business of Malfeasance

159   **LIBOR's background:** The BBA (or more recently ICE) LIBOR administration overview details the calculation of LIBOR. The number of contributions that are trimmed before averaging depends on the number of contributors with a 25 percent trimming

(i.e., top and bottom 4 contributors) occurring when there are 16 contributors for a rate calculation. For an enlightening overview of LIBOR, see Donald MacKenzie, "What's in a Number?" *London Review of Books, 30,* September 25, 2008, pp. 11–12. Managerial bias and LIBOR: Bazerman (2014).

160 **"where's young . . . ":** US Commodity Futures Trading Commission, "CFTC Orders the Royal Bank of Scotland plc and RBS Securities Japan Limited to Pay $325 Million Penalty to Settle Charges of Manipulation, Attempted Manipulation, and False Reporting of Yen and Swiss Franc LIBOR," Press Release PR6510–13, February 6, 2013. In the original release, the first Yen trader is referred to as "Yen Trader 4."

160 **LIBOR manipulation punishments:** James McBride, Christopher Alessi, and Mohammed Aly Sergie, "Understanding the Libor Scandal," Council on Foreign Relations, May 21, 2015.

160 **total cost of LIBOR's manipulation:** Phin et al. (2012).

161 **Financial industry's "crash board":** Fielding, Lo, and Yang (2011) and Andrew Lo, "The Financial Industry Needs Its Own Crash Safety Board," *Financial Times,* March 2, 2010.

162 **Prominence of female offenders in the United States:** Steffensmeier, Schwartz, and Roche (2013). Female offenders in Norway: Gottschalk and Glasø (2013). Analysis of Cressey's framework as it pertains to women: Zietz (1981).

162 **Prominent female offender:** Even one of the most prominent female offenders, Martha Stewart, is often incorrectly cited as having been convicted of insider trading; in actuality, she was convicted for obstruction of justice.

162 **False memories:** Loftus and Ketcham (1991), Shaw and Porter (2015), Baumeister and Newman (1994a), and Wilson and Ross (2003). Difference in memory between victim and perpetrator: Gordon and Miller (2000) and Baumeister, Stillwell, and Wotman (1990).

163 **"There is no attempt . . . ":** Zingales (2015), p. 1348.

Chapter 9: Misleading Disclosure

166 **Deception in real estate:** In the real estate industry, highly aggressive negotiating practices are common. Depending on the geographic market, these practices can be viewed as tolerable industry practices or as violations that could cause a broker to lose his or her real estate license. For example, to entice a buyer an agent may say that only one unit in a new development is available, when in fact there are other units available that are being shown to interested buyers. Such an example is featured in season 2, episode 10 of the show *Million Dollar Listings: New York,* in which one agent (Fredrik Eklund) deceptively tells another agent (Ryan Serhant) that supply is more limited than it actually is.

166 **Investors purchasing bonds from Litvak:** In his appeal, Litvak notes that customers' decisions to purchase bonds were based on valuation models that they had built and that did not take into account the dealer's costs. In addition, Litvak cites trial testimony that shows clients saying that purchasing the bonds from Litvak made financial sense regardless of his misstatements. Specifically, one testified that he "would do th[e] trade again at [the same] price" (J.A. 399) and another said that buying the bond at the final price "was a smart investment decision." For further discussion, see *United States of America, Appellee v. Jesse C. Litvak,* 14-2902-Cr, Brief of Defendant-Appellant, United States Court of Appeals for the Second Circuit (November 18, 2014).

167 **Litvak sentencing and appeal:** Litvak's actions were described in *SEC v. Jesse Litvak,* Civil Action No. 3:13-CV-00132, District of Connecticut (January 28, 2013), and

United States of America v. Jesse C. Litvak, No. 3:13CR19 (JCH) United States District Court District of Connecticut (January 25, 2013). His case was appealed and on December 8, 2015, several charges were reversed whereas others were sent for retrial.

167 **Lying during negotiations:** Peppet (2002), Shell (1991), White (1980), Strudler (1995), Wetlaufer (1990), and Norton (1989).

167 **Comparison between Litvak case and car sales:** Litvak's attorneys drew comparisons to standard negotiation practices. If Litvak's conviction was upheld, they said, "garden-variety statements that people make daily in negotiation . . . could support felony charges. Every car salesman who tells a customer that he cannot lower his price any further because he would earn only a miniscule profit on the sale as it is would be guilty of fraud" (*United States of America, Appellee v. Jesse C. Litvak,* 14-2902-Cr, Brief of Defendant-Appellant, United States Court of Appeals for the Second Circuit, November 18, 2014.)

168 **President Obama and insurance:** On June 6, 2009, President Obama similarly stated: "That means if you like the plan you have, you can keep it."

168 **"The whole episode . . . ":** Marc Thiessen, "Obama's Dishonest Presidency," *Washington Post,* November 4, 2013.

168 **Clutter the message on insurance:** During the passage of the legislation, several fact-checking organizations came up with evidence indicating that some individuals would not be able to keep their insurance. For example, see http://www.factcheck. org/2009/08/keep-your-insurance-not-everyone. The *Federal Register* described the expected disruptions in the insurance market in "Interim Final Rules for Group Health Plans and Health Insurance Coverage Relating to Status as a Grandfathered Health Plan Under the Patient Protection and Affordable Care Act" (*Federal Register,* Vol. 75, No. 116, June 17, 2010).

168 **President Obama and apology:** President Obama later apologized for these misstatements: "I am sorry that they, you know, are finding themselves in this situation based on assurances they got from me" (Juliet Eilperin, "President Obama Apologizes to Americans Who Are Losing Their Health Insurance," *Washington Post,* November 7, 2013).

168 **"will have to use . . . ":** Plato, edited and translated by Christopher Emlyn-Jones and William Preddy (2013), p. 485.

168 **Deception for a greater cause:** Bok (1978), Levine and Schweitzer (2014), and Mearsheimer (2011).

168 **"your president . . . ":** Franklin Delano Roosevelt, Remarks in Buffalo, New York, November 2, 1940.

168 **"I tell you . . . ":** Franklin Delano Roosevelt, Radio Address, September 11, 1941.

169 **Presidents and lying:** Alterman (2004), Carson (2010), and Dallek (1979).

169 **"FDR's deviousness . . . ":** Dallek (1979), p. 289.

169 **Altruism and lying:** Gino, Ayal, and Ariely (2013) and Levine and Schweitzer (2014).

169 **Lying in social settings:** Harris (2013). **Prosocial lies:** Levine and Schweitzer (2015).

170 **Disparity in stock prices and value in the oil industry:** Subcommittee on Fossil and Synthetic Fuels and the Subcommittee on Commerce, Transportation, and Tourism of the Committee on Energy and Commerce, House of Representatives, "Hearings on Oil Industry Mergers," 98th Congress, 2nd sess. (March 21 and May 16, 1984) (Testimony of Mark Gilman), pp. 238–252.

171 **Performance of "corporate raiders":** Holderness and Sheehan (1985), Coffee, Lowenstein, and Rose-Ackerman (1988), and Walsh and Kosnik (1993).

172 **"one of the more voracious . . . ":** Richard Behar, "The Special Talent of Paul Bilzerian," *Forbes,* December 15, 1986.

173 **"We use every trick . . . ":** Richard Behar, "Bilzerian's Talent," *Forbes,* June 13, 1988.

173 **Bilzerian charges:** Bilzerian was also charged with misreporting the source of funds used to fund the transaction. Bilzerian claimed that they were "personal funds" while prosecutors argued that they had been borrowed from investors whom he insulated against losses.

173 **Bilzerian defense:** Despite his conviction, Bilzerian was quick to point out that he did not believe the charges against him were appropriate or accurate.

Chapter 10: Financial Reporting Fraud

175 **"You show how much . . . ":** *United States of America v. Michael T. Rand,* No. 3:10-Cr-00182-RJC-DSC, United States District Court, Western District of North Carolina, Transcript of Jury Selection Before the Honorable Robert J. Conrad, Jr. (July 7, 2014), pp. 232–233. The trial transcript read "and then making the decision later" (p. 233). The use of "making" instead of "make" is either an unanticipated utterance or a transcription error; hence the substitution of "make" here. Discussion of earnings management from different perspectives: Dechow and Skinner (2000).

175 **Objective of financial reporting:** Kothari, Ramanna, and Skinner (2010) and Stickney et al. (2010).

176 **"Some of the other things . . . ":** Parfet (2000), p. 482.

176 **Your company is a defendant example:** Michael Rand provided this example during a conversation with me.

177 **Incentives to achieve benchmarks:** Healy and Wahlen (1999), Dechow and Skinner (2000), Barth, Elliott, and Finn (1999), Healy (1985), Johnson, Ryan, and Tian (2009), and Watts and Zimmerman (1990).

177 **Earnings targets and financial management:** Graham, Harvey, and Rajgopal (2005). In subsequent research, the authors found that 20 percent of firms they surveyed intentionally distorted earnings while still adhering to GAAP. Quality of reported earnings: Dichev et al. (2013) and Dichev et al. (2016).

178 **"we set an ambitious . . . ":** "Beazer Homes Announces December Quarter EPS of $2.47, Up 53 percent; EPS of $9.02 for Calendar 2001 Exceeds Five-Year Plan for 2004; Backlog of $815 Million Up 42," Beazer Homes, January 23, 2002.

179 **"Spoke to Ian . . . ":** *United States of America v. Michael T. Rand,* No. 3:10-Cr-00182-RJC-DSC, United States District Court, Western District of North Carolina, Transcript of Jury Selection Before the Honorable Robert J. Conrad, Jr. (July 7, 2014), pp. 2272–2273.

180 **"i'm relying on . . . ":** Ibid., p. 2345.

180 **"To achieve . . . ":** Ibid., pp. 1386–1387.

180 **"We may have . . . ":** Ibid., p. 1389. The original e-mail has "ant" instead of "any." The "ant" was a typographic error made at the time that Rand composed the e-mail.

180 **"Ian gave me . . . ":** Ibid., p. 721.

181 **"Set aside . . . ":** Ibid., p. 725.

183 **Symbol Technologies brand:** In 2007 Motorola acquired Symbol Technologies, and later, in 2014, Zebra Technologies acquired Motorola Solutions' enterprise business, which included Symbol. Symbol's scanning products are today labeled under the Zebra brand.

183 **"creating the global market . . . ":** United States Patent and Trademark Office, "The National Medal of Technology and Innovation 1999 Laureates."

183 **"unlike many technology companies . . . "**: Securities and Exchange Commission Complaint Against Symbol Technologies, Inc. (June 3, 2004), p. 13.

184 **"Bob Jones" alias:** Out of concern about future litigation, the name of this executive has been anonymized. "Bob Jones" is an alias.

186 **"as we discussed . . . "**: Securities and Exchange Commission Complaint Against Robert Asti (March 25, 2003), p. 4.

189 **Executives at Computer Associates:** Seven executives from Computer Associates faced sanctions related to backdating. An eighth individual, Thomas Bennett, who was senior vice-president of business development, was also charged with obstruction of justice.

190 **"This approach . . . "**: Alex Brown, "Computer Associates: A New Business Model, Closely Examined," Deutsche Bank, November 9, 2000, p. 5.

192 **"This was simply a timing issue . . . "**: Peter Griffin, "After Long Months, It's Long Years," *New Zealand Herald*, January 6, 2007.

194 **Figure 10.2:** The figure displays the distribution of earnings scaled by beginning-of-period market value of equity for publicly traded firms from 1976-2001. The discontinuity persists if the figure is updated until present, but as described by Gilliam, Heflin, and Paterson (2015), it does not arise in post-2002 data. The author appreciates the help of Jihwon Park for replicating this figure. Earnings discontinuity: Burgstahler and Dichev (1997), Durtschi and Easton (2005), Durtschi and Easton (2009), and Gilliam, Heflin, and Paterson (2015); Discontinuity in ROE in China: Liu and Lu (2007).

195 **Adjustment made by a different software firm around the same time:** This example was described to me by a participant in an executive education program at Harvard Business School. It also presumes that the provisions for these cancellations were released at the end of this quarter.

197 **"Transparent" earnings manipulation:** In theory, one could respond that investors would see this change in the financial statements, so the reporting decision wouldn't be deceptive. The presumption here is that investors and analysts would be able to unwind small adjustments to SG&A or other entries on the financial statements. In practice, however, it's not clear that investors and analysts would always correctly notice such changes.

198 **"that are growing . . . "**: Eric Pfeiffer, "Winner Profile: Critical Path," *Forbes ASAP*, April 3, 2000.

198 **Charges against David Thatcher:** *Securities and Exchange Commission v. David Thatcher and Timothy Ganley*, Civil Action No. C-02–0621 (SBA) Complaint (February 5, 2002).

Chapter 11: Insider Trading

201 **"'Did someone really compare what I built for shareholders with them?'"**: Transcripts from the trial show that one of the attorneys, rather than the judge, actually made this reference.

201 **Erbitux name:** Erbitux is one commercial name for IMC-C225; Cetuximab is another.

203 **Shares worth more than $140 million:** This was the value as of March 28, 2001. In addition, Waksal held over $700 million in unexercised in-the-money options as of December 31, 2000. By March 2002, Waksal had substantially reduced his ownership in the firm, but still held more than $15 million dollars in shares and options worth

nearly $40 million dollars (assuming a 5 percent appreciation of stock price over the option term).

203 **"Erbitux . . . ":** Toni Clarke, "Biotech Industry Gaining Maturity," *Los Angeles Times,* December 26, 2001.

203 **Waksal discussing news with family members:** Sam Waksal also told the news about the FDA's impending decision to other family members including his father, Jack. (See Securities and Exchange Commission Litigation Release No. 19039, January 19, 2005.)

204 **Stewart's involvement:** Martha Stewart would later be convicted of obstruction of justice and be sentenced to five months in prison (*Securities and Exchange Commission v. Martha Stewart and Peter Bacanovic,* 03-Civ-4070 (NRB), United States District Court Southern District of New York, June 17, 2004).

204 **"What's so bad about insider trading?":** Manne (1966a), p. 14.

204 **"Prior to the year 1910 . . . ":** Manne (1966b), p. 1. In referring to a 1910 critique, Manne was citing Wilgus (1910). Wilgus (1910) wrote: "That the director may take advantage of his position to secure the profits that all have won, offends the moral sense" (p. 297).

205 **"The tone . . . ":** Manne (1966b), p. 113. Emotion versus logic and insider trading: Berle (1927).

205 **"In small enterprises . . . ":** Manne (1966b), p. 1.

205 **"make more appropriate moral judgments":** Manne (1966b), p. 15.

205 **Reception to Manne:** Schotland (1967) and Baum (1967).

205 **More than four hundred successful civil and criminal cases:** The total number of civil and criminal cases was compiled on the basis of Morrison and Foerster's annual insider trading review.

206 **"bloody but brilliant":** *Gazette Extraordinary,* 5th ed., June 18, 1815, as cited in Cowles (1973).

207 **Rothschild's trading and the Battle of Waterloo:** Cowles (1973). An interesting empirical analysis of "insider trading" between traders in London and Amsterdam in the eighteenth century is described in Koudijs (2015).

207 **Verdict in favor of Organ:** On *Laidlaw v. Organ,* 15 U.S. 178 (1817), see Williams (1901) and Hoeflich (1991).

208 **History of trading on privileged information:** The history of trading on privileged information is discussed in Herzel and Katz (1987).

208 **90 percent of directors traded on information:** The frequency of insider trading in the early twentieth century is discussed in Manne (1966b), who cites the New York Times Company's *The Annalist* with respect to the 90 percent figure. However, the issue of *The Annalist* cited by Manne does not actually contain this figure but, instead, provides qualitative evidence that the majority of directors are willing to undertake such trading. Thus, it is inconclusive as to whether 90 percent is the appropriate figure to draw from *The Annalist*'s 1915 survey efforts.

208 **"if we were all . . . ":** "Should Directors Speculate?" *The Annalist,* July 19, 1915, p. 65.

208 **"They sent me word . . . ":** White (1910), p. 141. Subsequent rules created to regulate insider trading practices by directors: Bainbridge (2014), Dooley (1980), and Cook and Feldman (1953).

208 **Insider trading regulation around the world:** To determine the number of countries with insider trading prohibitions, I began with the data in Bhattacharya and Daouk (2002); then, with respect to countries without a prohibition, I examined the website

of the largest security exchange in the country for updated regulations. In cases where I did not locate information about a prohibition, I contacted the exchange directly.

209 **"Insider trading law . . . ":** Linda Chatman Thomsen, "U.S. Experience of Insider Trading Enforcement," Australian Securities and Investments Commission 2008 Summer School, Melbourne, Australia, February 19, 2008.

209 **United States and regulation against insider trading:** One exception is in the case of tender offers, which are explicitly prohibited under 17 CFR 240.14e-3.

210 **Regulation and equal access to information:** In the United States, the idea that all investors should have equal access to information was debated during one of the early formative insider-trading cases (*Securities and Exchange Commission v. Texas Gulf Sulpher Co.*, 401 F.2d 833, 2nd Cir., 1968).

210 **David Einhorn and insider trading:** Financial Services Authority, Final Notice to David Einhorn, February 15, 2012. European insider trading: Hostetter (1999).

210 **Enforcement of insider trading in the United States as compared with other countries:** Given the variations in what constitutes illicit insider trading around the world, I focus on the market where it's most vigorously enforced: the United States. The United States employs a narrower definition relative to other countries, but it enforces this position so intensely that the prohibition and especially the criminalization of insider trading are predominantly still an American phenomena.

211 **"The market is a victim":** Preet Bharara, "Insider Trading Is 'Rampant' on Wall Street," interview with *Frontline*, PBS (January 7, 2014).

211 **"Who's going to trade . . . ":** Roger Lowenstein, "The War on Insider Trading: Market-Beaters Beware," *New York Times Magazine*, September 22, 2011. Insider trading and the potential for market damage: Leland (1992) and Manove (1989).

211 **Equal access doctrine:** In *Chiarella v. United States*, 445 U.S. 222, U.S. Supreme Court (March 18, 1980), the Supreme Court rejected an equal access doctrine.

212 **Early access to corporate news:** Scott Patterson, "Speed Traders Get an Edge," *Wall Street Journal*, February 6, 2014.

212 **Innovative data sources:** Bradley Hope and Daniel Huang, "Firms Analyze Tweets to Gauge Stock Sentiment," *Wall Street Journal*, July 6, 2015; Bradley Hope, "Startups Mine Market-Moving Data from Fields, Parking Lots—Even Shadows," *Wall Street Journal*, November 20, 2014; and Michael Rothfeld and Scott Patterson, "Traders Seek an Edge with High-Tech Snooping," *Wall Street Journal*, December 19, 2013.

212 **"that a reasonable . . . ":** Securities and Exchange Commission, "Final Rule: Selective Disclosure and Insider Trading," October 23, 2000.

213 **Private meetings and informed trading:** Solomon and Soltes (2015), Bushee, Jung, and Miller (2014), Bushee, Gerakos, and Lee (2014), and Soltes (2014). Related research also explores the more informed trading by individuals with personal and professional connections: Cohen, Frazzini, and Malloy (2010) and Cohen, Frazzini, and Malloy (2008).

213 **Information disparities and consequences of insider trading regulation:** Bhattacharya and Daouk (2002) found that the cost of equity within a country falls after the first prosecution of insider trading (without distinguishing between civil and criminal cases). But as the authors noted, there is a concern that regulators' decisions to enforce regulation and the attractiveness of the country (e.g., credit rating) are endogenous. Consequently, it is difficult to accurately assess the impact of these prosecutions. A related question, as posed by Carlton and Fischel (1983), is why firms did not voluntarily seek to prohibit insider trading prior to regulation if such trading imposed significant costs on firms. Furthermore, regulators could require instantaneous

disclosure of insider trades, rather than a lag of days, if such informational differences were perceived to be an economically significant hindrance to market efficiency.

213 **Capital One insider trading case:** *Securities and Exchange Commission v. Bonan Huang and Nan Huang,* No. 2.15-Cv-00269, United States District Court for the Eastern District of Pennsylvania (January 21, 2015).

213 **Selling credit card data:** Several credit card companies including MasterCard and American Express already sell this type of data, albeit at the industry rather than firm level.

214 **Capital One trading on data:** Capital One may have a contract with customers that would prevent it from trading on these data. However, a related insider trading case raises the question of whether firms can trade on their own data. Foster Winans, a writer at the *Wall Street Journal,* was convicted of providing information to his broker about his upcoming column, which tended to be market moving. As provocatively noted by the court, the "*Wall Street Journal* or its parent, Dow Jones Company, might perhaps lawfully disregard its own confidentiality policy by trading in the stock of companies to be discussed in forthcoming articles" (*United States of America v. David Carpenter, Kenneth P. Felis, and R. Foster Winans,* United States Court of Appeals, Second Circuit, May 27, 1986). For further discussion of this case, see Winans (1984). Such concerns have been raised more recently in the context of venture funding and publishing; see L. Gordon Crovitz, "A Business Model Based on Conflict of Interest," *Wall Street Journal,* September 12, 2011.

214 **"all the honest people . . . ":** Preet Bharara, "Insider Trading Is 'Rampant' on Wall Street," interview with *Frontline,* PBS (January 7, 2014).

214 **Valid ways to trade on nonpublic news:** Two additional ways to acquire privileged nonpublic material information on which to trade are through luck (e.g., overhear conversation) and through government work. Insider trading based on luck: Green (2006). Government officials trading on insider information: Nagy (2011), Bainbridge (2011), and Ziobrowski et al. (2004).

214 **Differences needed to sustain investment markets:** Investors could have the same physical information about a firm, yet different interpretations of that information. Differences in interpretations could be generated by dissimilar analyses, prior knowledge, and beliefs that reflect other discrepancies between investors. But if not for informational differences caused by access or processing, trading would eventually arise only for liquidity reasons (e.g., to raise cash). Thus, efficient trading in markets is predicated on some informational differences between investors. In a carefully written piece, Grossman and Stiglitz (1980) describe the impossibility of fully informationally efficient markets.

214 **"If you have no . . . ":** Matt Levine, "Another Politician Wants to Ban Insider Trading," *Bloomberg,* April 1, 2015.

215 **"is a most serious offense . . . ":** Liman (1998), p. 270. Fairness and insider trading: Easterbrook (1981), McGee (2007), and Beams, Brown, and Killough (2003).

215 **"Make no mistake . . . ":** "Manhattan U.S. Attorney Charges Hedge Fund Managers, Fortune 500 Executives, and Management Consulting Director in $20 Million Insider Trading Case," US Attorney's Office, October 16, 2009.

216 **Trading if had information like insider:** As an example of a regulator noting that people would not trade if they had the same information as the insider, Preet Bharara commented that "you actually have identifiable counterparties who may not have engaged in the trade on the other side had they known what the information was"; see

Preet Bharara, "Insider Trading Is 'Rampant' on Wall Street," interview with *Frontline*, PBS (January 7, 2014).

216 **Insider trading changing prices in market:** One can contend that if an insider's trading sufficiently alters a price, then this price change may motivate an investor's decision to trade. To the extent that this occurs in some insider cases, it would be fair to describe those investors who transacted shares—and were motivated to do so by the price change—as victimized by the insider's trades.

216 **Trading can be deceptive:** Bonafide trading is not deceptive. However, traders can artificially act as though they are desiring to trade, but in fact do not necessarily have that intention (as in flash-trading, for example). Flash-trading: Lewis (2015).

217 **Aspect of deception with insider trading:** While the trading itself cannot be considered deceptive, the deliberate delay or nondisclosure of material information may be viewed as deceptive.

217 **Impersonal exchanges and insider trading:** Bainbridge (2013) and Bainbridge (2014).

217 **Matching on anonymous exchange:** If there was only one seller of a security, then victims would not arise from arbitrary matching. However, in a securities exchange with many buyers and sellers operating anonymously at the same time, the investor who is matched by an exchange to purchase securities from a specific seller is essentially arbitrary.

217 **Potential buyers/sellers and insider trading:** Herzel and Katz (1987).

218 **Journalists and insider trading:** Michael Wolff draws a provocative comparison between insider traders and journalists, inasmuch as both seek information often in violation of fiduciary duty (Michael Wolff, "How Hedge Funders Are Like Journalists—and Why We're Hated," *The Guardian*, November 26, 2012).

218 **Lehman Brothers firm name:** At the time of the transaction, the firm was called Lehman Brothers Kuhn Loeb Inc. Insider trading and Litton: *Litton Industries, Inc. v. Lehman Brothers Kuhn Loeb Incorporated,* United States Court of Appeals, Second Circuit, June 17, 1992; Diaz and Maxwell (1988); Frantz (1987); and Levine (1991).

219 **Announcement-day profits:** Second Amended Complaint, *Litton Industries, Inc. v. Lehman Brothers Kuhn Loeb, Inc.,* No. 86–6447, filed August 19, 1986, as cited in Diaz and Maxwell (1988).

219 **Overpricing and takeover premium:** The notion of appropriate price, and whether a firm "overpaid" for an acquisition, is subject to debate regarding efficient pricing. Takeover premiums: Stout (1990).

219 **Issuer damaged by insider trading:** A more recent example of damage to an issuer arising from insider trading is that of investors trading ahead of confidential marketed public offerings. For a discussion, see Matt Levine, "Insider Traders Made Some Easy Money on Stock Offerings," *Bloomberg,* June 3, 2015.

219 **Damage to companies and shareholders:** By harming a firm, one can by extension also hurt shareholders (e.g., the Litton shareholders who implicitly overpaid when Litton's board raised its price to purchase Itek).

220 **"Insider trading . . . ":** Michael W. Miller, "U.S. Prosecutor of Insider Trading Bluntly Labels the Offense as Theft," *Wall Street Journal,* December 24, 1986, p. 6.

220 **Who can damage reputation:** As the court noted, "Although the employer may perhaps lawfully destroy its own reputation, its employees should be and are barred from destroying their employer's reputation by misappropriating their employer's informational property" (*United States of America v. David Carpenter, Kenneth P. Felis, and R. Foster Winans,* United States Court of Appeals, Second Circuit, May 27, 1986).

222 **Dell providing information to outsiders:** Defendants argued that Dell routinely leaked information to preferential investors that many would view as more material in nature. See *United States of America against Jon Horvath, Danny Kuo, Hyung G. Lim, Michael Steinberg, Todd Newman, and Anthony Chiasson*, United States Court of Appeals, Brief of Defendant-Appellant Todd Newman (August 15, 2013), pp. 18–20.

222 **"There's still risk":** In some instances, the information about Dell that Tortora acquired from Goyal turned out to be quite useful in helping make better investment decisions, while at other times this information was far off the mark. For example, in August 2008, Ray provided Goyal a revenue number that was $400 million too low. Tortora "freaked" when he saw how far the number was off (*United States of America against Jon Horvath, Danny Kuo, Hyung G. Lim, Michael Steinberg, Todd Newman, and Anthony Chiasson*, United States Court of Appeals, Brief of Defendant-Appellant Todd Newman, August 15, 2013, p. 13).

223 **"This was a stark . . . ":** *United States of America v. Todd Newman and Anthony Chiasson*, No. 12-Cr-121 (RJS), United States District Court Southern District of New York (December 17, 2012).

224 **If a firm provides material information to investors in context of discussions:** To the extent that an executive of the firm selectively provides some investors material information that had not been publicly disclosed, this would be a violation of Regulation Fair Disclosure. See Securities and Exchange Commission, "Final Rule: Selective Disclosure and Insider Trading," October 23, 2000.

224 **Hypothetical about insider trading:** It is possible to construe an even more perverse example. Reporters often acquire information from corporate insiders. For instance, a *Wall Street Journal* article about Dell in 2013 noted that "according to a person briefed on the results" Dell planned to announce revenue and earnings far below analyst expectations, citing specific numbers to that effect. When Dell announced results two days later, the actual results were nearly identical to those reported by the *Journal* (Shira Ovide, "Dell to Miss Profit Estimates, Beat on Revenue," *Wall Street Journal*, May 14, 2013). If the additional condition that investors know about a violation of fiduciary duty was not imposed, anyone who had traded after reading this article (assuming that the confidential information was not now viewed as public since it was printed in a newspaper) could be seen as engaging in illicit insider trading.

225 **Restricting of insider trading:** Easterbrook and Fischel (1991).

226 **Reliability of inside information:** While the source of the information might not matter, one could argue that the certainty of the information would matter. As many insider trading cases make clear, even information conveyed illegally is often not without ambiguities and uncertainty. In many instances, the "inside information" turns out to be outdated or incorrect by the time it can be acted upon.

Chapter 12: Deceptive Financial Structures

228 **"We're not working with a base":** Matt Flegenheimer and Brian X. Chen, "As a Taxi-Hailing App Comes to New York, Its Legality Is Questioned," *New York Times*, September 4, 2012.

228 **Uber model:** Murad Ahmed, Jeevan Vasagar, and Tim Bradshaw, "Backseat Driver," *Financial Times*, September 16, 2015.

228 **Aereo's growth:** Peter Kafka, "Here's How Many Subscribers Aereo Had Last Year," *re/code*, July 21, 2014; J. J. Colao, "If Aereo Loses in Supreme Court, Can It Rise Again?"

Forbes, May 7, 2014; and Matt Buchanan and Nate Lavey, "Object of Interest: Aereo's Tiny Antennas," *New Yorker,* March 14, 2014.

228   **American Letter Mail Company:** Shively (1971).

229   **Thin political markets:** Regulatory capture is especially likely when markets are "thin," as described by Ramanna (2015).

229   **Taxi businesses versus Uber:** During periods of high demand, taxis may actually offer more economical rates, given Uber's surge pricing policies. Uber's dynamic pricing allows it to adjust the supply of drivers and demand from users more flexibly than taxi services that have fixed prices and numbers of vehicles on the road.

229   **Confronting regulatory obstacles:** In some instances, a business may enter a market facing regulatory obstacles that prevent it from officially operating. By rapidly expanding the business and gaining a large enough base of customers and/or suppliers, its executives hope that this will stimulate changes in regulation. Often, while defending against critics during the growth phase, these entrepreneurs find creative ways of interpreting current regulations that allow them to argue that their businesses are not operating illegally.

230   **Ship demolition and flag choice:** Anurag Kotoky, "Changing Flags to Use India's Ship Graveyard," *Bloomberg Businessweek,* February 12, 2015. For additional background, the NGO Shipbreaking Platform describes a significant amount of investigatory work around this issue.

230   **"If you take . . . ":** Andrew Pollack, "By 'Editing' Plant Genes, Companies Avoid Regulation," *New York Times,* January 1, 2015.

231   **Genetic modification of plants:** Andrew Pollack, "By 'Editing' Plant Genes, Companies Avoid Regulation," *New York Times,* January 1, 2015; Waltz (2015); and Waltz (2011). The distinction between exploiting leeway in a law's interpretation and engaging in a fraudulent scheme is often a dubious one. For example, officials at Nationwide created a policy specifying that a letter had only been received once the letter physically arrived in its building. Following this policy, if a letter just so happened to arrive in the building after 4 p.m., it would be marked at the following day's prices. But Nationwide didn't interpret "receive" in this matter simply because it viewed doing so the most obvious or appropriate way of processing orders; rather, it did so because it was a means to manage and adjust the timing of recording prices (Securities and Exchange Commission Administrative Proceeding in the Matter of Nationwide Life Insurance Company No. 3-16537, May 14, 2015).

231   **Creativity and dishonesty:** Gino and Ariely (2012) and Gino and Wiltermuth (2014). Kay (2015) explores some of the recent challenges created by regulatory arbitrage.

232   **"best demonstrates innovation, leadership, and social responsibility over the past year":** "Third Annual MIT Sloan eBusiness Awards Announce Winners," *MIT News,* April 23, 2001.

232   **Over $60 billion in market value vanished:** Enron's misstatements pertained to financial reports for the previous five years. While larger corporate bankruptcies have occurred since Enron, at the time it was deemed the largest (Richard Oppel and Andrew Ross Sorkin, "Enron's Collapse: The Overview," *New York Times,* December 3, 2001.) Description of Enron's rise and later collapse: McLean and Elkind (2003), Eichenwald (2005), Salter (2008), Niskanen (2005), Smith and Emshwiller (2003), and Markham (2002).

234   **"There was this anomaly . . . ":** *U.S. v. Jeffrey K. Skilling and Kenneth L. Lay,* Criminal No. H-04-25, United States District Court for the Southern District of Texas, Houston Division, Andrew Fastow Testimony (March 7–13, 2006). Pakaluk and Cheffers (2011) describe Fastow's testimony in the context of accounting ethics.

234   **Cheater's high:** Ruedy et al. (2013)

236   **Controls and LJM 2:** Additional controls were put into place to mitigate potential conflicts of interest when LJM 2 was created. This included the condition that all transactions would be subject to approval to Enron's chief accounting officer and chief risk officer. Furthermore, transactions would be reviewed by Enron's Audit and Compliance Committee annually. See William C. Powers, Jr., Raymond S. Troubh, and Herbert S. Winokur, Jr., "Report of Investigation by the Special Investigative Committee of the Board of Directors of Enron Corp.," February 1, 2002.

239   **"amazing transformation . . . ":** Russ Banham, "Andrew S. Fastow—Enron Corp.," *CFO Magazine,* October 1, 1999.

241   **Sustaining Enron:** Fastow explained that Enron needed to issue equity, but other executives were averse to doing so. It was this error in judgment, in his opinion, that led to Enron's rapid bankruptcy: "Lay decided that EPS was more important than credit rating. . . . At a time he should have been issuing equity, he engaged in a share buyback."

241   **"Enron so engineered . . . ":** United States Bankruptcy Court, Southern District of New York, In re: Enron Corp, et al., Debtors, Case No. 01–16034, Final Report of Neal Batson, Court-Appointed Examiner (November 4, 2003), p. 18.

242   **Defense attorneys' strategy:** Leo Katz eloquently describes this slippery-slope argument in Katz (1996).

243   **Breadth of regulation:** Buell (2008) points out that one of the rationales for the breadth in laws prohibiting fraud is to facilitate more flexible prohibitions of undesirable conduct.

243   **"over and over . . . ":** *Commissioner of Internal Revenue v. Newman,* 159 F. 2d 848, 2d Cir. (February 20, 1947).

243   **Obligations to pay tax globally:** In Britain, courts reached a similar conclusion: "Every man is entitled if he can order his affairs so that the tax attracting under the appropriate Acts is less than it would otherwise be" (IRC vs. Duke of Westminster, 19 TC 490, 1936).

243   **Window tax:** Dowell (1884), Ward (1952), Glantz (2008), and Oates and Schwab (2015).

243   **Russian poll tax:** Kort (2008).

244   **IRS and tax avoidance:** "Tax avoidance is perfectly legal and encouraged by the IRS," states an educational page on the Internal Revenue Service's website, "but tax evasion is against the law (see "Understanding Taxes" at IRS.gov).

244   **Tax code:** Wolters Kluwer, CCH Standard Federal Tax Reporter. Underscoring this complexity, the IRS states that "individuals and businesses spend about 6.1 billion hours a year complying with filing requirements. . . . If tax compliance were an industry, it would be one of the largest in the United States" (Taxpayer Advocate Service, 2012 Annual Report to Congress, Vol. I, December 31, 2012, p. 5).

244   **Gift of $10,000 and taxes:** Under IRS rules, the annual exclusion up to which a gift is nontaxable is $14,000 as of January 1, 2013. Thus, the $10,000 would be nontaxable.

244   **Generous-shoemaker example:** Katz (1996) and Katz (2011).

245   **"a deal done . . . ":** Graetz (2008), p. 116. "Tax shelter" is defined in Graetz and Schenk (2005).

245   **Objectives of tax planning:** Scholes et al. (2009).

245   **"Tax planning . . . ":** Weisbach (2002), p. 222.

245   **"Most people . . . ":** Gary Klott, "Giving Gifts Can Pay Off on Tax Return," *Sun-Sentinel,* December 13, 1999. Interestingly, however, Erickson, Hanlon, and Maydew (2004) show that firms with fraudulent income pay taxes on this overstated income.

246 **Another executive who frequently interacted with Watson and his colleagues at KPMG:** Out of concern for potential future litigation, this executive is described anonymously as "Bob Jones."

246 **Growth of tax sheltering businesses:** Ordower (2010).

246 **KPMG and aggressive tax-business:** Johnson (2005) and Rostain and Regan (2014).

246 **"the simple concept . . . ":** Memo of Randy Bickham, August 20, 1998. At the same time, KPMG had to limit the number of times a certain product could be sold. If the IRS saw many people carrying out the identical set of transactions, it might suspect—correctly—that those transactions represented a standardized tax shelter and not a solution to a client's particular problem.

247 **"dramatically accelerated . . . ":** US Senate, Committee on Governmental Affairs, "The Role of Professional Firms in the U.S. Tax Shelter Industry" (109th Congress), February 8, 2005, p. 17.

248 **How much "business purpose" is needed:** An analogous challenge is when firms seek to ostensibly distribute profits tax-free to investors, but need to include an active business to avoid taxation. Yahoo faced this challenge with its Alibaba stock in 2015. See Matt Levine, "Yahoo's Alibaba Spinoff Is in Tax Limbo," *Bloomberg*, September 9, 2015.

248 **"I would have thought . . . ":** US Senate, Committee on Governmental Affairs, "U.S. Tax Shelter Industry: The Role of Accountants, Lawyers, and Financial Professionals. Four KPMG Case Studies: FLIP, OPIS, BLIPS, and SC2" (108th Congress, 1st Session), November 18 and 20, 2003.

249 **"I don't like this product . . . ":** Ibid.

249 **"ready to proceed":** *United States of America v. John Larson, Robert Pfaff, Raymond J. Ruble, and David Greenberg*, S2-05-Cr-888 (LAK), United States District Court Southern District of New York (December 10, 2008).

249 **"Crimes like terrorism . . . ":** Statement of Senator Carl Levin Before U.S. Senate, Subcommittee on Investigations, "U.S. Tax Shelter Industry: The Role of Accountants, Lawyers, and Financial Professionals" (108th Congress, 1st Session), November 18, 2003, p. 1.

250 **"You're supposed to be an advocate . . . ":** Ruble (2003).

250 **Backflip shelter:** Weisbach (2002).

250 **Macroeconomic consequences of tax avoidance and evasion:** It is possible that some individuals who seek to aggressively minimize taxes do appreciate that this lowers government income *and* that this lower government spending is beneficial. Along a similar line of argument, some taxpayers believe that the use of complex structures to lower taxes is not really "aggressive" but, rather, simply a natural response to the needlessly complex tax code. For additional discussion on the tax shelter industry, see the excellent discussion in Rostain and Regan (2014).

251 **Legal consequences of BLIPS:** Ultimately, nineteen people were criminally indicted. However, only five received criminal sentences in the end (two with probation). The charges against thirteen people, including the most senior executives at KPMG (including Stein and Wiesner), were dropped when a judge deemed that prosecutors had violated the constitutional rights of many of the defendants by pressuring KPMG to not pay their legal costs.

252 **Apple most admired company since 2008:** As of this writing (in 2016).

252 **Apple's tax-reducing techniques:** Charles Duhigg and David Kocieniewski, "How Apple Sidesteps Billions in Taxes," *New York Times*, April 28, 2012. Social responsibility of tax avoidance: Dowling (2014).

252   **"Apple has conducted . . . "**: "Apple's Response on Its Tax Practices," *New York Times,*
      April 28, 2012.

252   **"The offshore tax avoidance . . . "**: Statement of Senator Carl Levin Before U.S. Sub-
      committee on Investigations, "Offshore Profit Shifting and the U.S. Tax Code—Part 2
      (Apple, Inc.)" (113th Congress, 1st Session), May 21, 2013, p. 6.

253   **Synthetic drugs:** *VICE* explored the creation of synthetic drugs in "Synthetic Drug
      Revolution," HBO, Season 3, Episode 5, April 10, 2015.

254   **"are merely put out . . . "**: As translated in Yoe (1882), p. 283, but originally described
      in Bastian (1866). Yoe (1882) discusses numerous other loopholes used to get around
      religious prohibitions, including not facing the sun to avoid knowing the time in or-
      der to create more flexibility with meals and wrapping one's hands in cloth to avoid
      physically touching money. For an excellent review of Yoe (1882), see Tylor (1882).

254   **Comfort developed over time with acts of evil:** More broadly, this is related to nor-
      malizing evil acts. Banality of evil: Arendt (1963).

254   **"So what's up . . . "**: Report of Anton R. Valukas, Examiner, United States Bankruptcy
      Court, Southern District of New York, In re Lehman Brothers Holdings Inc., et al.,
      Debtors, Chapter 11 Case no. 08–13555, March 11, 2010, Volume 3 of 9, p. 860–866.
      Lehman and LIBOR: Anette Mikes, Gwen Yu, and Dominique Hamel, "Lehman
      Brothers and Repo 105," Harvard Business School Case 112–050, October 2011 (re-
      vised 2013).

255   **"there was no substance . . . "**: Report of Anton R. Valukas, Examiner, United States
      Bankruptcy Court, Southern District of New York, In re Lehman Brothers Holdings
      Inc., et al., Debtors, Chapter 11 Case no. 08–13555, March 11, 2010, Volume 3 of 9,
      p. 735.

255   **UK opinion and Repo 105:** Linklaters' Repo 105 opinion letter is described in the
      Report of Anton R. Valukas, Examiner, United States Bankruptcy Court, Southern
      District of New York, In re Lehman Brothers Holdings Inc., et al., Debtors, Chapter 11
      Case no. 08–13555, March 11, 2010, Volume 3 of 9. As noted by the *Financial Times,*
      "the report does not suggest that Linklaters . . . acted illegally or unethically in any
      way" (Megan Murphy and Michael Peel, "Linklaters Faces Fall-Out from Repo 105,"
      March 12, 2010).

255   **"show me where it says I can't"**: Weil (2002), p. 2.

Chapter 13: The Pyramid Scheme

258   **"We are creative . . . "**: Tenbrunsel and Messick (2004), p. 225.

258   **Dreier LLP's history:** Robert Kolker, "The Impersonator," *New York Magazine,* April
      3, 2009.

259   **"This is not just a story . . . "**: Bryan Burrough, "Marc Dreier's Crime of Destiny,"
      Vanity Fair, November 2009, p. 4.

263   **Motivation of Dreier:** Dreier further explained what he believed motivated this sen-
      timent: "I think I was psychologically enabled to actually go ahead with the crime by
      that desperation as well as my despondence from my divorce, from the difficulty I was
      having meeting the challenges of keeping the firm afloat, and, to a not insignificant
      extent, from the aftermath of 9/11, which, more than I can explain, was very disturb-
      ing to me."

264   **"The initial misappropriation . . . "**: Bryan Burrough, "Marc Dreier's Crime of Des-
      tiny," *Vanity Fair,* November 2009, p. 12.

267   **Charles Ponzi:** Zuckoff (2005), Ponzi (2009), and Mary Darby, "In Ponzi We Trust," *Smithsonian Magazine*, December 1998. Investigation of Ponzi-type schemes: Frankel (2012).

268   **"I was getting accustomed . . . ":** Ponzi (2009), p. 103.

269   **Overconfidence and fraud:** While overconfidence is often present in Ponzi schemes, it is evident in other types of corporate misconduct as well. Schrand and Zechman (2012) explore executive overconfidence in the context of financial fraud.

269   **Hoffenberg's Ponzi as one of the largest in history:** Diana Henriques, "$450 Million Fraud by Bill Collector Is Charged by U.S," *New York Times*, February 18, 1994.

269   **Hoffenberg's business:** Ibid. and Hilary Rosenberg, "The Amazing Towers Financial Affair," *Institutional Investor*, June 1994.

270   **"leading . . . ":** George Anders, "Wall Street Hopes for Some Good in an Ill Wind," *Wall Street Journal*, December 4, 1992.

271   **"terrific business":** Hilary Rosenberg, "The Amazing Towers Financial Affair," *Institutional Investor*, June 1994.

274   **Sustaining losses and raising money:** The expectation of repayment would be characteristic of debt financing (e.g., from a bank or credit card) rather than from equity financing.

274   **"We expect to . . . ":** Webvan Group, Inc., Form S-1, August 6, 1999, p. 6. Although much of Webvan's financing came from selling equity, Webvan also had debt financing. Webvan's prospectus described its need to raise additional capital to fund its business: "If we are unable to obtain sufficient additional capital when needed . . . [it] would have a material adverse effect on our business, financial condition, and results of operation" (Webvan Group, Inc., Form S-1, August 6, 1999, p. 8).

274   **Webvan's prospects:** Although many people were quite enthusiastic about Webvan's prospects as suggested by its valuation, others were more skeptical. "I believe they were doomed from the start because their business model was one that was predicated on reinventing the entire system," noted Robert Mittelstaedt, vice-dean of Wharton's executive education program (Paul Abrahams and Andrew Edgecliffe-Johnson, "A Billion-Dollar Mistake," *Financial Times*, July 10, 2001).

274   **Multilevel marketing and Ponzi schemes:** The identification of a pyramid or Ponzi scheme is particularly difficult in the case of multilevel marketing businesses (see Valentine 1998 for a discussion of pyramid versus legitimate marketing). One example that generated considerable discussion is Herbalife (see William D. Cohen, "The Big Short War," *Vanity Fair*, April 2013, and Frank Partnoy, "Is Herbalife a Pyramid Scheme?" *The Atlantic*, June 2014).

275   **Stanford's Ponzi scheme:** Brame (2016), Kurdas (2016), Hoffman (2009), and Kotz (2014).

275   **"a fraud . . . ":** Securities and Exchange Commission, "SEC Charges R. Allen Stanford, Stanford International Bank for Multi-Billion Dollar Investment Scheme," (press release) February 17, 2009.

276   **41,000 feet comment:** Private commercial aircraft often fly several thousand feet higher than commercial aircraft to achieve a more direct routing. A common cruising altitude for a private jet is 41,000 feet, as compared to 36,000 feet for a commercial plane.

276   **Stanford's CD rates:** Matthew Goldstein, "Is Stanford Financial's Offer Too Good to Be True?" *Bloomberg Businessweek*, February 11, 2009.

276   **GIB and SIB:** Guardian International Bank (GIB) was the precursor to Stanford International Bank (SIB). For simplicity, I refer in dialogues with Stanford to SIB (where it may also apply to GIB).

276   **Referral fee:** There is some dispute about the size of the referral fee. Stanford describes this as a 1 percent fee with additional fees in the following years if the money is retained. The Stanford receiver estimates the total fee, beginning in 2005, as 3 percent of the face value of the CD.

277   **"a well-diversified . . . ":** Stanford International Bank Ltd., 2008, 20467 SIB, p. 3.

277   **"First and foremost . . . ":** *United States of America v. Robert Allen Stanford,* No. H-09-342, United States District Court for the Southern District of Texas, Volume 27 of Transcript of Jury Trial (February 29, 2012), p. 7967. In the printed transcript, the final sentiment "And those businesses . . . " is typed as its own sentence at the beginning of a new paragraph. Placing this remark as continuing from the prior sentence reflects the spoken argument more clearly.

278   **AAA ratings downgrade:** US Senate, Committee on Homeland Security and Governmental Affairs, "Wall Street and the Financial Crisis: Anatomy of a Financial Collapse" (112th Congress, 1st Session), April 13, 2011, p. 31.

278   **Informing investors of risks:** The disclosures available to Stanford's investors did not provide specific details about the nature of the investments. Consequently, it would be difficult to assert that they were fully informed about the risks of their investments.

278   **Estimated Stanford assets:** *Ralph S. Janvey, in His Capacity as Court-Appointed Receiver for the Stanford International Bank, Ltd., et al. v. James R. Alguire et al.,* 03:09-CV-0724-N, United States District Court for the Northern District of Texas, Dallas Division, "Declaration of Karyl Van Tassel" (March 26, 2010).

279   **Private equity investments:** The nature of the private equity investment seems contrary to the advertised portfolio of highly marketed securities provided to investors in at least some offering documents.

279   **Valued at $3.2 billion:** Different valuations of the Antigua real estate, including one supporting Stanford's argument, are described in Brame (2016).

280   **Subsisting only on the inflows from additional CDs:** *Ralph S. Janvey, in His Capacity as Court-Appointed Receiver for the Stanford International Bank, Ltd., et al. v. James R. Alguire, et al.,* 03:09-CV-0724-N, United States District Court for the Northern District of Texas, Dallas Division, "Declaration of Karyl Van Tassel" (May 24, 2010), p. 9, says the receiver found that new CDs payed off old through an analysis of the cash flows. This itself does not necessarily indicate that Stanford's bank was a Ponzi scheme if illiquid assets could have been sold, but for business reasons were not. The aggregate value of the assets would need to be insufficient for it to definitively be described as a Ponzi. According to the receiver, that was the case as of 2004.

280   **"protect investors . . . ":** *Securities and Exchange Commission v. Stanford International Bank, Ltd.,* Stanford Group Company, Stanford Capital Management, LLC, R. Allen Stanford, James M. Davis, and Laura Pendergest-Holt, Memorandum of Law in Support of Motion for Ex Parte Temporary Restraining Order (February 16, 2009), p. 4.

280   **"The bank's claims are improbable":** Ibid., p. 2.

281   **"It's difficult . . . ":** James Stewart, "Solvency, Lost in the Fog at the Fed," *New York Times,* November 7, 2014.

281   **"disclosure very cleverly crafted . . . ":** Securities and Exchange Commission, Office of Inspector General, Report of Investigation, "Investigation of the SEC's Response to Concerns Regarding Robert Allen Stanford's Alleged Ponzi Scheme," Case No. OIG-526, March 31, 2010, p. 86.

281   **"unlike a lot of Ponzi schemes . . . ":** Securities and Exchange Commission, Office of Inspector General, Report of Investigation, "Investigation of the SEC's Response to Concerns Regarding Robert Allen Stanford's Alleged Ponzi Scheme," Case No. OIG-526, Appendix, Vol. II, Exhibit 30, p. 34.

283   **"Neal . . . ":** *Ralph S. Janvey, in His Capacity as Court-Appointed Receiver for the Stanford International Bank, Ltd., et al. v. James R. Alguire et al.,* 03:09-CV-0724-N, United States District Court for the Northern District of Texas, Dallas Division, "Declaration of Karyl Van Tassel" (March 26, 2010), pp. 24–25.

283   **Which executives understood value of assets:** When Laura Pendergest-Holt pointed out to Stanford and other executives that the assets were far lower than expected in a meeting on February 5, 2009, Stanford allegedly began pounding on the table, insisting that the assets were there (see *United States of America v. Laura Pendergest-Holt,* 3-09-MJ-56, United States District Court Northern District of Texas, Criminal Complaint, February 25, 2009).

284   **Final reckoning of bank's assets:** As of December 31, 2013, the receiver had collected $899.5 million in assets from Stanford's businesses. Even if some of the assets (e.g., illiquid assets) were disposed of more quickly and realized lower values, the assets were far lower than the outstanding CD obligations of the bank.

284   **Conversation with Stanford about my impressions of his case:** In my discussions with Stanford, he raised a number of concerns (e.g. time, resources, and physical condition) about his ability to fully defend himself against the charges against him. The opportunity for a vigorous defense is a critical right within the US judicial system, and I found these arguments among the most compelling he made in his defense.

285   **Who created loss in bank:** Undoubtedly, investors in Stanford's bank have incurred losses on their investments. However, the issue of whether these losses were incurred before or after the bank was placed in receiverships differs between Stanford and the regulators. Stanford contends that investors had not incurred any losses until regulators took over his bank ("no one lost a dime until the government took over Stanford's U.S. operations"). In contrast, the regulators contend that the bank had already incurred significant losses (through its poor investments and consumption of resources by Stanford) and was insolvent, but that this was simply not evident to investors yet. The verdict at Stanford's trial supports the government's allegation that these losses were due to Stanford's decisions and activities.

Chapter 14: Bernie Madoff

287   **Madoff narrative books:** Arvedlund (2009), Henriques (2011), Oppenheimer (2009), Kirtzman (2009), Ross (2009), and Sandell (2011).

287   **Misappropriation of capital:** Some of this $20 billion in principal would more accurately be described as lost rather than misappropriated. Proceeds that the trustee overseeing the liquidation of Madoff's firm recovered (in excess of 60 percent of the estimated principal by fall 2015) would be deemed misappropriated, while principal that was consumed by Madoff and his firm would be best viewed as "lost" in the Ponzi scheme.

288   **Madoff's victims:** Arvedlund (2010) and Sandell (2011).

288   **Madoff and NYSE trading:** Gary Slutsker, "If You Can't Beat 'Em . . . ," *Forbes,* January 6, 1992.

288   **"the successful securities . . . ":** Blume, Siegel, and Rottenberg (1993), p. 240.

289   **"I know the rules . . . ":** Hearing in the Matter of Certain Hedge Fund Trading Practices, Witness Bernard Madoff, Securities and Exchange Commission, May 19, 2006, p. 53.

290 **"pink sheets" and other OTC "sheets":** Different parts of the country actually had differently colored sheets. The "pink sheets" referred to the popular Eastern Section. "Pink sheets": Ingebretsen (2002).

291 **Early deception by Madoff:** Henriques (2011) suggests that this incident was the beginning of Madoff's fraudulent investment business. With little documentation of these purchases and few details about what investors understood about their investments with Madoff, it is difficult to ascertain the precise nature of these buybacks.

291 **SEC's study on the securities market:** US House, Committee on Interstate and Foreign Commerce, "Report of Special Study of Securities Markets of the Securities and Exchange Commission, Part 1" (88th Congress, 1st Session), April 3, 1963.

292 **Madoff's use of technology:** Weiner (2005) and Peter Chapman, "Before the Fall," *Traders Magazine,* March 2009.

292 **Paying for order flow:** Mayer (1992), Richard Stern, "Living Off the Spread," *Forbes,* July 10, 1989, and Gary Slutsker, "If You Can't Beat 'Em . . . ," *Forbes,* January 6, 1992.

293 **Execution speed and cost:** Blume, Siegel, and Rottenberg (1993) and Battalio (1995).

293 **"this much is clear . . . ":** Gary Slutsker, "If You Can't Beat 'Em . . . ," *Forbes,* January 6, 1992, p. 48.

294 **"More than any single individual . . . ":** Robert Flaherty, "Bernard Madoff: OTC Man of the Year," *OTC Review,* December 1989.

294 **"was considered . . . ":** Peter Chapman, "Before the Fall," *Traders Magazine,* March 2009.

295 **Regulators and "naked short" sales:** The market maker may be purchasing the security or borrowing it. In regards to the appropriateness of "naked" short sales, the SEC notes that "because it may take a market maker considerable time to purchase or arrange to borrow the security, a market maker engaged in bona fide market making, particularly in a fast-moving market, may need to sell the security short without having arranged to borrow shares." See Securities and Exchange Commission, "Key Points about Regulation SHO."

297 **" . . . then I would have been all right":** Madoff's statement presumes he actually believed, at the time, that he was trading with clients. It is not possible to assess whether this is an ex-post rationalization or an accurate reflection of how he thought about these transactions at the time.

301 **S&P 100 stock on hedge fund statement:** Fairfield held $2.5 billion in securities according to statements in 2005 (Securities and Exchange Commission, "Investigation of Failure of the SEC to Uncover Bernard Madoff's Ponzi Scheme," August 31, 2009, p. 332).

301 **"the staff found no evidence of fraud":** SEC Division of Enforcement, "Case Closing Recommendation," *Certain Hedge Fund Trading Practices,* Case No. NY-07563, November 21, 2007.

302 **Wrongdoing in the workplace:** Andrew Ross Sorkin, "Many on Wall Street Say It Remains Untamed," *New York Times,* May 18, 2015; and Labaton Sucharow (2015). Chibnall and Saunders (1977) noted one businessman on trial for corruption arguing that "I will never believe I have done anything criminally wrong. I did what is business. If I bent the rules, who doesn't?" The "everyone-does-it defense" and the normalization of conduct: Gabor (1995), Husak (1996), Ashforth and Anand (2003), and Lynn Stout, "How Hedge Funds Create Criminals," HBR Blog Network, December 13, 2010.

303 **Madoff and front-running:** An article in *Barron's* (Erin Arvedlund, "Don't Ask, Don't Tell," *Barron's,* May 7, 2001) fueled speculation that Madoff was front-running trades based on client trading in his market-making operations.

306 **Variations in empathy:** Baron-Cohen (2011). Extraordinary altruists: Marsh et al. (2014).

307   **Madoff and psychopathy:** The most widely used psychological tool to assess psychopathy is the revised PCL-R. In the introductory session of the PCL-R training course, numerous public figures who display characteristics consistent with scoring high on the PCL-R are described. One such figure is Bernard Madoff. Psychopathy characteristics, measurement, and diagnosis: Cleckley (1941), Hare (1993), Blair, Mitchell, and Blair (2005), and Schouten and Silver (2012). Sources of sociopathy: Mealey (1995). Moderating effects of attention on psychopathy: Baskin-Sommers, Curtin, and Newman (2013).

307   **Madoff's character is different from other executives:** Madoff's lower capacity to empathize makes him different from many other executives described in this book. For most of the former executives, their failure in intuitions were strongly influenced by the distance between themselves and their victims. Yet, Madoff was close to his victims. His character, rather than the nature of his actions, heavily distanced his victims. Although there is variation in the capacity to empathize across people, Madoff provides an acute case of when character may prove to be a more significant driver of conduct than the situation.

308   **"There's plenty of ways . . . ":** Hearing in the Matter of Certain Hedge Fund Trading Practices, Witness Bernard Madoff, July 24, 2006, p. 53.

Conclusion: Toward Greater Humility

309   **"business was simple . . . ":** Young (1927), p. 389.

309   **"with tears acknowledge . . . ":** Innes (1995), p. 161. Robert Keayne: Bailyn (1950).

309   **Apple margin:** Recode reported that Apple's gross margin for its iPhones ranged between 55–70 percent in September 2014.

310   **"A man could not sell . . . ":** Young (1927), p. 389.

310   **Aggregate cost of fraud:** Dyck, Morse, and Zingales (2014).

311   **Identifying ethical dilemma:** In some instances students are not given the issue but, rather, are asked to identify it from reading the case. One well-regarded business ethics textbook (Ferrell, Fraedrich, and Ferrell 2015), for example, asks students to "Identify the ethical issues in this case" after each short vignette. While not explicitly identifying the moral issues in question for students, the condensed nature of case-based narratives, which strip out much of the context for the protagonists' actions, necessarily illuminates the moral question on which the authors mean to focus.

312   **The difficulty of identifying or "noticing":** Bazerman (2014).

312   **"I now argue . . . ":** Gioia (1992), p. 388. Gioia explains how he, like others, relied on predetermined scripts that did not include ethical dimensions. He notes that while the Pinto incident was ongoing, he even continued driving a Pinto himself and later sold it to his sister—thus suggesting the difficulty of identifying the problem while actually "in" it.

313   **Argumentation among people with different opinions and viewpoints:** Even if the participants are initially of a similar mind, the instructor leading the discussion can foster argumentation and suggest alternatives to foster a revision of judgments.

313   **Less ethical in practice:** Bazerman and Tenbrunsel (2011) provide extensive evidence on our "bounded ethicality" by describing our tendency to believe that we are more ethical than we actually are and explaining why we tend to ignore unethical behavior.

314   **Individual differences and the propensity to engage in malfeasance:** Some executives described in the book, like Bernard Madoff, may have a greater proclivity to engage in crime due to a lower capacity to appreciate the harm of their decisions. Their

inability to understand the harm of their decisions can still be described as a failure of intuition. However, rather than being driven by the distance between themselves and their victims, this failure of intuition arises more from their innate character. Nevertheless, with appropriate controls put in place, it is possible to minimize the propensity that individuals with such innate vulnerabilities will engage in deviant conduct.

For instance, one hedge fund sought to hire an assistant to work with a talented trader who was prone to antisocial behaviors. Beyond making the trader more sociable, this assistant could help reduce the proclivity of the trader to potentially engage in malfeasance that would be related to vulnerabilities arising from his developmental disorder (Kibbie 2012).

The advertisement, "Unique Job: Help Hedge Fund Trader with Asperger's Syndrome" (November 15, 2010, http://teachers.net), read:

> We're a top tier hedge fund seeking an assistant to help one of our traders with Aspergers Syndrome.
>
> He has a PHD in mathematics from an Ivy League University and is a genius at applying stochastic calculus to the derivatives markets. However, he has Aspergers syndrome and sometimes struggles with his social skills. He's aware of his limitations and has requested an assistant.
>
> We would like someone to help him prioritize his tasks, avoid anti-social behaviors, and help him interact with his coworkers.
>
> Candidates must have Masters/PHD in education or educational psychology and 10+ years experience working with gifted people with Aspergers. A background in math/finance is preferred, but not necessary. Ideally, candidates will have experience working with gifted adults with Apsergers [sic] in a professional setting.
>
> We're willing to pay what it takes to get right person. At a minimum, we'll pay a 125k Base Salary and a bonus. We're willing to pay relocation expenses for the right candidate.

315 **Prevalence of speeding:** Skszek (2004) and Joseph White, "Why 70 Miles Per Hour Is the New 55," *Wall Street Journal,* March 17, 2010.

316 **$250–350 million in sales:** During Kozlowski's last year at Tyco, 2002, total revenue was $33 billion. This would imply that the sales on an average workday (i.e., excluding weekends and holidays) totaled approximately $140 million. Given that contract sales would not be distributed evenly, $250–350 million of sales in a day—though not unreasonable—wouldn't be representative of daily average sales.

316 **Tyco board members' reaction:** Suraj Srinivasan and Aldo Sesia, "The Crisis at Tyco— A Director's Perspective," Harvard Business School Case 111–035, May 2011 (revised June 2011).

316 **Power and response to others:** Galinsky et al. (2006), Hogeveen, Inzlicht, and Obhi (2014), Fiske and Depret (1996), and Kraus, Côté, and Keltner (2010). In contrast, Mast, Jonas, and Hall (2009) argue that power improves interpersonal sensitivity. Conditional on an individual having a strong moral identity, power can also enhance moral awareness and lessen self-interest (DeCelles et al. 2012).

317 **"She asked several . . . ":** Whitacre (2014), p. 526. ADM and price-fixing: White (2001) and Eichenwald (2000).

318 **"If it was not for . . . ":** Whitacre (2014), p. 527.

318 **Angels and demons:** An early instance of this depiction of angels and demons is in *The Shepherd of Hermas* (c. AD 140).

318   **Lawyer and scientist analogy:** Haidt (2001) and Baumeister and Newman (1994b). **Confirmation bias:** Nickerson (1998).

318   **Options-backdating scandal:** Dechow and Tan (2016) find 171 companies that filed backdating related restatements. "Backdating" itself is not illicit. The firms and executives that faced sanctions pertaining to the backdating process primarily did so for violations of tax rules concerning the change in option dates. Firms can also face sanctions for improper disclosure if dates are changed and not disclosed to shareholders. Options backdating: Fried (2008), Bernile and Jarrell (2009), Armstrong and Larcker (2009), Bizjak, Lemmon, and Whitby (2009), and Collins, Gong, and Li (2009).

319   **Horowitz and backdating:** This specific story was removed from Horowitz (2014). Horowitz described the story on his website in a post entitled "Why I Did Not Go to Jail" (Ben Horowitz, *Ben's Blog*, February 6, 2014). In that post, he referred to the executive as "Michelle." However, the evidence he provided in the same post indicates that the name of the executive to whom he is referring is actually "Sharlene Abrams." Ms. Abrams was identified in William Alden, "How Ben Horowitz Avoided an Options Backdating Scandal," *New York Times*, February 6, 2014.

319   **"One area . . . ":** Ben Horowitz, "Why I Did Not Go to Jail," *Ben's Blog*, February 6, 2014.

319   **"I told . . . ":** Ibid.

319   **"I've gone over . . . ":** Ibid.

320   **"The only thing . . . ":** Ibid.

320   **Avoiding prison is not simply a function of values:** Often people argue that failed leadership decisions that land executives in prison arise from a lack of "authenticity" or a less principled set of values. In this example, staying out of prison has little to do with principles or authenticity and, instead, everything to do with setting up the appropriate internal controls.

320   **Whitacre additional misconduct:** Whitacre would later go to prison for engaging in money laundering for ADM while he was an FBI informant. Unlike the price-fixing, this money laundering was not something about which he engaged in outside deliberation with his spouse.

320   **Ethics hotlines:** Trevino and Weaver (2003) and Paul Healy, V. G. Narayanan, and Penelope Rossano, "Guiding Professional Accountants to Do the Right Thing," Harvard Business School Case 115–028, March 2015.

320   **Leadership and humility:** Supporting this observation, the Stanford management scholar Jeffrey Pfeffer wrote "once people believe they are better leaders . . . they are less likely to be as vigilant about their subsequent behavior" (Pfeffer 2015, p. 55). One psychological explanation for this phenomenon is moral-licensing (Merritt, Effron, and Monin 2010).

320   **Power and moral identity:** Whether power enables or corrupts depends on the strength of that individual's moral identity. See DeCelles et al. (2012).

321   **"nobody is ever the villain . . . ":** In conversation with the author, February 2016.

321   **"they come across . . . ":** Vaughan (1996), p. 63. Vaughan articulately describes the normalization of deviance in situations where people carry on "as if nothing was wrong when they continually faced evidence that something was wrong" (Vaughan 1996, p. 62).

321   **Reasoning and argumentation:** Mercier and Sperber (2011).

321   **Group decision making:** A related advantage is that groups, as opposed to individuals, tend to make decisions that are consistent with hypothesis testing. See Moshman and Geil (1998).

322 **Deliberation is not always superior:** Of course, even when forced to deliberate, individuals may still make decisions that are no better than their intuitive ones. Advantages of intuitive decision making: Klein (2013), Gigerenzer, Todd, and ABC Research Group (1999), and Gladwell (2005).

322 **Best way to reduce crime:** "In contrast to street criminals who generally have little to risk, white-collar criminals would seem especially susceptible to the threat of punishment," Weisburd, Waring, and Chayet (1995), p. 589. Some scholars argue that fines would be sufficient to achieve the desired deterrence; see, for example, Posner (1980).

322 **Deterrence and white-collar crime:** Mann, Wheeler, and Sarat (1980), Richman (2013), and Dutcher (2005). The clearest study on the potential deterrence effect of punishing white-collar criminals is Weisburd, Waring, and Chayet (1995), in the context of reoffending. These authors conclude that: "It has often been assumed by scholars and policymakers that white-collar criminals will be particularly affected by imprisonment. Our analyses suggest that this assumption is wrong, at least as regards official reoffending among those convicted of white-collar crimes in the federal courts" (p. 601).

322 **Enforcement and driving:** Hauer, Ahlin, and Bowser (1982).

323 **Scandinavian law enforcement:** US Department of Transportation (1985) and Ross (1984).

323 **Tax aggressiveness and deterrence:** Several researchers examined tax aggressiveness after firms were audited by regulators. They found that aggressiveness increased in the years following an audit, before later decreasing.

323 **Tax audits and aggressiveness:** DeBacker et al. (2015).

323 **Deterrence and level of fraud:** Ball (2009). Future of fraud: Harrington (2012).

323 **Driving enforcement in Sweden:** Ross (1982). Making deterrence sanctions relevant: Robinson and Darley (1997) and Tyler (1997b).

324 **Managerial attitudes toward deterrence:** Simpson (1992) surveyed managers to understand their attitudes on deterrence. She points out that "quizzing managers about the ethical choices they make while on the job leads one to conclude that managers, do not, for the most part, think in deterrence terms" (p. 303).

324 **Legal sanction and managerial deterrence:** Smith, Simpson, and Huang (2007) provide evidence that legal sanctions do not directly deter managers from engaging in misconduct.

324 **Marketing of Justice Department convictions:** Matthews (2001).

324 **Enforcing norms and norm conformity:** Brennan et al. (2013), Posner and Rasmusen (1999), and Feldman (1984).

324 **Orthodox Judaism and enforcement of Sh'tarei Siruv:** Rabbinical Council of America (1993), Cohn, Levitats, and Drori (2007), and Harriet Sherwood, "Jewish Court Names and Shames Man for Denying Wife a Religious Divorce," *The Guardian,* November 8, 2015.

324 **Utah and white-collar criminal database:** Legislators in Utah have created a white-collar crime registry. This online database displays offenders' photos and other information for a decade after their offense. While the objective of creating the database is to help others avoid falling prey to potential repeat offenders, the greater visibility and shaming of offenders may also increase the salience of these offenses to the public. Critics worry, however, that profiling offenders in the same manner as pedophiles will unduly stigmatize individuals.

324 **Shaming and white-collar crime:** Kahan and Posner (1999), Kostelnik (2012), and Jacquet (2015).

325 **"The thief . . . ":** Shaw (1922), p. xl.

325 **"no soul . . . ":** Edward, First Baron Thurlow, quoted in King (1977), p. 1. Corporate criminal liability outside the United States: Diskant (2008) and Hefendehl (2000).

325 **Life-long effects of being a felon:** It has been estimated that there are more than 38,000 statutes in the United States imposing additional consequences on individuals convicted of crimes. Collateral consequences: Love, Roberts, and Klingele (2013). Corporate criminal/civil sanctions: Coffee (1981), Fischel and Sykes (1996), Khanna (1996), and Edgerton (1927).

325 **"no impact on . . . ":** Credit Suisse Group AG Conference Call, May 20, 2014.

325 **Unintended effects of corporate sanctions:** The famous exception is Arthur Andersen, Enron's accountant, which was effectively put out of business by its prosecution. The federal government seems to have responded to the company's closing by reducing full prosecution of corporate offenders (i.e., that could lead to the closing of the firm). Concerns about corporate rather than individual prosecution: Rakoff (2015).

325 **Airplane disaster investigators:** Angers (2010).

326 **"I don't feel . . . ":** Testimony to the Treasury Committee as reported in *The Guardian* (Patrick Wintour, "HSBC Scandal Caused Horrible Damage to Reputation, says Chairman," *The Guardian*, February 25, 2015). In the article describing the testimony, Flint notes that he felt "very ashamed" of the events at the bank and believed in personal accountability for "what they have direct oversight over."

326 **Investigation of HSBC:** HSBC's private bank was under investigation by regulators in ten jurisdictions (Harry Davies, "HSBC Files: 10 Days On, Bank Faces 10 Separate Inquires," *The Guardian*, February 18, 2015). French magistrates launched a formal criminal investigation into the private bank for tax-related offenses (Noemie Bisserbe, "French Magistrates Open Criminal Investigation of HSBC," *Wall Street Journal*, April 9, 2015).

326 **Additional consideration and externalities of adjusted recruiting policy:** There would be additional externalities to consider before implementing such a policy. Preventing these firms from recruiting students at leading universities would disadvantage employees at the firms who did not engage in misconduct. It would push recruiting off campus, where recruiting students would be less accountable to the school and would also disadvantage shareholders who commit capital. These costs would need to be weighed against the potential future reduction in fines from less misconduct that shareholders would not later bear.

326 **Criminal conviction or deferred prosecution and recruiting:** The firms whose parent or a subsidiary recruited on Harvard's campus (i.e., hosting an information session, participating in campus activities, or posting a job on an internal Harvard job portal) with a conviction, deferred prosecution agreement, or non-prosecution agreement include BNP Paribas, Credit Suisse, Deutsche Bank, Duke Energy, General Motors, Genzyme, Hewlett Packard, JP Morgan, Schlumberger, and UBS. The data on convictions and prosecution agreements were kindly provided to me by Brandon Garrett. Garrett describes the extraordinary rate of corporate settlements and criminal fines paid by organizations in Garrett (2014).

327 **Accountability for actions of all employees:** It would be less viable to hold the attitude once expressed by HSBC's chief: "Can I know what every one of 257,000 people is doing? Clearly I can't. If you want to ask the question 'could it ever happen again?'— that is not reasonable" (Martin Arnold and George Parker, "Bankers Held to Higher Standards Than Bishops, Claims HSBC chief," *Financial Times,* February 23, 2015).

327 **Influence of new work environment:** Consider this another way. In just your first sixty-hour work week, you'd be more heavily exposed to the culture of that firm's

environment and norms than during all your previous time explicitly trying to cultivate better intuitions.

327   **Selection mechanism to sort employees based on pre-existing norms:** In the fall
      of 2015, Goldman Sachs and JP Morgan fired thirty analysts for cheating on inter-
      nal tests (Sofia Horta E. Costa, "Goldman, JPMorgan Said to Fire 30 Analysts for
      Cheating on Tests," *Bloomberg Businessweek,* October 16, 2015). While this single step
      isn't going to provide assurance that every banker will always abide by the law, it's a
      promising start to identify potential employees who are most likely to disregard ba-
      sic compliance procedures and create risks for themselves and the firm. Motivating
      more firms to take actions like this one can serve as the impetus for greater and more
      industry-wide changes in norms.

328   **"They all feel deeply . . . ":** Nitin Nohria, "Practicing Moral Humility," TEDxNewEn-
      gland, November 1, 2011.

328   **Moral humility:** Nitin Nohria, "You're Not as Virtuous as You Think," *Washington
      Post,* October 15, 2015.

328   **Mistaken belief in one's own ethicality:** Bazerman and Tenbrunsel (2011), Gino
      (2013), and Ariely (2012).

328   **"How could that . . . ":** Bazerman (2014), p. xxi.

329   **"Is it easy to say . . . ":** *Unraveled,* a documentary directed by Marc H. Simon in 2011.

330   **Appreciating our lack of invincibility:** *New York Times* columnist David Brooks ex-
      plores leadership and the value of humility in Brooks (2015).

330   **Suspicions about new intuitions:** Sunstein (2005), Slovic (2007), Singer (1974), and
      Woodward and Allman (2007).

BIBLIOGRAPHY

Adams, J. S., Tashchian, A., & Shore, T. H. 2001. Codes of Ethics as Signals for Ethical Behavior. *Journal of Business Ethics, 29,* 199–211.

Additions and Corrections in Former Obituaries. 1802. *The Gentleman's Magazine, 71,* 182–184.

Adler, F., Mueller, G., & Laufer, W. 2013. *Criminology* (8th ed.). New York: McGraw-Hill.

Akerlof, G. A., & Kranton, R. E. 2000. Economics and Identity. *The Quarterly Journal of Economics, 115,* 715–753.

———. 2005. Identity and the Economics of Organizations. *Journal of Economic Perspectives, 19,* 9–32.

Akerlof, G. A., & Shiller, R. J. 2015. *Phishing for Phools.* Princeton, NJ: Princeton University Press.

Åkerlund, D., Golsteyn, B. H., Gronqvist, H., & Lindahl, L. 2014. *Time Preferences and Criminal Behavior.* IZA Discussion Paper No. 8168.

Akers, R. L. 1990. Rational Choice, Deterrence, and Social Learning Theory in Criminology: The Path Not Taken. *Journal of Criminal Law and Criminology, 81,* 653–676.

———. 1991. Self-Control as a General Theory of Crime. *Journal of Quantitative Criminology, 7,* 201–211.

Albrecht, W. 1991. Fraud in Governmental Entities: The Perpetrators and the Types of Fraud. *Government Finance Review, 7,* 27–30.

———. 2014. Iconic Fraud Triangle Endures. *Fraud Magazine,* 1–7.

Albrecht, W., Romney, M., Cherrington, D., Payne, I., & Roe, A. 1982. *How to Detect and Prevent Business Fraud.* Englewood Cliffs, NJ: Prentice-Hall.

Alger, G. W. 1904. Unpunished Commercial Crime. *The American Lawyer, 12,* 379.

Alterman, E. 2004. *When Presidents Lie: A History of Official Deception and Its Consequences.* New York: Viking.

Andrews, J. M. 1941. The Varieties of Human Physique by W. H. Sheldon, with the collaboration of S. S. Stevens and W. B. Tucker. *American Anthropologist, 43,* 470–474.

Andrighetto, G., Zhang, N., Ottone, S., Ponzano, F., D'Attoma, J., & Steinmo, S. 2016. Are Some Countries More Honest than Others? Evidence from a Tax Compliance Experiment in Sweden and Italy. *Frontiers in Psychology, 7.*

Angers, B. S. 2010. The Go Team. *Boeing Frontiers,* July, 35–36.

Apicella, C. L., Carré, J. M., & Dreber, A. 2015. Testosterone and Economic Risk Taking: A Review. *Adaptive Human Behavior and Physiology, 1,* 358–385.

Archer, J. 1991. The Influence of Testosterone on Human Aggression. *British Journal of Psychology, 82,* 1–28.

Arendt, H. 1963. *Eichmann in Jerusalem: A Report on the Banality of Evil.* New York: Viking Press.

Ariely, D. 2012. *The (Honest) Truth About Dishonesty.* New York: Harper.

Aristotle. 1984. Physiognomonics. In J. Barnes (Ed.), *The Complete Works of Aristotle* (Vol. 1), 1237–1250. Princeton, NJ: Princeton University Press.

Armstrong, C. S., & Larcker, D. F. 2009. Discussion of "The Impact of the Options Backdating Scandal on Shareholders" and "Taxes and the Backdating of Stock Option Exercise Dates." *Journal of Accounting and Economics, 47,* 50–58.

Armstrong, M. B. 1987. Moral Development and Accounting Education. *Journal of Accounting Education, 5,* 27–43.

Arnulf, J., & Gottschalk, P. 2013. Heroic Leaders as White-Collar Criminals: An Empirical Study. *Journal of Investigative Psychology and Offender Profiling, 10,* 96–113.

Arvedlund, E. 2009. *Too Good to Be True: The Rise and Fall of Bernie Madoff.* New York: Portfolio.

———. (Ed.). 2010. *The Club No One Wanted to Join: Madoff Victims in Their Own Words.* Andover, MA: The Doukathsan Press.

Ash, B. 1969. *Tiger in Your Tank.* London: Cassell.

Ashforth, B. E., & Anand, V. 2003. The Normalization of Corruption in Organizations. *Research in Organizational Behavior, 25,* 1–52.

Axelrod, R. 1984. *The Evolution of Cooperation.* New York: Basic Books.

Axelrod, R., & Hamilton, W. D. 1981. The Evolution of Cooperation. *Science, 211,* 1390–1396.

Babiak, P. 1995. When Psychopaths Go to Work: A Case Study of an Industrial Psychopath. *Applied Psychology, 44,* 171–188.

Babiak, P., & Hare, R. D. 2006. *Snakes in Suits: When Psychopaths Go to Work.* New York: Regan Books.

Babiak, P., Neumann, C., & Hare, R. D. 2010. Corporate Psychopathy: Talking the Walk. *Behavioral Sciences and the Law, 28,* 174–193.

Bacon, F. 1825. *The Works of Francis Bacon, Lord Chancellor of England,* Ed. B. Montagu. London: William Pickering.

Bacon, S. 1950. White Collar Crime by Edwin H. Sutherland. *American Sociological Review, 15,* 309–310.

Badaracco, J. L. 2013. *The Good Struggle: Responsible Leadership in an Unforgiving World.* Boston: Harvard Business Review Press.

Badaracco, J. L., & Webb, A. 1995. Business Ethics: A View from the Trenches. *California Management Review, 37,* 8–28.

Baer, M. 2008. Linkage and the Deterrence of Corporate Fraud. *Virginia Law Review, 94,* 1295–1365.

Bahrani, M. 2012. The Economics of Crime with Gary Becker. *The Chicago Maroon,* May 25.

Bailyn, B. 1950. The Apologia of Robert Keayne. *The William and Mary Quarterly, 7,* 568–587.

———. 1955. *The New England Merchants in the Seventeenth Century.* Cambridge, MA: Harvard University Press.

Bainbridge, S. M. 2011. Insider Trading Inside the Beltway. *The Journal of Corporation Law,* *36,* 281–307.

———. 2013. *Research Handbook on Insider Trading.* Northampton, MA: Edward Elgar.

———. 2014. *Insider Trading Law and Policy.* New York: Foundation Press.

Baird, B. A., & Vinson, C. P. 1990. RICO Pretrial Restraints and Due Process: The Lessons of Princeton/Newport. *Notre Dame Law Review, 65,* 1009–1054.

Baker, W. E., & Faulkner, R. R. 1993. The Social Organization of Conspiracy: Illegal Networks in the Heavy Electrical Equipment Industry. *American Sociological Review, 58,* 837–860.

Ball, R. 2009. Market and Political/Regulatory Perspectives on the Recent Accounting Scandals. *Journal of Accounting Research, 47,* 277–323.

Balleisen, E. J. 2009. Private Cops on the Fraud Beat: The Limits of American Business Self-Regulation, 1895–1932. *Business History Review, 83,* 113–160.

Baltrušaitis, J. 1989. *Aberrations: An Essay on the Legend of Forms.* Cambridge, MA: MIT Press.

Banham, R. 1999. Andrew S. Fastow-Enron Corp. *CFO Magazine,* October.

Bargh, J. A., & Chartrand, T. L. 1999. The Unbearable Automaticity of Being. *American Psychologist, 54,* 462–479.

Baron-Cohen, S. 2011. *The Science of Evil.* New York: Basic Books.

Barrett, S. R. H., Speth, R. L., Eastham, S. D., Dedoussi, I. C., Ashok, A., Malina, R., & Keith, D. W. 2015. Impact of the Volkswagen Emissions Control Defeat Device on US Public Health. *Environmental Research Letters, 10,* 1–10.

Bartal, I. B., Decety, J., & Mason, P. 2011. Empathy and Pro-Social Behavior in Rats. *Science, 334,* 1427–1430.

Barth, M. E., Elliott, J., & Finn, M. W. 1999. Market Rewards Associated with Patterns of Increasing Earnings. *Journal of Accounting Research, 37,* 387–413.

Baskin-Sommers, A. R., Curtin, J. J., & Newman, J. P. 2013. Emotion-Modulated Startle in Psychopathy: Clarifying Familiar Effects. *Journal of Abnormal Psychology, 122,* 458–468.

Bastian, A. 1866. *Die Geschichte der Indochinesen: aus einheimischen Quellen.* Leipzig: Verlag Van Otto Wigand.

Batson, C. D. 1990. How Social an Animal? The Human Capacity for Caring. *American Psychologist, 45,* 336–346.

Batson, C. D., Ahmad, N., Lishner, D. A., & Tsang, J. A. 2002. Empathy and Altruism. In C. R. Snyder & S. Lopez (Eds.), *Handbook of Positive Psychology,* 495–499. Oxford: Oxford University Press.

Batson, C. D., & Shaw, L. L. 1991. Evidence for Altruism: Toward a Pluralism of Prosocial Motives. *Psychological Inquiry, 2,* 107–122.

Battalio, R. H. 1995. *Does Increased Competition in Securities Markets Always Lower Trading Costs? Theory and Evidence.* Indiana University. Dissertation.

Baum, D. D. 1967. Book Review: Insider Trading and the Stock Market. *Duke Law Journal, 16,* 456–461.

Baumeister, R. F. 1999. *Evil: Inside Human Violence and Cruelty.* New York: Henry Holt.

Baumeister, R. F., & Newman, L. S. 1994a. How Stories Make Sense of Personal Experiences: Motives That Shape Autobiographical Narratives. *Personality and Social Psychology Bulletin, 20,* 676–690.

———. 1994b. Self-Regulation of Cognitive Inference and Decision Processes. *Personality & Social Psychology Bulletin, 20,* 3–19.

Baumeister, R. F., Stillwell, A., & Wotman, S. R. 1990. Victim and Perpetrator Accounts of Interpersonal Conflict: Autobiographical Narratives About Anger. *Journal of Personality & Social Psychology, 59,* 994–1005.

Baumhart, R. C. 1961. How Ethical Are Businessmen? *Harvard Business Review*, July-August, 7–19, 156–176.

Bazerman, M. H. 2014. *The Power of Noticing: What the Best Leaders See.* New York: Simon and Schuster.

Bazerman, M. H., & Moore, D. A. 2013. *Judgment in Managerial Decision Making* (8th ed.). Hoboken, NJ: John Wiley & Sons, Inc.

Bazerman, M. H., & Tenbrunsel, A. E. 2011. *Blind Spots: Why We Fail to Do What's Right and What to Do About It.* Princeton, NJ: Princeton University Press.

Beams, J. D., Brown, R. M., & Killough, L. N. 2003. An Experiment Testing the Determinants of Non-Compliance with Insider Trading Laws. *Journal of Business Ethics, 45,* 309–323.

Beaver, K. M., DeLisi, M., Vaughn, M. G., & Wright, J. P. 2010. The Intersection of Genes and Neuropsychological Deficits in the Prediction of Adolescent Delinquency and Low Self-Control. *International Journal of Offender Therapy and Comparative Criminology, 54,* 22–42.

Bechara, A., & Damasio, A. R. 2005. The Somatic Marker Hypothesis: A Neural Theory of Economic Decision. *Games and Economic Behavior, 52,* 336–372.

Bechara, A., Damasio, A. R., Damasio, H., & Anderson, S. W. 1994. Insensitivity to Future Consequences Following Damage to Human Prefrontal Cortex. *Cognition, 50,* 7–15.

Bechara, A., Damasio, H., Tranel, D., & Damasio, A. R. 1997. Deciding Advantageously Before Knowing the Advantageous Strategy. *Science, 275,* 1293–1295.

Becker, G. S. 1968. Crime and Punishment: An Economic Approach. *Journal of Political Economy, 76,* 169–217.

———. 1976. *The Economic Approach to Human Behavior.* Chicago: University of Chicago Press.

———. 1993. Nobel Lecture: The Economic Way of Looking at Behavior. *Journal of Political Economy, 101,* 385–409.

———. 1995. The Economics of Crime. *Cross Sections,* Fall.

Becker, G. S., & Becker, G. N. 1997. *The Economics of Life.* New York: McGraw-Hill.

Beirne, P. 1993. *Inventing Criminology: Essays on the Rise of "Homo Criminalis."* Albany: State University of New York Press.

Bell, D. 1960. *The End of Ideology.* Glencoe, IL: The Free Press.

Benson, M. L., & Moore, E. 1992. Are White-Collar and Common Offenders the Same? An Empirical and Theoretical Critique of a Recently Proposed General Theory of Crime. *Journal of Research in Crime and Delinquency, 29,* 251–272.

Bentham, J. 1789. *An Introduction to the Principles of Morals and Legislation.* Oxford: Clarendon Press.

———. 1830. *The Rationale of Punishment.* London: Robert Heward.

Berle, A. A. 1927. Publicity of Accounts and Directors' Purchases of Stock. *Michigan Law Review, 25,* 827–838.

Berle, A. A., & Means, G. C. 1932. *The Modern Corporation and Private Property.* New York: Harcourt, Brace & World.

Bernard, T., Snipes, J., & Gerould, A. 2010. *Vold's Theoretical Criminology* (6th ed.). New York: Oxford University Press.

Bernile, G., & Jarrell, G. A. 2009. The Impact of the Options Backdating Scandal on Shareholders. *Journal of Accounting and Economics, 47,* 2–26.

Bettenhausen, K., & Murnighan, J. K. 1985. The Emergence of Norms in Competitive Decision-Making Groups. *Administrative Science Quarterly, 30,* 350–372.

Bhattacharya, U., & Daouk, H. 2002. The World Price of Insider Trading. *Journal of Finance, 57,* 75–108.

Bizjak, J., Lemmon, M., & Whitby, R. 2009. Option Backdating and Board Interlocks. *Review of Financial Studies, 22,* 4821–4847.

Blair, J., Mitchell, D. R., & Blair, K. 2005. *The Psychopath.* Malden, MA: Blackwell Publishing Inc.

Blair, R. J. 1995. A Cognitive Developmental Approach to Mortality: Investigating the Psychopath. *Cognition, 57,* 1–29.

Blakey, G. R., Coffee, J. C., Coffey, P. E., & Crovitz, L. G. 1990. What's Next: The Future of RICO. *Notre Dame Law Review, 65,* 1073–1105.

Blasi, A. 1980. Bridging Moral Cognition and Moral Action: A Critical Review of the Literature. *Psychological Bulletin, 88,* 257–272.

Blatt, M. M., & Kohlberg, L. 1975. The Effects of Classroom Moral Discussion upon Children's Level of Moral Judgment. *Journal of Moral Education, 4,* 129–161.

Blickle, G., Schlegel, A., Fassbender, P., & Klein, U. 2006. Some Personality Correlates of Business White-Collar Crime. *Applied Psychology, 55,* 220–233.

Bloom, P. 2013. *Just Babies: The Origins of Good and Evil.* London: The Bodley Head.

Blume, M., Siegel, J. J., & Rottenberg, D. 1993. *Revolution on Wall Street: The Rise and Decline of the New York Stock Exchange.* New York: W. W. Norton & Company.

Board, B. J., & Fritzon, K. 2005. Disordered Personalities at Work. *Psychology, Crime & Law, 11,* 17–32.

Bogaert, V., Taes, Y., Konings, P., Van Steen, K., De Bacquer, D., Goemaere, S., Zmierczak, H., Crabbe, P., & Kaufman, J. M. 2008. Heritability of Blood Concentrations of Sex-Steroids in Relation to Body Composition in Young Adult Male Siblings. *Clinical Endocrinology, 69,* 129–135.

Bok, S. 1978. *Lying: Moral Choice in Public and Private Life.* New York: Pantheon Books.

Book, A. S., Starzyk, K. B., & Quinsey, V. L. 2001. The Relationship Between Testosterone and Aggression: A Meta-Analysis. *Aggression and Violent Behavior, 6,* 579–599.

Bouchard, T. J., & Loehlin, J. 2001. Genes, Evolution, and Personality. *Behavior Genetics, 313,* 243–273.

Bouchard, T. J., & McGue, M. 2003. Genetic and Environmental Influences on Human Psychological Differences. *Journal of Neurobiology, 54,* 4–45.

Bower, M. 1966. *The Will to Manage.* New York: McGraw-Hill.

Bowman, F. O. 2004. The Curious History and Distressing Implications of the Criminal Provisions of the Sarbanes-Oxley Act and the Sentencing Guidelines Amendments That Followed. *Ohio State's Journal of Criminal Law, 23,* 373–442.

Boyd, D. P. 1981. Improving Ethical Awareness Through the Business and Society Course. *Business & Society, 20,* 27–31.

Braithwaite, J. 1982. Challenging Just Deserts: Punishing White-Collar Criminals. *The Journal of Criminal Law and Criminology, 73,* 723–763.

———. 1985. White Collar Crime. *Annual Review of Sociology, 11,* 1–25.

———. 1989. Criminological Theory and Organizational Crime. *Justice Quarterly, 6,* 333–358.

Brame, R. H. 2016. *Brutal Takeover.* CreateSpace Independent Publishing Platform.

Brennan, G., Eriksson, L., Goodin, R. E., & Southwood, N. 2013. *Explaining Norms.* Oxford: Oxford University Press.

Brooks, D. 2015. *The Road to Character.* New York: Random House.

Brower, H. H., & Shrader, C. B. 2000. Moral Reasoning and Ethical Climate: Not-for-Profit vs. For-Profit Boards of Directors. *Journal of Business Ethics, 26,* 147–167.

Brown, A. 2000. *Computer Associates: A New Business Model, Closely Examined.* Deutsche Bank.

Brown, D. E. 1991. *Human Universals.* Philadelphia: Temple University Press.

———. 2004. Human Universals, Human Nature & Human Culture. *Daedalus, 133,* 47–54.

Bucy, P., Formby, E., Raspanti, M., & Rooney, K. 2008. Why Do They Do It? The Motives, Mores, and Character of White Collar Criminals. *St. John's Law Review, 82,* 401–571.

Buell, S. W. 2008. Upside of Overbreadth. *New York University Law Review, 83,* 1491–1564.

Buelow, M. T., and Suhr, J. A. 2009. Construct Validity of the Iowa Gambling Task. *Neuropsychology Review,* 19(1), 102–114.

Burgstahler, D., & Dichev, I. 1997. Earnings Management to Avoid Earnings Decreases and Losses. *Journal of Accounting and Economics, 24,* 99–126.

Bushee, B. J., Gerakos, J., & Lee, L. F. 2014. Corporate Jets and Private Meetings with Investors. Chicago Booth Research Paper, 12–43.

Bushee, B. J., Jung, M. J., & Miller, G. S. 2014. Do Investors Benefit from Selective Access to Management? Working Paper.

Cahill, J. 1952. The Sherman Act and Big Business: Must We Brand American Business as Criminal? *Section of Antitrust Law, 1,* 26–59.

Caldwell, R. 1958. A Reexamination of the Concept of White-Collar Crime. *Federal Probation Quarterly, 22,* 30–36.

Calkins, E. 1928. *Business the Civilizer.* Boston: Little, Brown and Company.

Camerer, C., Loewenstein, G., & Prelec, D. 2005. Neuroeconomics: How Neuroscience Can Inform Economics. *Journal of Economic Literature, 43,* 9–64.

Candea, M. 2010. *The Social After Gabriel Tarde: Debates and Assessments.* New York: Routledge.

Cannon, A. M. 1956. Other People's Money by Donald R. Cressey: Review. *The Accounting Review, 31,* 156–157.

Carey, N. 2012. *The Epigenetics Revolution.* New York: Columbia University Press.

Carlton, D. W., & Fischel, D. R. 1983. The Regulation of Insider Trading. *Stanford Law Review,* 857–895.

Carré, J. M., & McCormick, C. M. 2008. In Your Face: Facial Metrics Predict Aggressive Behaviour in the Laboratory and in Varsity and Professional Hockey Players. *Proceedings of the Royal Society Biological Sciences, 275,* 2651–2656.

Carré, J. M., McCormick, C. M., & Mondloch, C. J. 2009. Facial Structure Is a Reliable Cue of Aggressive Behavior. *Psychological Science, 20,* 1194–1198.

Carson, T. 2010. *Lying and Deception: Theory and Practice.* Oxford: Oxford University Press.

Chamber of Commerce of the United States of America. 1974. *A Handbook on White Collar Crime: Everyone's Problem, Everyone's Loss.* Washington, DC.

Chen, M., & Bargh, J. 1999. Consequences of Automatic Evaluation: Immediate Behavioral Predispositions to Approach or Avoid the Stimulus. *Personality and Social Psychology Bulletin, 25,* 215–224.

Chibnall, S., & Saunders, P. 1977. Worlds Apart: Notes on the Social Reality of Corruption. *The British Journal of Sociology, 28,* 138–154.

Christensen, A., & Eining, M. 1991. Factors Influencing Software Piracy: Implications for Accountants. *Journal of Information Systems, 5,* 67–80.

Christensen, C., Allworth, J., & Dillon, K. 2012. *How Will You Measure Your Life?* London: HarperCollins.

Christiansen, K. 1977. A Preliminary Study of Criminality Among Twins. In S. A. Mednick & K. Christiansen (Eds.), *Biosocial Bases of Criminal Behavior*, 89–108. New York: Gardner Press.

Chu, M., & Magraw, D. 1978. The Deductibility of Questionable Foreign Payments. *Yale Law Journal, 87*, 1091–1124.

Chugh, D. 2004. Societal and Managerial Implications of Implicit Social Cognition: Why Milliseconds Matter. *Social Justice Research, 17*, 203–222.

Cialdini, R. B., Demaine, L. J., Sagarin, B. J., Barrett, D. W., Rhoads, K., & Winter, P. L. 2006. Managing Social Norms for Persuasive Impact. *Social Influence, 1*, 3–15.

Cialdini, R. B., & Trost, M. R. 1998. Social Influence: Social Norms, Conformity and Compliance. In D. T. Gilbert, S. Fiske, & G. Lindzey (Eds.), *The Handbook of Social Psychology*, 151–192. Boston: McGraw-Hill.

Cleckley, H. 1941. *The Mask of Sanity*. St. Louis: Mosby.

Clinard, M. 1952. *The Black Market: A Study of White Collar Crime*. New York: Rinehart & Co.

———. 1954. Review of Other People's Money: A Study in the Social Psychology of Embezzlement by Donald R. Cressey. *American Sociological Review, 19*, 362–363.

Clinard, M., & Yeager, P. 1980. *Corporate Crime*. New York: Free Press.

Cloninger, C. R., Sigvardsson, S., Bohman, M., & von Knorring, A. L. 1982. Predisposition to Petty Criminality in Swedish Adoptees. *Archives of General Psychiatry, 39*, 1242–1247.

Coates, J. M. 2012. *The Hour Between Dog and Wolf*. New York: Penguin Press.

Coates, J. M., & Herbert, J. 2008. Endogenous Steroids and Financial Risk Taking on a London Trading Floor. *Proceedings of the National Academy of Sciences of the United States of America, 105*, 6167–6172.

Coffee, J. C. 1977. Beyond the Shut-Eyed Sentry: Toward a Theoretical View of Corporate Misconduct and an Effective Legal Response. *Virginia Law Review, 63*, 1099–1278.

———. 1981. "No Soul to Damn: No Body to Kick": An Unscandalized Inquiry into the Problem of Corporate Punishment. *Michigan Law Review, 79*, 386–459.

Coffee, J. C., Lowenstein, L., & Rose-Ackerman, S. (Eds.). 1988. *Knights, Raiders, and Targets: The Impact of the Hostile Takeover*. New York: Oxford University Press.

Cohen, A. 2016. *Imbeciles: The Supreme Court, American Eugenics, and the Sterilization of Carrie Buck*. New York: Penguin Press.

Cohen, A. K. 1966. *Deviance and Control*. London: Prentice-Hall.

Cohen, A., Lindesmith, A., & Schuessler, K. (Eds.). 1956. *The Sutherland Papers*. Bloomington: Indiana University Press.

Cohen, J., Ding, Y., Lesage, C., & Stolowy, H. 2010. Corporate Fraud and Managers' Behavior: Evidence from the Press. *Journal of Business Ethics, 95*, 271–315.

Cohen, L., Frazzini, A., & Malloy, C. 2008. The Small World of Investing: The Use of Social Networks in Bank Decision-Making. *Journal of Political Economy, 116*, 951–979.

———. 2010. Sell-Side School Ties. *Journal of Finance, 65*, 1409–1437.

Cohn, H. H., Levitats, I., & Drori, M. 2007. Bet Din and Judges. In *Encyclopaedia Judaica* (2nd ed., 512–524). Detroit, MI: Macmillan Reference USA.

Colby, A., & Kohlberg, L. 1987. *The Measure of Moral Judgment*. New York: Cambridge University Press.

Coleman, J. 1987. Toward an Integrated Theory of White-Collar Crime. *American Journal of Sociology, 93*, 406–439.

———. 2002. *The Criminal Elite: Understanding White-Collar Crime* (5th ed.). New York: St. Martin's Press.

Coleman, R., & Wilkins, L. 2004. The Moral Development of Journalists: A Comparison with Other Professions and a Model for Predicting High Quality Ethical Reasoning. *Journalism and Mass Communication Quarterly, 81*, 511–527.

Collins, D., Gong, G., & Li, H. 2009. Corporate Governance and Backdating of Executive Stock Options. *Contemporary Accounting Research, 26*, 403–445.

Comer, M. 1977. *Corporate Fraud*. London: McGraw-Hill.

Commission on Law Enforcement and Administration of Justice. 1967. *The Challenge of Crime in a Free Society*. Washington, DC.

Conti, R. M., Bernstein, A. C., Villaflor, V. M., Schilsky, R. L., Rosenthal, M. B., & Bach, P. B. 2013. Prevalence of Off-Label Use and Spending in 2010 Among Patent-Protected Chemotherapies in a Population-Based Cohort of Medical Oncologists. *Journal of Clinical Oncology, 31*, 1134–1139.

Cook, D. C., & Feldman, M. 1953. Insider Trading Under the Securities Exchange Act. *Harvard Law Review, 66*, 385–422.

Cornish, D., & Clarke, R. 1986. *The Reasoning Criminal: Rational Choice Perspectives on Offending*. New York: Springer-Verlag.

Corporate Fraud Task Force. 2008. *Report to the President*.

Cosmides, L., & Tooby, J. 1989. Evolutionary Psychology and the Generation of Culture, Part II: Case Study: A Computational Theory of Social Exchange. *Ethology and Sociobiology, 10*, 51–97.

———. 1997. *Evolutionary Psychology: A Primer*.

Coughlan, R. 1951. What Manner of Morph Are You? *Life*, June.

Cowles, V. 1973. *The Rothschilds: A Family of Fortune*. New York: Knopf.

Crane, M., Raiswell, R., & Reeves, M. 2004. *Shell Games: Studies in Scams, Frauds, and Deceits (1300–1650)*. Toronto: Centre for Reformation and Renaissance Studies.

Craswell, R. 1985. Interpreting Deceptive Advertising. *Boston University Law Review, 65*, 657–732.

Cressey, D. 1951a. Criminological Research and the Definition of Crimes. *American Journal of Sociology, 56*, 546–551.

———. 1951b. Why Do Trusted Persons Commit Fraud? *Journal of Accountancy, 92*, 576–581.

———. 1953. *Other People's Money*. Glencoe, IL: Free Press.

———. 1965. The Respectable Criminal. *Criminologica, 3*, 11–15.

———. 1973. *Other People's Money*. Montclair, NJ: Patterson Smith.

———. 1986. Why Managers Commit Fraud. *Australian and New Zealand Journal of Criminology, 19*, 195–209.

Cueva, C., Roberts, R. E., Spencer, T., Rani, N., Tempest, M., Tobler, P. N., Herbert, J., & Rustichini, A. 2015. Cortisol and Testosterone Increase Financial Risk Taking and May Destabilize Markets. *Scientific Reports, 5*, 1–16.

Cullen, F. T., Clark, G., Link, B., Mathers, R., Niedospial, J. L., & Sheahan, M. 1985. Dissecting White-Collar Crime: Offense Type and Punitiveness. *International Journal of Comparative and Applied Criminal Justice, 9*, 15–28.

Cullen, F. T., Clark, G., Mathers, R. A., & Cullen, J. B. 1983. Public Support for Punishing White Collar Crime: Blaming the Victim Revisited? *Journal of Criminal Justice, 11*, 481–493.

Cullen, F. T., Hartman, J. L., & Jonson, C. L. 2009. Bad Guys: Why the Public Supports Punishing White-Collar Offenders. *Crime, Law and Social Change, 51*, 31–44.

Cullen, F. T., Link, B. G., & Polanzi, C. W. 1982. The Seriousness of Crime Revisited. *Criminology, 20*, 83–102.

Cullen, F. T., Maakestad, W. J., & Cavender, G. 1987. *Corporate Crime Under Attack: The Ford Pinto Case and Beyond*. Cincinnati: Anderson Publishing Company.

Cushman, F., Gray, K., Gaffey, A., & Mendes, W. B. 2012. Simulating Murder: The Aversion to Harmful Action. *Emotion, 12*, 2–7.

Daemmrich, A., & Radin, J. 2007. *Perspectives on Risk and Regulation: The FDA at 100*. Philadelphia, PA: Chemical Heritage Foundation.

Dallek, R. 1979. *Franklin D. Roosevelt and American Foreign Policy, 1932–1945*. New York: Oxford University Press.

Damasio, A. 1994. *Descartes' Error: Emotion, Reason, and the Human Brain*. New York: Putnam.

Damasio, A., & Carvalho, G. B. 2013. The Nature of Feelings: Evolutionary and Neurobiological Origins. *Nature Reviews. Neuroscience, 14*, 143–152.

Darby, M. 1998. In Ponzi We Trust. *Smithsonian Magazine*, December.

Darley, J. M., & Batson, C. D. 1973. From Jerusalem to Jericho: A Study of Situational and Dispositional Variables in Helping Behavior. *Journal of Personality and Social Psychology, 27*, 100–108.

Darwin. 1871. *The Descent of Man*. London: John Murray.

Das, G. 2009. *The Difficulty of Being Good*. New York: Oxford University Press.

Davidson, R., Dey, A., & Smith, A. J. 2014. Executives' Legal Records, Lavish Lifestyles and Insider Trading Activities. Working Paper.

———. 2015. Executives' "Off-the-Job" Behavior, Corporate Culture, and Financial Reporting Risk. *Journal of Financial Economics, 117*, 5–28.

Davis, M. 1906. *Gabriel Tarde: An Essay in Sociological Theory*. New York: Columbia University.

Dawkins, R. 1976. *The Selfish Gene*. Oxford: Oxford University Press.

Deal, T., & Kennedy, A. 1982. *Corporate Cultures: The Rites and Rituals of Corporate Life*. Reading, MA: Addison-Wesley Publishing Co.

Deb, S. 2013. *Fallen Angel: The Making and Unmaking of Rajat Gupta*. New Delhi: Rupa Publications.

DeBacker, J., Heim, B. T., Tran, A., & Yuskavage, A. 2015. Legal Enforcement and Corporate Behavior: An Analysis of Tax Aggressiveness After an Audit. *Journal of Law and Economics, 58*, 291–324.

DeCelles, K. A., DeRue, D. S., Margolis, J. D., & Ceranic, T. L. 2012. Does Power Corrupt or Enable? When and Why Power Facilitates Self-Interested Behavior. *Journal of Applied Psychology, 97*, 681–689.

Decety, J., Michalska, K. J., & Kinzler, K. D. 2011. The Developmental Neuroscience of Moral Sensitivity. *Emotion Review, 3*, 305–307.

Dechow, P. M., Ge, W., Larson, C. R., & Sloan, R. G. 2011. Predicting Material Accounting Misstatements. *Contemporary Accounting Research, 28*, 17–82.

Dechow, P. M., & Skinner, D. J. 2000. Earnings Management: Reconciling the Views of Accounting Academics, Practitioners, and Regulators. *Accounting Horizons, 14*, 235–250.

Dechow, P., & Tan, S. 2016. How Do Accounting Practices Spread? An Examination of Law Firm Networks and Stock Option Backdating. Working paper.

Dershowitz, A. 1961. Increasing Community Control over Corporate Crime: A Problem in the Law of Sanctions. *Yale Law Journal, 71*, 289–306.

de Waal, F. de. 1996. *Good Natured: The Origins of Right and Wrong in Humans and Other Animals*. Cambridge, MA: Harvard University Press.

———. 2006. *Primates and Philosophers: How Morality Evolved*. Princeton, NJ: Princeton University Press.

———. 2012. The Antiquity of Empathy. *Science, 336*, 874–876.

Diaz, P., & Maxwell, R. 1988. Insider Trading and the Corporate Acquirer: Private Actions Under Rule 10b-5 Against Agents Who Trade on Misappropriated Information. *Washington Law Review, 56,* 600–657.

Dichev, I., Graham, J., Harvey, C. R., & Rajgopal, S. 2013. Earnings Quality: Evidence from the Field. *Journal of Accounting and Economics, 56,* 1–33.

———. 2016. The Misrepresentation of Earnings. *Financial Analysts Journal, 72,* 22–35.

Dilulio, J. J. 1996. Help Wanted: Economists, Crime and Public Policy. *The Journal of Economic Perspectives, 10,* 3–24.

Dimmock, S. G., Gerken, W. C., & Graham, N. P. 2015. *Is Fraud Contagious? Career Networks and Fraud by Financial Advisors.* Working paper.

Diskant, E. B. 2008. Comparative Corporate Criminal Liability: Exploring the Uniquely American Doctrine Through Comparative Criminal Procedure. *Yale Law Journal, 118,* 126–176.

Dooley, M. P. 1980. Enforcement of Insider Trading Restrictions. *Virginia Law Review, 66,* 1–83.

Dorminey, J., Fleming, A. S., Kranacher, M. J., & Riley, R. A. 2010. Beyond the Fraud Triangle. *CPA,* July, 16–24.

———. The Evolution of Fraud Theory. *Issues in Accounting Education, 27,* 555–579.

Dorris, J. 2002. *Lack of Character: Personality and Moral Behavior.* Cambridge: Cambridge University Press.

Dowell, S. 1884. *A History of Taxation and Taxes in England: From the Earliest Times to the Present Day.* London: Longmans, Green and Co.

Dowling, G. R. 2014. The Curious Case of Corporate Tax Avoidance: Is It Socially Irresponsible? *Journal of Business Ethics, 124,* 173–184.

Duckworth, K. L., Bargh, J. A., Garcia, M., & Chaiken, S. 2002. The Automatic Evaluation of Novel Stimuli. *Psychological Science, 13,* 513–519.

Dunn, B. D., Dalgleish, T., & Lawrence, A. D. 2006. The Somatic Marker Hypothesis: A Critical Evaluation. *Neuroscience and Biobehavioral Reviews, 30,* 239–271.

Durtschi, C., & Easton, P. 2005. Earnings Management? The Shapes of the Frequency Distributions of Earnings Metrics Are Not Evidence Ipso Facto. *Journal of Accounting Research, 43,* 557–592.

———. 2009. Earnings Management? Erroneous Inferences Based on Earnings Frequency Distributions. *Journal of Accounting Research, 47,* 1249–1281.

Dutcher, J. S. 2005. From the Boardroom to the Cellblock: The Justifications for Harsher Punishment of White-Collar and Corporate Crime. *Arizona State Law Journal, 37,* 1295–1319.

Dyck, A., Morse, A., & Zingales, L. 2014. How Pervasive Is Corporate Fraud? Working Paper.

Easterbrook, F. H. 1981. Insider Trading, Secret Agents, Evidentiary Privileges, and the Production of Information. *The Supreme Court Review, 1981,* 309–365.

Easterbrook, F. H., & Fischel, D. R. 1991. *The Economic Structure of Corporate Law.* Cambridge, MA: Harvard University Press.

Edgerton, H. W. 1927. Corporate Criminal Responsibility. *Yale Law Journal, 36,* 827–844.

Edmonds, D. 2014. *Would You Kill the Fat Man? The Trolley Problem and What Your Answer Tells Us About Right and Wrong.* Princeton, NJ: Princeton University Press.

Edwards, K. 1990. The Interplay of Affect and Cognition in Attitude Formation and Change. *Journal of Personality and Social Psychology, 59,* 202–216.

Edwards, K., & von Hippel, W. 1995. Hearts and Minds: The Priority of Affective Versus Cognitive Factors in Person Perception. *Personality and Social Psychology Bulletin, 21*, 996–1011.

Eichenwald, K. 2000. *The Informant.* New York: Broadway Books.

———. 2005. *Conspiracy of Fools: A True Story.* New York: Broadway Books.

Eisenberg, N., Valiente, C., & Champion, C. 2004. Empathy-Related Responding: Moral, Social, and Socialization Correlates. In A. Miller (Ed.), *The Social Psychology of Good and Evil,* 386–415. New York: Guilford Press.

Ellis, H. 1914. *The Criminal.* New York: Scribner & Welford.

Elm, D. R., & Nichols, M. L. 1993. An Investigation of the Moral Reasoning of Managers. *Journal of Business Ethics, 12*, 817–833.

Elm, D. R., & Weber, J. 1994. Measuring Moral Judgment: The Moral Judgment Interview or the Defining Issues Test? *Journal of Business Ethics, 13*, 341–355.

Erickson, M., Hanlon, M., & Maydew, E. L. 2004. How Much Will Firms Pay for Earnings That Do Not Exist? Evidence of Taxes Paid on Allegedly Fraudulent Earnings. *The Accounting Review, 79*, 387–408.

Eskenazi, P., Hartmann, F., & Rietdijk, W. 2016. Why Controllers Compromise on Their Fiduciary Duties: EEG Evidence on the Role of the Human Mirror Neuron System. *Accounting, Organizations and Society, 50*, 41–50.

Evans, J. 2003. In Two Minds: Dual-Process Accounts of Reasoning. *Trends in Cognitive Sciences, 7*, 454–459.

———. 2008. Dual-Processing Accounts of Reasoning, Judgment, and Social Cognition. *Annual Review of Psychology, 59*, 255–278.

Evans, J., & Stanovich, K. E. 2013. Theory and Metatheory in the Study of Dual Processing: Reply to Comments. *Perspectives on Psychological Science, 8*, 263–271.

Fara, P. 2003. Marginalized Practices. In R. Porter (Ed.), *The Cambridge History of Science,* 485–508. Cambridge: Cambridge University Press.

Faulkner, R. 2011. *Corporate Wrongdoing and the Art of the Accusation.* New York: Anthem Press.

Feldman, D. C. 1984. The Development and Enforcement of Group Norms. *The Academy of Management Review, 9*, 47–53.

Ferarra, R. 2008. Securities and Exchange Commission Historical Society Interview with Ralph Ferrara.

Ferguson, C. J. 2010. Genetic Contributions to Antisocial Personality and Behavior: A Meta-Analytic Review from an Evolutionary Perspective. *The Journal of Social Psychology, 150*, 160–180.

Ferguson, M. J., & Zayas, V. 2009. Automatic Evaluation. *Current Directions in Psychological Science, 18*, 362–366.

Fernie, G., & Tunney, R. J. 2006. Some Decks Are Better than Others: The Effect of Reinforcer Type and Task Instructions on Learning in the Iowa Gambling Task. *Brain and Cognition, 60*, 94–102.

Ferrell, O. C., Fraedrich, J., & Ferrell, L. 2015. *Business Ethics: Ethical Decision Making & Cases.* Stamford, CT: Cengage Learning.

Festinger, L. 1954. A Theory of Social Comparison Processes. *Human Relations, 7*, 117–140.

———. 1957. *A Theory of Cognitive Dissonance.* Evanston, IL: Row Peterson.

Fielding, E., Lo, A. W., & Yang, J. H. 2011. The National Transportation Safety Board: A Model for Systemic Risk Management. *Journal of Investment Management, 9*, 17–49.

Fischel, D. R. 1995. *Payback: The Conspiracy to Destroy Michael Milken and His Financial Revolution.* New York: HarperCollins.

Fischel, D. R., & Sykes, A. O. 1996. Corporate Crime. *The Journal of Legal Studies, 25,* 319–349.

Fiske, A. P. 1999. Learning a Culture the Way Informants Do: Observing, Imitating, and Participating. Working Paper.

Fiske, S. T., & Dépret, E. 1996. Control, Interdependence and Power: Understanding Social Cognition in Its Social Context. *European Review of Social Psychology, 7,* 31–61.

Fisman, R., & Miguel, E. 2007. Corruption, Norms, and Legal Enforcement: Evidence from Diplomatic Parking Tickets. *Journal of Political Economy, 115,* 1020–1048.

Fisse, B., & Braithwaite, J. 1983. *The Impact of Publicity on Corporate Offenders.* Albany: State University of New York Press.

Flack, J. C., & de Waal, F. 2000. Being Nice Is Not a Building Block of Morality. *Journal of Consciousness Studies, 7,* 67–78.

———. 2002. "Any Animal Whatever": Darwinian Building Blocks of Morality in Monkeys and Apes. In L. Katz (Ed.), *Evolutionary Origins of Morality,* 1–30. Thorverton: Imprint Academic.

Fleming, T. R. 2010. Clinical Trials: Discerning Hype from Substance. *Annals of Internal Medicine, 153,* 400–406.

Foot, P. 1967. The Problem of Abortion and the Doctrine of the Double Effect. *Oxford Review, 5,* 1–6.

Forte, A. 2004. Antecedents of Managers Moral Reasoning. *Journal of Business Ethics, 51,* 315–347.

Frank, R. 1988. *Passions Within Reason: The Strategic Role of the Emotions.* New York: Norton.

———. 1990. Rethinking Rational Choice. In R. Friedland & A. F. Robertson (Eds.), *Beyond the Marketplace: Rethinking Economy and Society,* 53–87. New Brunswick, NJ: Transaction Publishers.

Frankel, T. 2006. *Trust and Honesty: America's Business Culture at a Crossroad.* New York: Oxford University Press.

———. 2012. *Ponzi Scheme Puzzle: A History and Analysis of Con Artists and Victims.* Oxford: Oxford University Press.

Franklin, B. 1887. *The Complete Works of Benjamin Franklin,* Ed. J. Bigelow. New York and London: G. P. Putnam's Sons.

———. 1956. *Mr. Franklin: A Selection from His Personal Letters,* Ed. W. J. Bell & L. W. Labaree. New Haven, CT: Yale University Press.

Frankopan, P. 2015. *The Silk Roads: A New History of the World.* New York: Knopf.

Frantz, D. 1987. *Levine and Co.: Wall Street's Insider Trading Scandal.* New York: Holt.

Frederick, S. 2005. Cognitive Reflection and Decision Making. *Journal of Economic Perspectives, 19,* 25–42.

Fried, J. M. 2008. Option Backdating and Its Implications. *Washington and Lee Law Review, 65,* 853–888.

Friedman, M. 1953. The Methodology of Positive Economics. In *Essays in Positive Economics,* 3–43. Chicago: University of Chicago Press.

Friedman, M., & Savage, L. J. 1948. The Utility Analysis of Choices Involving Risk. *Journal of Political Economy, 56,* 279–304.

Friedrichs, D. 2010. *Trusted Criminals: White Collar Crime in Contemporary Society* (4th ed.). Belmont, CA: Wadsworth Cengage Learning.

Frijda, N., & Mesquita, B. 1994. The Social Roles and Functions of Emotions. In S. Kitayama & H. R. Markus (Eds.), *Emotion and Culture: Empirical Studies of Mutual Influence,* 51–87. Washington, DC: American Psychological Association.

Fuller, J. G. 1962. *The Gentlemen Conspirators.* New York: Grove Press.

Gabor, T. 1995. *Everybody Does It! Crime by the Public*. Toronto: University of Toronto Press.

Galambos, L. 1975. *The Public Image of Big Business in America, 1880–1940*. Baltimore: Johns Hopkins Press.

Galbraith, J. 1954. *The Great Crash 1929*. Boston: Mariner Books.

Galinsky, A. D., Magee, J. C., Inesi, M. E., & Gruenfeld, D. H. 2006. Power and Perspective Not Taken. *Psychological Science, 17*, 1068–1074.

Gall, F. J. 1835. *On the Functions of the Brain and of Each of Its parts: With Observations on the Possibility of Determining the Instincts, Propensities, and Talents, Or the Moral and Intellectual Dispositions of Men and Animals, by the Configuration of the Brain and Head*. Boston: Marsh, Capen & Lyon.

Gao, Y., & Raine, A. 2010. Successful and Unsuccessful Psychopaths: A Neurobiological Model. *Behavioral Sciences and the Law, 28*, 194–210.

Garrett, B. 2014. *Too Big to Jail: How Prosecutors Compromise with Corporations*. Cambridge, MA: The Belknap Press of Harvard University Press.

Geis, G. 1962. Toward a Delineation of White-Collar Offenses. *Sociological Inquiry, 32*, 160–171.

———. 1977. The Heavy Electrical Equipment Antitrust Cases of 1961. In G. Geis & R. Meier (Eds.), *White Collar Crime*, 117–133. New York: Free Press.

———. 1992. White-Collar Crime: What Is It? In K. Schlegel & D. Weisburd (Eds.), *White-Collar Crime Reconsidered*, 31–52. Boston: Northeastern University Press.

———. 2000. On the Absence of Self-Control as the Basis for a General Theory of Crime: A Critique. *Theoretical Criminology, 4*, 35–53.

Geis, G., & Goff, C. 1983. Introduction. In *White Collar Crime: The Uncut Version*, ix–xxxiii. New Haven, CT: Yale University Press.

———. 1986. Edwin H. Sutherland's White-Collar Crime in America: An Essay in Historical Criminology. In *Criminal Justice History: An International Annual*, 1–31.

Gellerman, S. W. 1986. Why "Good" Managers Make Bad Ethical Choices. *Harvard Business Review*, July-August, 85–90.

Genego, W. J. 1988. The New Adversary. *Brooklyn Law Review, 54*, 781–892.

Gibson, E. L. 2007. Carbohydrates and Mental Function: Feeding or Impeding the Brain? *Nutrition Bulletin, 32*, 71–83.

Gibson, E. L., & Green, M. W. 2002. Nutritional Influences on Cognitive Function: Mechanisms of Susceptibility. *Nutrition Research Reviews, 15*, 169–206.

Gigerenzer, G., Todd, P. M., & ABC Research Group. 1999. *Simple Heuristics That Make Us Smart*. Oxford: Oxford University Press.

Gilliam, T. A., Heflin, F., & Paterson, J. S. 2015. Evidence That the Zero-Earnings Discontinuity Has Disappeared. *Journal of Accounting and Economics, 60*, 117–132.

Gilligan, C. 1982. *In a Different Voice*. Cambridge, MA: Harvard University Press.

Gino, F. 2013. *Sidetracked: Why Our Decisions Get Derailed, and How We Can Stick to the Plan*. Boston: Harvard Business Review Press.

———. 2015. Understanding Ordinary Unethical Behavior: Why People Who Value Morality Act Immorally. *Behavioral Sciences, 3*, 107–111.

Gino, F., & Ariely, D. 2012. The Dark Side of Creativity: Original Thinkers Can Be More Dishonest. *Journal of Personality and Social Psychology, 102*, 445–459.

Gino, F., Ayal, S., & Ariely, D. 2013. Self-Serving Altruism? The Lure of Unethical Actions That Benefit Others. *Journal of Economic Behavior & Organization, 93*, 285–292.

Gino, F., & Galinsky, A. D. 2012. Vicarious Dishonesty: When Psychological Closeness Creates Distance from One's Moral Compass. *Organizational Behavior and Human Decision Processes, 119*, 15–26.

Gino, F., Schweitzer, M. E., Mead, N. L., & Ariely, D. 2011. Unable to Resist Temptation: How Self-Control Depletion Promotes Unethical Behavior. *Organizational Behavior and Human Decision Processes, 115,* 191–203.

Gino, F., & Wiltermuth, S. S. 2014. Evil Genius? How Dishonesty Can Lead to Greater Creativity. *Psychological Science, 25,* 973–981.

Gioia, D. A. 1992. Pinto Fires and Personal Ethics: A Script Analysis of Missed Opportunities. *Journal of Business Ethics, 11,* 379–389.

Gladwell, M. 2005. *Blink: The Power of Thinking Without Thinking.* New York: Little, Brown and Company.

Glantz, A. E. 2008. A Tax on Light and Air: Impact of the Window Duty on Tax Administration and Architecture, 1696–1851. *Penn History Review, 15,* 18–23.

Glenn, A. L., & Raine, A. 2014. Neurocriminology: Implications for the Punishment, Prediction and Prevention of Criminal Behaviour. *Nature Reviews Neuroscience, 15,* 54–63.

Glueck, S., & Glueck, E. 1956. *Physique and Delinquency.* New York: Harper and Brothers.

Goldman, A. 2006. *Simulating Minds.* Oxford: Oxford University Press.

Goldman, A., & Sripada, C. S. 2005. Simulationist Models of Face-Based Emotion Recognition. *Cognition, 94,* 193–213.

Goldman, S., & Arbuthnot, J. 1979. Teaching Medical Ethics: The Cognitive-Developmental Approach. *Journal of Medical Ethics, 5,* 170–181.

Gordon, A. K., & Miller, A. G. 2000. Perspective Differences in the Construal of Lies: Is Deception in the Eye of the Beholder? *Personality and Social Psychology Bulletin, 26,* 46–55.

Goring, C. 1913. *The English Convict.* London: HM Stationery Office.

Gottfredson, M., & Hirschi, T. 1990. *A General Theory of Crime.* Stanford, CA: Stanford University Press.

Gottschalk, P., & Glasø, L. 2013. Gender in White-Collar Crime: An Empirical Study of Pink-Collar Criminals. *International Letters of Social and Humanistic Sciences, 4,* 22–34.

Graetz, M. J. 2008. *100 Million Unnecessary Returns.* New Haven, CT: Yale University Press.

Graetz, M. J., & Schenk, D. 2005. *Federal Income Taxation: Principles and Policies.* Westbury, NY: Foundation Press.

Graham, J. 1960. *The Development of the Use of Physiognomy in the Novel.* Johns Hopkins University.

———. 1979. *Lavater's Essays on Physiognomy.* Berne: P. Lang.

Graham, J. R., Harvey, C. R., Popadak, J., & Rajgopal, S. 2015. Corporate Culture: Evidence from the Field. Working Paper.

Graham, J. R., Harvey, C. R., & Rajgopal, S. 2005. The Economic Implications of Corporate Financial Reporting. *Journal of Accounting and Economics, 40,* 3–73.

Grasmick, H., & Bursik, R. 1990. Conscience, Significant Others, and Rational Choice: Extending the Deterrence Model. *Law & Society Review, 24,* 837–861.

Grasmick, H., & Green, D. 1980. Legal Punishment, Social Disapproval and Internalization as Inhibitors of Illegal Behavior. *Journal of Criminal Law and Criminology, 71,* 325–335.

Green, S. P. 1997. Why It's a Crime to Tear the Tag off a Mattress: Overcriminalization and the Moral Content of Regulatory Offenses. *Emory Law Journal, 46,* 1533–1615.

———. 2006. *Lying, Cheating, and Stealing: A Moral Theory of White-Collar Crime.* Oxford: Oxford University Press.

Greenberg, J. D., & Brotman, E. C. 2014. Strict Vicarious Criminal Liability for Corporations and Corporate Executives: Stretching the Boundaries of Criminalization. *American Criminal Law Review, 658,* 79–98.

Greene, J. D. 2013. *Moral Tribes*. New York: The Penguin Press.

Greene, J. D., Sommerville, R. B., Nystrom, L. E., Darley, J. M., & Cohen, J. D. 2001. An fMRI Investigation of Emotional Engagement in Moral Judgment. *Science, 293*, 2105–2108.

Greenspan, A. 2013. *The Map and the Territory*. New York: Penguin Books.

Grossman, D. 2009. *On Killing*. New York: Little, Brown and Company.

Grossman, S., & Stiglitz, J. E. 1980. On the Impossibility of Informationally Efficient Markets. *American Economic Review, 70*, 393–408.

Grove, W. M., Eckert, E. D., Heston, L., Bouchard, T. J., Segal, N., & Lykken, D. T. 1990. Heritability of Substance Abuse and Antisocial Behavior: A Study of Monozygotic Twins Reared Apart. *Biological Psychiatry, 27*, 1293–1304.

Guzzardi, W. J. 1976. An Unscandalized View of Those "Bribes" Abroad. *Fortune*, July, 118–182.

Haan, P., & Berkey, C. 2002. A Study of the Believability of the Forms of Puffery. *Journal of Marketing Communications, 8*, 243–256.

Hagan, J. 2010. *Who Are the Criminals?: The Politics of Crime Policy from the Age of Roosevelt to the Age of Reagan*. Princeton, NJ: Princeton University Press.

Hagger, M. S., Wood, C., Stiff, C., & Chatzisarantis, N. L. D. 2010. Ego Depletion and the Strength Model of Self-Control: A Meta-Analysis. *Psychological Bulletin, 136*, 495–525.

Haidt, J. 2001. The Emotional Dog and Its Rational Tail: A Social Intuitionist Approach to Moral Judgment. *Psychological Review, 108*, 814–834.

———. 2006. *The Happiness Hypothesis*. New York: Basic Books.

———. 2012. *The Righteous Mind: Why Good People Are Divided by Politics and Religion*. New York: Pantheon.

Haidt, J., Bjorklund, F., & Murphy, S. 2000. Moral Dumbfounding: When Intuition Finds No Reason. Unpublished manuscript, University of Virginia, Charlottesville, VA.

Haidt, J., & Joseph, C. 2004. Intuitive Ethics: How Innately Prepared Intuitions Generate Culturally Variable Virtues. *Daedalus, 133*, 55–66.

———. 2007. The Moral Mind: How 5 Sets of Innate Intuitions Guide the Development of Many Culture-Specific Virtues, and Perhaps Even Modules. In P. Carruthers, S. Laurence, & S. Stich (Eds.), *The Innate Mind, Vol. 3*, 367–391. New York: Oxford University Press.

Haier, R. J., Siegel, B. V, MacLachlan, A., Soderling, E., Lottenberg, S., & Buchsbaum, M. S. 1992. Regional Glucose Metabolic Changes After Learning a Complex Visuospatial/Motor Task: A Positron Emission Tomographic Study. *Brain Research, 570*, 134–143.

Haller, M. 1984. *Eugenics: Hereditarian Attitudes in American Thought*. New Brunswick: Rutgers University Press.

Hamilton, W. D. 1964. The Genetical Evolution of Social Behaviour. *Journal of Theoretical Biology, 7*, 1–16.

Hamlin, J. K., Wynn, K., & Bloom, P. 2007. Social Evaluation by Preverbal Infants. *Nature, 450*, 557–559.

———. 2010. Three-Month-Olds Show a Negativity Bias in Their Social Evaluations. *Developmental Science, 13*, 923–929.

Hammond, J. S., Keeney, R. L., & Raiffa, H. 1999. *Smart Choices*. Boston: Harvard Business School Press.

Harden, K. P., Kretsch, N., Tackett, J. L., & Tucker-Drob, E. M. 2014. Genetic and Environmental Influences on Testosterone in Adolescents: Evidence for Sex Differences. *Developmental Psychobiology, 56*, 1278–1289.

Hare, R. 1993. *Without Conscience*. New York: Pocket Books.

Harlow, J. M. 1869. *Recovery from the Passage of an Iron Bar Through the Head*. Boston: David Clapp & Son.

Harrington, E. B. 2012. The Sociology of Financial Markets. In K. Knorr-Cetina & A. Preda (Eds.), *The Oxford Handbook of the Sociology of Finance*, 393–410. Oxford: Oxford University Press.

Harris, J. R. 1995. Where Is the Child's Environment? A Group Socialization Theory of Development. *Psychological Review, 102,* 458–489.

Harris, S. 2013. *Lying.* Opelousas, LA: Four Elephants Press.

Harrison, A. A. 1977. Mere Exposure. In L. Berkowitz (Ed.), *Advances in Experimental Social Psychology,* 40–83. New York: Academic Press.

Hartley, L. 2001. *Physiognomy and the Meaning of Expression in Nineteenth-Century Culture.* Cambridge: Cambridge University Press.

Hartshorne, H., & May, M. 1928. *Studies in the Nature of Character.* New York: The MacMillan Company.

Hartung, F. 1950. White-Collar Offenses in the Wholesale Meat Industry in Detroit. *American Journal of Sociology, 56,* 25–34.

Haselhuhn, M. P., & Wong, E. M. 2012. Bad to the Bone: Facial Structure Predicts Unethical Behaviour. *Proceedings of the Royal Society: Biological Sciences, 279,* 571–576.

Haskins, B. G., & Silva, J. A. 2006. Asperger's Disorder and Criminal Behavior: Forensic-Psychiatric Considerations. *Journal of the American Academy of Psychiatry and the Law, 34,* 374–384.

Hatfield, E., Cacioppo, J. T., & Rapson, R. L. 1993. Emotional Contagion. *Current Direction in Psychological Science, 2,* 96–99.

Hatfield, E., Rapson, R. L., & Le, Y. C. 2011. Emotional Contagion and Empathy. In J. Decety & W. Ickes (Eds.), *The Social Neuroscience of Empathy,* 19–29. Cambridge, MA: MIT Press.

Hauer, E., Ahlin, F. J., & Bowser, J. S. 1982. Speed Enforcement and Speed Choice. *Accident Analysis and Prevention, 14,* 267–278.

Haugh, T. 2014. Sentencing the Why of White Collar Crime. *Fordham Law Review, 82,* 3143–3188.

Hauser, M. 2006. *Moral Minds.* New York: Ecco.

Hauser, M., Cushman, F., Young, L., Jin, R. K. X., & Mikhail, J. 2007. A Dissociation Between Moral Judgments and Justifications. *Mind and Language, 22,* 1–21.

Hay, D., & Cooke, K. 2007. The Transformation of Prosocial Behavior from Infancy to Childhood. In C. Brownell & C. Kopp (Eds.), *Socioemotional Development in the Toddler Years,* 100–131. New York: Guilford Press.

Head, M. L., Holman, L., Lanfear, R., Kahn, A. T., & Jennions, M. D. 2015. The Extent and Consequences of P-Hacking in Science. *PLOS Biology,* 1–15.

Healy, P. M. 1985. The Effect of Bonus Schemes on Accounting Decisions. *Journal of Accounting and Economics, 7,* 85–107.

Healy, P. M., & Wahlen, J. M. 1999. A Review of the Earnings Management Literature and Its Implications for Standard Setting. *Accounting Horizons, 13,* 365–383.

Heath, J. 2008. Ethics and Moral Motivation: A Criminological Perspective. *Journal of Business Ethics, 83,* 595–614.

Hechter, M., & Kanazawa, S. 1997. Sociological Rational Choice Theory. *Annual Review of Sociology, 23,* 191–214.

Hefendehl, R. 2000. Corporate Criminal Liability: Model Penal Code Section 2.07 and the Development in Western Legal Systems. *Buffalo Criminal Law Review, 4,* 283–300.

Heineke, J. 1978. *Economic Models of Criminal Behavior.* Amsterdam: North-Holland Publishing.

Henrich, J., Ensminger, J., McElreath, R., Barr, A., Barrett, C., Bolyanatz, A., Cardenas, J. C., Gurven, M., Gwako, E., Henrich, N., Lesorogol, C., Marlowe, F., Tracer, D., & Ziker, J.

2010. Markets, Religion, Community Size, and the Evolution of Fairness and Punishment. *Science, 327,* 1480–1484.

Henriques, D. B. 2011. *The Wizard of Lies: Bernie Madoff and the Death of Trust.* New York: St. Martin's Press.

Herling, J. 1962. *The Great Price Conspiracy.* Washington, DC: Robert B. Luce, Inc.

Hersey, G. 1996. *The Evolution of Allure.* Cambridge, MA: MIT Press.

Herzel, L., & Katz, L. 1987. Insider Trading: Who Loses? *Lloyds Bank Review,* July, 15–26.

Hill, C. A., & Painter, R. W. 2015. *Better Bankers, Better Banks.* Chicago: University of Chicago Press.

Hilt, E. 2008. When Did Ownership Separate from Control? Corporate Governance in the Early Nineteenth Century. *The Journal of Economic History, 68,* 645–685.

Hirshleifer, J. 1985. The Expanding Domain of Economics. *The American Economic Review, 75,* 53–68.

Hobson, J. L., Mayew, W. J., & Venkatachalam, M. 2012. Analyzing Speech to Detect Financial Misreporting. *Journal of Accounting Research, 50,* 349–392.

Hochfelder, D. 2006. "Where the Common People Could Speculate": The Ticker, Bucket Shops, and the Origins of Popular Participation in Financial Markets, 1880–1920. *The Journal of American History, 93,* 335–358.

Hodges, L. 1963. *The Business Conscience.* Englewood Cliffs, NJ: Prentice-Hall.

Hoeflich, M. H. 1991. Laidlaw V. Organ, Gulian C. Verplanck, and the Shaping of Early Nineteenth Century Contract Law: A Tale of a Case and a Commentary. *University of Illinois Law Review,* 55–66.

Hoffman, D. A. 2006. The Best Puffery Article Ever. *Iowa Law Review, 91,* 1395–1448.

Hoffman, M. L. 1981. Is Altruism Part of Human Nature? *Journal of Personality and Social Psychology, 40,* 121–137.

Hoffman, R. 2009. *Sir Allen & Me: An Insider's Look at R. Allen Stanford and the Island of Antigua.* Christiansted, US Virgin Islands: Southern Cross Publication.

Hogan, R., & Hogan, J. 2001. Assessing Leadership: A View from the Dark Side. *International Journal of Selectin and Assessment, 9,* 40–51.

Hogarth, R. 2001. *Educating Intuition.* Chicago: University of Chicago Press.

Hogeveen, J., Inzlicht, M., & Obhi, S. S. 2014. Power Changes How the Brain Responds to Others. *Journal of Experimental Psychology: General, 143,* 755–762.

Holderness, C. G., & Sheehan, D. P. 1985. Raiders or Saviors? The Evidence on Six Controversial Investors. *Journal of Financial Economics, 14,* 555–579.

Hooton, E. A. 1939a. *The American Criminal: Volume 1.* Cambridge, MA: Harvard University Press.

———. 1939b. *Crime and the Man.* Cambridge, MA: Harvard University Press.

Horn, D. 2003. *The Criminal Body: Lombroso and the Anatomy of Deviance.* New York: Routledge.

Hornstein, H. A., Fisch, E., & Holmes, M. 1968. Influence of a Model's Feeling About His Behavior and His Relevance as a Comparison Other on Observers' Helping Behavior. *Journal of Personality and Social Psychology, 10,* 222–226.

Horowitz, B. 2014. *The Hard Thing About Hard Things.* New York: Harper Business.

Hostetter, V. 1999. Turning Insider Trading Inside Out in the European Union. *California Western International Law Journal, 30,* 175–208.

Hurtado, J. 2008. Jeremy Bentham and Gary Becker: Utilitarianism and Economic Imperialism. *Journal of the History of Economic Thought, 30,* 337–357.

Husak, D. 1996. The "But-Everyone-Does-That!" Defense. *Public Affairs Quarterly, 10,* 307–334.

Huxley, A. 1944. Who Are You? *Harper's Magazine,* November, 512–522.

Ingebretsen, M. 2002. *NASDAQ: A History of the Market That Changed the World.* Roseville, CA: Forum.

Innes, S. 1995. *Creating the Commonwealth: The Economic Culture of Puritan New England.* New York: W. W. Norton & Company.

Ito, T. A., & Cacioppo, J. T. 2000. Electrophysiological Evidence of Implicit and Explicit Categorization Processes. *Journal of Experimental Social Psychology, 36,* 660–676.

Jackson, R. H., & Dumbauld, E. 1938. Monopolies and the Courts. *University of Pennsylvania Law Review, 86,* 231–257.

Jacquet, J. 2015. *Is Shame Necessary?: New Uses for an Old Tool.* New York: Pantheon Books.

Jia, Y., van Lent, L., & Zeng, Y. 2014. Masculinity, Testosterone, and Financial Misreporting. *Journal of Accounting Research, 52,* 1195–1246.

Johnson, C. H. 2005. Tales from the KPMG Skunk Works: The Basis-Shift or Defective-Redemption Shelter. *Tax Notes,* 431–443.

Johnson, G. R., Beer, F. A., van den Berghe, P. L., & Rushton, J. P. 1986. Kin Selection, Socialization, and Patriotism: An Integrating Theory. *Politics and the Life Sciences, 4,* 127–154.

Johnson, J., & Douglas, J. 1978. *Crime at the Top.* Philadelphia: Lippincott.

Johnson, S. A., Ryan, H. E., & Tian, Y. S. 2009. Managerial Incentives and Corporate Fraud: The Sources of Incentives Matter. *Review of Finance, 13,* 115–145.

Jones, T. M. 1991. Ethical Decision Making by Individuals in Organizations: An Issue-Contingent Model. *Academy of Management Review, 16,* 366–395.

Kadish, S. H. 1962. Some Observations on the Use of Criminal Sanctions in Enforcing Economic Regulations. *The University of Chicago Law Review, 30,* 423–449.

Kahan, D. M. 2013. A Risky Science Communication Environment for Vaccines. *Science, 342,* 53–55.

———. 2014. Vaccine Perceptions and Ad Hoc Risk Communication: An Empirical Assessment. *Cultural Cognition Project, 17,* 1–81.

Kahan, D. M., & Posner, E. A. 1999. Shaming White-Collar Criminals: A Proposal for Reform of the Federal Sentencing Guidelines. *Journal of Law and Economics, 42,* 365–392.

Kahneman, D. 2011. *Thinking, Fast and Slow.* New York: Farrar, Straus and Giroux.

Kahneman, D., & Thaler, R. H. 2006. Anomalies: Utility Maximization and Experienced Utility. *Journal of Economic Perspectives, 20,* 221–234.

Karpoff, J. M., Lee, D. Scott, & Martin, G. S. 2008. The Consequences to Managers for Financial Misrepresentation. *Journal of Financial Economics, 88,* 193–215.

Kassem, R., & Higson, A. 2012. The New Fraud Triangle Model. *Journal of Emerging Trends in Economics and Management Sciences, 3,* 191–195.

Katz, J. 1980. The Social Movement Against White-Collar Crime. In E. Bittner & S. L. Messinger (Eds.), *Criminology Review Yearbook, Volume 2,* 161–185. Beverly Hills: Sage Publications.

Katz, L. 1996. *Ill-Gotten Gains.* Chicago: University of Chicago Press.

———. 2011. *Why the Law Is So Perverse.* Chicago: University of Chicago Press.

Katz, R. 2004. FDA: Evidentiary Standards for Drug Development and Approval. *NeuroRx, 1,* 307–316.

Kay, J. 2015. *Other People's Money.* New York: PublicAffairs.

Kedia, S., Koh, K., Rajgopal, S. 2015. Evidence on Contagion in Earnings Management. *The Accounting Review,* 90, 2337–2373.

Kellens, G. 1968. Du Crime en Col Blanc. *Annales de La Faculté de Droit de Liege,* 61–124.

Keller, E., & Gehlmann, G. A. 1988. Introductory Comment: A Historical Introduction to the Securities Act of 1933 and the Securities Exchange Act of 1934. *Ohio State Law Journal, 49,* 329–352.

Keltner, D., Haidt, J., & Shiota, M. 2006. Social Functionalism and the Evolution of Emotions. In M. Schaller, J. Simpson, & D. Kenrick (Eds.), *Emotion and Social Psychology,* 115–142. New York: Psychology Press.

Keltner, D., & Lerner, J. S. 2010. Emotion. In S. T. Fiske, D. T. Gilbert, & G. Lindzey (Eds.), *Handbook of Social Psychology,* 317–352. Hoboken, NJ: Wiley.

Kets de Vries, M., & Miller, D. 1985. Narcissism and Leadership: An Object Relations Perspective. *Human Relations, 38,* 583–601.

Khanna, V. S. 1996. Corporate Criminal Liability: What Purpose Does It Serve? *Harvard Law Review, 109,* 1477–1534.

Khurana, R. 2007. *From Higher Aims to Hired Hands.* Princeton, NJ: Princeton University Press.

Kibbie, K. 2012. Maleficent or Mindblind: Questioning the Role of Asperger's in Quant Hedge Fund Malfeasance and Modeling Disasters. *American Criminal Law Review, 49,* 367–402.

King, M. 1977. *Public Policy and the Corporation.* London: Chapman and Hall.

King, M. C., & Wilson, A. C. 1975. Evolution at Two Levels in Humans and Chimpanzees. *Science, 188,* 107–116.

Kirtzman, A. 2000. *Rudy Giuliani: Emperor of the City.* New York: HarperCollins.

———. 2009. *Betrayal: The Life and Lies of Bernie Madoff.* New York: Harper.

Klaus, I. 2014. *Forging Capitalism: Rogues, Swindlers, Frauds, and the Rise of Modern Finance.* New Haven, CT: Yale University Press.

Klein, G. 2013. *Seeing What Others Don't: The Remarkable Ways We Gain Insights.* New York: PublicAffairs.

Klein, L. 2010. Rational Choice and White-Collar Crime. In *Encyclopedia of Criminological Theory* (Vol. 2, 774–776). Sage Publications.

Kohlberg, L. 1958. The Development of Modes of Moral Thinking and Choice in the Years 10 to 16. University of Chicago. Dissertation.

———. 1969. Stage and Sequence: The Cognitive-Developmental Approach to Socialization. In D. A. Goslin (Ed.), *Handbook of Socialization: Theory and Research,* 347–480. Chicago: Rand McNally.

———. 1981. *The Philosophy of Moral Development: Moral Stages and the Idea of Justice.* New York: Harper and Row.

———. 1991. My Personal Search for Universal Morality. In *The Kohlberg Legacy for the Helping Professions,* 11–17. Birmingham, AL: R.E.P.

Kort, M. 2008. *A Brief History of Russia.* New York: Facts On File.

Kostelnik, J. 2012. Sentencing White-Collar Criminals: When Is Shaming Viable? *Global Crime, 13,* 141–159.

Kotchian, A. C. 1976. *Lockheed Sales Mission.* University of California.

———. 1978. Rokkiedo Jiken. Los Angeles. Personal manuscript.

Kothari, S. P., Ramanna, K., & Skinner, D. J. 2010. Implications for GAAP from an Analysis of Positive Research in Accounting. *Journal of Accounting and Economics, 50,* 246–286.

Kotter, J. P., & Heskett, J. L. 1992. *Corporate Culture and Performance.* New York: Free Press.

Kotz, H. D. 2014. *Why Ponzi Schemes Work and How to Protect Yourself from Being Defrauded.* Eagan, MN: Thomson Reuters.

Koudijs, P. 2015. Those Who Know Most: Insider Trading in Eighteenth-Century Amsterdam. *Journal of Political Economy, 123,* 1356–1409.

Kramer, R. 1989. Criminologists and the Social Movement Against Corporate Crime. *Social Justice, 16,* 146–164.

Kraus, M. W., Côté, S., & Keltner, D. 2010. Social Class, Contextualism, and Empathic Accuracy. *Psychological Science, 21,* 1716–1723.

Krogman, W. M. 1939. Crime and the Man by Earnest Albert Hooton. *American Anthropologist, 41,* 504–509.

———. 1976. Fifty Years of Physical Anthropology: The Men, the Material, the Concepts, the Methods. *Annual Review of Anthropology, 5,* 1–14.

Kunst-Wilson, W. R., & Zajonc, R. B. 1980. Affective Discrimination of Stimuli That Cannot Be Recognized. *Science, 207,* 557–558.

Kurdas, C. 2016. *Political Sticky Wicket: The Untouchable Ponzi Scheme of Allen Stanford.* CreateSpace Independent Publishing Platform.

Kurzban, R. 2010. *Why Everyone (Else) Is a Hypocrite.* Princeton, NJ: Princeton University Press.

Labaton Sucharow. 2015. *The Street, The Bull and The Crisis: A Survey of the US and UK Financial Services Industry.* University of Notre Dame.

Ladd, S. L., Toscano, W. B., Cowings, P. S., & Gabrieli, J. D. E. 2014. Cardiovascular Change During Encoding Predicts the Nonconscious Mere Exposure Effect. *The American Journal of Psychology, 127,* 157–182.

Lane, R. E. 1953. Why Business Men Violate the Law. *Journal of Criminal Law, Criminology, and Political Science, 44,* 151–165.

Langer, E. 1989a. Minding Matters: The Consequences of Mindlessness-Mindfulness. *Advances in Experimental Social Psychology, 22,* 137–173.

———. 1989b. *Mindfulness.* Reading, MA: Addison-Wesley Publishing Co.

Langer, E. J., Blank, A., & Chanowitz, B. 1978. The Mindlessness of Ostensibly Thoughtful Action: The Role of "Placebic" Information in Interpersonal Interaction. *Journal of Personality and Social Psychology, 36,* 635–642.

Largent, M. 2008. *Breeding Contempt: The History of Coerced Sterilization in the United States.* New Brunswick, NJ: Rutgers University Press.

Larrick, R. P., Nisbett, R. E., & Morgan, J. N. 1993. Who Uses the Cost-Benefit Rules of Choice? Implications for the Normative Status of Microeconomic Theory. *Organizational Behavior and Human Decision Processes, 56,* 331–347.

Laufer, W. S. 2014. Where Is the Moral Indignation over Corporate Crime? In D. Brodowski, M. Espinoza de los Monteros de la Parra, K. Tiedemann, & J. Vogel (Eds.), *Regulating Corporate Criminal Liability,* 19–31. New York: Spring International Publishing.

Lavater, J. 1817. *The Pocket Lavater, or, the Science of Physiognomy.* New York: Van Winkle and Wiley.

LeDoux, J. 1996. *The Emotional Brain: The Mysterious Underpinning of Emotional Life.* New York: Simon and Schuster.

———. 2000. Emotion Circuits in the Brain. *Annual Review of Neuroscience, 23,* 155–184.

Lee, H. 1960. *To Kill a Mockingbird.* Philadelphia, PA: J. B. Lippincott Company.

Lee, J. J. 2011. Demystify Statistical Significance—Time to Move On from the *P* Value to Bayesian Analysis. *Journal of the National Cancer Institute, 103,* 2–3.

Lee, J. J., Gino, F., Jin, E. S., Rice, L. K., & Josephs, R. A. 2015. Hormones and Ethics: Understanding the Biological Basis of Unethical Conduct. *Journal of Experimental Psychology: General, 144,* 891–897.

Lee, T. M. C., Chan, S. C., & Raine, A. 2008. Strong Limbic and Weak Frontal Activation to Aggressive Stimuli in Spouse Abusers. *Molecular Psychiatry, 13,* 655–660.

Lefevre, C. E., Lewis, G. J., Perrett, D. I., & Penke, L. 2013. Telling Facial Metrics: Facial Width Is Associated with Testosterone Levels in Men. *Evolution and Human Behavior, 34,* 273–279.

Leland, H. 1992. Insider Trading: Should It Be Prohibited? *The Journal of Political Economy, 100,* 859–887.

Lennie, P. 2003. The Cost of Cortical Computation. *Current Biology, 13,* 493–497.

Levenson, R. W. 1992. Autonomic Nervous System Differences Among Emotions. *Psychological Science, 3,* 23–27.

———. 1999. The Intrapersonal Functions of Emotion. *Cognition and Emotion, 13,* 481–504.

Levine, D. 1991. *Inside Out: An Insider's Account of Wall Street.* New York: G. P. Putnam's Sons.

Levine, E. E., & Schweitzer, M. E. 2014. Are Liars Ethical? On the Tension Between Benevolence and Honesty. *Journal of Experimental Social Psychology, 53,* 107–117.

———. 2015. Prosocial Lies: When Deception Breeds Trust. *Organizational Behavior and Human Decision Processes, 126,* 88–106.

Levitt, A. 1922. Extent and Function of the Doctrine of Mens Rea. *Illinois Law Review, 17,* 578–595.

Levitt, S. D. 1998. Why Do Increased Arrest Rates Appear to Reduce Crime: Deterrence, Incapacitation, or Measurement Error? *Economic Inquiry, 36,* 353–372.

———. 2002. Deterrence. In J. Q. Wilson & J. Petersilia (Eds.), *Crime: Public Policies for Crime Control,* 435–450. Oakland, CA: ICS Press.

Levitt, S. D., & List, J. A. 2007. What Do Laboratory Experiments Measuring Social Preferences Reveal About the Real World? *The Journal of Economic Perspectives, 21,* 153–174.

Levitt, T. 1958. Are Advertising and Marketing Corrupting Society? *Advertising Age,* October, 89–92.

Lewis, M. 2015. *Flash Boys.* New York: W. W. Norton & Company.

Lieberman, M. D. 2000. Intuition : A Social Cognitive Neuroscience Approach. *Psychological Bulletin, 126,* 109–137.

———. 2007. Social Cognitive Neuroscience: A Review of Core Processes. *Annual Review of Psychology, 58,* 259–289.

Liman, A. 1998. *Lawyer: A Life of Counsel and Controversy.* New York: PublicAffairs.

Lindesmith, A. R. 1954. Review of Other People's Money: A Study in the Social Psychology of Embezzlement by Donald R. Cressey. *The Annals of the American Academy of Political and Social Science, 291,* 180.

Lipartito, K., & Morii, Y. 2010. Rethinking the Separation of Ownership from Management in American History. *Seattle University Law Review, 33,* 1025–1063.

Liu, Q., & Lu, Z. 2007. Corporate Governance and Earnings Management in the Chinese Listed Companies: A Tunneling Perspective. *Journal of Corporate Finance, 13,* 881–906.

Lo, A. W., & Repin, D. V. 2002. The Psychophysiology of Real-Time Financial Risk Processing. *Journal of Cognitive Neuroscience, 14,* 323–339.

Loewenstein, G. 1996. Behavioral Decision Theory and Business Ethics: Skewed Trade-Offs Between Self and Others. In D. Messick & A. Tenbrunsel (Eds.), *Codes of Conduct: Behavioral Research into Business Ethics,* 214–227. New York: Russell Sage Foundation.

Loewenstein, G., & Thaler, R. H. 1989. Anomalies: Intertemporal Choice. *Journal of Economic Perspectives, 3,* 181–193.

Loftus, E., & Ketcham, K. 1991. *Witness for the Defense.* New York: St. Martin's Press.

Lombroso, C. 1895–1896. Criminal Anthropology: Its Origins and Application. In *The Forum* (Vol. XX, 33–49). New York: The Forum Publishing Co.

———. 1911. *Criminal Man According to the Classification of Cesare Lombroso.* New York: G. P. Putnam's Sons.

Lonigan, E. 1929. Wanted: A New Criticism of Business. *The New Republic,* June 26.

Lord, C. G., Ross, L., & Lepper, M. R. 1979. Biased Assimilation and Attitude Polarization: The Effects of Prior Theories on Subsequently Considered Evidence. *Journal of Personality and Social Psychology, 37,* 2098–2109.

Louis, M. R. 1986. Sourcing Workplace Cultures: Why, When, and How. In *Gaining Control of the Corporate Culture,* 126–136. San Francisco: Jossey-Bass Publishers.

Love, M. C., Roberts, J., & Klingele, C. 2013. *Collateral Consequences of Criminal Convictions.* Washington, DC: NACDL Press.

Lucas, P., & Sheeran, A. 2006. Asperger's Syndrome and the Eccentricity and Genius of Jeremy Bentham. *Journal of Bentham Studies, 8,* 1–37.

MacCoun, R. J. 1993. Drugs and the Law: A Psychological Analysis of Drug Prohibition. *Psychological Bulletin, 113,* 497–512.

Macey, J. 2013. *The Death of Corporate Reputation.* Upper Saddle River, NJ: FT Press.

MacKay, M. 2013. *Impeccable Connections: The Rise and Fall of Richard Whitney.* New York: Brick Tower Press.

Maier, N. R. F. 1931. Reasoning in Humans. *Journal of Comparative Psychology, 12,* 181–194.

Mann, H., Garcia-Rada, X., Houser, D., & Ariely, D. 2014. Everybody Else Is Doing It: Exploring Social Transmission of Lying Behavior. *PloS ONE, 9.*

Mann, K., Wheeler, S., & Sarat, A. 1980. Sentencing the White-Collar Offender. *American Criminal Law Review, 17,* 479–500.

Manne, H. 1966a. In Defense of Insider Trading. *Harvard Business Review,* November-December, 113–122.

———. 1966b. *Insider Trading and the Stock Market.* New York: Free Press.

———. 1967. What's So Bad About Insider Trading? *Challenge, 15,* 14–16, 42.

Mannheim, H. 1949. White Collar Crime by Edwin H. Sutherland. *Annals of the American Academy of Political and Social Science, 266,* 243–244.

Manove, M. 1989. The Harm from Insider Trading and Informed Speculation. *Quarterly Journal of Economics,* 823–845.

March, J. 1994. *A Primer on Decision Making: How Decisions Happen.* New York: Simon and Schuster.

Marcus, G. 2004. *The Birth of the Mind.* New York: Basic Books.

Margolis, H. 1987. *Patterns, Thinking, and Cognition: A Theory of Judgment.* Chicago: University of Chicago Press.

Markham, J. 2002. *A Financial History of the United States.* Armonk, NY: M. E. Sharpe.

———. 2006. *A Financial History of Modern U.S. Corporate Scandals.* Armonk, NY: M. E. Sharpe.

Marlowe, F. W. 2005. Hunter-Gatherers and Human Evolution. *Evolutionary Anthropology: Issues, News, and Reviews, 14,* 54–67.

Marsh, A. A., Stoycos, S. A., Brethel-Haurwitz, K. M., Robinson, P., VanMeter, J. W., & Cardinale, E. M. 2014. Neural and Cognitive Characteristics of Extraordinary Altruists. *Proceedings of the National Academy of Sciences, 111,* 15036–15041.

Marshall, S. L. 1947. *Men Against Fire: The Problem of Battle Command in Future War.* Washington, DC: Combat Forces Press.

Masserman, J., Wechkin, S., & Terris, W. 1964. "Altruistic" Behavior in Rhesus Monkeys. *American Journal of Psychiatry, 171,* 584–585.

Mast, M. S., Jonas, K., & Hall, J. A. 2009. Give a Person Power and He or She Will Show Interpersonal Sensitivity: The Phenomenon and Its Why and When. *Journal of Personality and Social Psychology, 97,* 835–850.

Matthews, A. F. 1971. Criminal Prosecutions Under the Federal Securities Laws and Related Statutes: The Nature and Development of SEC Criminal Cases. *George Washington Law Review, 39,* 901–970.

Matthews, M. E. 2001. What Has Changed for IRS Criminal Investigation and Our Relationship with the Department of Justice? *IRS Reorganization and Tax Prosecutions, 49,* 1–4.

Mayer, M. 1992. *Stealing the Market: How the Giant Brokerage Firms, with Help from the SEC, Stole the Stock Market from Investors.* New York: Basic Books.

Mayer, R. 1989. *The Consumer Movement: Guardians of the Marketplace.* Boston: Twayne Publishers.

Mayo, A., & Nohria, N. 2005. *In Their Time: The Greatest Business Leaders of the Twentieth Century.* Boston: Harvard Business School Publishing.

McCarthy, B. 2002. New Economics of Sociological Criminology. *Annual Review of Sociology, 28,* 417–442.

McCraw, T. (Ed.). 1981. *Regulation in Perspective: Historical Essays.* Cambridge, MA: Harvard University Press.

McDonald, D. 2013. *The Firm.* New York: Simon and Schuster.

McDonald, N. M., & Messinger, D. S. 2011. The Development of Empathy: How, When, and Why. In J. J. Sanguineti, A. Acerbi, & J. A. Lombo (Eds.), *Moral Behavior and Free Will,* 333–360. Rome: IF Press.

McGee, R. W. 2007. Two Approaches to Examining the Ethics of Insider Trading. Working Paper.

McLean, B., & Elkind, P. 2003. *The Smartest Guys in the Room: The Amazing Rise and Scandalous Fall of Enron.* New York: Portfolio.

McKenna, C. 2006. *The World's Newest Profession: Management Consulting in the Twentieth Century.* Cambridge: Cambridge University Press.

McMahon, T. 1975. *Report on the Teaching of Socio-Ethical Issues in Collegiate Schools of Business.* Chicago: Loyola University.

McPhee, C., & Orenstein, N. 2011. *Infinite Jest: Caricature and Satire from Leonardo to Levine.* New York: The Metropolitan Museum of Art.

Mead, N. L., Baumeister, R. F., Gino, F., Schweitzer, M. E., & Ariely, D. 2009. Too Tired to Tell the Truth: Self-Control Resource Depletion and Dishonesty. *Journal of Experimental Social Psychology, 45,* 594–597.

Mealey, L. 1995. The Sociobiology of Sociopathy: An Integrated Evolutionary Model. *Behavioral and Brain Sciences, 18,* 523–599.

Mearsheimer, J. 2011. *Why Leaders Lie: The Truth About Lying in International Politics.* Oxford: Oxford University Press.

Mercier, H., & Sperber, D. 2011. Why Do Humans Reason? Arguments for an Argumentative Theory. *The Behavioral and Brain Sciences, 34,* 57–111.

Merritt, A. C., Effron, D. A., & Monin, B. 2010. Moral Self-Licensing: When Being Good Frees Us to Be Bad. *Social and Personality Psychology Compass, 5,* 344–357.

Merton, R. K., & Ashley-Montagu, M. F. 1940. Crime and the Anthropologist. *American Anthropologist, 42,* 384–408.

Metcalfe, J., & Miscel, W. 1999. A Hot/Cool-System Analysis of Delay of Gratification: Dynamics of Willpower. *Psychological Review, 106,* 3–19.

Michael, R. T., & Becker, G. S. 1973. On the New Theory of Consumer Behavior. *The Swedish Journal of Economics, 75,* 378–396.

Micklethwait, J., & Woolridge, A. 2003. *The Company: A Short History of a Revolutionary Idea.* London: Weidenfeld & Nicolson.

Mihm, S. 2007. *A Nation of Counterfeiters: Capitalists, Con Men, and the Making of the United States*. Cambridge, MA: Harvard University Press.

Mikhail, J. 2007. Universal Moral Grammar: Theory, Evidence and the Future. *Trends in Cognitive Sciences, 11,* 143–152.

———. 2011. *Elements of Moral Cognition*. Cambridge: Cambridge University Press.

Milgram, S. 1963. Behavioral Study of Obedience. *Journal of Abnormal and Social Psychology, 67,* 371–378.

———. 1974. *Obedience to Authority: An Experimental View*. New York: Harper and Row.

Miller, A. G., Gordon, A. K., & Buddie, A. M. 1999. Accounting for Evil and Cruelty: Is to Explain to Condone? *Personality and Social Psychology Review, 3,* 254–268.

Miller, J. D., Lynam, D., & Leukefeld, C. 2003. Examining Antisocial Behavior Through the Lens of the Five Factor Model of Personality. *Aggressive Behavior, 29,* 497–514.

Minoura, Y. 1992. A Sensitive Period for the Incorporation of a Cultural Meaning System: A Study of Japanese Children Growing Up in the United States. *Ethos, 20,* 304–339.

Mintzberg, H. 1973. *The Nature of Managerial Work*. New York: Harper and Row.

———. 1975. The Manager's Job: Folklore and Fact. *Harvard Business Review*, July-August, 49–61.

———. 1989. *Mintzberg on Management*. New York: Free Press.

Mischel, W. 2014. *The Marshmellow Test*. New York: Little, Brown and Company.

Mischel, W., Ayduk, O., Berman, M. G., Casey, B. J., Gotlib, I. H., Jonides, J., Shoda, Y. 2011. "Willpower" over the Life Span: Decomposing Self-Regulation. *Social Cognitive and Affective Neuroscience, 6,* 252–256.

Mischel, W., Ebbesen, E. B., & Zeiss, A. R. 1972. Cognitive and Attentional Mechanisms in Delay of Gratification. *Journal of Personality and Social Psychology, 21,* 204–218.

Mitchell, W. C. 1918. Bentham's Felicific Calculus. *Political Science Quarterly, 33,* 161–183.

Mokhiber, R. 2013. Top 100 Corporate Criminals of the Decade. *Corporate Crime Reporter*, 1–56.

Morris, A. 1935. *Criminology*. New York: Longmans, Green and Co.

Moshman, D., & Geil, M. 1998. Collaborative Reasoning: Evidence for Collective Rationality. *Thinking & Reasoning, 4,* 231–248.

Mother Teresa. 1983. *Words to Love By*. Notre Dame, IN: Ave Maria Press.

Muraven, M., & Baumeister, R. F. 2000. Self-Regulation and Depletion of Limited Resources: Does Self-Control Resemble a Muscle? *Psychological Bulletin, 126,* 247–259.

Muraven, M., Tice, D. M., & Baumeister, R. F. 1998. Self-Control as Limited Resource: Regulatory Depletion Patterns. *Journal of Personality and Social Psychology, 74,* 774–789.

Murphy, P. R., & Dacin, M. T. 2011. Psychological Pathways to Fraud: Understanding and Preventing Fraud in Organizations. *Journal of Business Ethics, 101,* 601–618.

Myrseth, K. O. R., & Fishbach, A. 2009. Self-Control: A Function of Knowing When and How to Exercise Restraint. *Current Directions in Psychological Science, 18,* 247–252.

Nadel, M. V. 1971. *Politics of Consumer Protection*. Indianapolis: Bobbs-Merrill.

Nader, R. 1965. *Unsafe at Any Speed*. New York: Knightsbridge Publishing Company.

———. 1973. *The Consumer and Corporate Accountability*. New York: Harcourt Brace Jovanovich.

Nagy, D. M. 2011. Insider Trading, Congressional Officials, and Duties of Entrustment. *Boston University Law Review, 91,* 1105–1163.

Neal, C. 2014. *Taking Down the Lion*. New York: St. Martin's Press.

Neff, T., & Citrin, J. 1999. *Lessons from the Top: The Search for America's Best Business Leaders*. New York: Currency/ Doubleday.

Nesse, R. M. 1990. Evolutionary Explanations of Emotions. *Human Nature, 1,* 261–289.

Newman, D. 1957. Public Attitudes Toward a Form of White Collar Crime. *Social Problems, 4*, 228–232.

———. 1958a. Research Interviewing in Prison. *The Journal of Criminal Law, Criminology, and Political Science, 49*, 127–132.

———. 1958b. White-Collar Crime. *Law and Contemporary Problems, 23*, 735–753.

Newman, M. L., & Josephs, R. A. 2009. Testosterone as a Personality Variable. *Journal of Research in Personality, 43*, 258–259.

Nickerson, R. S. 1998. Confirmation Bias: A Ubiquitous Phenomenon in Many Guises. *Review of General Psychology, 2*, 175–220.

Nisbett, R. E., & Wilson, T. D. 1977. Telling More Than We Can Know: Verbal Reports on Mental Processes. *Psychological Review, 84*, 231–259.

Niskanen, W. 2005. *After Enron: Lessons for Public Policy*. Lanham, MD: Rowman & Littlefield.

Noonan, J. T. 1984. *Bribes*. Berkeley: University of California Press.

Nørretranders, T. 1998. *The User Illusion: Cutting Consciousness Down to Size*. New York: Viking.

Norton, E. H. 1989. Bargaining and the Ethic of Process. *New York University Law Review, 64*, 493–577.

Nyhan, B., Reifler, J., Richey, S., & Freed, G. L. 2014. Effective Messages in Vaccine Promotion: A Randomized Trial. *Pediatrics, 133*, e835–e842.

O'Hare, J. 1998. The Resurrection of the Dodo: The Unfortunate Re-emergence of the Puffery Defense in Private Securities Fraud Actions. *Ohio State Law Journal, 59*, 1697–1740.

Oakley, B. 2007. *Evil Genes*. Amherst, NY: Prometheus Books.

Oates, W. E., & Schwab, R. M. 2015. The Window Tax: A Case Study in Excess Burden. *Journal of Economic Perspectives, 29*, 163–180.

Obermaier, O. G., & Morvillo, R. G. 1990. *White Collar Crime: Business and Regulatory Offenses*. New York: Law Journal Seminars-Press.

Ogren, R. 1973. The Ineffectiveness of the Criminal Sanction in Fraud and Corruption Cases. *American Criminal Law Review, 11*, 959–988.

Ohlsson, C., Wallaschofski, H., Lunetta, K. L., Stolk, L., Perry, J. R. B., Koster, A., . . . Haring, R. 2011. Genetic Determinants of Serum Testosterone Concentrations in Men. *PLoS Genetics, 7*, 1–11.

Olson, J., & Dover, P. 1978. Cognitive Effects of Deceptive Advertising. *Journal of Marketing Research, 15*, 29–38.

Oppenheimer, J. 2009. *Madoff with the Money*. Hoboken, NJ: Wiley.

Ordower, H. 2010. The Culture of Tax Avoidance. *Saint Louis University Law Journal, 55*, 47–128.

Ornstein, R., & Ehrlich, P. 1989. *New World New Mind: Moving Toward Conscious Evolution*. New York: Doubleday.

Ostas, D. T. 2007. When Fraud Pays: Executive Self-Dealing and the Failure of Self-Restraint. *American Business Law Journal, 44*, 571–601.

Over, H., & Carpenter, M. 2009. Eighteen-Month-Old Infants Show Increased Helping Following Priming With Affiliation. *Psychological Science, 20*, 1189–1193.

Padfield, S. J. 2008. Is Puffery Material to Investors? Maybe We Should Ask Them. *University of Pennsylvania Journal of Business and Employment Law, 10*, 339–381.

Paine, L. S. 1994. Managing for Organizational Integrity. *Harvard Business Review*, March-April, 106–117.

Pakaluk, M., & Cheffers, M. 2011. *Accounting Ethics*. Sutton, MA: Allen David Press.

Pamental, G. 1988. *Ethics in the Business Curriculum: A Preliminary Survey of Undergraduate Business Programs.* Lanham, MD: University Press of America.

Panizzon, M. S., Hauger, R., Jacobson, K. C., Eaves, L. J., York, T. P., Prom-Wormley, E., & Kremen, W. S. 2013. Genetic and Environmental Influences of Daily and Intra-Individual Variation in Testosterone Levels in Middle-Aged Men. *Psychoneuroendocrinology, 38,* 2163–2172.

Parfet, W. U. 2000. Accounting Subjectivity and Earnings Management: A Preparer Perspective. *Accounting Horizons, 14,* 481–488.

Parkin, D., Appleby, J., & Maynard, A. 2013. Economics: The Biggest Fraud Ever Perpetrated on the World? *The Lancet, 382,* 11–15.

Parkinson, B., Fischer, A., & Manstead, A. S. R. 2005. *Emotion in Social Relations.* New York: Psychology Press.

Partnoy, F. 2009. *The Match King: Ivar Krenger, the Financial Genius Behind a Century of Wall Street Scandals.* New York: PublicAffairs.

Paternoster, R. 1987. The Deterrent Effect of the Perceived Certainty and Severity of Punishment: A Review of the Evidence and Issues. *Justice Quarterly, 4,* 173–217.

Paternoster, R., & Iovanni, L. 1986. The Deterrent Effect of Perceived Severity: A Reexamination. *Social Forces, 64,* 751–777.

Paternoster, R., Saltzman, L. E., Waldo, G. P., & Chiricos, T. G. 1983. Perceived Risk and Social Control: Do Sanctions Really Deter? *Law & Society Review, 17,* 457–479.

Paternoster, R., & Simpson, S. S. 1993. A Rational Choice Theory of Corporate Crime. In R. V. Clarke & M. Felson (Eds.), *Routine Activity and Rational Choice,* 37–58. New Brunswick: Transaction Publishers.

———. 1996. Sanction Threats and Appeals to Morality: Testing a Rational Choice Model of Corporate Crime. *Law & Society Review, 30,* 549–584.

Paulhus, D. L. 2014. Toward a Taxonomy of Dark Personalities. *Current Directions in Psychological Science, 23,* 421–426.

Paxton, J. M., & Greene, J. D. 2010. Moral Reasoning: Hints and Allegations. *Topics in Cognitive Science, 2,* 511–527.

Paxton, J. M., Ungar, L., & Greene, J. D. 2011. Reflection and Reasoning in Moral Judgment. *Cognitive Science, 36,* 163–177.

Penn, W. Y., & Collier, B. D. 1985. Current Research in Moral Development as a Decision Support System. *Journal of Business Ethics, 4,* 131–136.

Peppet, S. R. 2002. Can Saints Negotiate? A Brief Introduction to the Problems of Perfect Ethics in Bargaining. *Harvard Negotiation Law Review, 7, 83,* 92–95.

Pettegree, A. 2014. *The Invention of News: How the World Came to Know About Itself.* London: Yale University Press.

Pfaff, D. 2015. *The Altruistic Brain.* Oxford: Oxford University Press.

Pfeffer, J. 2015. *Leadership BS: Fixing Workplaces and Careers One Truth at a Time.* New York: HarperCollins.

Phin, M., Stimpson, A., Moreno, V., & Birtwistle, L. 2012. *European Banks: LIBOR—Sizing the Potential Damage.* Keefe, Bruyette & Woods.

Pinker, S. 1997. *How the Mind Works.* New York: Norton.

———. 2002. *The Blank Slate.* New York: Viking.

———. 2004. Why Nature and Nurture Won't Go Away. *Daedalus, 133,* 5–17.

———. 2011. *The Better Angels of Our Nature.* New York: Viking.

Piper, T. E., Gentile, M., & Parks, S. D. 1993. *Can Ethics Be Taught? Perspectives, Challenges, and Approaches at Harvard Business School.* Boston: Harvard Business Press.

Piquero, A. R., Jennings, W. G., & Farrington, D. P. 2010. On the Malleability of Self-Control: Theoretical and Policy Implications Regarding a General Theory of Crime. *Justice Quarterly, 27,* 803–834.

Piquero, A. R., & Tibbetts, S. G. 2002. *Rational Choice and Criminal Behavior.* New York: Routledge.

Piquero, N. L., Exum, M. L., & Simpson, S. S. 2005. Integrating the Desire-for-Control and Rational Choice in a Corporate Crime Context. *Justice Quarterly, 22,* 252–280.

Plato. 2013. *Republic, Volume I, Books 1–5,* Ed. C. Emlyn-Jones & W. Preddy. Cambridge, MA: Harvard University Press.

Podgor, E. S. 2003. Extraterritorial Criminal Jurisdiction: Replacing "Objective Territoriality" with "Defensive Territoriality." *Studies in Law, Politics and Society, 28,* 117–135.

———. 2007a. Throwing Away the Key. *Yale Law Journal, 116,* 279–285.

———. 2007b. White Collar Crime: A Letter from the Future. *Ohio State Journal of Criminal Law, 5,* 247–255.

———. 2016. "White Collar Crime": Still Hazy After All These Years." *Georgia Law Review, 50.*

Podgor, E., & Dervan, L. 2016. "White-Collar Crime": Still Hazy After All These Years. *Georgia Law Review, 50,* forthcoming.

Ponemon, L. A. 1992. Ethical Reasoning and Selection-Socialization in Accounting. *Accounting, Organizations and Society, 17,* 239–258.

Ponzi, C. 2009. *The Rise of Mr. Ponzi.* Austin, TX: Despair, Inc.

Porter, G. 1992. *The Rise of Big Business, 1860–1920.* Arlington Heights, IL: Harlan Davidson, Inc.

Posner, B. Z., & Schmidt, W. H. 1987. Ethics in American Companies: A Managerial Perspective. *Journal of Business Ethics, 6,* 383–391.

Posner, R. A. 1980. Optimal Sentences for White-Collar Criminals. *American Criminal Law Review, 17,* 409–418.

———. 2011. *Economic Analysis of Law* (8th ed.). New York: Aspen Publishers.

Posner, R. A., & Rasmusen, E. B. 1999. Creating and Enforcing Norms, with Special Reference to Sanctions. *International Review of Law and Economics, 19,* 369–382.

Poveda, T. 1992. White-Collar Crime and the Justice Department: The Institutionalization of a Concept. *Crime, Law and Social Change, 17,* 235–252.

Power, F. C., Higgins, A., & Kohlberg, L. 1989. *Lawrence Kohlberg's Approach to Moral Education.* New York: Columbia University Press.

Pozen, R. C. 2009. Is It Fair to Blame Fair Value Accounting for the Financial Crisis? *Harvard Business Review,* November, 85–92.

Prentice, R. A. 2007. Ethical Decision Making: More Needed Than Good Intentions. *Financial Analysts Journal, 63,* 17–30.

Preston, I. 1998. Puffery and Other "Loophole" Claims: How the Law's "Don't Ask, Don't Tell" Policy Condones Fraudulent Falsity in Advertising. *Journal of Law and Commerce, 18,* 49–114.

Preston, S. D., & de Waal, F. B. M. 2002. Empathy: Its Ultimate and Proximate Bases. *Behavioral and Brain Sciences, 25,* 1–71.

Pyle, D. 1983. *The Economics of Crime and Law Enforcement.* New York: St. Martin's Press.

Rabbinical Council of America. 1993. *Resolution: Matter of Pre-Nuptial Agreements and Recalcitrant Spouses.* Pre-Nuptial Agreements and Recalcitrant Spouses, June 1.

Rabin, M., & Thaler, R. H. 2001. Anomalies: Risk Aversion. *Journal of Economic Perspectives, 15,* 219–232.

Rabin, R. L. 1972. Agency Criminal Referrals in the Federal System: An Empirical Study of Prosecutorial Discretion. *Stanford Law Review, 24,* 1036–1091.

Radley, D. C., Finkelstein, S. N., & Stafford, R. S. 2006. Off-Label Prescribing Among Office-Based Physicians. *Archives of Internal Medicine, 166,* 1021–1026.

Radzinowicz, L. 1948. *A History of English Criminal Law and Its Administration from 1950* (Volume 1). London: Stevens and Sons.

Rafter, N. 1997. *Creating Born Criminals.* Urbana: University of Illinois Press.

———. 2008. *The Criminal Brain.* New York: New York University Press.

Raghavan, A. 2013. *The Billionaire's Apprentice.* New York: Business Plus.

Raine, A. 1993. *The Psychopathology of Crime.* New York: Academic Press.

———. 2002. Biosocial Studies of Antisocial and Violent Behavior in Children and Adults: A Review. *Journal of Abnormal Child Psychology, 30,* 311–326.

———. 2013. *The Anatomy of Violence.* New York: Pantheon Books.

Raine, A., Brennan, P., & Mednick, S. A. 1994. Birth Complications Combined with Early Maternal Rejection at Age 1 Year Predispose to Violent Crime at Age 18 Years. *Archives of General Psychiatry, 51,* 984–988.

Raine, A., Laufer, W. S., Yang, Y., Narr, K. L., Thompson, P., & Toga, A. W. 2012. Increased Executive Functioning, Attention, and Cortical Thickness in White-Collar Criminals. *Human Brain Mapping, 33,* 2932–4290.

Rajgopal, S., & White, R. 2015. Cheating When in The Hole: The Case of New York City Taxis. Working Paper.

Rakoff, J. J. 2014. Why Have No High Level Executives Been Prosecuted in Connection with the Financial Crisis? *New York Review of Books,* January.

———. 2015. Justice Deferred Is Justice Denied. *New York Review of Books,* February.

Ramamoorti, S. 2008. The Psychology and Sociology of Fraud: Integrating the Behavioral Sciences Component into Fraud and Forensic Accounting Curricula. *Issues in Accounting Education, 23,* 521–533.

Ramamoorti, S., Morrison, D., Koletar, J., & Pope, K. 2013. *A.B.C.'s of Behavioral Forensics.* Hoboken, NJ: John Wiley & Sons.

Ramanna, K. 2015. *Political Standards: Corporate Interest, Ideology, and Leadership in the Shaping of Accounting Rules for the Market Economy.* Chicago: University of Chicago Press.

Rappleye, C. 2010. *Robert Morris: Financier of the American Revolution.* New York: Simon and Schuster.

Reed, J. P., & Reed, R. S. 1975. "Doctor, Lawyer, Indian Chief": Old Rhymes and New on White Collar Crime. *International Journal of Criminology and Penology, 3,* 279–293.

Reimann, M., & Bechara, A. 2010. The Somatic Marker Framework as a Neurological Theory of Decision-Making: Review, Conceptual Comparisons, and Future Neuroeconomics Research. *Journal of Economic Psychology, 31,* 767–776.

Rest, J. R. 1982. A Psychologist Looks at the Teaching of Ethics. *The Hastings Center Report, 12,* 29–36.

———. 1983. Morality. In *Handbook of Child Psychology* (4th ed., 556–629). New York: Wiley.

———. 1986. *Moral Development.* New York: Praeger.

———. 1988. Can Ethics Be Taught in Professional Schools? The Psychological Research. *Easier Said Than Done,* 22–26.

Rest, J. R., Power, C., & Brabeck, M. 1988. Lawrence Kohlberg (1927–1987). *American Psychologist, 43,* 399–400.

Rettig, S., & Pasamanick, B. 1959. Changes in Moral Values as a Function of Adult Socialization. *Social Problems, 7,* 117–125.

Reuter, E. B. 1939. Crime and the Man by Earnest Albert Hooton. *Journal of Sociology, 45,* 123–126.

Rhee, S. H., & Waldman, I. D. 2002. Genetic and Environmental Influences on Antisocial Behavior: A Meta-Analysis of Twin and Adoption Studies. *Psychological Bulletin, 128,* 490–529.

Richards, J. 2012. *Federal Prison: A Comprehensive Survival Guide.* SK Enterprises.

Richman, D. 2013. Federal White Collar Sentencing in the United States: A Work in Progress. *Law and Contemporary Problems, 76,* 53–73.

Riedweg, C. 2005. *Pythagoras: His Life, Teaching, and Influence.* Ithaca, NY: Cornell University Press.

Rijsenbilt, A., & Commandeur, H. 2013. Narcissus Enters the Courtroom: CEO Narcissism and Fraud. *Journal of Business Ethics, 117,* 412–429.

Ritchie, D. 1980. *James M. Landis: Dean of the Regulators.* Cambridge, MA: Harvard University Press.

Roberts, R. 2014. *How Adam Smith Can Change Your Life.* New York: Penguin.

Robinson, P. H., & Darley, J. M. 1995. *Justice, Liability, and Blame: Community Views and the Criminal Law.* Boulder, CO: Westview Press.

———. 1997. The Utility of Desert. *Northwestern University Law Review, 91,* 453–499.

Robitscher, J. 1973. *Eugenic Sterilization.* Springfield, IL: Charles Thomas.

Ross, B. 2009. *The Madoff Chronicles: Inside the Secret World of Bernie and Ruth.* New York: Hyperion.

Ross, E. A. 1907. *Sin and Society.* Boston: Houghton Mifflin Company.

Ross, H. L. 1982. *Deterring the Drinking Driver: Legal Policy and Social Control.* Lexington, MA: Lexington Books.

———. 1984. Social Control Through Deterrence: Drinking-and-Driving Laws. *Annual Review of Sociology, 10,* 21–35.

Ross, L. 1977. The Intuitive Psychologist and His Shortcomings: Distortions in the Attribution Process. In L. Berkowitz (Ed.), *Advances in Experimental Social Psychology,* 173–214. New York: Academic Press.

Ross, L., & Nisbett, R. E. 1991. *The Person and the Situation: Perspectives of Social Psychology.* Philadelphia, PA: Temple University Press.

Rostain, T., & Regan, M. C. 2014. *Confidence Games: Lawyers, Accountants, and the Tax Shelter Industry.* Cambridge, MA: MIT Press.

Rotfeld, H., & Rotzoll, K. 1980. Is Advertising Puffery Believed? *Journal of Advertising, 9,* 16–20.

Rousseau, P. L., & Sylla, R. 2005. Emerging Financial Markets and Early US Growth. *Explorations in Economic History, 42,* 1–26.

Rowan, C. T., & Mazie, D. M. 1980. New Look at the FBI. *Reader's Digest,* 142–146.

Rubin, R. 2000. *Rudy, Rudy, Rudy.* New York: Holmes & Meier.

Ruble, R. J. 2003. *The Professional Responsibilities of a Tax Lawyer in the Context of Corporate Tax Shelters.* Practising Law Institute.

Ruedy, N. E., Moore, C., Gino, F., & Schweitzer, M. E. 2013. The Cheater's High: The Unexpected Affective Benefits of Unethical Behavior. *Journal of Personality and Social Psychology, 105,* 531–548.

Salter, M. 2008. *Innovation Corrupted: The Origins and Legacy of Enron's Collapse.* Cambridge, MA: Harvard University Press.

Sandell, L. 2011. *Truth and Consequences: Life Inside the Madoff Family.* New York: Little, Brown and Company.

Santoro, M., & Strauss, R. 2013. *Wall Street Values.* New York: Cambridge University Press.

Schauer, F. 2015. *The Force of Law.* Cambridge, MA: Harvard University Press.

Schein, E. H. 2010. *Organizational Culture and Leadership*. San Francisco: John Wiley & Sons.

Schiffrin, A. 2002. Avoiding Future Enrons. *Columbia Journalism Review, 40*, 29.

Schmitthoff, M. 1939. The Origin of the Joint-Stock Company. *The University of Toronto Law Journal, 3*, 74–96.

Scholes, M. S., Wolfson, M. A., Erickson, M. M., Hanlon, M. L., Maydew, E. L., & Shevlin, T. J. 2009. *Taxes and Business Strategy: A Planning Approach* (4th ed.). Upper Saddle River, NJ: Pearson/Prentice-Hall.

Schotland, R. A. 1967. Unsafe at Any Price: A Reply to Manne, Insider Trading and the Stock Market. *Virginia Law Review, 53*, 1425–1478.

Schouten, R., & Silver, J. 2012. *Almost a Psychopath*. Silver City, MN: Hazelden.

Schrand, C. M., & Zechman, S. L. C. 2012. Executive Overconfidence and the Slippery Slope to Financial Misreporting. *Journal of Accounting and Economics, 53*, 311–329.

Schuessler, K. F. 1954. Review of Other People's Money: A Study in the Social Psychology of Embezzlement by Donald R. Cressey. *American Journal of Sociology, 59*, 604.

Schwarzkopf, S. 2005. They Do It with Mirrors: Advertising and British Cold War Consumer Politics. *Contemporary British History, 19*, 133–150.

Schwitzgebel, E. 2009. Do Ethicists Steal More Books? *Philosophical Psychology, 22*, 711–725.

Schwitzgebel, E., & Cushman, F. 2015. Philosophers' Biased Judgments Persist Despite Training, Expertise and Reflection. *Cognition, 141*, 127–137.

Schwitzgebel, E., & Rust, J. 2014. The Behavior of Ethicists. Working Paper.

Scofield, S. B 1997. *Re-Examination of the Application of Cognitive Development Theory to the Study of Ethics and Socialization in the Accounting Profession*. Dissertation.

Seligman, J. 2003. *The Transformation of Wall Street: A History of the Securities and Exchange Commission and Modern Corporate Finance* (3rd ed.). New York: Aspen Publishers.

Seligman, M. 1970. On the Generality of the Laws of Learning. *Psychological Review, 77*, 406–418.

Sellers, J. G., Mehl, M. R., & Josephs, R. A. 2007. Hormones and Personality: Testosterone as a Marker of Individual Differences. *Journal of Research in Personality, 41*, 126–138.

Sellin, J. T. 1958. Pioneers in Criminology XV—Enrico Ferri (1856–1929). *Journal of Criminal Law and Criminology, 48*, 479–490.

Shah, A. K., & Ludwig, J. 2016. The Cognitive Accessibility of Crime: Behavioral Science and Criminal Behavior. Working Paper.

Shalvi, S., Gino, F., Barkan, R., & Ayal, S. 2015. Self-Serving Justifications: Doing Wrong and Feeling Moral. *Current Directions in Psychological Science, 24*, 125–130.

Shank, M. J. 2005. *The Impact of Moral Reasoning on the Performance of Salespeople*. Dissertation.

Shapiro, H. L. 1954. Earnest A. Hooton: 1887–1954. *Science, 119*, 861–862.

Shavitt, S. 1990. The Role of Attitude Objects in Attitude Functions. *Journal of Experimental Social Psychology, 26*, 124–148.

Shaw, B. 1922. Preface. In *English Prisons Under Local Government*, vii–lxxiii. London: Longmans, Green and Co.

Shaw, J., & Porter, S. 2015. Constructing Rich False Memories of Committing Crime. *Psychological Science, 26*, 291–301.

Sheldon, W. H. 1949. *Varieties of Delinquent Youth*. New York: Harper and Brothers.

———. 1954. *Atlas of Men*. New York: Harper.

Sheldon, W. H., Stevens, S., & Tucker, W. B. 1940. *The Varieties of Human Physique*. New York: Harper and Brothers.

Sheldon, W. H., & Tucker, W. B. 1938. The Anthrotyping Technique, unpublished manuscript, Harvard University, Cambridge, MA.

Shell, G. R. 1991.When Is It Legal to Lie in Negotiations? *Sloan Management Review, 32,* 93–101.

Sherman, S. 2002. Enron: Uncovering the Uncovered Story. *Columbia Journalism Review, 40,* 22–28.

Shermer, M. 2004. *The Science of Good and Evil.* New York: Times Books.

Shively, C. 1971. Chapter 4. In *The Collected Works of Lysander Spooner: Biography.* Weston, MA: M & S Press.

Shover, N., & Hochstetler, A. 2006. *Choosing White-Collar Crime.* Cambridge: Cambridge University Press.

Shu, L., Mazar, N., Gino, F., Ariely, D., & Bazerman, M. 2012. Signing at the Beginning Makes Ethics Salient and Decreases Dishonest Self-Reports in Comparison to Signing at the End. *Proceedings of the National Academy of Sciences, 109,* 15197–15200.

Shweder, R. A., Turiel, E., & Much, N. C. 1981. The Moral Intuitions of the Child. In J. H. Flavell & L. Ross (Eds.), *Social Cognitive Development: Frontiers and Possible Futures,* 288–305. Cambridge: Cambridge University Press.

Silverglate, H. 2009. *Three Felonies a Day: How Feds Target the Innocent.* New York: Encounter Books.

Simmons, J. P., Nelson, L. D., & Simonsohn, U. 2011. False-Positive Psychology: Undisclosed Flexibility in Data Collection and Analysis Allows Presenting Anything as Significant. *Psychological Science, 22,* 1359–1366.

Simon, D., & Eitzen, D. S. 1990. *Elite Deviance.* Boston: Allyn and Bacon.

Simon, D., & Swart, S. 1984. The Justice Department Focuses on White Collar Crime. *Crime & Delinquency, 30,* 107–119.

Simon, H. A. 1956a. Rationality and Administrative Decision Making. In *Models of Man,* 196–206. London: John Wiley & Sons.

———. 1956b. Rational Choice and the Structure of the Environment. *Psychological Review, 63,* 196–198.

———. 1990. A Mechanism for Social Selection and Successful Altruism. *Science, 250,* 1665–1668.

Simons, R. 2010. *Seven Strategy Questions: A Simple Approach for Better Execution.* Boston: Harvard Business Review Press.

Simpson, E. 1974. Moral Development Research. *The Journal of Social Issues, 29,* 81–106.

Simpson, S. S. 1992. Corporate Crime Deterrence and Corporate Control Policies: Views from the Inside. In K. Schlegel & D. Weisburd (Eds.), *White-Collar Crime Reconsidered,* 289–308. Boston: Northeastern University Press.

———. 2013. White-Collar Crime: A Review of Recent Developments and Promising Directions for Future Research. *Annual Review of Sociology, 39,* 309–331.

Singer, P. 1974. Sidgwick and Reflective Equilibrium. *The Monist, 58,* 490–517.

———. 2005. Ethics and Intuitions. *The Journal of Ethics, 9,* 331–352.

———. 2011. *Practical Ethics.* New York: Cambridge University Press.

Skszek, S. L. 2004. *Actual Speeds on the Roads Compared to the Posted Limits.* Arizona Department of Transportation. Final Report 551.

Slovic, P. 2007. "If I Look at the Mass I Will Never Act": Psychic Numbing and Genocide. *Judgment and Decision Making, 2,* 79–95.

Slovic, P., & Västfjäll, D. 2010. Affect, Moral Intuition, and Risk. *Psychological Inquiry, 21,* 387–398.

Small, D. A., Loewenstein, G., & Slovic, P. 2007. Sympathy and Callousness: The Impact of Deliberative Thought on Donations to Identifiable and Statistical Victims. *Organizational Behavior and Human Decision Processes, 102,* 143–153.

Smith, A. 1761. *The Theory of Moral Sentiments* (2nd ed.). London: A. Millar.

Smith, A., Lohrenz, T., King, J., Montague, P. R., & Camerer, C. F. 2014. Irrational Exuberance and Neural Crash Warning Signals During Endogenous Experimental Market Bubbles. *Proceedings of the National Academy of Sciences, 111,* 10503–10508.

Smith, N. C., Simpson, S. S., & Huang, C. 2007. Why Managers Fail to Do the Right Thing: An Empirical Study of Unethical and Illegal Conduct. *Business Ethics Quarterly, 17,* 633–667.

Smith, R. A. 1961. The Incredible Electrical Conspiracy. *Fortune,* April, 132–180.

———. 1961. The Incredible Electrical Conspiracy-Part II. *Fortune,* May, 161–224.

Smith, R., & Emshwiller, J. 2003. *24 Days: How Two Wall Street Journal Reporters Uncovered the Lies That Destroyed Faith in Corporate America.* New York: HarperBusiness.

Snyder, C., Higgins, R. L., & Stucky, R. J. 1983. *Excuses: Masquerades in Search of Grace.* New York: Wiley.

Sober, E. 1988. What Is Evolutionary Altruism? *Canadian Journal of Philosophy, Supplement,* 75–99.

Solomon, D. H., & Soltes, E. F. 2015. What Are We Meeting For? The Consequences of Private Meetings with Investors. *Journal of Law and Economics, 58,* 325–355.

Solomons, L. M., & Stein, G. 1896. Normal Motor Automatism. *Psychological Review, 3,* 492–512.

Soltes, E. F. 2014. Private Interaction Between Firm Management and Sell-Side Analysts. *Journal of Accounting Research, 52,* 245–272.

Sonnenfeld, J., & Lawrence, P. R. 1978. Why Do Companies Succumb to Price Fixing? *Harvard Business Review,* July-August.

Sorenson, R. C. 1950. White Collar Crime by Edwin H. Sutherland. *Journal of Criminal Law and Criminology, 41,* 80–82.

Spiller, R. 1988. S. L. A. Marshall and the Ratio of Fire. *The RUSI Journal, 134,* 63–71.

Sporkin, S. 2003. Securities and Exchange Commission Historical Society Interview with Stanley Sporkin.

———. 2004. The Foreign Corrupt Practices Act-Then and Now. Washington, DC: 12th National Foreign Corrupt Practices Act Conference.

Srinivasan, S. 2004. Consequences of Financial Reporting Failure for Outside Directors: Evidence from Accounting Restatements and Audit Committee Members. *Journal of Accounting Research, 43,* 291–334.

Starkman, D. 2008. Boiler Room. *Columbia Journalism Review, 47,* 49–53.

Steffensmeier, D. J., Schwartz, J., & Roche, M. 2013. Gender and Twenty-First-Century Corporate Crime: Female Involvement and the Gender Gap in Enron-Era Corporate Frauds. *American Sociological Review, 78,* 448–476.

Stein, G. 1898. Cultivated Motor Automatism; A Study of Character in its Relation to Attention. *Psychological Review, 5,* 295–306.

Stice, J., & Stice, E. 2014. *Intermediate Accounting.* Mason, OH: Cengage Learning.

Stickney, C., Weil, R., Schipper, K., & Francis, J. 2010. *Financial Accounting: An Introduction to Concepts, Methods, and Uses* (13th ed.). Mason, OH: South-Western Cengage Learning.

Stigall, S. 1995. Preventing Absurd Application of RICO. *Temple Law Review, 68,* 223–243.

Stigler, G. 1950. The Development of Utility Theory. I. *Journal of Political Economy, 58,* 307–327.

Stirrat, M., & Perrett, D. I. 2010. Valid Facial Cues to Cooperation and Trust: Male Facial Width and Trustworthiness. *Psychological Science, 21,* 349–354.

Stout, L. A. 1990. Are Takeover Premiums Really Premiums? Market Price, Fair Value, and Corporate Law. *Yale Law Journal, 99,* 1235–1296.

Strudler, A. 1995. On the Ethics of Deception in Negotiation. *Business Ethics Quarterly, 5,* 805–822.

Sunstein, C. R. 2005. Moral Heuristics. *Behavioral and Brain Sciences, 28,* 531–573.

Sutherland, E. 1934. *Principles of Criminology.* Chicago: J. B. Lippincott.

———. 1940. White-Collar Criminality. *American Sociological Review, 5,* 1–12.

———. 1945. Is "White Collar Crime" Crime? *American Sociological Review, 10,* 132–139.

———. 1948. Crime of Corporations. *The Sutherland Papers,* 78–96.

———. 1949. *White Collar Crime.* New York: The Dryden Press.

———. 1951. Critique of Sheldon's Varieties of Delinquent Youth. *American Sociological Review, 16,* 10–13.

———. 1968. Crime of Corporations. In G. Geis (Ed.), *White-Collar Criminal.* New York: Atherton Press.

———. 1983. *White Collar Crime: The Uncut Version.* New Haven, CT: Yale University Press.

Sylla, R. 1998. U.S. Securities Markets and the Banking System, 1790–1840. *Federal Reserve Bank of St. Louis Review,* 83–98.

Tangney, J. P., Baumeister, R. F., & Boone, A. L. 2004. High Self-Control Predicts Good Adjustment, Less Pathology, Better Grades, and Interpersonal Success. *Journal of Personality, 72,* 271–324.

Tappan, P. W. 1947. Who Is the Criminal? *American Sociological Review, 12,* 96–102.

Tarde, G. 1962. *The Laws of Imitation* (2nd ed.). Gloucester, MA: Peter Smith.

Tavris, C., & Aronson, E. 2007. *Mistakes Were Made (But Not by Me).* Orlando: Harcourt, Inc.

Taylor, J. 2013. *Boardroom Scandal: The Criminalization of Company Fraud in Nineteenth-Century Britain.* Oxford: Oxford University Press.

Tellegen, A., Lykken, D. T., Bouchard, T. J., Wilcox, K. J., Segal, N. L., & Rich, S. 1988. Personality Similarity in Twins Reared Apart and Together. *Journal of Personality and Social Psychology, 54,* 1031–1039.

Temporary National Economic Committee. 1940. *Investigation of Concentration of Economic Power.* Washington, DC.

Tenbrunsel, A. E., & Messick, D. M. 1999. Sanctioning Systems, Decision Frames, and Cooperation. *Administrative Science Quarterly, 44,* 684–707.

———. 2004. Ethical Fading: The Role of Self-Deception in Unethical Behavior. *Social Justice Research, 17,* 223–236.

Tenbrunsel, A. E., & Smith-Crowe, K. 2008. Ethical Decision Making: Where We've Been and Where We're Going. *The Academy of Management Annals, 2,* 545–607.

Thaler, R. H. 1980. Toward a Positive Theory of Consumer Choice. *Journal of Economic Behavior and Organization, 1,* 39–60.

———. 2000. From Homo Economicus to Homo Sapiens. *Journal of Economic Perspectives, 14,* 133–141.

Thoma, S. 1985. On Improving the Relationship Between Moral Reasoning and External Criteria. Minneapolis: University of Minnesota.

Thoma, S. & Dong, Y. 2014. The Defining Issues Test of Moral Judgment Development. *Behavior Development Bulletin, 19,* 55–61.

Thomson, J. J. 1985. The Trolley Problem. *Yale Law Journal, 94,* 1395–1415.

———. 1986. *Rights, Restitution, and Risk: Essays in Moral Theory.* Cambridge, MA: Harvard University Press.

Thornburgh, D. 2003. *Where the Evidence Leads.* Pittsburgh: University of Pittsburgh Press.

Thornton, T. D. 2015. *My Adventures with Your Money: George Graham Rice and the Golden Age of the Con Artist.* New York: St. Martin's Press.

Toffler, B. 1986. *Tough Choices.* New York: Wiley.

Tooby, J., & Cosmides, L. 1989. Evolutionary Psychology and the Generation of Culture, Part I. *Ethology, 10,* 29–49.

Tracy, E. J. 1976. How United Brands Survived the Banana War. *Fortune,* July, 144–151.

Trevino, L. K. 1992. Moral and Business Ethics: Reasoning Implications for Research, Education, and Management. *Journal of Business Ethics, 11,* 445–459.

Trevino, L. K., & Weaver, G. R. 2003. Has Business Ethics Come of Age? In *Managing Ethics in Business Organizations,* 71–88. Stanford, CA: Stanford Business Books.

Trevino, L. K., & Youngblood, S. A. 1990. Bad Apples in Bad Barrels: A Causal Analysis of Ethical Decision-Making Behavior. *Journal of Applied Psychology, 75,* 378–385.

Trivers, R. L. 1971. The Evolution of Reciprocal Altruism. *The Quarterly Review of Biology, 46,* 35–57.

Trompeter, G. M., Carpenter, T. D., Jones, K. L., & Riley, R. A. 2014. Insights for Research and Practice: What We Learn About Fraud from Other Disciplines. *Accounting Horizons, 28,* 769–804.

Tucker, W. B. 1940. Is There Evidence of a Physical Basis for Criminal Behavior. *Journal of Criminal Law and Criminology, 31,* 427–437.

Turkle, S. 2015. *Reclaiming Conversation: The Power of Talk in a Digital Age.* New York: Penguin Press.

Turnbull, C. 1972. *The Mountain People.* New York: Simon and Schuster.

Tyler, T. R. 1990. *Why People Obey the Law.* New Haven, CT: Yale University Press.

Tyler, T. R. 1997a. Citizen Discontent with Legal Procedures: A Social Science Perspective on Civil Procedure Reform. *American Journal of Compliance Law, 45,* 871–904.

———. 1997b. Procedural Fairness and Compliance with the Law. *Swiss Journal of Economics and Statistics, 133,* 219–240.

———. 2006. Psychological Perspectives on Legitimacy and Legitimation. *Annual Review of Psychology, 57,* 375–400.

Tyler, T. R., & Darley, J. M. 1999. Building a Law-Abiding Society: Taking Public Views About Morality and the Legitimacy of Legal Authorities into Account When Formulating Substantive Law. *Hofstra Law Review, 28,* 707–739.

Tylor, E. B. 1882. Review of The Burman: His Life and Notions by Shway Yoe. *Nature, 26,* 593–595.

Tytler, G. 1982. *Physiognomy in the European Novel.* Princeton, NJ: Princeton University Press.

Uddin, N., & Gillett, P. R. 2002. The Effects of Moral Reasoning and Self-Monitoring on CFO Intentions to Report Fraudulently on Financial Statements. *Journal of Business Ethics, 40,* 15–32.

Ulen, T. S. 1998. Rational Choice Theory in Law and Economics. In *Encyclopedia of Law and Economics,* 790–818. Ghent, Belgium: University of Ghent.

United States Federal Bureau of Investigation. 1989. *White-Collar Crime: A Report to the Public.* Washington, DC: US Department of Justice Federal Bureau of Investigation.

Unnever, J. D., Cullen, F. T., & Pratt, T. C. 2003. Parental Management, ADHD, and Delinquent Involvement: Reassessing Gottfredson and Hirschi's General Theory. *Justice Quarterly, 20,* 471–500.

US Department of Transportation National Highway Traffic Safety Administration. 1985. *Alcohol and Highway Safety 1984: A Review of the State of the Knowledge.*

Valentine, D. A. 1998. Pyramid Schemes. *International Monetary Fund's Seminar on Current Legal Issues Affecting Central Banks.* Washington, DC, May 13.

Van den Berg, C. J. 1986. On the Relation Between Energy Transformations in the Brain and Mental Activities. In R. Hockey, A. Gaillard, & M. Coles (Eds.), *Energetics and Human Information Processing,* 131–135. Dordrect: M. Nijhoff.

Vaughan, D. 1996. *The Challenger Launch Decision*. Chicago: University of Chicago Press.

Vogel, D. 1979. *Lobbying the Corporation: Citizen Challenges to Business Authority*. New York: Basic Books.

———. 1981. The "New" Social Regulation in Historical and Comparative Perspective. In T. McCraw (Ed.), *Regulation in Perspective*, 155–185. Cambridge, MA: Harvard University Press.

Vold, G. B. 1951. Criminology at the Crossroads. *Journal of Criminal Law and Criminology*, 42, 155–162.

Walker, C. E. 1931. The History of the Joint Stock Company. *The Accounting Review*, 6, 97–105.

Waller, J. 2007. *Becoming Evil*. Oxford: Oxford University Press.

Walsh, A., & Beaver, K. M. 2009. *Biosocial Criminology*. New York: Routledge/Taylor and Francis Group.

Walsh, J. P., & Kosnik, R. D. 1993. Corporate Raiders and Their Disciplinary Role in the Market for Corporate Control. *The Academy of Management Journal*, 36, 671–700.

Waltz, E. 2011. GM Grass Eludes Outmoded USDA Oversight. *Nature Biotechnology*, 29, 772–773.

———. 2015. USDA Approves Next-Generation GM Potato. *Nature Biotechnology*, 33, 12–13.

Wang, L., Malhotra, D., & Murnighan, J. K. 2011. Economics Education and Greed. *Academy of Management Learning & Education*, 10, 643–660.

Wang, L., Zhong, C., & Murnighan, J. K. 2011. The Ethical and Social Consequences of a Calculative Mindset. Working Paper.

Ward, W. R. 1952. The Administration of the Window and Assessed Taxes, 1696–1798. *The English Historical Review*, 67, 522–542.

Warneken, F., & Tomasello, M. 2009. The Roots of Human Altruism. *British Journal of Psychology*, 100, 455–471.

Warren, D., Gaspar, J., & Laufer, W. 2014. Is Formal Ethics Training Merely Cosmetic? A Study of Ethics Training and Ethical Organizational Culture. *Business Ethics Quarterly*, 24, 85–117.

Wasserman, D., & Wachbroit, R. 2001. *Genetics and Criminal Behavior*. New York: Cambridge University Press.

Wasserstein, R. L., & Lazar, N. A. 2016. The ASA's Statement on P-Values: Context, Process, and Purpose. *The American Statistician*, 70, 129–133.

Waters, J., Bird, F., & Chant, P. 1986. Everyday Moral Issues Experienced by Managers. *Journal of Business Ethics*, 5, 373–384.

Watts, R. L., & Zimmerman, J. L. 1990. Positive Accounting Theory: A Ten Year Perspective. *The Accounting Review*, 65, 131–156.

Weaver, G. R., Trevino, L. K., & Cochran, P. L. 1999. Corporate Ethics Practices in the Mid-1990s : An Empirical Study of the Fortune 1000. *Journal of Business Ethics*, 18, 283–294.

Weber, J. 1990. Managers' Moral Reasoning: Assessing Their Responses to Three Moral Dilemmas. *Human Relations*, 43, 687–702.

Wegner, D. 2002. *The Illusion of Conscious Will*. Cambridge, MA: MIT Press.

Weil, R. L. 2002. Fundamental Causes of the Accounting Debacle at Enron: Show Me Where It Says I Can't, Summary of Testimony for Presentation.

Weiner, E. J. 2005. *What Goes Up*. New York: Little, Brown and Company.

Weisbach, D. A. 2002. Ten Truths About Tax Shelters. *Tax Law Review*, 55, 215–254.

Weisburd, D., Waring, E., & Chayet, E. 1995. Specific Deterrence in a Sample of Offenders Convicted of White-Collar Crimes. *Criminology*, 33, 587–607.

Weisburd, D., Wheeler, S., Waring, E., & Bode, N. 1991. *Crimes of the Middle Classes: White Collar Offenders in the Federal Courts.* New Haven, CT: Yale University Press.

Welch, J. 2001. *Jack: Straight from the Gut.* New York: Warner Business Books.

Wells, J. 2011. *Principles of Fraud Examination* (3rd ed.). Hoboken, NJ: Wiley.

Westen, D., Blagov, P. S., Harenski, K., Kilts, C., & Hamann, S. 2006. Neural Bases of Motivated Reasoning: An fMRI Study of Emotional Constraints on Partisan Political Judgment in the 2004 U.S. Presidential Election. *Journal of Cognitive Neuroscience, 18,* 1947–1958.

Weston, E. M., Friday, A. E., & Liò, P. 2007. Biometric Evidence That Sexual Selection Has Shaped the Hominin Face. *PloS ONE, 2,* 1–8.

Wetlaufer, G. B. 1990.The Ethics of Lying in Negotiations. *Iowa Law Review, 75,* 1219–1273.

Whitacre, M. 2014. When Good Leaders Lose Their Way. *Loyola University Chicago Law Journal, 45,* 525–536.

White, B. 1910. *The Book of Daniel Drew.* New York: George H. Doran Co.

White, J. J. 1980. Machiavelli and the Bar: Ethical Limitations on Lying in Negotiation. *American Bar Foundation Research Journal, 1980,* 926–938.

White, L. J. 2001. Lysine and Price Fixing: How Long? How Severe? *Review of Industrial Organization, 18,* 23–31.

Wicker, B., Keysers, C., Plailly, J., Royet, J., Gallese, V., & Rizzolatti, G. 2003. Both of Us Disgusted in My Insula: The Common Neural Basis of Seeing and Feeling Disgust. *Neuron, 40,* 655–664.

Wilgus, H. L. 1910. Purchase of Shares of Corporation by a Director from a Shareholder. *Michigan Law Review, 8,* 267–297.

Williams, G. C. 1989. A Sociobiological Expansion of Evolution and Ethics. In J. Paradis & G. C. Williams (Eds.), *Evolution and Ethics: T. H. Huxley's Evolution and Ethics,* 179–214. Princeton, NJ: Princeton University Press.

Williams, J. H., Whiten, A., Suddendorf, T., & Perrett, D. I. 2001. Imitation, Mirror Neurons and Autism. *Neuroscience and Biobehavioral Reviews, 25,* 287–295.

Williams, S. K. 1901. *Reports of Cases Argued and Decided in the Supreme Court of the United States, 1815–1819.* Rochester, NY: The Lawyers Co-operative Publishing Company.

Wilson, A. E., & Ross, M. 2003. The Identity Function of Autobiographical Memory: Time Is on Our Side. *Memory, 11,* 137–149.

Wilson, E. 1975. *Sociobiology.* Cambridge, MA: Belknap Press.

———. 1978. *On Human Nature.* Cambridge, MA: Harvard University Press.

———. 1998. Consilience: The Unity of Knowledge. New York: Knopf.

Wilson, J. Q. 1993. *The Moral Sense.* New York: First Free Press Paperbacks.

Wilson, J. Q., & Herrnstein, R. J. 1998. *Crime and Human Nature: The Definitive Study of the Causes of Crime.* New York: The Free Press.

Wilson, S. 2014. *The Origins of Modern Financial Crime.* London: Routledge.

Winans, R. F. 1984. *Trading Secrets: Seduction and Scandal at the Wall Street Journal.* New York: St. Martin's Press.

Winerman, M. 2003. The Origins of the FTC: Concentration, Cooperation, Control, and Competition. *Antitrust Law Journal, 71,* 1–97.

Winkielman, P., & Berridge, K. C. 2004. Unconscious Emotion. *Current Direction in Psychological Science, 13,* 120–123.

Wolfe, B. D. T., & Hermanson, D. R. 2004. The Fraud Diamond: Considering the Four Elements of Fraud. *CPA Journal, 74,* 38–42.

Wolfgang, M. E. 1961. Pioneers in Criminology: Cesare Lombroso (1825–1909). *Journal of Criminal Law and Criminology, 52,* 361–391.

Woodward, J., & Allman, J. 2007. Moral Intuition: Its Neural Substrates and Normative Significance. *Journal of Physiology-Paris, 101,* 179–202.

Wright, J. P., & Beaver, K. M. 2005. Do Parents Matter in Creating Self-Control in Their Children? A Genetically Informed Test of Gottfredson and Hirschi's Theory of Low Self-Control. *Criminology, 43,* 1169–1202.

Wright, R. 1994. *The Moral Animal: Evolutionary Psychology and Everyday Life.* New York: Pantheon Books.

Wright, R., Logie, R. H., & Decker, S. H. 1995. Criminal Expertise and Offender Decision Making: An Experimental Study of the Target Selection Process in Residential Burglary. *Journal of Research in Crime and Delinquency, 32,* 39–53.

Yoder, S. A. 1978. Criminal Sanctions for Corporate Illegality. *The Journal of Criminal Law and Criminology, 69,* 40–58.

Yoe, S. 1882. *The Burman: His Life and Notions.* London: Macmillan and Co.

Young, O. 1927. Dedication Address. *Harvard Business Review, 5,* 387–394.

Young, R. M. 1970. *Mind, Brain, and Adaptation in the Nineteenth Century: Cerebral Localization and Its Biological Context from Gall to Ferrier.* Oxford: Clarendon Press.

Zahra, S. A., Priem, R. L., & Rasheed, A. A. 2007. Understanding the Causes and Effects of Top Management Fraud. *Organizational Dynamics, 36,* 122–139.

Zajonc, R. B. 1968. Attitudinal Effects of Mere Exposure. *Journal of Personality and Social Psychology Monograph Supplement, 9,* 1–27.

———. 1980. Feeling and Thinking: Preferences Need No Inferences. *American Psychologist, 35,* 151–175.

———. 2001. Mere Exposure: A Gateway to the Subliminal. *Current Directions in Psychological Science, 10,* 224–228.

Zeleny, L. D. 1933. Feeble-Mindedness and Criminal Conduct. *American Journal of Sociology, 38,* 564–576.

Ziesche, R., Hofbauer, E., Wittmann, K., Petkov, V., & Block, L. H. 1999. A Preliminary Study of Long-Term Treatment with Interferon Gamma-1b and Low-Dose Prednisolone in Patients with Idiopathic Pulmonary Fibrosis. *New England Journal of Medicine, 341,* 1264–1269.

Zietz, D. 1981. *Women Who Embezzle or Defraud: A Study of Convicted Felons.* New York: Praeger Publishers.

Zimbardo, P. 2007. *The Lucifer Effect.* New York: Random House.

Zimmerman, M. 1989. The Nervous System in the Context of Information Theory. In R. F. Schmidt & G. Thews (Eds.), *Human Physiology* (2nd ed., 166–173). New York: Springer-Verlag.

Zimring, F., & Hawkins, G. 1973. *Deterrence: The Legal Threat in Crime Control.* Chicago: University of Chicago Press.

Zingales, L. 2015. Presidential Address: Does Finance Benefit Society? *The Journal of Finance, 70,* 1327–1363.

Ziobrowski, A. J., Cheng, P., Boyd, J. W., & Ziobrowski, B. J. 2004. Abnormal Returns from the Common Stock Investments of the U. S. Senate. *Journal of Financial and Quantitative Analysis, 39,* 661–677.

Zuckoff, M. 2005. *Ponzi's Scheme: The True Story of a Financial Legend.* New York: Random House.

INDEX

Eugene Soltes is the Jakurski Family Associate Professor of Business Administration at Harvard Business School. His research on corporate malfeasance has been cited by the *Wall Street Journal, Financial Times, USA Today,* and *Bloomberg News.* Professor Soltes teaches in Harvard Business School's executive education programs and is the recipient of the Charles M. Williams Award for Outstanding Teaching. He received his PhD and MBA from the University of Chicago Booth School of Business and his AM in statistics and AB in economics from Harvard University.

Photograph by Stuart Cahill

PublicAffairs is a publishing house founded in 1997. It is a tribute to the standards, values, and flair of three persons who have served as mentors to countless reporters, writers, editors, and book people of all kinds, including me.

I. F. STONE, proprietor of *I. F. Stone's Weekly*, combined a commitment to the First Amendment with entrepreneurial zeal and reporting skill and became one of the great independent journalists in American history. At the age of eighty, Izzy published *The Trial of Socrates*, which was a national bestseller. He wrote the book after he taught himself ancient Greek.

BENJAMIN C. BRADLEE was for nearly thirty years the charismatic editorial leader of *The Washington Post*. It was Ben who gave the *Post* the range and courage to pursue such historic issues as Watergate. He supported his reporters with a tenacity that made them fearless and it is no accident that so many became authors of influential, best-selling books.

ROBERT L. BERNSTEIN, the chief executive of Random House for more than a quarter century, guided one of the nation's premier publishing houses. Bob was personally responsible for many books of political dissent and argument that challenged tyranny around the globe. He is also the founder and longtime chair of Human Rights Watch, one of the most respected human rights organizations in the world.

•   •   •

For fifty years, the banner of Public Affairs Press was carried by its owner Morris B. Schnapper, who published Gandhi, Nasser, Toynbee, Truman, and about 1,500 other authors. In 1983, Schnapper was described by *The Washington Post* as "a redoubtable gadfly." His legacy will endure in the books to come.

Peter Osnos, *Founder and Editor-at-Large*